Clickstream
Data Warehousing

Clickstream
Data Warehousing

Mark Sweiger
Mark R. Madsen
Jimmy Langston
Howard Lombard

WILEY COMPUTER PUBLISHING

John Wiley & Sons, Inc.
NEW YORK • CHICHESTER • WEINHEIM • BRISBANE • SINGAPORE • TORONTO

Publisher: Robert Ipsen
Editor: Robert Elliott
Developmental Editor: Emilie Herman
Managing Editor: John Atkins
Associate New Media Editor: Brian Snapp
Text Design & Composition: ProImage

This book is printed on acid-free paper.

Published by John Wiley & Sons, Inc.

Published simultaneously in Canada.

This publication is designed to provide accurate and authoritative information in regard to the subject matter covered. It is sold with the understanding that the publisher is not engaged in professional services. If professional advice or other expert assistance is required, the services of a competent professional person should be sought.

Library of Congress Cataloging-in-Publication Data:

ISBN: 0-471-08377-1

Printed in the United States of America.

10 9 8 7 6 5 4 3 2 1

Advance Praise for
Clickstream Data Warehousing

"*Clickstream Data Warehousing* is a great read for the serious data warehouse designer grappling with clickstream data. With a clear style, the authors explain the intricacies of this important source of customer behavior data. They combine engineering knowledge of the clickstream with state-of-the-art dimensional data warehouse design techniques to produce a very useful book."

Ralph Kimball
President, Ralph Kimball Associates

"Mark Sweiger and his co-authors have created a foundation and architecture for profiting from all of the clickstream data produced in an e-business environment. The proliferation of clickstream data requires the ability to capture this data in a data warehouse to ensure that the needs of your customers are being satisfied. They begin by characterizing a typical e-business architecture and explain how it can be fortified by the creation of a clickstream data warehouse. This book is a must-read for corporations that have a tremendous investment in their e-business infrastructure and are trying to increase their ROI."

Ron Powell
Publisher and Editorial Director, **DM Review**

"The clickstream data warehouse is among the most important assets of any modern, competitive business. But unfortunately, the lack of available, actionable information about planning, developing, deploying, and managing this still relatively exotic asset—to say nothing of the challenges involved in maximizing its business value—can raise uncertainties that will intimidate the most experienced data warehousing and application development teams. In their new book, Mark Sweiger, Mark Madsen, Jimmy Langston, and Howard Lombard pick up where Ralph Kimball and Richard Merz's groundbreaking work *The Data Webhouse Toolkit* left off. They provide detailed, hands-on advice about every aspect of the clickstream data warehousing continuum—from architecture, to data sources, to user-identity tracking, to project management, to infrastructure. *Clickstream Data Warehousing* could become the classic handbook on the subject."

Justin Kestelyn
Editor-in-Chief, **Intelligent Enterprise**

"This book comprehensively covers the process required to ensure that companies receive the greatest possible benefit from their Web site clickstream data. The insight to be gained by properly capturing and analyzing clickstream data can easily spell competitive advantage for companies that implement a clickstream data warehouse. In addition to describing all architectural components required for a clickstream data warehouse, this book also provides advice for designing a Web site so that the most advantageous clickstream data will be available for analysis. As an aid for those beginning the process or as a reference for those already building a clickstream data warehouse, this book will be the only non-software tool they need."

Jean Schauer
Editor-in-Chief, **DM Review**

"*Clickstream Data Warehousing* should be read by everyone working with e-commerce data. It provides in one place a welcome reference that not only illuminates the potential pitfalls of building data warehouses from Web data, but also suggests some good solutions. It is sufficiently technical to be of help to an audience of practitioners, while clear and concise enough to be of use to their managers. It is a welcome addition to my bookshelf."

Herb Edelstein
President, Two Crows Corporation

"If you are wondering how to avoid repeating the failure of many dot-coms, you must read this book. Successful business management requires good business intelligence, and building a clickstream data warehouse is the only way to obtain actionable business intelligence in an e-business environment."

Elizabeth Schaedler
Enterprise Systems Business Development Manager, Sun Microsystems

"If you are a practitioner who is considering or is currently engaged in a clickstream data warehouse project, the knowledge you need is in this book. The subject matter is presented in logical steps with each chapter building on the last, enabling the reader to mentally construct a picture of clickstream data warehouse architecture, its components, project best practices, and success factors. The direct and understandable treatment of Web architecture, Web transactions, and what should happen behind the scenes to capture, organize, and use valuable clickstream data is extremely useful to those who are new to data warehousing as well as those who have more experience. And the numerous how-to examples and suggestions have the detail required to address many of the difficult technical problems encountered when implementing a clickstream data warehouse."

John Gensler
Senior Consultant, KPMG Consulting, Inc.

"This book is a model for how implementation guides should be written. Building on the proven foundation of Dr. Ralph Kimball's 'Toolkit' books, Mark Sweiger and his co-authors drill down into the real-world complexities of Web data and e-business. What makes this book especially powerful is its combination of breadth and depth. If you are responsible for implementing a clickstream data warehouse, this book is the closest thing you can get to an insurance policy for success."

Warren Thornthwaite
Founding Partner, InfoDynamics, LLC

"This book provides the reader with practical guidance on how to address specific challenges facing project teams who are working on clickstream data warehouses. It offers the overall context and, more importantly, the details that the project team needs to know. Web developers should read this book to understand what data the business really needs and why the data warehouse team keeps asking for more. "

Laura L. Reeves
Principal, StarSoft Solutons, Inc.

"Any data warehousing professional that needs to get a firm handle on how to deliver an effective clickstream data warehouse will find this book to be an excellent guide through the technical maze of the Web site clickstream. Rather than introducing their own data warehousing vernacular, the authors embrace the by now familiar knowledge base of dimensional data modeling and warehouse development practices to serve as the foundation for delivering an effective clickstream solution."

Bob Becker
Vice President, DecisionWorks Consulting, Inc.

"*Clickstream Data Warehousing* builds on the data warehousing concepts introduced in the past few years, adding the critical data elements that today's marketers are so hungry for—the clicks. Some of us may fondly remember the days when we could take weekly data extracts from our transaction systems and provide all the decision support needed to run the business. Like it or not, those days are gone forever; business managers are demanding a view of data accumulating in Web logs at a furious pace. The authors do a terrific job of introducing the new concepts, revisiting the tried and true, and exploring solutions in great depth. Highly recommended."

Dave Stauffer
Director of Site Development, Walmart.com

"This book takes traditional data warehousing into a whole new dimension. If your business has a Web presence and you're serious about success, then this is a must-read. It is designed for literally everyone involved in a data warehousing development project and provides you with the nuts and bolts from A to Z for a successful implementation. I'm really looking forward in anticipation to putting my newfound knowledge to work on our very next project!"

Curtis McClendon
Oracle Team Manager, Qwest Cyber.Solutions Inc.

"*Clickstream Data Warehousing* adds new Web dimensions to traditional data warehousing, enabling analysts to track and forecast customer behavior in addition to product sales and promotions."

Gary Hallmark
Architect, Oracle Corporation

Contents

Introduction

This book describes how to design and build a clickstream data warehouse to analyze user behavior on your Web site. Every user click on your Web site is already recorded in Web server log files and that historical clickstream can be turned into a treasure trove of business intelligence by loading it into an appropriately designed clickstream data warehouse environment. The techniques described in this book can be used whether you have a pure e-business or a so-called brick-and-mortar business that happens to have a Web site as one of its many business channels. The resultant clickstream data warehouse can be a stand-alone entity, or it can be integrated as part of a larger enterprise data warehouse installation.

Clickstream data warehousing is quite different from earlier data warehousing disciplines, like financial data warehousing, sales and marketing data warehousing, or even data warehousing in support of customer relationship management (CRM). For example, clickstream data warehouses incorporate new Web-based technologies and infrastructure that are unfamiliar to many organizations with more traditional data warehouses. Furthermore, clickstream data warehouses have a much richer set of source data than the typical brick-and-mortar data warehouse environment, adding new complexity to both data extraction and the schema design. And, finally, clickstream data warehouses can be truly enormous, often containing billions of fact table rows that stress the underlying hardware and software technology infrastructure to its limits.

If you have a Web site, a clickstream data warehouse is also a business necessity. What happens on that Web site will be completely opaque to the enterprise unless it loads and analyzes the resultant clickstream. Not having a clickstream data warehouse is like flying an airplane without windows or instruments in the cockpit—you are flying blind and you will crash. It is only a matter of time. We have been surprised by the number of organizations that operate without clickstream data warehouses. We have *not* been surprised that many of those same organizations have subsequently failed because they did not have insight into where the business was going. Taking the liberty of using some industry vernacular, clickstream data warehousing is a *no-brainer* because without it you are probably heading toward the ground at terminal velocity.

Who Should Read This Book

This book is for everyone who will be working on a data warehouse project that includes Web-based data. It will be particularly useful to architects and designers, database administrators, data modelers, and project managers because it provides a wealth of details on Web-based data topics that is not found elsewhere. The knowledge in this book provides team members with a common framework that is the necessary basis for any clickstream data warehouse project. The book is also essential reading for consultants who are going to implement a clickstream data warehouse project, since they will be key members of the project team.

We also suggest that Web site developers and Webmasters read this book to get a better understanding of the analytical requirements of business users and some of the data issues involved. This information will show how to implement Web sites so that they enhance, rather than hinder, clickstream analysis. The Web site developers are often in charge of e-business information technology initiatives, and if the site is not designed so that user behavior can be analyzed, implementing the appropriate Web analytics can be very difficult or impossible.

One group that should really read this book is the designers of Web application server products and personalization tools. Many of these products do not support clickstream data capture very well. As these products dynamically generate their Web pages, they need to remember to provide the capability to log any clickstream information generated by these pages so that historical user behavior can be tracked and analyzed. Without that ability, the businesses using these tools face enormous challenges managing their e-business endeavors.

Prerequisite Knowledge

The book assumes that the reader is already familiar with basic dimensional data modeling and star schema designs. A good source for this knowledge is *The Data Warehouse Toolkit* by Ralph Kimball (Wiley, 1996). The book also assumes basic knowledge of data warehouse development practices and techniques. An excellent reference is *The Data Warehouse Lifecycle Toolkit* by Ralph Kimball, Laura Reeves, Margy Ross, and Warren Thornthwaite (Wiley, 1998).

As of this writing, there is only one other book on the topic of clickstream data warehousing, *The Data Webhouse Toolkit* by Ralph Kimball and Richard Merz (Wiley, 2000). We consider our book to be a solid practitioner's guide or how-to companion volume to the *The Data Webhouse Toolkit,* containing much more detail on the underlying Web technologies and design techniques required to implement a clickstream data warehouse.

The Structure of the Book

The book is in two parts. Part 1, called "Clickstream Data Warehouse Architectural Foundations," explains in careful detail Web technology and infrastructure as it relates to a clickstream data warehouse. In many cases, the authors have found that the data warehouse project team is unfamiliar with new Web technology and infrastructure. This lack of knowledge can result in slipped schedules, lukewarm user acceptance, and even project failure. Without this knowledge, the project team may also find it difficult to communicate with the Web site development side of the house, making problem resolution even more uncertain.

Part 1 has four chapters:

- Chapter 1, "A Typical E-Business Architecture," describes the components of an e-business information system architecture and shows how they relate to clickstream data warehousing. The environment includes client user systems, Internet service providers (ISPs), Web servers, applications servers, cached content servers, advertising engines, search engines, business transaction servers, the public Internet, common carriers, private intranets, and of course, clickstream data warehouses. This canonical architecture is used throughout the rest of the book.

- Chapter 2, "The Web Application Environment," describes the unusual stateless Web application environment, and introduces basic concepts like

HyperText Transfer Protocol (HTTP), HTTP header fields, query strings, Common Gateway Interface (CGI), cookies, Web server log records, scripting languages, Web servers, and application servers. The rest of the book assumes that the reader is familiar with these concepts, making this a critical architectural foundation chapter.

- Chapter 3, "Clickstream Data Sources and Web Server Log Files," is an in-depth analysis of the Web-based data sources for a clickstream data warehouse. It covers the basics of Web server log files and standard log file formats and provides a detailed analysis of the many issues one encounters with Web-based data, before moving on to other data sources like cache servers, Web application servers, and media servers. Log file data is the major clickstream data source, and we consider this chapter to be the benchmark source for information on the formats and use of log file data.

- Chapter 4, "Using Cookies and Other Mechanisms to Track User Identity," delves into the critical issue of establishing and tracking user identity on the Web and in the data. This chapter describes the mechanisms used to manage user sessions, identify users and track them across visits, as well as some of the data management issues involved. It also discusses the business and ethical issues surrounding user identity and user privacy, which have to be carefully thought through in any clickstream data warehouse implementation.

Armed with the insight into the Web-based infrastructure and data available from Part 1, the reader is ready to tackle Part 2, "Building a Clickstream Data Warehouse, Step-by-Step." This part, which covers the remainder of this volume, is a handbook on how to design and implement a clickstream data warehouse. It covers all the issues, from project staffing and management, to schema design, to extract transformation and load, to end-user analysis. Just as data warehouse-oriented staff can learn about important Web architecture issues in Part 1, Web site-oriented staff, like site designers and Webmasters, can learn in Part 2 what Web site design features are required to support a good clickstream data warehouse. We sincerely hope that this book can be used as a communication bridge between the Web site and data warehouse staff members, producing much better outcomes for clickstream data warehouse projects. That said, the main audience for Part 2 is, of course, the clickstream data warehouse project team.

Part 2 has five chapters:

- Chapter 5, "Planning, Managing, and Staffing a Clickstream Data Warehouse Project," contains a nutshell description of all the phases of a clickstream data warehouse project. In a series of "Lessons Learned the Hard Way" sections, we provide insight into how to avoid the problems and pitfalls of a typical project. The chapter ends with a discussion of project roles, staffing needs, and how to organize the project team, including potential organization charts.

- Chapter 6, "The Clickstream Data Warehouse Meta-Schema," is one of the most important chapters in the book. This chapter describes the click-stream data warehouse meta-schema, a universal template used to guide the logical design of any clickstream data warehouse schema. The schema includes the User Activity Fact table, and 10 possible dimensions, including User, Content, Activity, User Time, Fiscal Time, Physical Geography, Web Geography, Site Geography, Internal Promotion, and External Promotion. This template is used as a vehicle to bridge the communication gap between business users and the schema designers, and it ensures that all the important facts, dimensions, and attributes of a clickstream data ware-house will be considered in the course of the logical schema design.

- Chapter 7, "Implementing the Appropriate Clickstream Data Warehouse Technology Infrastructure," contains information you will find nowhere else on the physical database design and technology infrastructure of a clickstream data warehouse. We find that most books on data warehous-ing gloss over physical design and technology infrastructure issues, leav-ing this very complex subject as an exercise for the reader. This chapter discusses:

  - Efficient bulk and batch load techniques.
  - Table partitioning, including range, hash, and composite partitioning.
  - Indexing, including b-tree, bitmapped, function, and partitioned indexes.
  - Joins, including star joins, the Oracle star transformation, and parti-tion-wise joins.
  - Dimensional aggregate management, including aggregate creation candidates, database optimizer aggregate awareness, aggregate navi-gation, and materialized views.
  - Database parallelism, including tips on how to parallelize database operations using block, key, and hash partitioning, as well as parallel database processes.
  - New extensions to SQL to support clickstream data warehousing, including Top-N ranking inside SQL statements, the ROLLUP opera-tor for aggregate creation, the CUBE operator for cross-tabulation.
  - Disk drive and logical volume management including concatenation, striping, mirroring, RAID plexes, etc., and how database objects like tables, indexes, tablespaces, log volumes, and temporary tablespaces map onto volumes and disk drives.

- A section on choosing products from various vendors including database software vendors, logical volume management software vendors, and disk subsystem vendors.

- Chapter 8, "Building the Clickstream Extract, Transformation, and Load Mechanism," describes the fundamentals of clickstream data warehouse extract, transformation, and load. The chapter includes a detailed discussion of the eight steps needed to build a clickstream extract, transformation, and load (ETL) mechanism. It also has a very detailed example, based on the meta-schema, that shows how source data is processed into the clickstream data warehouse during ETL.

- Chapter 9, "Analyzing the Data in the Clickstream Data Warehouse," offers practical solutions to the problem of querying very large clickstream data warehouses, including a discussion of relational online analytical processing (OLAP), multidimensional OLAP, and hybrid OLAP query environments. The chapter also shows how the chosen OLAP query environment can utilize efficient query techniques like partition elimination, materialized views, and server-side Group By calculations to meet end-user performance expectations.

The Companion Web Site

This book has a companion Web site at www.wiley.com/compbooks/sweiger. This Web site has been designed to extend the information in this book and offer the clickstream data warehouse community a place to go for more enlightenment and interaction. Although this site will certainly evolve over time, the site has additional information that is best presented in an electronic format, like a Microsoft Project clickstream data warehouse project plan, useful scripts, and links to articles written by the authors and others. We have also included information that is more topical or subject to frequent changes that would be inappropriate for this book, as well as information on more general data warehousing topics.

Acknowledgments

I would like to acknowledge Elizabeth Schaedler of Sun Microsystems, whose initial encouragement provided the genesis for writing this book. I would also like to acknowledge Mark Madsen for his major contribution as a co-author of this text, without which it could never have been completed.

I would also like to thank Stuart and Vinita Nelson, and John and Linda Gensler for their support during the long and difficult process of writing this book.

Finally, I would like to acknowledge Bob Elliott of John Wiley & Sons for his instrumental efforts in helping us get this book published.

Mark Sweiger
January 2002

I would like to first thank my wife Kim, who has supported me throughout my career and put up with late nights of noisy typing for many months. Next in line are Rob Kondoff and Ralph Kimball. Without Rob's encouragement and mentoring, I never would have entered this field or been successful at it. Ralph Kimball, though he may not realize it, taught me nearly everything I know about schema design on my very first data warehouse project. What he didn't teach me, I probably learned from Bob Becker of DecisionWorks.

Thanks go also to Tom Dopirak, who has patiently answered questions from me over the years. JP Gordon and Alice Liu both supplied me with product information, saving me from embarrassing mistakes. I must also acknowledge Alex Lubarov, Dave Stauffer and Larry Murdock, who worked with me on my first Web development project and answered technical questions for this book.

Last and not least, thanks to Mark Sweiger, whom I've worked with over the years and who approached me with the idea of writing this book together.

Mark Madsen
January 200

Clickstream Data Warehousing

PART ONE

Clickstream Data Warehouse Architectural Foundations

CHAPTER 1

A Typical E-Business Architecture

No matter what kind of e-business you operate, one thing is clear: information systems dominate the enterprise. This a fundamental switch from pre-Web days when information systems simply served various brick-and-mortar business functions that were largely executed through human labor. In an e-business, information technology (IT) doesn't just serve the business, it executes the business—it *is* the business, which is a big shift from older business models.

The biggest obstacle to understanding clickstream data warehousing is an IT mindset rooted inside older brick-and-mortar business information system models. The vast majority of existing enterprises are brick-and-mortar businesses, and while their existing information system architectures have served them adequately, the brick-and-mortar IT mindset does not translate well to an e-business environment. In order to create a successful clickstream data warehouse, one needs to move away from this old way of thinking and thoroughly understand the many new architectural components of an e-business information system.

In this chapter we introduce all of the components of a typical e-business architecture, and show how they relate to the clickstream data warehouse. The terminology and architecture presented here will be used throughout the rest of this book. This canonical architecture is explained in a series of steps, each with an associated figure to help the reader visualize the architecture as it unfolds.

Simplistic View of E-Business Architecture

The first unusual aspect of an e-business information system architecture is the autonomous nature of the users of the e-business, over which IT has almost no control. One of the hallmarks of older information system architectures has been IT's very high level of control over the end-user application environment. IT would dictate the functionality, data access rights, security level, etc., of all end-user applications, creating a tightly controlled environment that could be evolved in a fairly well-planned fashion.

This tightly controlled end-user environment is gone forever in the Internet environment. Now users run Web browsers as their principal end-user application, and these users and their browsers are not controlled by IT in any meaningful way. Users are spread around the world, and it is likely that most are not employees of the enterprise. They can request pages and services from your Web site 24 hours a day, 365 days a year, and your enterprise has no control over the timing or the nature of their activity. They can swamp your site with hits or they can ignore it. It is up to them, and you have to build an extremely flexible architecture that can deal with whatever they might decide to do. This new architectural environment is illustrated in Figure 1.1.

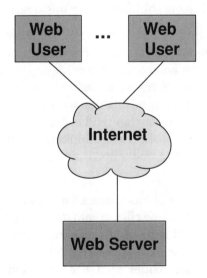

Figure 1.1 A simple view of an e-business architecture.

Another unusual aspect of an e-business architecture is the kind of network Web users use to access the Web site. Instead of the tightly controlled internal networks of older IT architectures, users use the public Internet for all their network access. IT cannot control this network, they can only adapt to it. In this environment there are no more finely tuned corporate Local Area Networks (LANs) and Wide Area Networks (WANs). The users use the Internet to get to your e-business, and your enterprise had better find a way to make Internet connectivity reliable and snappy.

In this uncontrolled environment, your Web server would seem to be an oasis of comfort, because IT does control this entity. The e-business creates all Web server content, sizes the Web server, and administers the Web server. But although IT controls the content and operations of the Web server, they have very little control over who accesses it. Web servers may be behind a router/firewall, but its level of security is quite weak. The level of user access to Web servers is comparable to that of publicly accessible email servers, which are already a notorious entry point for hackers and viruses. Web servers are similar public entities and your enterprise has to make provisions to thwart undesirable access without restricting legitimate users. This is a very difficult balancing act, but it is also the everyday reality of the Web environment.

The simple e-business information system architecture explained above lacks a lot of important architectural details. Let's start to fill in those details.

Internet Service Providers

It wasn't very long ago that almost every enterprise maintained its own network, including banks of modems for its corporate users to use to dial in to the private company LAN. Because the Internet completely decouples user network access from these internal corporate networks, Web users need some other mechanism to get access to target Web servers. While the public Internet provides most of the legs of the path to the target server, the last few miles between the Web user system and the Internet itself must be bridged by something, and that entity is usually the user's Internet Service Provider, or ISP, as shown in Figure 1.2.

ISPs have racks of proxy servers that attach to common carriers like telephone networks, cable TV networks, and satellite networks. Users use everything from dialup, to DSL, to wireless protocols to get at the ISP servers, which then forward their requests over the Internet to the appropriate Web servers. Examples of ISPs include such stalwarts as AOL, Earthlink, and Terra Lycos, as well as cable TV services like @Home and Roadrunner, satellite services like the

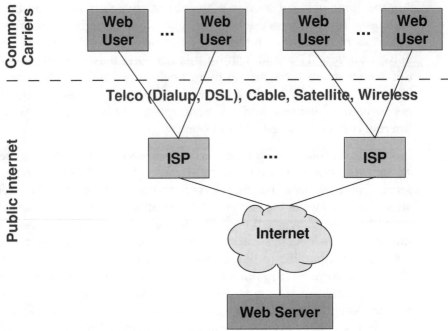

Figure 1.2 Internet Service Providers (ISPs).

Echostar/Dish, Hughes Satellite System and Starband, and various wireless services. It should be noted that in a corporate campus environment, an enterprise's LAN or WAN can also function as a dedicated ISP for your corporate users.

Multiple Internet-Connected Services

The assumption that all user interactions are confined to your enterprise's Web servers is natural but not correct. A typical user requesting a Web page can hit your enterprise's Web server and many additional Internet attached servers, including the following:

- How did your user find your Web site? There are many ways this can happen but one of the most important is via a search engine query, whose results link users to your site. These search engines are external to your enterprise.

- Your site's Web pages may contain externally provided advertising content, such as banner advertisements and sponsor buttons. These are typically provided by an external advertising service like DoubleClick's DART system.

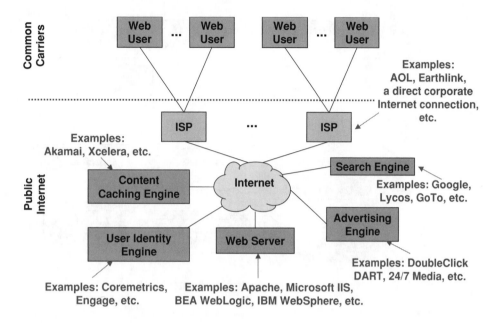

Figure 1.3 Third-party Internet services provide a significant portion of a user's Web site experience.

- Your site may strive to personalize the user's Web experience by providing content that is specific to that user. You can't do this if you can't identify the user, so your site's pages may call user identification engines or use other Web-based mechanisms to establish user identity.

Many sites include large-sized content like images and file downloads that may overwhelm the site's Internet connectivity bandwidth. One way to improve the user load time performance of these large objects is to give them to external content caching services like Akamai, who use a worldwide network of servers to deliver this type of content quickly to the end users. These kinds of external Internet services are shown in Figure 1.3.

Multiple Physical Web Servers

What if user Web traffic load overwhelms the capacity of a particular kind of server? The answer is multiple physical Web servers with replicated content, another hallmark of the e-business environment.

If your Web site is medium to large in terms of user traffic, it is probably housed on multiple Web servers with replicated site content on each server. Site traffic load is spread over the server pool rather than overwhelming a single server, as shown in Figure 1.4

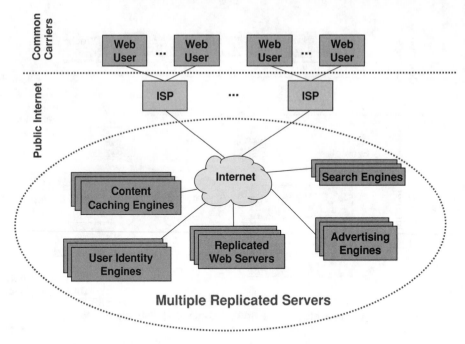

Figure 1.4 All types of Web servers are subject to replication.

External services use multiple servers by definition, since they tend to be large, Web-wide aggregators of user traffic. From a clickstream data warehousing perspective, this means that many servers and their corresponding multitude of log files, both internal and external, are potential data sources for the clickstream data warehouse.

Different Types of Replicated Web Servers

Inside an e-business Web site there is likely to be more than one type of Web server. A typical site almost certainly has at least one traditional Web page server of either the Apache or Microsoft IIS variety. Apache is open source freeware that runs on Linux and UNIX, and Microsoft IIS is bundled with the server versions of Windows 2000, formerly known as NT. But many sites also contain other types of Web servers. Examples of these other types of Web servers include:

Internal Cached Web Page Servers. These servers store the most commonly accessed pages of the Web site in memory in order to satisfy user page requests without the latency of a disk lookup.

Secure Servers. These specialized servers use secure protocols like Hypertext Transfer Protocol Secure (HTTPS) or Secure Socket Layer (SSL) to perform secure HTTP transactions between the Web user and the Web server.

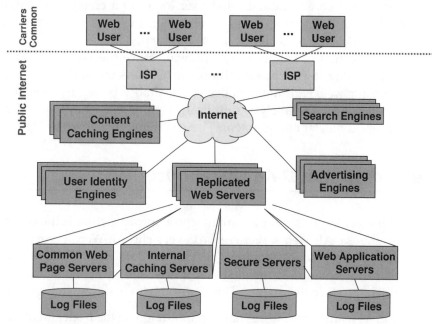

Figure 1.5 The different types of replicated Web servers.

Secure transactions would include things like user registration and login as well as financial and confidential information.

Web Application Servers. These specialized servers are offered by vendors like BEA WebLogic, IBM WebSphere, Blue Martini, Art Technology Group, etc. They usually offer some kind of specialized vertical application logic, like an online store, or a business-to-business (B2B) marketplace, speeding up the development time for the resultant application. They often sit behind common Web page servers like Apache or Microsoft IIS, as shown in Figure 1.5.

Each type of Web server can record server activity as records in its Web server log file. But what types of data can be recorded and the format of those records can vary widely between different types of Web servers. If an e-business site uses multiple kinds of Web servers to record clickstream history, it is very important to reconcile the different types and formats of data that each kind of server records. Unless all types of servers record the same types and formats of data, there may be certain types of user activity that cannot be properly recorded and analyzed.

Clustered Business Transaction Systems

Your site's replicated Web servers can dish out content, but what happens when a user wants to do a business transaction? A business transaction can be anything from an authenticated user logon to a credit card validation, to a check on the shipping status of an order. Business transactions need to be secure and they occur on business transaction servers, which are behind the secure portion of the enterprise firewall. Since the Web user environment is 24/7 365 days a year by definition, the business transaction servers cannot be down for weekend maintenance. They should be highly available clustered systems, which is likely a significant step above what would be done in a brick-and-mortar environment. These systems are shown in Figure 1.6.

The Clickstream Data Warehouse

Sitting behind this complex architectural infrastructure is the clickstream data warehouse. All Web servers record every click in Web server log files, which are extracted and loaded into a clickstream data warehouse. Additional transaction information from business transaction systems is normally used to enrich the clickstream data. This environment is shown in Figure 1.7.

To date, many e-businesses have concentrated on the front end of the e-business information system architecture, namely the Web server content and delivery infrastructure. While we would be the last to argue against a good front-

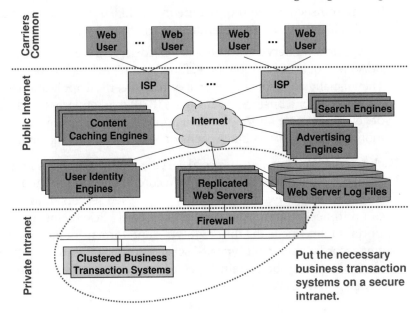

Figure 1.6 Business transaction systems are typically behind the firewall on a secure intranet.

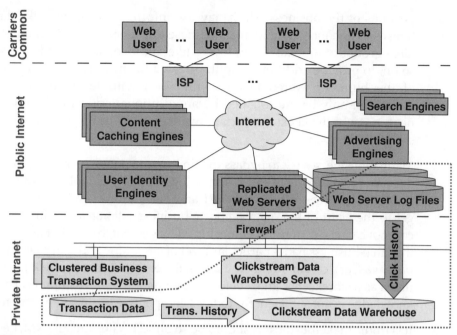

Figure 1.7 Historical Web server log file data and business transaction server data are the primary data sources for the clickstream data warehouse.

end implementation, we have noted the widespread and often fatal inattention to the corresponding back-end infrastructure. Back-end systems like the business transaction servers and the clickstream data warehouse are IT differentiators that are the key to the long-term success of an e-business. Because of the low barriers to entry for Internet businesses, almost anyone can implement a good front-end environment with a relatively small investment of time and money. Without the corresponding critical back-end components, e-business transactions are likely falling very short on operational fulfillment. Without a clickstream data warehouse the e-business is flying absolutely blind in terms of understanding its business relationship with its users. While the failure to operationally fulfill e-business transactions usually results in the relatively quick death of an e-business, the failure to manage an e-business's electronic relationship with its users using a clickstream data warehouse results in a lingering, systemic competitive disadvantage that only rewards its competitors.

Clickstream data warehouses are even more important to an e-business than the corresponding traditional data warehouses are to their brick-and-mortar competitors. You see, in an e-business environment there really isn't any other type of feedback or business-intelligence mechanism as there usually is in the brick-and-mortar world. In a brick-and-mortar enterprise, an executive can ask his functional reports—who are real people—what is going on with their portions of the business. They may use information systems like data warehouses to enhance their answers to these questions, but they can also rely on large groups of functional employees like salespeople, purchasing agents, and so on, to provide additional input. But an e-business typically replaces much of the human-powered business functions with technology components, which can only be interrogated by an additional critical technology component, namely the clickstream data warehouse. Without it, your e-business is simply flying blind.

Many e-businesses try to bypass the time and expense of creating a clickstream data warehouse by using Web server log file analysis tools to produce regular site traffic analyses. While such site traffic analyses are surely useful, they do not get to the heart of the matter: your e-business relationship with your users, a concept called electronic Relationship Management, or eRM. If all one knows is that an e-business had a particular level of site traffic and that a certain product page was hit a certain number of times, the electronic enterprise knows about as much as a storekeeper knew before the invention of the computer. This level of knowledge is not sufficient for today's competitive business environment.

It is ironic that e-businesses should be so blind to clickstream eRM, because the information is at their fingertips—much more so than it would be in the traditional brick-and-mortar environment. In a brick-and-mortar world it is not unusual to spend months developing screen-scraping legacy applications to obtain data to load into the data warehouse. But in the much more friendly Web environment, Web servers automatically record the details of all the HTTP transactions that comprise every page view. The Web environment is rich in eRM data—the challenge is to exploit it.

While your enterprise's Web site may or may not currently have a clickstream data warehouse, other external content providers almost certainly do. The business intelligence they gather is used for everything from what advertising banner to paint on a particular user's page to the user identity and psychographic profiles provided by user identity engines. Your ISP may also be using clickstream data warehousing to analyze the scope of an entire browser session, which encompasses all the sites viewed by a user during that session. This session-wide analysis of the ISP-level clickstream gives an ISP a very deep view into the behavior and preferences of its user population. This situation is shown in Figure 1.8.

Different ISPs have different policies regarding the tracking of user behavior. AOL, which is by far the largest ISP with tens of millions of users, tracks user behavior and personalizes content using clickstream analysis. Earthlink, the second largest ISP in the United States, explicitly does not track user behavior and its user anonymity is marketed as a major differentiator by Earthlink. But unless there is an explicit guarantee against it, you should assume that third-

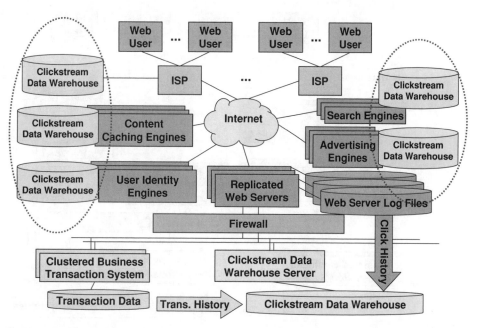

Figure 1.8 Other entities also keep clickstream data warehouses on their portions of the user clickstreams.

party services are tracking their view of the user clickstream. And it is likely that they are sharing their portion of the clickstream or the results of its analysis with others.

The Canonical E-Business Architecture

Putting all the pieces together from the previous sections we come up with the canonical e-business information system architecture that will be used throughout the rest of this book.

The canonical architecture shown in Figure 1.9 is complex, and the exact nature of its components has a great deal of influence on the design and implementation of the resultant clickstream data warehouse. We will explore each component of this architecture in more detail as the rest of this book unfolds.

Summary

In this chapter we established the components of the typical e-business information system architecture, and we showed how they relate to a clickstream

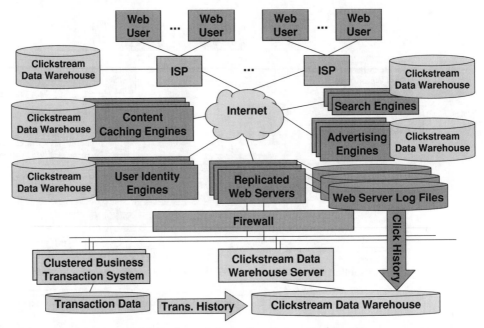

Figure 1.9 The Canonical E-Business Information System Architecture.

data warehouse. The terminology and architecture presented here is used throughout the rest of this book.

Continuing our quest to establish the foundational knowledge required for clickstream data warehousing, the next chapter investigates the unusual, stateless Web application environment.

CHAPTER 2

The Web Application Environment

With the components of a Web information system architecture established in Chapter 1, we are now well on our way in our quest to remove the brick-and-mortar mindset obstacles to understanding clickstream data warehousing. The next obstacle to remove is the familiar, very stateful, client/server software application model.

Unlike the client/server application model, the basic web application model is completely stateless. This unusual application model uses new programming paradigms that are alien to the client/server programming environment, and they need to be completely understood before you begin any attempt to capture clickstream data generated by Web application environment.

The Stateless HTTP Transaction Model

Before the Web, almost every important application architecture was based on application state. Application design methodologies used state diagrams to map out functionality. Programming languages used activation record stacks to preserve state between subroutine calls. Simple data structures were built into complicated control blocks, which became the skyscrapers of complex application state.

But then the Web arrived and whisked away this application complexity. On the Web, information is stored as HyperText Markup Language (HTML) pages. In order to access a Web page, a client's Web browser executes a Hyper-

Text Transfer Protocol (HTTP) transaction whose primary argument is the Universal Resource Locator (URL), the hypertext link to the desired Web page.

HTTP transactions are completely stateless. A client's Web browser can access a Web page at one site, disconnect from the network, reconnect, and then access the next page on the Web site with no loss of continuity. The only information required to access a page is the URL, and no state from any prior activity is required to display that URL.

Since the inception of the Web, the functionality of HTTP has remained fairly static with just two versions of the protocol, HTTP 1.0 and HTTP 1.1, in use. HTTP 1.1 has nine different methods (which is object-oriented terminology for transaction types) of which only three are relevant to this book:

- GET
- HEAD
- POST

We will now discuss each in greater detail.

1. **GET:** A GET gets a Web page
   Syntax: GET URL HTTP-Version-Number
   Example: GET / HTTP/1.1

   Note that all URL paths are relative to the domain specified in the full URL. For example, a GET of the home page URL of the author's Web site at *http://www.ClickstreamConsulting.com/* would first use directory name service (DNS to resolve the domain name *www.ClickstreamConsulting.com* to its real IP address, and then the actual GET is done on the relative URL of / .

2. **HEAD:** Returns only the HTTP headers and not the Web page contents. This operation is used to test a Web page to see if it has been modified since the last time it was cached locally by the requesting client or since it was indexed by a search engine indexing robot.
   Syntax: HEAD URL HTTP-Version-Number
   Example: HEAD /index.html/ HTTP/1.1

3. **POST**: A way to send the fields in an HTML form from the client to the Web server. The form fields are sent by name in the input HTTP header fields
   Syntax: POST URL HTTP-Version-Number
   Example: POST /login-userID.html SHTTP/1.1

   For example, the concatenated HTTP header for the POST could contain the encrypted headers "UserID=sweiger" and "Password=guessme" sent via the secure HTTP connection (SHTTP) to the site's secure server where such logins are processed.

In general, the HTTP transactions are executed by Web browsers, which issue HTTP transactions on behalf of their clients, and the transactions are in turn fulfilled by Web servers who return the content requested by the browsers. Each transaction is stateless and *idempotent*, which means that no matter how many times a transaction is reapplied, the result is always the same.

Passing Information between HTTP Transactions

HTTP may be stateless and idempotent, but that has not prevented it from implementing several interesting ways to pass parameters between HTTP transactions. The first method is via HTTP header fields, illustrated in Figure 2.1.

In this example, the client browser HTTP requests and their headers are on the left, and Web server response headers are on the right. For the sake of brevity, we do not show the body of the Web page requests.

The first GET is for the page /mysite/entrypage.html. But what do the header fields tell us? The If-Modified-Since field helps the browser and its proxies optimize for browser or proxy caching of Web pages. Most Web browsers and many proxy servers, like the ones used by your ISP, cache the most recently accessed

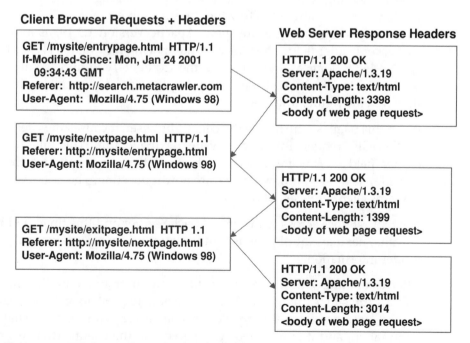

Figure 2.1 HTTP interaction using header fields.

pages on behalf of the client. This means that using the If-Modified-Since header field, we can do what is called a conditional GET of the page/mysite/entrypage.html. If the page has not been modified since Monday, January 24, 2001, at 9:34:43 GMT, then the version in our local browser or proxy cache is the most recent and the server need not return any new page data, because it hasn't changed. If not the new version of the page must be sent again.

The misspelled Referer field indicates the URL, if any, from which the current HTTP request was obtained. In this case, the referrer that is causing this GET of /mysite/entrypage.html is the search engine results page http://search .metacrawler.com. The user who visited this page searched using Metacrawler and the browser window displayed the search results including one hit for /mysite/entrypage.html, which is the subject of the current GET.

User-Agent indicates which type of browser issued the current HTTP request. In this case the browser is Netscape version 4.7, running on Windows 98.

All of this header information is passed to mysite's Web server as part of the HTTP transaction to GET the page.

The Web server for mysite receives the request and returns the result to the requesting client. The result format includes a status, any HTTP header fields in the response, and the body of the request, which can be text, images, or even something executable like JavaScript. Looking at the first response block, we see a status of 200, which means success (OK). The type of Web server software running at mysite is Apache Version 1.3.19, as indicated by the Server header field. The type of content being returned is HTML text, and is 3398 bytes long as indicated by the Content-Type and Content-Length header fields. The byte string containing the actual page text, which is not shown in the figure, follows.

When this page is returned to the client's browser, it causes the client to make another GET request for page /mysite/nextpage.html. This time the Referer header field is /mysite/entrypage because that page contains the link to /mysite/nextpage.html, which we are now requesting. The User-Agent is still the same client browser, of course.

The request goes across to mysite's Apache server and this time the 1399 byte /mysite/nextpage.html page is sent back with a success status and the other header information.

After examining /mysite/nextpage.html, the user finds another interesting link at /mysite/exitpage.html, and issues a request to get that page. The request goes across to the mysite Apache server with all the usual header information, and it is returned with success to the client. After this request, there are no more GETs for this client.

Using Query Strings

Another way to pass parameters between HTTP transactions is via the "query string" of parameters that can be appended to an URL. Any URL can be extended with any number of parameters. The parameters begin after a question mark (?) appended to the end of the URL and the parameters are separated by ampersands (&). Since URLs and their query strings are not permitted to have any blanks in them, the plus sign (+) is used as a substitute for every blank in the query string. An example of a referring URL from the Google search engine, with a parameterized search string that was used to find the authors' Web site, is shown below:

```
http://www.google.com/search
    ?hl=en&lr=lang_en&safe=off&q=clickstream+data+model
```

Notice that the search string value "clickstream+data+model" is assigned to the last parameter, q, and that the three other variables hl, lr, and $safe$ are also set by the query string.

Cookies, User Identity, and Web Server Log Records

A more persistent mechanism for passing state information from one HTTP transaction to another is the client-side cookie for a particular Web site. Cookies are most commonly used to store persistent user identity information on the client's system, like UserID=203983, for example. Once set, this information is automatically passed to the Web server by each client HTTP request, as an additional header field like this:

```
Cookie: UserID=203983
```

But cookies can be used to store any number of variables and their values, and these variables can persist for as little as the duration of the current browser session, or as long as the current UNIX epoch, which started January 1, 1970, at 00:00:00 GMT and ends January 19, 2038, at 03:14:07. The duration of the cookie is specified when the cookie is set. The default is no duration, which means the cookie expires at the end of the current browser session, but a more persistent cookie can be created by specifying an expiration date far into the future.

Most larger Web sites, and many smaller ones, set persistent user identification cookies upon first access by a client system. All subsequent accesses by that client system pass the persistent identification cookie as part of their HTTP header fields, and this information is used to track client access to the site over time.

In fact, all these mechanisms for passing state information—the HTTP header fields, referring and target URLs and their query strings, and the cookies—can all be recorded in Web server log records, which are written for each HTTP transaction that reaches the target Web server. This recorded history of HTTP state information, the clickstream history, is the primary data source for a clickstream data warehouse. We will go into much more depth about log records, URLs, query strings, cookies, and user identity in Chapters 3 and 4.

Site Hits, Page Visits, and User Sessions

A client's clickstream history can be divided into site visits of various durations, starting out with the simple page view. You may think that a page view is one HTTP transaction like:

```
GET clickstreamconsulting.com/index.html
```

But most page views generate multiple embedded HTTP transactions in order to display images like logos and pictures, as well as advertisements and dynamically generated page content. This means that a "single page view" actually generates the same number of Web server log records as the number of HTTP transactions required to present all the content on the page.

The slang term for a single HTTP transaction is a site "hit" and each site hit results in one Web server log file record. If one is counting site hits and thinking that these equate to page views by site users, one is probably overestimating the number of actual page views by an order of magnitude, assuming that, on average, there are approximately 10 HTTP transactions required to create a single page.

A site visit by a user, also called a user session, is the set of all the HTTP transactions that comprise a particular user's actions during his visit to a site. The log records for this set of transactions reveal all the HTTP activity by the user on the Web server, including interesting information like the first page the user visited, called the entry page, and the page upon which he left the site, called the exit page. By comparing the time stamps on successive log records, one can calculate the length of time the user spent on a given page for every page but the exit page. This is because the exit page has no successor log record from which to calculate the duration of time the user spent on that page. The time a user spends on a page is often called the *dwell time*.

If the client has a persistent cookie that does not expire after he exits his browser, the cookie value can be used as an identifier to track multiple visits by that user. If one only wants to track the activity that has occurred within a session, the Web server can create a temporary session cookie, and only HTTP transactions within that user session will have that cookie in their log records.

A browser session is the collection of all site visits by a user while the browser is active. Unlike the individual Web sites, which can only track visits to their pages, the user's Internet Service Provider (ISP) can track all user activity during a browser session. ISPs like AOL and MSN can track all of the sites visited by a user because they issue all browser requests on behalf of their clients as their Internet proxy. Because of this, ISPs have unique visibility into the entire spectrum of cross-site Web behavior of their users.

Only HTTP transactions that make it to a site's Web server are logged and therefore trackable in a site's clickstream data warehouse. Because of browser-level Web page caching or upstream content caching at user proxies like ISPs, many HTTP requests for popular pages may never make it to the Web server. Instead, the requests are satisfied by a page cache earlier in the network pathway to the page. This phenomenon can cause page hit statistics for popular pages like a site's home page to be underreported by large margins. It is not uncommon to see site traffic statistics that show the home page having half the hits of some internal site page that sits beneath it, because of caching activity earlier in the path to the home page. The challenge for the clickstream analyst is to determine whether the home page really is being cached upstream, and therefore underreported, or whether users have instead found a new point of entry into the site that bypasses the home page, meaning that the reported shortfall in home page hits is truly accurate. We will have much more to say on this issue in Chapter 3.

Calling Other Executables Using CGI

Early in the life of the Web it became apparent that it would be useful to have a mechanism to call another executable entity within HTML, and the Common Gateway Interface (CGI) was the result. By convention, Web servers house CGI-callable executable files in the default directory *cgi-bin*, which typically sits just beneath the root directory of the Web site. Parameters are passed to the executable program by the query string or by setting the values of various CGI environment variables using HTTP header field values passed from the client.

Although one often hears Web programmers talk about CGI scripts, CGI itself is not a scripting language. It is simply a standard mechanism to call programs within HTML, and executable scripts called using CGI are written in some other popular scripting language like Perl. Part of the confusion stems from the fact that CGI programs can have the file extension .cgi. If the program is not a binary, but is truly a script then the first line of the executable script file must specify which interpreter to execute, like:

```
#!/usr/bin/perl
```

Server-side scripts are typically invoked as a child process or as a thread of the Web or application server receiving the request. For example, the following HTML executes a server-side Perl script called UserID_Pwd_Validation.pl when the client POSTs a form that contains the client userID and password:

```
<FORM METHOD=POST ACTION="/cgi-bin/UserID_Pwd_Validation.pl">
   Username: <INPUT TYPE=text NAME=username VALUE="" SIZE=24
     MAXLENGTH=24>
   <br>
   Password: <INPUT TYPE=password NAME=password VALUE="" SIZE=12
     MAXLENGTH=12>
   <br>
   <INPUT TYPE=submit VALUE="Submit">
</FORM>
```

This HTML code will cause two text boxes, Username and Password, to be displayed on the client system, along with a Submit button. When the client enters the text "jsmith" and "yulnvrguess" into these boxes and presses Submit, the values username=jsmith and password=yulnvrguess are passed as standard input to the CGI script UserID_Pwd_Validation.pl on the server, for userID and password validation. If the userID and password are instead passed using the GET method, by altering the form method to METHOD=GET, the values are appended to the ACTION URL as a query string. This is shown in the line below:

```
/cgi-bin/UserID_Pwd_Validation.pl?username=jsmith+password=yulnvrguess
```

Since the full text of the URL is always logged for every HTTP transaction, the GET method of passing parameters using the query string will ensure that the log contains a record of the parameters passed to the script. If the POST method is used, the parameters will not be logged in the URL because the parameters are passed as standard input and there is no query string. Since parameter values are key to understanding what the client has done on the site, using POST instead of GET can greatly diminish the value of the data in the Web server log file. Unfortunately, many HTML style guides recommend using POST over GET. If your site uses POST, you may have to develop a custom logging mechanism to record form parameters so that you can get the full picture of user behavior.

CGI is not the only way to execute code in response to page requests. It is also possible to use a scripting language executed by an *HTML preprocessor*, like Microsoft Active Server Pages or UNIX/Linux-oriented Hypertext Pre-Processor (called PHP), which embed scripting language functionality inside HTML. Another option is Java, which can be used in similar fashion with Java Server Pages (JSP).

Most sites execute their code on the server, although JavaScript is often used to do HTML form field validation, mouse rollover menus, and other client-side dynamic programming logic. Because JavaScript is platform independent, it should run in any client environment, and all popular browsers support it, even Microsoft's Internet Explorer.

Using Scripting Languages to Log User Behavior

One of the biggest trends in Web programming is the use of embedded scripting languages like PHP or Microsoft's Active Server Pages. Scripted Web pages can have dynamic content and other forms of program logic that enhance their functionality. Scripting can also be used to log information that is not automatically captured by Web server log files, as shown in the following PHP script example.

One of the most nettlesome areas of clickstream analysis surrounds the *exit page* of a user session. At the end of every user session, the client follows some link that takes him away from the site. The click on that link is *not recorded* in the site's log file. Instead, it is recorded in the log of the destination site because that is where the client's HTTP request went. In many cases, the HTML that takes a client to a new destination site is coded directly into the originating site as a hypertext link like the one shown below:

```
<a href="http://www.ExternalSite.com/coollink.html">
  Click Here to go to ExternalSite.com </a>
```

If the client clicks on this link, he goes to ExternalSite.com, ending his session and leaving no final log record of his exit. We can rectify this situation by replacing the hypertext link with a PHP script that logs the fact that the client went to ExternalSite.com as well as redirecting him to that location once the necessary information has been logged. The new link would look like this:

```
<a href="/cgi-bin/redirect.php
  ?ExtURL=http://www.ExternalSite.com/coollink.html&SessionCookie=13284">
  Click Here to go to ExternalSite.com </a>
```

The script, redirect.php, which is shown below, is called using CGI with method GET when the user clicks on the modified link above:

```php
<?php
$extURL = $HTTP_GET_VARS["ExtURL"]
$SessionCookie = $HTTP_GET_VARS["SessionCookie"]
mysql_connect("127.0.0.1", "ScriptUser", "ScriptPassword")
  or die("Cannot connect to the database. Please try again")
mysql_select_db("RedirectLog")
$timestamp = time();
mysql_query("INSERT INTO ExternalLinks
  COLUMNS (SessionID, ExtURL, Timestamp)
  VALUES ($SessionCookie, $ExtURL, $timestamp)");
Header("Location: $ExtURL");
?>
```

When a user clicks on the link, the redirect.php script is executed with the two query string arguments:

```
ExtURL=http://www.ExternalSite.com/coolink.html
   SessionCookie=13284
```

PHP automatically takes these arguments and puts them into an associative array, $HTTP_GET_VARS, with a key of the variable name and a value of the variable value. The PHP script above begins by assigning the external URL variable, $extURL, the URL passed by the original call using the associative array. Similarly the value of the session's cookie is assigned to the PHP variable $SessionCookie.

Next PHP uses the freeware MySQL database to connect and open a database called RedirectLog. After that, it uses the UNIX time() function to get the latest timestamp. Then it uses MySQL to INSERT the cookie SessionID, the external URL, and the timestamp into the table called ExternalLinks, which is the actual log record of the user's request to go to the external link.

To get to the actual external link, the last line of the PHP script emits an HTTP header that resolves to the passed URL:

```
Location: http://www.ExternalSite.com/coolink.html
```

This causes the user's browser to get automatically redirected to the coollink .html page at ExternalSite.com, completing the redirection.

The site administrator can then write another PHP script that calls MySQL to count the number of clickthroughs to each external URL:

```php
<?php
mysql_connect("127.0.0.1", "ScriptUser", "ScriptPassword")
  or die("Cannot connect to the database. Please try again")
mysql_select_db("RedirectLog")
```

```
mysql_query("SELECT ExtURL, count(*) FROM ExternalLinks
  GROUP BY ExtURL");
?>
```

which produces output like that shown in Table 2.1.

By combining the information in the SessionID and Timestamp columns in the ExternalLinks table with information in the Web server log records, one can calculate the time the user spent on the exit page by subtracting the timestamp of the external link clickthrough from the last record of the session in the Web server log file. Knowing how much time a user spent on an exit page can be very revealing. A very short time may indicate that content is not interesting, while a longer time can indicate that the user found what they were looking for and then moved on. Chapters 3 and 4 contain much more information on the use of redirection, logging, and scripting to log user behavior.

Web Servers, Application Servers, and Dynamically Generated Web Pages

Many sites use two types of replicated Web servers to implement their site's functionality. The first type, the regular *Web server*, is the familiar Apache or Microsoft IIS Web server that services external HTTP transaction requests. Web servers are fine for serving up static Web page data, but they do not implement more sophisticated functionality like dynamic Web page generation and application-specific functionality. The Web application server, usually simply called the *application server*, implements further functionality like that needed by a retail e-commerce site designed to show a product catalog and complete product purchase transactions, or by a customer service site designed to track user requests for customer service and resolve them. While some Web servers have configurable logging functionality that can record user identity information like persistent cookies, application servers typically assign their own persistent cookies and log only certain data items that may not be sufficient for complete clickstream analysis of user activity inside the application engine.

Table 2.1 External URL Clickthrough Counts

ExtURL	COUNT(*)
http://www.ExternalSite.com/coollink.htm	47
http://www.AffiliatedSite.com/index.html	139
http://www.AdSite.com/SpringAd.html	312
etc.	

Web server log records and application server log records can be linked during data extract, transformation, and load by using a nonpersistent session cookie that is set on the initial request of a user's visit. The Web server will log the session cookie for every HTTP request after the initial hit, and if the application server logs the same session cookie for each of its log records, then the two log record streams can be merged together into a complete picture of session activity.

In our experience, many popular application servers give little thought to clickstream analysis. Consequently, their event and object logging functionality is not very useful or robust. Many application servers require custom code to log even a simple session cookie, and they also need custom code to log other information like the types of dynamically generated content presented by a particular Web page or the result of a call to a credit card transaction processing server. When choosing application server software, sites must make sure that all standard and custom-created application objects and events can be logged directly through a centralized, configurable logging interface similar to that provided by the Web servers. Otherwise, a great deal of additional custom code may be required to log the right information for analysis and to link application server log records to Web server log records.

Another problematic issue that has arisen with application servers is dynamically generated Web pages. On the surface, dynamically generated Web pages seem like a wonderful idea. Page content can be generated on the fly, personalizing it for the user. In addition, site content revisions become easier, because content blocks can be replaced at will without changing the style of the page. Dynamic pages have URLs that include a query string with every page that contains the parameters used to create these pages. Because dynamically created URLs have no fixed address, even counting page hits on dynamic pages can be quite problematic. We have seen several extreme cases where the entire Web site was implemented as a set of dynamic pages or frames under single URL.

Dynamically Generated Web Pages and Search Engines

In addition to problems with clickstream analysis, search engines do not index dynamically generated Web pages. As soon as most search engines see the "?" in a URL, they stop indexing. Since the content of such a page is dynamic, indexing it is futile from the perspective of a search engine. This is often quite ironic, because many so-called dynamic sites really don't have personalized or changing-content pages. They just use a publishing tool or application server that makes all pages but the root dynamic for the convenience of the software or programming staff.

A Dynamic Application Server Logging Horror Story

Here is an all too common example of what can go wrong when application servers fail to implement proper logging functionality for clickstream analysis:

A popular retail Web site decided to redo the entire site as dynamic Web pages using a major, brand-name e-business application server. The application server vendor's implementation consultants were to do most of the work of converting the site to the new dynamic page implementation. After signing the contract and getting part of the way through the implementation, the retailer realized that getting the clickstream analytics that had been previously available in the old site design would be problematic in the new dynamic environment. We were called in to analyze the situation and make recommendations.

The application server could only log certain data items like the session cookie and the beginning and end of a session. Amazingly, they could not log the persistent user identification cookie created by the overlying Web server, nor any application-specific information like shopping basket contents, dynamic page content types, or sales transaction information! Since the application server could not log the data, the only way to log this information was to insert these variables into the Java-based application code and pass the data as a gigantic concatenated query string so it would appear in the Web server's log file. This required a great deal of custom code to implement and would be a maintenance nightmare going forward.

The additional code to support logging was outside the scope of the original implementation contract, and our engagement ended with the retailer and the application server vendor threatening one another with legal action.

Before you decide to implement a Web site using an application server, you should verify that it is able to log *any standard or custom-created variables using a standard, configurable, centralized logging mechanism*. The Apache and Microsoft IIS Web servers use this kind of centralized logging mechanism already for basic Web server data, and there is no reason why application servers cannot do the same. Some, like Blue Martini, do have centralized logging functionality, but the majority of application servers do not. Writing custom code to log variables as query strings attached to every page is not appropriate, because it is costly, error prone, and will probably have to be redone completely when the application server software is revised or the site has major revisions in content.

If a site uses dynamic page generation, tracing a user's path through the site may involve parsing the URL parameter list of each HTTP request. The clickstream data warehouse designers must have a clear understanding of what these parameters mean. The resulting requirement is that application servers must expose the semantic meaning of the parameters in the dynamically generated URLs to the clickstream data warehouse extract, transformation, and load process. Many application server implementation specialists are extremely reluctant to do this, because the parameter string may change over time, as the site evolves or new revisions of application server software are released.

A way around this problem is to manually create "hallway" and "doorway" pages to dynamic content with fixed URLs. These pages are only for the consumption of search engines, and when a user clicks on one, they are led to the appropriate dynamically generated page. Without hallway and doorway pages, a dynamically generated Web site can become invisible from the perspective of search engines. Given that search engines are the number one user mechanism to find Web content, being invisible is not a good idea. Dynamically generated sites need to consider funding at least a parallel effort to create static hallway and doorway pages that can be indexed by search engines.

For content intensive sites like online magazines, hallway and doorway pages will not solve the indexing problem. For these sites, all content needs to be indexed, and the content changes rapidly, usually every day or even every hour or minute. But once created, this content remains on the site for a long period of time, never changing. These sites need to create static URLs for all new content pages, as the pages are published. The process of creating the page content can be dynamic, but the resultant content should be static. By using style sheets, the look of these pages can be kept current with the site design even though the URLs are static.

Summary

This chapter provided an overview of the Web application environment, including such topics as HTTP, query strings, cookies, log records, CGI, scripting languages, Web servers, and application servers. The next two chapters explore the implications of using the data produced by these Web technologies in a clickstream data warehouse. Chapter 3 provides an in-depth explanation of the details of Web and application server data formats and log records, which are the major data sources for a clickstream data warehouse. Chapter 4 explores the many nuances of tracking user identity, including a detailed explanation of how cookies are used in a clickstream data warehouse environment.

Clickstream Data Sources and Web Server Log Files

T he primary data source for a clickstream warehouse is the set of log files generated by a site's Web servers. These log files contain a record of most of the HTTP transactions performed on behalf of every visitor to the Web site. Although server logs contain a lot of useful information, they rarely encompass the entire scope of the data required for a complete clickstream analysis.

Web server logs were originally designed to provide administrative statistics for Web site and system administrators, not as a complete data source for clickstream data warehouses. The kind of information needed by site administrators was smaller in scope and more technical in nature than what is now required for business-oriented clickstream analysis. Today, the Web site is frequently the first point of contact between an enterprise and its prospective or current customers. Enterprise management wants to know much more about user activity than just the administrative statistics. They want to know who is visiting the site, what the visitors do while on the site, and what business—if any—is being transacted there.

In this chapter we discuss the typical data sources for a clickstream warehouse. The first section reviews the data available from Web servers, the standard formats of log files, some of the uses and pitfalls associated with log data, and concludes with a discussion of how to extend server logs and what data ought to be recorded. The subsequent sections cover some of the other common internal and external data sources, concluding with some of the important third-party data sources like advertising engines.

Web Server Logs

As mentioned above, the data contained in the server logs forms the core of the information in the clickstream warehouse. The extent of data logged determines the quality and completeness of the information available in the warehouse. Fortunately, most Web server software allows quite a bit of control over what data elements can be logged.

Every time you view a page from a Web site the Web server writes one or more records containing data about the page view into log files. This data is written in a specific format that either adheres to one of the standard log file formats or is customized to fit the needs of a particular site.

It is important to know exactly what log file format your Web server uses so you can make basic design decisions about components of your clickstream data warehouse. The scope of data contained in the log file dictates the kinds of analyses that can be performed against the clickstream data warehouse. By thoroughly understanding the data available in your logs, you can set appropriate end-user analysis expectations early in the project. Setting appropriate expectations early is often a key element to a successful project.

Standard Log File Formats

There are dozens of log file formats used by commonly implemented Web servers. Instead of reviewing all of these, we'll focus on the most frequently used standard formats and provide information on how to customize the log file format for a few of the more popular Web servers.

Most commonly used Web server software is capable of logging in at least one of three open log file format standards: NCSA Common Log Format (CLF), NCSA Extended Log Format (ECLF) or W3C Extended Log File Format (ExLF). The first of these standards is the oldest and contains the least amount of data, but almost all Web servers are capable of logging in this format. Apache, NCSA, and Netscape all use CLF as their default format.

NCSA Common Log Format

The seven data elements contained in the Common Log Format are described below. The field names as shown are from the NCSA Common Log Format standard and so they may be somewhat obscure. If data is not available to the

Web server for a particular field then the Web server will place a dash ("-") in the empty field.

1. **remotehost.** This is the fully qualified hostname of the machine making the request. This will contain the IP address of the client if the Web server does not perform name resolution when logging. Most Web servers will log the IP address because of the overhead associated with resolving names.

2. **rfc931.** This field contains the remote login name of the user as identified by identd. This is a carryover from multiuser systems and will almost always contain a dash.

3. **authuser.** If the document being requested by the client is password protected on the Web server then this field will contain the login name of the user.

4. **date.** The Date field contains the date and time that the request was served.

5. **request.** The first line of the HTTP request as it came from the client. This field will specify the URL of the file requested including the query string if present, and the method used to retrieve the file.

6. **status.** The Status field contains the status code indicating whether or not the file was successfully retrieved, and if not, the error message was returned. The status code is a three digit code, with the first digit indicating the result type. There are five status code types, each described below. A comprehensive list of HTTP status codes is listed in Table 3.1.

   ■ Codes starting with 1 are informational codes that can be used by the server's administrator or developers to provide extra information.

   ■ Codes starting with 2 indicate a successful operation.

   ■ Codes starting with 3 are for redirection and usually indicate that the requested file is in a different location from that specified by the URL.

   ■ Codes starting with 4 mean that there has been an error due to the client. The most common errors are unauthorized attempts to access documents or nonexistent files. A bad link on the Web site is treated as a client error (the 404 error code).

   ■ Codes starting with 5 indicate that the Web server can't complete a request due to either a Web server or network problem.

7. **bytes.** The Bytes-sent field indicates the actual number of bytes transferred. For a successful transfer this is normally equal to the size of the document, and does not include the HTTP header information.

Table 3.1 HTTP 1.1 Status Codes

STATUS CODE	DESCRIPTION
100	Continue
101	Switching Protocols
200	OK
201	Created
202	Accepted
203	Non-Authoritative Information
204	No Content
205	Reset Content
206	Partial Content
300	Multiple Choices
301	Moved Permanently
302	Found
303	See Other
304	Not Modified
305	Use Proxy
307	Temporary Redirect
400	Bad Request
401	Unauthorized
402	Payment Required
403	Forbidden
404	Not Found
405	Method Not Allowed
406	Not Acceptable
407	Proxy Authentication Required
408	Request Time-out
409	Conflict
410	Gone
411	Length Required
412	Precondition Failed
413	Request Entity Too Large
414	Request-URI Too Large
415	Unsupported Media Type
416	Requested Range Not Satisfiable

(continued)

Table 3.1 *(Continued)*

STATUS CODE	DESCRIPTION
417	Expectation Failed
500	Internal Server Error
501	Not Implemented
502	Bad Gateway
503	Service Unavailable
504	Gateway Time-out
505	HTTP Version Not Supported

These status codes are taken from RFC 2616, the HTTP 1.1 Request For Comment. For more information on how to interpret the meanings of these codes, refer to the RFC 2616 document, which should be available online at http://www.cis.ohio-state.edu/htbin/rfc/rfc2616.html.

Figure 3.1 shows a record in the Common Log Format. The interpretation of this record is as follows: we know that the user "hal" is logged in to the Web site and that Hal successfully retrieved the file "index.php" from IP address 255.188.33.227 on January 12 of 2001 at 6:20 P.M., and that the 110 bytes were transferred.

NCSA Extended Log Format

The NCSA Extended Log Format, also called the Combined Log Format, is almost identical to the Common Log Format. The only difference between the two formats is the addition of the Referrer and User-agent fields to the end of the log record.

The Referrer field contains the URL that the user clicked on to access the current page. If there is no link—the user typed the URL of the current page into the browser's location window, for example—then the field will contain a dash. The data for this field is actually extracted from the HTTP Referer header sent with the page request. And yes, the term *referer* is misspelled in the standard.

The User-agent field contains the name and version of the Web browser that is making the request. This information comes from the HTTP User-agent header. The field will contain a dash if the client does not transmit the User-agent header. The User-agent field is useful when optimizing Web pages for a particular browser, or when trying to weed out indexing robot page views from those of real users. There aren't a lot of other uses for this field.

| 255.188.33.227 | - | hal | [12/Jan/2001:20:20:11 -0700] | "GET /index.php HTTP/1.0" | 200 | 110 |

Figure 3.1 Record in Common Log Format.

Below is a section of the log file from our Web site (IP addresses altered to protect privacy). We'll review some of the fields and records in this example so it is easier to visualize what a server log file looks like. All relative URLs are from the base http://www.clickstreamconsulting.com/.

```
255.219.77.29 - - [19/Feb/2001:08:06:19 -0600] "GET /robots.txt
   HTTP/1.1" 200 7 "-" "Gulliver/1.3"
255.219.77.29 - - [19/Feb/2001:08:20:57 -0600] "HEAD /bios.html
   HTTP/1.1" 200 0 "-" "Gulliver/1.3"
255.219.77.29 - - [19/Feb/2001:08:22:13 -0600] "HEAD /index.html
   HTTP/1.1" 200 0 "-" "Gulliver/1.3"
255.13.64.204 - - [25/Feb/2001:06:12:11 -0600] "GET /services.html
   HTTP/1.0" 200 5903 "http://alltheweb.com/cgi-bin/search
   ?type=all&query=clickstream+database"
   "Mozilla/4.0 (compatible; MSIE 5.01; Windows NT; QXW0330v)"
255.13.64.204 - - [25/Feb/2001:06:12:15 -0600] "GET /logo1.gif
   HTTP/1.0" 200 1900
   http://www.clickstreamconsulting.com/services.html
   "Mozilla/4.0 (compatible; MSIE 5.01; Windows NT; QXW0330v)"
255.13.64.203 - - [25/Feb/2001:06:13:22 -0600] "GET /index.html
   HTTP/1.0" 200 8437
   http://www.clickstreamconsulting.com/services.html
   "Mozilla/4.0 (compatible; MSIE 5.01; Windows NT; QXW0330v)"
255.13.64.201 - - [25/Feb/2001:06:15:07 -0600] "GET /why_csdw2.html
   HTTP/1.0" 200 9576
   "http://www.clickstreamconsulting.com/index.html"
   "Mozilla/4.0 (compatible; MSIE 5.01; Windows NT; QXW0330v)"
255.13.64.201 - - [25/Feb/2001:06:18:19 -0600] "GET /articles.html
   HTTP/1.0" 200 7363
   "http://www.clickstreamconsulting.com/why_csdw2.html"
   "Mozilla/4.0 (compatible; MSIE 5.01; Windows NT; QXW0330v)"
255.199.225.190 - - [26/Feb/2001:00:37:02 -0600] "GET /
   HTTP/1.0" 200 8437 "http://search.dogpile.com/texis/search
   ?q=features+of+data+warehouse&geo=no&fs=web"
   "Mozilla/4.75 [en] (Win98; U)"
255.199.225.190 - - [26/Feb/2001:00:37:04 -0600] "GET /logo1.gif
   HTTP/1.0" 200 1900 "http://www.clickstreamconsulting.com/"
   "Mozilla/4.75 [en] (Win98; U)"
255.34.109.190 - - [01/Mar/2001:21:11:19 -0600] "GET /robots.txt
   HTTP/1.1" 200 7 "-" "Gulliver/1.3"
255.34.109.190 - - [01/Mar/2001:21:12:23 -0600] "GET /articles.html
   HTTP/1.1" 200 7363 "-" "Gulliver/1.3"
255.34.109.190 - - [01/Mar/2001:21:13:23 -0600] "GET /bios.html
   HTTP/1.1" 200 7601 "-" "Gulliver/1.3"
255.34.109.190 - - [01/Mar/2001:21:14:24 -0600] "GET /contact.html
   HTTP/1.1" 304 - "-" "Gulliver/1.3"
255.34.109.190 - - [01/Mar/2001:21:15:38 -0600] "GET /index.html
   HTTP/1.1" 304 - "-" "Gulliver/1.3"
255.34.109.190 - - [01/Mar/2001:21:16:54 -0600] "GET /overview.html
   HTTP/1.1" 304 - "-" "Gulliver/1.3"
```

```
255.34.109.190 - - [01/Mar/2001:21:17:56 -0600] "GET /services.html
   HTTP/1.1" 304 - "-" "Gulliver/1.3"
255.34.109.190 - - [01/Mar/2001:21:18:57 -0600] "GET /why_csdw2.html
   HTTP/1.1" 304 - "-" "Gulliver/1.3"
```

According to this log fragment, there were four different visits to the site by three different visitors. The first visit is from the Northern Light search engine. This visit checked our robots.txt file, then checked the file information on a number of documents. The next visit was from someone who visited the site and read through several pages before departing. The third visit was from someone who landed on our home page and apparently did not find what they were looking for, as there were no more hits from this user. The last visit was from the search engine again, looking for more modified pages.

We'll take each visitor in turn and look at the details. The first visit is from a spider indexing our site. We know this because the User-agent field contains "Gulliver/1.3" and a quick check showed us that this is the NorthernLight site indexing robot. We'll look at robot identification in more detail in a later section in this chapter.

During this visit the spider downloaded the robots.txt file to see if there was anything it should not index. We know this because the request line is "GET/ robots.txt HTTP/1.1" showing that it issued a GET for /robots.txt using the HTTP version 1.1 protocol. The spider then checked the metadata of several documents by using HEAD. There were no subsequent accesses so we can assume that the search engine was up to date.

The next visit is from a user running Internet Explorer version 5.01 on Windows NT, as shown by the User-agent field of "Mozilla/4.0 (compatible; MSIE 5.01; Windows NT; QXW0330v)." The user came via a proxy server at the University of Karlsruhe in Germany, which we know because the IP address goes back to this location. We resolved the address to a hostname as one would normally do when processing logs during a warehouse load.

This is an interesting visit because it highlights an IP address problem we'll discuss later in the chapter. This user comes to us from three different addresses: 255.13.64.204, 255.13.64.203, and 255.13.64.201. We believe this is one visitor because all addresses resolve to proxy servers at the same location, and because of the time log and the trail of referrers.

Using the trail of referrers we can see the user's path through the site. This person first came to the page "services.html" and linked here from the search engine at alltheweb.com. We know this because the base URL in the Referrer field is the CGI program "http://alltheweb.com/cgi-bin/search" and the query string in the URL is "type=all&query=clickstream+database."

Once on our site, their browser loaded the logo on the services.html page. Shortly thereafter, the user linked to the home page "index.html". Here we have another piece of evidence supporting our assertion that these different IP addresses are one user: the logo was not loaded for any subsequent page views, most likely because it was cached in the user's browser. We know the user linked to the home page because the referrer for index.html is "http://www .clickstreamconsulting.com/services.html". Our home page has the start of an informational article on it. This leads to why_csdw2.html, where the user linked to next.

The user apparently read all of these pages based on the time between hits in the log. Finally, the user linked to the articles page. From here, we assume the user left our site to read some of the magazine articles we point to at an affiliated site.

The next visit is from a user via a dialup ISP in India, based on the domain we resolved their IP address to. The User-agent field contains "Mozilla/ 4.75–(Win98; U)" showing that the user is running version 4.75 of Netscape, in English on Windows 98. This user also came from a search engine as the base URL from the Referrer field is "http://search.dogpile.com/texis/search" and there is a query string showing the search terms. The logo for the home page was also loaded, but there are no subsequent hits.

The last visit is from the search engine spider. This time it fetched the page articles.html and bios.html pages, as indicated by the 200 in the HTTP Status field. The subsequent GETs for the remaining URLs show a status of 304, or "Not Modified," and a dash in the Bytes field, implying that the spider is fetching pages only if they've been modified since the last time it visited the site.

One last thing to note is that none of these visits placed data into the Ident and Authuser fields. This is because the former field is rarely used, and the latter field is only used with Web site logins, which our site did not require.

W3C Extended Log Format

The last log format, W3C Extended Log File Format (or ExLF for short), is not as commonly used as the previously described formats. W3C is shorthand for the World Wide Web Standards Committee, and all of its specifications are online at www.w3c.org. The ExLF format is the most complex of the standard log formats. It is the only standardized format that can be customized to specify which fields are logged, and it provides a much more detailed set of fields to choose from. This flexibility allows ExLF to be used by many different types of software, including firewalls, cache servers, and other applications.

Table 3.2 W3C Extended Log Format Directives

DIRECTIVE	DESCRIPTION
Version:	The version of ExLF used
Fields:	A white space delimited list of fields that are present in the log file
Software:	Identifies the software that created the log
Start-Date:	The date and time the log was started
End-Date:	The date and time the log was completed
Date:	The date and time an entry was added
Remark:	Comments placed in the log by the software or person administering the software

In order to specify what is logged, an ExLF log file contains two different kinds of records. The first type of record is a directive record that contains metadata about the content of the log file. The second type of record is a data record containing the data fields actually logged.

A line in the log file beginning with the pound character ("#") indicates that this line is a directive providing some information about the format of log file records or about the log file itself. There are two directives that are required and must be present at the beginning of a log file. These are the Version and Fields directives. Table 3.2 describes the directives available.

Instead of defining a fixed format, the ExLF specifies logs that may contain any of a set of fields. To make the data even more interesting, one may specify the logging of transfers between types of participants. For instance, you might choose to log the Referer header that the server sends to the client as well as the Referer header the client sends to you. Table 3.3 lists all of the field prefixes that may be used.

Table 3.3 W3C Extended Log Format Field Prefixes

PREFIX	MEANING
c-	Client
s-	Server
r-	Remote server
cs-	Client-to-server
sc-	Server-to-client
sr-	Server to remote server
rs-	Remote server to server
x-	Application

The remote server prefix is not used for normal browser to Web server transactions. This prefix is intended for use with proxy servers and Web servers.

The field prefixes are required for most fields. These prefixes are combined with the field identifiers on the Fields directive line to indicate what data is being logged. There are 20 different field identifiers to choose from. These are described in Table 3.4.

Table 3.4 W3C Extended Log Format Fields

FIELD IDENTIFIER	PREFIX REQUIRED	DESCRIPTION
Date	No	The date the transaction completed
Time	No	The time the transaction completed
Ip	Yes	The IP address and port of the host specified by the prefix
Dns	Yes	The fully qualified hostname of the host specified by the prefix
Method	Yes	The action being performed (for example, a GET)
Uri	Yes	The full URI of the resource being accessed
uri-stem	Yes	The portion of the URL excluding the query string
uri-query	Yes	The query string portion of the URL, if present in the request
Cookie	Yes	The content of cookies sent, if any
Username	Yes, cs only	User name sent if the visitor is logged into the Web site
cs(referer)	Yes, cs only	The URL of the last page visited, if present
cs(user-agent)	Yes, cs only	The client browser type
From	Yes, cs only	The email address of the user; no longer sent by most browsers
Protocol	Yes	The Internet protocol used, e.g., HTTP, FTP
Version	Yes	The version of the protocol used
Status	Yes	The HTTP status code
Comment	Yes	The comment returned with the HTTP status code
Bytes	No	The number of bytes transferred
time-taken	No	The length of time the transaction took to complete, in seconds
Cached	No	Indicates whether a cache hit occurred; a zero is a cache miss

The simplest way to describe this format is to review a sample log file and discuss some of the records from this file:

```
#Software: Microsoft Internet Information Services 5.0
#Version: 1.0
#Date: 2001-03-01 17:42:15
#Fields: c-ip date time cs-method cs-uri-stem sc-status sc-bytes
   cs-referer cs-user-agent
255.191.63.124 2001-03-01 08:30:20 GET /articles.html 200 6919
   http://www.alltheweb.com/cgi-bin/search?
   type=all&query=clickstream+data
   "Mozilla/4.0 (compatible; MSIE 5.01; Windows NT)"
255.191.63.124 2001-03-01 08:30:22 GET /logo1.gif 200 1900
   http://www.clickstreamconsulting.com./
   "Mozilla/4.0 (compatible; MSIE 5.01; Windows NT)"
```

In the example we see four directives at the beginning of the log file. The first three directives tell us that the Web site is running Microsoft IIS as the Web server, that we're using version 1.0 of ExLF and that the log file was generated on March 1 of 2001 at 5:42 P.M.

The fourth directive is the most interesting to us because it specifies what this log file contains. This line is a Fields directive with a list of field identifiers telling us that the log file records contain the following data:

- The client's IP address (c-ip).
- The date the transaction was completed (date).
- The time the transaction was completed (time).
- The method used by the client to communicate with the Web server (cs-method).
- The stem portion of the URL requested by the client (cs-uri-stem).
- The status of the response by the server (sc-status).
- The number of bytes transferred by the server to the client (sc-bytes).
- The referring URL that got us this client (cs-referer).
- The client's browser type (cs-user-agent).

The first line of the log file tells us that the user at IP address 255.191.63.124 running Microsoft Internet Explorer 5.01 successfully retrieved all 6919 bytes of the document "articles.html" at 8:30:20 A.M. and was referred to us by the search engine at www.alltheweb.com. The second line tells us that this same user also successfully loaded the logo associated with the HTML page.

The comprehensive data content and the self-documenting nature of the log files make this format great for warehouse developers. If the Web servers and other applications support ExLF, it is worthwhile to ask the site administrator to make use of this format.

Other Log Formats

You might encounter one of many other log file formats. For example, while IBM's Websphere supports both the NCSA Combined and W3C Extended formats, it also has some special purpose logging capabilities. If the Web server is running on an Apple Macintosh then one might encounter the WebStar format. This is another highly configurable format that provides some data not available in other formats.

As is often the case, Microsoft is an exception. Microsoft decided to create a proprietary format for IIS that is comma delimited. This is the *only* comma-delimited format. Similar to the WebStar format on the Macintosh, the IIS format provides a number of Windows-specific data fields. One field of interest is the Microsoft GUID. We will discuss this data element in more detail later.

Another situation you might find is a Web site running older software and hardware. The original Web logging formats put different information into four different log files: the access log, referrer log, agent log, and error log. Most Web servers now allow one to place the access, referrer, and agent data into the same log, with the error log usually placed in a separate file.

In these older formats the access log generally contains the information found in the Common Log Format. The referrer log records the document the user requested and the referring URL that linked to this document, assuming there is one. The example below shows a referrer log example from an older version of the NCSA HTTPd Web server.

```
[02/Mar/2001:13:03:29] http://www.google.com/search?q=clickstream+crm
  -> /articles.html
[02/Mar/2001:13:03:29] http://www.google.com/ search
  ?q=clickstream+junk+food -> /ding_dong_order.php
[02/Mar/2001:13:03:34] http://www.spins.com/marketing/partners.html
  -> /Index.html
```

The agent log lists the browser type (the User-agent HTTP header) for each access to the Web site. The example below shows a sample Agent log from the same NCSA HTTPd server.

```
[02/Mar/2001:13:03:29] Mozilla/4.76 [en] (Win98; U)
[02/Mar/2001:13:03:29] Mozilla/4.76 [en]C-CCK-MCD {Sony}(Win98; U)
[02/Mar/2001:13:03:34] Mozilla/1.22 (Windows; I; 16bit)
[02/Mar/2001:13:08:22] Mozilla/4.0 (compatible; MSIE 5.5; AOL 6.0;
  Windows 98)
[02/Mar/2001:14:00:02] Mozilla/4.0 (compatible; MSIE 5.01; Windows NT)"
[02/Mar/2001:14:11:30] 1NCSA Mosaic for the X Window System/2.4
[02/Mar/2001:14:12:34] Mercator-Scrub-1.1
```

One thing to note is that the timestamp should be synchronized for related records between the different logs. This is not an entirely dependable mechanism to tie records back together because it is possible to have multiple records with the same timestamp. This will occur if the Web server gets many hits at one time. Usually you can put the records back together.

Most of the time, Web servers will be configured with one transfer log and one error log. If not, you may want to request this of your site administrator. Alternatively, you may find it easier to deal with each set of data discretely and assemble them together in the database. This is one of the design decisions discussed in Chapter 8.

Realities of Log File Data

Now that we've reviewed some of the common log file formats and what they contain, we need to look at some of the data elements in more depth. On the surface, many of these elements seem to be of obvious utility and others seem to be of no use in the warehouse. When examined in the context of the stateless HTTP protocol and how browsers and Web servers work you may find that this initial assessment is inaccurate.

As mentioned earlier, the date and time are the date and time the server completed a given transaction. Apart from indicating when the transaction occurred, we might need to use them to link records across multiple log files.

IP Address and Hostname

The client's IP address is an interesting field. Most Web servers are capable of translating the address into a full hostname, but do not perform the reverse lookup because of the performance degradation. This is not a problem for the warehouse because the IP addresses can be translated during the extract and load processing.

Apart from the basic IP Address and Hostname fields, it is possible to infer other information based on the address. This information can be processed at the same time and loaded into the warehouse along with the IP address and hostname.

Using domain name service (DNS) lookup, a client IP address can be converted into its corresponding full domain and hostname, revealing the network origin of the visitor. The top level of the domain name (the trailing .com, .edu, .org, etc.) also reveals interesting information about user demographics. For example, if there are a lot of visits from the .edu top level domain (TLD), then that would indicate a great deal of student interest in a site, but if the bulk of the visits come from .gov, then the site must be of interest to government workers. Because many countries have their own TLD it is also possible to infer the geography and language characteristics of site visitors.

One might assume that an IP address in the Web server log always equates to an individual client system. If so, counting the number of unique IP addresses would reveal the total number of visitors to a site during a particular time period. Unfortunately, this is absolutely wrong.

In the good old days, IP addresses were statically assigned to individual computers, creating a one-to-one mapping between an IP address and a computer. But today most Internet users use Internet Service Providers (ISPs) to access the Internet. ISPs multiplex client requests over massive server installations, and as a result, users will likely have a different IP address each time they dial in. The same user might visit your Web site three times and have a different IP address each time. This means that many different IP addresses can map to the same hostname. Furthermore, many enterprises use Dynamic Host Configuration Protocol (DHCP) to manage IP address assignment for computers on their networks, resulting in a different IP address each time the computer is connected to the network. These IP addresses are often unresolvable into a hostname using DNS.

Don't make the mistake of translating addresses to names and loading only these hostnames into the warehouse. You need to keep both the IP Address and the Hostname fields to handle the cases where DNS cannot resolve an IP address into a hostname. The number of unresolvable IP addresses in a log file can be surprisingly large. It is not uncommon to fail to resolve the IP address in 25 percent or more of one's log records.

Proxies, firewalls, and network address translation (NAT) also interfere with the use of IP addresses to distinguish unique users. Depending on how proxies or firewalls are configured at an enterprise, one might find that every user from a given Internet domain shows up with the same IP address, meaning the logged IP address cannot be used to distinguish one visitor from another.

Network address translation creates the same situation. If you want to share an Internet connection at home, you can purchase a small network hub that allows you to share the same connection to your ISP across multiple computers. This works by using NAT to map each machine's internal IP address to the same externally visible IP address. To the Web site, two home users visiting the same site look like they are coming from the same IP address. A number of online gaming services still have problems allowing more than one user to log in if they have the same IP address due to NAT.

The most insidious problem with IP addresses is that some ISPs use multiple IP addresses for a single computer during a user session. Both AOL and MSN do this. The result is that each request by a given client will come from a different IP address. For example, if a Web site's home page contains a logo graphic and two navigation graphics, the server log will record each HTTP request with a different IP address, making it appear that there were several different visitors for just one page view.

In order to accurately count users and sessions, the Web site must implement some type of session management or user tracking system. When dealing with commerce-oriented sites, chances are very good that this has already been done.

Ident

The Ident field in these formats is almost always a dash (indicating no value was supplied). The original intent of this field was to record the login name of the user accessing the Web site. The login name of the user would be provided by the ident demon (identd), usually running on the client host, which was often a multiuser UNIX system or UNIX workstation at a university. Identd is almost never used these days because of security risks, nor do personal computers provide this facility, so no data is sent to the Web server.

Authorized User

The Authorized user field is only used when the Web site makes use of Web server authentication. If the site authenticates users this way—rare for most commercial sites—then the Authuser field will contain the login name provided by the user. Most of the time this field will contain a dash since most Web sites use application-based logins rather than Web server logins.

Request and the Request Components

Some log formats such as the W3C Extended Format separate the request into each of its components: the HTTP method, the URL for the document, the query string, and the protocol and version. In CLF or ECLF the request line will be a single field containing all of these parts in order. Figure 3.2 provides an example of the request field divided into components.

When using ExLF, the components of the request map to fields as follows: the URL and query string make up the *uri* field, *uri-stem* is the URL without the query string, *uri-query* is just the query string, *method* is the method at the beginning of the URL, *protocol* is the protocol at the end of the URL without the version number, and *version* is the version number by itself.

Placing the method, URL and query string in separate fields makes processing the log files simpler. It is worth checking to see if your Web server can record the request data this way. Doing so can save time when developing the extract and load programs.

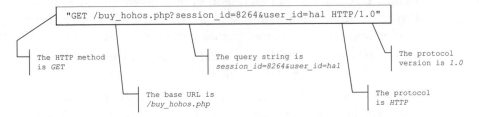

Figure 3.2 Components of the request field.

Status and Comment

As mentioned earlier in this chapter, the status is the HTTP status of the transfer. If using the W3C log format then the associated comment may be added, showing the text of the message sent to the client. The comment is not normally a useful field for the warehouse, but the status code is. The status code will help to determine exactly what transpired during different transactions. It is very important to note that a 200 (OK) status is not necessarily an indication that the page transfer to the client was completed normally. Hitting the browser Back button in the middle of a page load may still result in a 200 status for the HTML page even though all the page components may not have been completely displayed before the button was hit.

Bytes Sent

The Bytes field contains the total number of bytes transferred for the request and should be the exact same count as the document size. This transfer size excludes the data sent in the HTTP headers, including cookies. One might question why bytes would be interesting when doing warehouse analysis, other than knowing how much data was sent.

There are several uses for the size of the transfer. If the user is downloading a document and stops the transfer, either by hitting the Stop button, closing the browser, or otherwise disconnecting from the site, then the bytes transferred will be smaller than the document size, giving the vital clue that the transfer was prematurely ended.

Knowing this, we can do an analysis of the number of times pages were not fully transferred. If the same page shows up consistently then it could be that the page takes too long to load and people get frustrated. It might also indicate that users get to the page and realize that it isn't what they expect or want. An analyst could look through more information to determine what is really happening with these pages.

There are some anomalies that one might see when looking at the log files. For instance, one might see a partial transfer, then a later transfer for the same document, with the sum of both Bytes fields adding up to the actual size of the document. One might also see a record where the Bytes field is a dash, indicating no data was recorded. This entry catches up a lot of people who assume the transfers are always numeric.

To reconcile these anomalies one must examine the URL, time, HTTP status, and bytes. In the first case, it is possible that the transfer was interrupted. If the user reloads the page or visits the same page a little later the browser can continue the page load where it left off, because a portion of the page is already in the browser's cache. Assuming that the HTTP status is 206, the timestamp for the second request is close to the prior timestamp for the same URL and the bytes from the two records add up to the correct size for the document, one can assume that is what happened. This type of transfer is termed a *partial GET.*

Another common occurrence is a status of 304 in the record, and no data (a dash) for the Bytes field. This indicates that a client checked to see if the document was changed since the last time it was loaded, and the Web server did not send the document because there was no change. This is termed a *conditional GET.* Instead of requesting the document again, the browser displays the unchanged document from the local browser cache. The good thing about this behavior is that we know the user was accessing this particular URL so we can include it in the clickstream data and count it as a page view in the user's session.

All of this brings up a key point about clickstream-relevant data that is not in the log files. If possible, one should load the Web site's document names and sizes into the warehouse so it is possible to deduce the information we've been discussing here. Unfortunately this is not always possible, particularly in dynamic page generation environments where the page content may be generated on the fly rather than assembled from prebuilt components.

Referrer

The Referrer field is used for a number of different purposes and should always be present in the warehouse. The Referrer field will be a complete URL and will include a query string if one was used. That means the field should be divided into its constituent parts during the warehouse load.

The referrer will usually contain the URL of the page the user was last visiting before they linked to your Web site. If the user is already on your site, the Referrer field works the same way. Instead of an outside URL, the field will contain the URL of the page the user was last viewing on your site. The Referrer field thus provides a trail of information about where a user has been during his session. The referrer may be blank because the browser may mask or not send the referrer information, although this is not common.

It is possible that there was no referrer for the document sent to the client. There would be no referrer if the user typed the URL in the address window of their browser, or had their browser set to load this page on startup, or if they used a bookmark. In these cases, the referrer would contain a dash *most of the time*.

The problem is that the referrer may be a number of things if the browser used a bookmark. On older versions of certain browsers the referrer can be the full path to their bookmark file. Finding a bookmark file location in the referrer is a rare occurrence and you should consider yourself lucky. There will be a dash if the browser is a recent version of Internet Explorer. Access from current versions of Netscape will result in the text "[unknown origin]" being recorded.

We mentioned that the Referrer field contains the complete URL including the query string. The query string contains useful information if the page was accessed via a search engine. If the search was local to your site, it means the user was having difficulty finding what they needed. Examining their search terms from the query string can tell you something about how they think of the site and may help you design a better site organization. Searches from external sites will show what terms people are using to search for content similar to that on your site. We'll discuss more about search engines and search logs later in this chapter.

User Agent

The User-agent field is one of those fields that is interesting to Web designers, but probably not that useful for most of your end users. The field is intended for three purposes: tracing protocol violations; statistical information-gathering purposes; and to help Web developers work around the shortcomings of specific browsers or browser versions. Analysis of user-agent data is how many of the Internet data analysis companies estimate the market share held by browser companies.

In general, the only data warehouse users who care about the browser data are the site designers and developers. When doing analysis with the User-agent field, one should be careful not to draw incorrect conclusions. For example, assuming that the breakdown of browser types is 65 percent Netscape Navigator, 15 percent Internet Explorer, and 10 percent other, the Web designers might decide to optimize the site for Netscape.

While this might be valid, it is also possible that one could generate an increase in site traffic by focusing more on some of the 10 percent of "other" browsers. If these visitors are using a text-based browser or an alternative viewing device then better serving this audience might be more valuable to the enterprise. One interesting note about the User-agent field is that some browsers will lie about what type of browser they are. There are reasonable explanations for why they do this, but it can be misleading when analyzing logs.

This field is also useful as part of the mechanism to differentiate visits by users from visits by search engines. We'll discuss these search engine robots and how to identify them in a later section.

Time-Taken

Time-taken is the amount of time in seconds that the server took to process the request. The primary use for this field is in determining how well the site is performing on average. When combined with document access frequency and information from content caches, you can provide site administrators with useful performance information.

Cached

This field is generally available only when using the W3C extended format. Even then, the Web server may not support it. The more likely use of this field is with proxy and cache servers, where monitoring caching information is of more use. When incorporating the data into the warehouse, combining this information with the time-taken field may provide useful information about how well the site is performing and whether more investment in content caching would be worthwhile.

Protocol and Version

The protocol in Web server logs will usually be HTTP, but not in every case. For example, firewalls, proxy servers, and cache servers can be configured to log information about access via different ports. If one is processing these kinds of log files then the protocol may be more important. For example, if your Web site permits downloading of files via File Transfer Protocol (FTP) and email then you should also load these log records into the clickstream data warehouse.

A more technical use of the protocol and version is in Web site design and capacity planning. HTTP 1.1 is much more efficient than HTTP 1.0. If the trend is toward increasing access via HTTP 1.1 (or later) protocols then this information could help the systems administrators save money on equipment upgrades.

Cookies

Cookies are transmitted as part of the HTTP header, so any Web server that can log headers should be able to log cookies. Cookies frequently play a very important role in assembling and analyzing data in the warehouse. We will discuss cookies in more detail later in this chapter, and revisit the topic in Chapter 4.

Other Data and Data-Related Issues

In this section we'll describe a few of the data issues one will likely encounter when working with log files. Chapter 8 will cover processing techniques to consider when selecting or designing the data warehouse extract and transformation software.

Apart from specific fields, there are some other important things to keep in mind when dealing with Web server logs. A key concept is that the logs record discrete transactions. HTTP is stateless; a client makes a request and receives a response from the server, and that is the end of any state kept between the two parties. There are some challenges resulting from this, and some challenges resulting from the architecture of the Web and design of Web browsers.

Data Separation

Statelessness causes a number of problems to crop up when processing logs into the warehouse. One problem was mentioned earlier: the use of Web load balancers means that a single visit may happen across multiple Web servers. This means that the data for a single session appears in log files from multiple servers.

To further complicate the load, it is possible that a visit will cross over a single log file boundary. Log files are of a finite size and must be rotated out and new logs started. The warehouse will contain partial visit information for a user if the log change happens in the middle of a visit. The remaining data will not be available until the next data load, which might be a day away. This problem applies to both multiserver and single server sites.

Browser Buttons and Missed Pages

The stateless nature of HTTP creeps in when we look at browser functionality as well. When a person hits the Back button in the browser there is no contact with the server to tell it that the user went back to an earlier page. The page will be loaded from the browser's cache unless the site makes an explicit effort to prevent caching.

The implication of this shows up when reviewing a series of user actions as they click through the Web site. If a user clicks on a link on our home page, then hits the Back button and clicks on a different link on our home page, we will see the following in the Web server log:

```
255.2.248.190 - - [02/Mar/2001:012:37:02 -0600] "GET /homepage.html
  HTTP/1.0" 200 8437 "-" "Mozilla/4.75 [en] (Win98; U)"
255.2.248.190 - - [02/Mar/2001:012:37:42 -0600] "GET /second_page.html
  HTTP/1.0" 200 2198
  "http://www.clickstreamconsulting.com/homepage.html"
  "Mozilla/4.75 [en] (Win98; U)"
```

```
255.2.248.190 - - [02/Mar/2001:012:40:26 -0600] "GET /third_page.html
   HTTP/1.0" 200 2198
   "http://www.clickstreamconsulting.com/homepage.html"
   "Mozilla/4.75 [en] (Win98; U)"
```

The first record is the first page the user requested from our site. The second record shows that the user linked from the home page to the second page on the site. The third record shows that the user linked from the home page to the third page on the site, but there is no data showing that the user went back to the home page and forward to the third page. This is why one must be careful when examining the paths users take through the site.

There are techniques one can use to attempt to better record the user path. One possibility is to prevent pages from being cached. This can be done by setting the expiration date to a time in the past or by using cache directives on the HTML pages. The downside is that site performance will be worse, so one is unlikely to find sites of any scale disabling the caching of all the site's pages.

Another technique is to include a logging element on the page. A way to accomplish this is by embedding an element on the page that is different every time, for example a reference to an image with a random number in the query string. If the element contains the page's URL as part of its query string then you will see a hit because the browser thinks the element is different due to the random name. The log sample below shows what the records might look like. The Ident, Authuser, and User-agent fields were left off and open lines were added to make the example more readable.

```
255.2.248.190 [02/Mar/2001:12:37:02 -0600] "GET /homepage.php
   HTTP/1.0" 200 8437 "-"
255.2.248.190 [02/Mar/2001:12:37:04 -0600] "GET /cgi-bin/tracker
   ?page=/homepage.php&rand=123702 HTTP/1.0" 200 64
   "http://www.clickstreamconsulting.com/homepage.php"

255.2.248.190 [02/Mar/2001:12:37:42 -0600] "GET /second_page.php
   HTTP/1.0" 200 2198
   "http://www.clickstreamconsulting.com/homepage.php"
255.2.248.190 [02/Mar/2001:12:37:44 -0600] "GET /cgi-bin/tracker
   ?page=/second_page.php&rand=123742 HTTP/1.0" 200 64
   "http://www.clickstreamconsulting.com/homepage.php"

255.2.248.190 [02/Mar/2001:12:40:22 -0600] "GET /cgi-bin/tracker
   ?page=/homepage.php&rand=123827 HTTP/1.0" 200 64
   "http://www.clickstreamconsulting.com/homepage.php"

255.2.248.190 [02/Mar/2001:12:40:26 -0600] "GET /third_page.php
   HTTP/1.0" 200 2198
   "http://www.clickstreamconsulting.com/homepage.php"
255.2.248.190 [02/Mar/2001:12:40:28 -0600] "GET /cgi-bin/tracker
   ?page=/third_page.php&rand=124026 HTTP/1.0" 200 64
   "http://www.clickstreamconsulting.com/third.php"
```

Now the log contains two records per page. Each pair consists of the page and the associated tracking element. The query string contains the page name of the referring page and a changing ID. The fifth record in the file is just for the tracker. This is because, while the home page was cached, the tracker was not. We assume that the user loaded a page from cache, and we know that it was the home page thanks to the query string.

It is possible to embed a logging element on every page. Depending on the implementation, the technique may only work the first time the Back button is used. Very few sites use this technique because of the extra development effort, because it is not perfect and can still be confounded by caching, and because the utility of seeing every page view is not always worth the expense.

Content Caching

That brings us to the next item, caching. With caching, a file is kept locally and the Web server doesn't receive a hit for the file. Documents can be cached in many places. Each browser has a local cache where it stores the files it has recently accessed. The Web browser checks its local cache before sending a request out. If the URL requested matches the URL of an item in the cache then no request is sent and the local copy is used. Depending on the browser settings, the browser may check to see if the file has been modified before displaying the page in the cache.

Cache servers work in fundamentally the same way. With cache servers, if you request a page from a Web site and any other user from the same ISP requested that same page recently, the page will be served from the cache and the Web site will not receive a hit. ISPs use cache servers to improve the service to their users and to decrease the amount of traffic on their networks.

If a request makes it past the ISP's cache then it may hit a content cache elsewhere. Many businesses with high-traffic sites use content delivery networks provided by companies like Akamai and Inktomi. These content delivery networks will cache data on servers closer (in network topology terms) to end users, decreasing the load on a Web site and improving performance to the end user. The ISP for a business may also use cache servers at their site, just like an end user ISP. Finally, the Web site may also run its own cache or caching proxy servers to improve performance.

If caching is employed at every point between a user and a Web site, there are at least five locations where a page may be cached. Based on all this caching, one can see why counting page views in the Web server logs could significantly underreport site traffic.

The caches can also cause you to lose referring site information. If someone uses a search engine and clicks on the link to your site, and the page they are linking to is in a cache, then the Web site will not see the referrer. If the user clicks on a link from this page to another page that is not cached, the referrer will show up in the logs as either the prior page or as a dash. This means that the original referrer has been lost.

Missed hits because of caching can lead to improper conclusions. Caching hides the hits from the more popular pages. The more popular a page, the more likely it is to be cached somewhere between your Web site and the visitors. If you judge page hits based only on data in your log files, you may find that less popular pages show more logged hits than the more popular pages that get cached upstream from your Web servers.

Finally, we note that the failure to log page hits because of caching only further confounds attempts to map a given user's path through a Web site.

Dwell Time

An important element of visitor behavior is the time spent on a given page, called the dwell time. The dwell time for a page is calculated by subtracting the timestamp value of the current log record from the timestamp of the next log record for the visit.

As usual, there are problems that can distort the interpretation of the dwell time. Although we have no idea what the user really does between page views, we tend to assume it was time spent reading the page. However, a user might have gone out to lunch before returning to read the next page, and the hour-long page view would be a gross distortion of his actual behavior. Page views by a user that take longer than some predetermined time are usually used to indicate the end of a user session and the beginning of a new session. This decision will show two sessions rather than a single session containing extraordinarily long page views.

Another issue is page caching. Because of the caching we may not see page views between one record and the next in our log. To make matters worse, we don't know anything about what the user did for the time between. It's possible the user read three other pages that were delivered by a cache before we saw them hit an uncached page. It appears that the user spent five minutes reading a single page when they really read four pages in that time.

Identifying Exit Pages

One final problem when combining records from the log into a picture of a user's visit is knowing when the user's session is over. There is no record in the server log that says the user left the site. This is true if the person hit their Home button, turned off their browser, or went to another site by clicking a link on the page they were viewing.

This means that the records for a visit simply stop. If the site does some form of user tracking and the person returns later, the records start again. Because of this problem, many companies and many log analysis tools assume that a thirty minute gap between records indicates that a session has terminated. This may be a bad assumption, since the user may have linked to another site, taken a phone call, or had the good fortune to hit a series of pages cached by their ISP.

There are two instances where it may be possible to track a user leaving the site. The first is if the site forces users to log in to gain access. Users who log out will leave a record that they logged out of the system.

The second possible way to track users who leave the site is to change how links to external sites are configured. Instead of having a link to another site on one of the pages, every link off the site is actually a call to a program with the URL of the link as a parameter. For example, the following link would accomplish this:

```
<A HREF="/cgi-bin/redirector?link=www.OtherSite.com">
   This link goes to OtherSite.com</A>
```

The link is actually a call to the CGI program *redirector*. It takes the link parameter as input and redirects the user's browser to the appropriate site. By doing external links this way, the Web server will record every access to the redirector program. The result is that it is possible to determine where people link to by examining the query string associated with these records.

Extending the Web Server Logs

The probability is high that when you get your first look at your site's Web server log files they will be configured to the Web server's default setting. This setting will most likely be Common Log Format because so many servers use it as the default. Unfortunately, the Common Log Format does not contain enough information to deliver what we need in a clickstream warehouse. Even the NCSA Combined Log Format, although an improvement, may be too limited.

The design of the Web applications running the Web site will dictate whether the Combined format provides enough information. If your Web site uses cookies for session or user tracking then you must extend the log file to include this data or you will not be able to provide the information the warehouse users need.

Logging Additional Data

The NCSA Combined Log Format (ECLF) contains most of the information we might need for our clickstream data warehouse. The only other item that is almost certain to be a necessity is the user's cookie data, which is passed in the Cookie HTTP header field. Since most Web servers can be configured to also log any of the fields passed in the HTTP headers, the user's cookie and other header fields can be appended to a standard format log record.

The Content-type header field is another field that would be interesting to log. The server sends this header to tell the browser what the media type of the document is. For example, if the Web site contains documents in Adobe's PDF format then the MIME type sent will be *application/pdf*. If the document type information doesn't come from some other data source then logging the Content-type header will capture it for you.

If possible, one should log the time required to serve requests (this is the Time-taken field in the ExLF). As was just mentioned, cookies should be logged if the Web site uses them. Cookies usually contain the information needed to match records in the Web server's log with user profile information stored in other databases.

One other data element that can be helpful, particularly when there are problems with log file processing, is the hostname of the Web server that produced the logs or its IP address. This is the *s-ip* or *s-dns* field in the W3C Extended format. Some Web servers provide facilities for logging this type of local server information, even if they do not explicitly support the W3C Extended format.

The reason we may want to have the Web server hostname is that many Web sites use multiple Web servers for load-balancing and for special-purpose site activities. An upgrade or change in the configuration of one of the Web servers may cause problems with the data sent to the warehouse, and the server name can help in tracking down the problem server. The hostname will also help if site administrators want to examine performance of the Web server farm.

One situation you might encounter with Web server logs is virtual servers. Using virtual servers means that a single Web server has been configured to answer for multiple Web sites with different domain names. For example, the Web site might contain one URL for customers at http://www.company.com and one for remote salespeople at http://sales.company.com.

The common practice is to log each virtual server into its own log file, but most servers do not default to this automatically. If the site administrator can't or won't configure logging this way, the server IP address or name will be vital— without it there is no way to differentiate records from the different Web sites.

In general, changing the data a Web server records is not difficult. It usually entails editing a configuration file, or in some cases, going through a user interface to alter some information on a form. For example, the following line is the default configuration line for Apache:

```
LogFormat "%h %l %u %t \"%r\" %s %b"
```

Each field is denoted by a percent sign and a letter indicating the data element to record. The above line is the default for Apache, the Common Log Format. The format string shows the fields for host (%h), ident (%l), authuser (%u), date (%t), requested URL (%r) in quotes, HTTP status (%s) and bytes sent (%b). To change the configuration for Apache so it logs in the NCSA Combined Log Format and includes cookies, the only work to do is to edit the configuration file and change the above sample line to the following:

```
LogFormat "%h %l %u %t \"%r\" %s %b %{referer}i %{user-agent}i %{cookie}i"
```

All we've done is added the Referrer, User-agent, and Cookie headers into the string. Making changes will generally not be much more complex than this for most other types of Web servers.

Error Logs

The error log is a separate log that can be a useful source of information for the warehouse. Apart from basic data about attempts to access files that are not present, generally due to broken links, the data may tell you something about the site design or how people are attempting to navigate the site. The error log format can vary between Web servers but is generally close to format in the records shown below.

```
Thu Aug 31 17:34:51 2000] [notice] Apache/1.3.12 (Unix) configured
   - resuming normal operations
[Thu Aug 31 17:48:31 2000] [notice] caught SIGTERM, shutting down
[Thu Aug 31 18:15:26 2000] [notice] Apache/1.3.12 (Unix) configured
   - resuming normal operations
[Thu Aug 31 21:12:06 2000] [warn] pid file /logs/httpd.pid overwritten
   - Unclean shutdown of previous Apache run?
[Thu Aug 31 21:12:06 2000] [notice] Apache/1.3.12 (Unix)
   PHP/4.0.2 configured - resuming normal operations
[Fri Sep  1 14:16:31 2000] [error] [client 255.168.11.65]
   File does not exist: /usr/local/apache/htdocs/big_stuf.html
[Fri Sep  1 14:42:57 2000] [error] [client 255.168.11.65]
   File does not exist: /usr/local/apache/htdocs/ /dingdongs.php
[Thu Sep 21 11:31:19 2000] [notice] caught SIGTERM, shutting down
[Fri Oct  6 17:35:56 2000] [error] [client 255.16.74.76]
   user conchita: authentication failure
   for "/php4/logintest.php": password mismatch
[Fri Oct  6 17:36:04 2000] [error] [client 255.16.74.76]
   user notme not found: /php4/logintest.php
```

The above error log shows some notices or warnings from the Apache Web server telling us that it started up, was shut down, and was shut down incorrectly or crashed. The data that might be interesting in the warehouse is the error messages. The first two messages show that a user attempted to access files that are not present on the Web site. The second two messages show that a user tried to log in with a bad password, and a user provided an invalid login name.

The *file not found* errors might indicate a link problem within the site or from a partner's Web site. If one were to see consistent messages of this type for the same page then combining the error data with the referrer data could help us pinpoint where those visitors are coming from and why they are being given a bad link.

The failed login information could indicate a security problem, but there is more interesting analysis that could be done. If there are a lot of failed logins and this data is combined with customer service email or phone call data, one might find that the site is suffering from a design flaw that makes it hard for users to log in. Perhaps adding the option to remember users' passwords would decrease failed logins and help to improve the user experience.

Alternative Logging Techniques

It is possible to extend the capabilities of a Web server logging by applying some alternative techniques. When we discussed data problems due to the browser's Back button in an earlier section we described one such technique. The idea was to embed a logging element that would not be cached by the browser to capture some of the missing page views.

The technique can be extended to provide a better mechanism for logging data for the clickstream warehouse. A Web page consists of many elements, and those elements do not have to be served by the same Web server. It is easy to embed an image from one Web site in a page on your own site. The Web page contains HTML tags that tell the browser where to find the image, and all of this is transparent to the user. In fact, this is how most banner ads are placed on Web sites.

To turn this into a logging mechanism we need to do a few things. First, we want to place something on the Web page that won't affect page layouts. We can use a transparent gif, an image that is one pixel in size and is set to be transparent rather than colored. If the Web developers place this image somewhere on each Web page we want to track then the image will be loaded when the Web page loads.

To make this a more useful logging mechanism we should dedicate a Web server to serving up only the transparent gif. This makes the Web server log file much easier to process because we are now looking at a record of requests from only the pages we are interested in. We no longer have to filter out the requests for items like navigation bars and image spacers that show up in a normal Web server log.

We need to look for the URL in a different field because the log file from this Web server is only serving the transparent gif, therefore showing only the single URL in the request field. The referrer field now contains the URL instead of the request field.

There are some drawbacks to using this technique. We do not have access to the query string on the originating URL. This can be a serious problem if our site uses query strings for something we need to store. We also lose visibility into requests checking to see if documents changed, since HEAD requests and conditional GETs will not cause the image to be loaded. Robots typically do not load images, so we will probably not see any robot activity in our log.

There are many Web sites and third party services that use variations on this basic technique to provide site analytics. One common variation involves using mechanisms that prevent the image from being cached so that one will see page views even if the actual HTML page is cached. Seeing all page views can be a big plus over the standard Web server log.

Another common variation is to place additional data in the query string for the transparent gif when the page is generated. This allows the Web application to send useful information to the logging server. For example, one might place the content type of the page or the user identifier in the query string. When the image is loaded this data will appear in the log file records. The HTML fragment displayed here results in all of the data shown being logged.

```
<IMG SRC="http://www. clickstreamconsulting.com/logging/hidden.gif
    ?page_type=catalog&category_type=junk_food&userID=mark">
```

If our logging server is in the same domain as the Web site then we will see any cookies the Web site is using in the log file. If the logging server is in a different domain then we can't see those cookies. However, there is nothing to prevent setting cookies from this logging server. A few Web site analysis services make use of JavaScript code you embed in your Web pages to set cookies that will be transmitted back to their logging server.

This is the point where one can start to cross into the realm of shady ethics and abuse of the technique. There is nothing essentially wrong with this technique, provided you are doing this to support analysis for your Web site. The problem is that this mechanism is typically done without the user's awareness. Because of its surreptitious nature, transparent gifs used in this manner are commonly termed *web bugs*.

The problem with ethics enters when the technique is used in other venues. It is possible to send any data you want to the logging server via either the query string or cookies. It will work in *any* HTML page no matter where it is displayed.

For example, you could send out emails to everyone on a mailing list and embed a web bug with the person's email address in the query string. The moment a user views that email message in an HTML-capable mail reader, which covers more than 90 percent of the mail clients on the market, the image is retrieved and you have a log of the event. Some might consider that an invasion of their privacy.

In fact, spammers frequently use web bugs that send back the email address of the recipient to test whether messages are read. By viewing the message, the user is advertising the fact that they have a valid email address, thus ensuring a steady flow of spam in the future.

What makes web bugs particularly insidious is that they can be used across multiple Web sites. If the provider of this bug sets a unique cookie when the image is first retrieved then the provider can identify that user over repeat visits to every Web site that embeds the web bug. This allows the provider of the bug to track a user's activities from one Web site to the next. This is a practice used extensively by online advertising networks to build user profiles. We will revisit this topic again in Chapter 4.

Differentiating Between Visitors and Search Engines

As we saw in one of the earlier log file samples, search engines will visit the site periodically to index the information on the Web site. The programs search engines use to index sites are called spiders or robots. When loading Web server log records into the warehouse it is important to flag the visits from robots, to distinguish them from normal users. Since robots typically crawl all the pages in a Web site, unless they are properly identified, they seem to be avid users of the site visiting most content on a regular basis. If robot data were loaded into a clickstream data warehouse without proper identification, marketing users of the data warehouse will likely be sending many special offers to the robots because of their apparent zeal for site content.

In order to identify visits by robots we need to know how their records might show up in the logs. There are only three ways to identify the robots. If the log files contain unresolved IP addresses we can use a list of search engine IP domains and match the records to these. If the log files contain hostnames then we can use a list of search engine domain names instead. If we are logging the User-agent data then we can examine this.

Well-behaved robots will identify themselves by sending information that is logged in the User-agent field. The problem is that not all companies have well-behaved robots so it will not be possible to use this to track every visit. Identifying robots is a multistep process.

If we have a list of registered robots then we can identify most robot visits. For the misbehaving 'bots the next step is to attempt to match the IP domain address or domain name to a list of robot data. The odds are good that some will still slip through. There is one last thing we can do, again based on one of the actions of most robots.

When a robot first visits a site, it *should* attempt to access a file named "robots.txt" at the root of the Web site. In the case of the authors' site, the file is located at http://www.clickstreamconsulting.com/robots.txt. This file is used to tell robots where they should not search. For example, you might not want any robots to wander through certain areas of the site because it would be unproductive or because it would soak up a lot of site resources.

We can use this information when processing logs. Whether or not there is a robots.txt file present, there should be a record in the log showing an attempted GET of the file. By searching for these records it is possible to then record the IP address or hostname and flag all remaining records in the log with that address or hostname.

Fortunately for clickstream data warehouse developers, a number of people have gone to great lengths to work out things like robot identification, lists of known robot user-agent responses and search engine IP addresses. There are also freely available programs, BotWatch for example, that can process the log file and identify all the robot records. By making some simple modifications to one of these programs we can incorporate them into the data transformation process of loading the clickstream data warehouse.

With search engine data flagged as a distinct class of visitor it is possible to see what portion of the total page views are from robots, how much bandwidth they consumed, and which engines index the site most frequently. When coupled with an investigation of search results, the latter data can be useful in determining whether to register the site with more search engines or whether changes are needed to search-related information on the site's pages.

Cookies

Netscape originally developed the cookie protocol as a solution to the stateless nature of the HTTP protocol, namely the problem of an application not knowing what happens from one page view to the next during a user session at a Web site. Simply put, a cookie is a variable stored on the client system by the browser on behalf of a particular site. It is the primary mechanism that most Web sites use to manage client sessions and to keep track of users.

A cookie has a number of values that require some explanation. Six parameters that may be set in a cookie:

Name. The name of the cookie variable. This is how the cookie is referenced and used. The name is a required field and has no default values.

Value. The value assigned to the cookie variable. For example, if the cookie name is "UserID" the cookie value might be set to something like "080112."

Domain. The Internet domain of the server that created the cookie. Only servers that are part of that domain can read the cookie. Cookies can be assigned so that they are valid for a single server, a subdomain of an enterprise, or an entire domain. For example, if the domain is set to ".mydomain .com" then any server within mydomain.com will be able to access the cookie. If the domain were set to "sales.mydomain.com" then only servers within sales.mydomain.com would have access. If the domain is not set explicitly then it defaults to the full domain of the document request that created the cookie. Cookies may not be set for top-level domains like .com, .net, .org, etc.

Path. The top level of the file system tree within the domain for which the cookie is valid. A request by the Web browser for any page from the path specified will send the cookie to the Web server. For example, a path of "/" means the cookie is good for all pages in the Web site, while a more qualified path, like "/ClickstreamConsulting/articles" means the cookie only applies pages in the /articles subtree. An URL request higher in the path would not send the cookie. The path defaults to "/" if it is not set explicitly.

Expires. The expiration date of the cookie. This lets the Web site determine how long a cookie will remain in the browser. If this value is not set then it defaults to the length of time the client's Web browser is running. When the browser is shut down the cookie will be deleted.

Secure. A flag set to indicate that a secure connection using Secure Sockets Layer (SSL) is required to send the cookie. The default value is FALSE.

The original intent of the cookie specification was to allow an application to keep state information from one page view to the next, such as a list of products selected for purchase. One thing that became apparent early on was that sending all this data back and forth in cookies is usually not necessary and is quite inefficient. A better technique is to pass a single session ID in the cookie. This session ID is used by a Web application running on the server to access the session data that has been stored locally.

The most common use of cookies is tracking a user's session during a visit to the site. The next most common use of cookies is the persistent tracking of a user from one visit to the next. These cookies are often called *persistent* cookies as opposed to *session* cookies that expire at the end of a browser session. When tracking a user with cookies, we would like the information to show up in the Web server log files. This information is the key to reassembling all of the records for a given visit, and differentiating one visit from another.

The techniques for using cookies to track sessions and users will be completely described in Chapter 4. In this chapter we will only examine the fields in a cookie and how they are stored and sent.

Cookies on the Browser Side

Cookies are set and stored by browsers in one of two ways. They can be set by the Web server itself, or they can be set from within a Web page via one of the client-side scripting languages such as JavaScript. Cookies are sent back and forth between the client and Web server in HTTP header fields. The HTTP standard does not define how cookies are stored on the Web server or browser. The standard simply specifies what is transmitted in the cookie-related headers.

We'll take a quick look at cookie storage in the Netscape and Microsoft browsers to provide an example of how they may be stored on the client and what they contain.

Netscape stores its cookies in a single file named "cookies.txt" in the user's profile directory. For example, on the author's Windows 98 PC the cookies are stored in:

```
C:\Program Files\Netscape\Users\MarkM\cookies.txt
```

Netscape stores the cookies in a tab-delimited format, one cookie to a line. Note that there are actually seven fields in the file format, as opposed to the six specified in the standard. Below are several records from the cookie file above.

```
.netscape.com TRUE / FALSE 1293840097 UID 255.16.74.73:09822760:793670
.flycast.com  TRUE / FALSE 1293753600 atf 1_74467616417
.cnet.com     TRUE / FALSE 2145830497 aid D8C8F7843A8C5A0F0003CE1300002
.cnet.com     TRUE / FALSE 2145830497 s_cur_1_0
```

The fields are laid out in the following order: domain, creating agent, path, secure flag, expiration date, cookie name, and cookie value. The extra field in the file is the creating agent. This field is set to FALSE if the cookie was created locally and TRUE if set by a server.

If we look at the first cookie, we see that Netscape placed a cookie valid for the entire Netscape domain, the cookie was created by a server at Netscape, the cookie is valid for any URL within the domain because the path is "/", the cookie expires at 1:55:02 P.M. on August 30 of 2018 (a very persistent cookie), the name of the cookie is "UIDC" and the value is"255.16.74.73:09822760: 793670". The value is interesting because it is an IP address from my service provider, and the values appear to be the date and time the cookie was set.

Different versions of Internet Explorer store cookies in different directories. The version of Windows also affects where IE stores cookies. On the author's system running Windows 98 and IE 5.5 the cookies can be found in "C:\ Windows \Cookies" as well as "C:\Windows\Temporary Internet Files." Unlike Netscape, IE stores cookies for each domain in a separate file. The files are named for the computer user and the domain. For example, the cookie contents below come from a cookie stored in "C:\Windows\Cookies\ markm@excite.txt."

```
registered
no
excite.com/
0
1073733632
30124258
145922848
29402612
*
UID
F8237C893A46A11
excite.com/
0
1073733632
30124258
145922848
29402612
*
```

In IE, each cookie created by a domain is stored on a separate line in the site's cookie file, and each cookie created by the Web site is separated from the next by an asterisk. Note that there are eight fields stored for each cookie. The fields are organized as follows: cookie name, cookie value, domain and path combined into one field, secure flag, expiration date, expiration time, date last used, and time last used.

For the first cookie above the name is "registered" and the value is "no." The cookie is valid for all servers in the excite.com domain, it is not secure (IE uses zero for not secure and one for secure), it will expire on December 31 of 2010 at 12:00 P.M., and it was last accessed on March 6 of 2001 at 4:15:10 A.M. The second cookie is like the first, but it contains a UID instead.

Browsers impose a number of limitations on cookies. They generally limit the number of cookies that may be set from a given server. Most browsers also limit the total number of cookies that can be stored. For example, Netscape limits the total number of cookies to 300, and the number of cookies from a single domain to 20.

Cookies on the Server Side

Where do cookies get logged? Depending on the Web server and how it's configured, the cookies may show up in the standard log file, or they may be logged into a separate log file specifically for cookies. For example, the Apache Web server provides a directive that tells it to log cookies into a separate file:

```
CookieLog filename
```

Logging cookies separately is not a good practice. Logging data into multiple log files makes the data extraction process more complex because you will need to attempt the difficult job of synchronizing both the standard log file and the cookie log file when loading data into the warehouse. A better practice is to configure a single log file that places the cookie data in the same record as the originating request. In the section above on extending log file formats, we gave an example of an Apache log format string that extends the Combined Log Format to include cookies.

By design, cookies may be read or set only by the originating server or by any server within the domain that is set in the domain field in the cookie. This means that a Web server in "yourdomain.com" can't set a cookie that is visible to servers in "mydomain.com."

When looking at the logged data there are a few points to keep in mind. The first point is that the value of a cookie is stored as a text string. This means that developers are not forced to use multiple cookies to store multiple values. Web developers can choose how they want to store values in this string. For example, a developer could store all of the values they wanted to persistently track as a concatenated string in a single cookie. If the site needed to track both user ID and session ID, it could store both values as a concatenated string in one cookie. The entire text of this string would be appended to the records in the Web server log. When parsing the log file, the parsing process would have to understand that the cookie value is actually multiple values strung together and would need to be separated into its component values.

Alternatively, a site could choose to assign each discrete persistent variable to a separate cookie. This would result in many separate cookies being passed for each access. When the Web server receives multiple cookies for a request it will place all of those cookies together in the cookie fields of the record. Each cookie will be stored in the log record as a "cookie name=value" pair, separated from the other cookies by a semicolon.

For security reasons or to hide how a particular Web site uses cookies, it is fairly common for the Web server to encrypt the cookie name and value. Cold Fusion is an example of a development tool that allows one to encrypt cookie values before setting cookies. Instead of a simple name and value, the encrypted Name and Value fields passed in the Cookie header will contain garbled text. This garbled text is what will show up in the Web server log. The data warehouse load programs may not be able to decrypt the cookie unless they have access to the original encryption and decryption routines. Without access to these routines processing log files with encrypted cookies can be challenging.

Internal Data Sources

The clickstream warehouse usually contains data from sources other than Web server logs. As you can see from the prior discussion of log files, there are some significant gaps in the data necessary for a complete job of clickstream analysis. Simple information about business transactions, such as the item purchased or purchase price, may not be available. Nor is there any enriched user identity information to help the business learn more about customer behavior.

The incompleteness of server log data is one of the primary reasons for building a clickstream warehouse rather than using packaged Web site analysis software as the sole e-business intelligence mechanism. Web log file analysis tools are not sufficient to deliver the kinds of information required by most Web enterprises because the source of data is so limited. More detailed information about the site content, user activities, and user profiles is required. This information comes from numerous additional sources that can be inside or outside the enterprise.

Typically, there are many additional sources of data that are internal to an enterprise. It would be impossible to review them all, so we'll focus instead on some of the data sources that are more closely related to the Web-based activities of an enterprise.

Web Site and Log File Analysis Tools

The purpose of all Web site and log file analysis tools is to transform the Web server log data into straightforward reports and graphs for subsequent analysis. These products process Web server log files and store the data into output files or in a database. Products that use databases either store their data in a product-internal database or they store data to an open relational database.

There are many products on the market, ranging from free tools such as Analog, to costly tools that completely ignore the log files and obtain data in real time by capturing network traffic going to and from a site's Web servers. Most of the tools tend toward the lower end of analytical capability, providing useful but basic site traffic metrics. The downside is that these products do not support the deeper levels of clickstream analysis that are possible if you have a clickstream warehouse.

It is quite likely that your enterprise will already have one or more Web site analysis tools in-house. Most site administrators make use of their basic reporting features to manage the Web site and to provide basic site traffic information to other departments. It is helpful to know what log file analysis tools are already in use at your enterprise, because you will be able to familiarize yourself with what information is currently provided and you will be able to determine some of the gaps in reporting.

Keep in mind that there is often initial resistance to implementing a clickstream data warehouse if a log file analysis tool is already in use. Some may believe that there is no need for a more comprehensive solution and the enterprise may have already spent considerable time and money on the existing reporting and analysis infrastructure.

Assuming your enterprise already uses a Web log file analysis product, it is important to familiarize yourself with how it works and what kinds of analyses can be performed on its output. It is possible that the tool might be usable as a component of the clickstream data warehouse extract and load process. The other reason to learn the tool is that there may be some helpful reports that could be delivered out of the data warehouse better than from the tool.

Web Site Analysis Product Characteristics

Most Web log file analysis products are capable of importing and processing Web server logs in a wide variety of formats. Any of them should be able to handle the Common and Combined Log Formats. Even the network traffic-based products can import log files so they can fill in a history for trend reporting.

There are a few basic design decisions that the product designers make when implementing one of these products. A key decision is which approach to use for data collection, log file processing, or network traffic analysis. With the former, the Web server log files are parsed, filtered, and loaded into a database or flat files. The vast majority of these products process the actual log files.

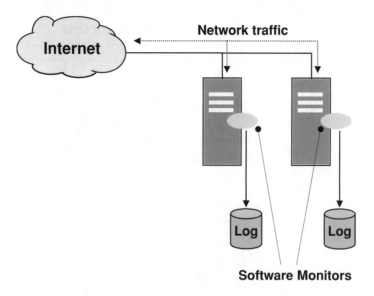

Figure 3.3 Server traffic monitoring.

Network analyzers are generally more sophisticated and expensive products than log-based products. There are two approaches that are used, although both use packet sniffing techniques. The first is to use a piece of software that sits on each Web server and intercepts traffic as it comes in to that server. This is depicted in Figure 3.3.

The server monitoring option is best for site environments that have only one or at most a few servers. If there are many Web servers then the additional licensing, installation, and management costs of the software installed over all those servers becomes a big issue. Depending on the product, one might also have to manually assemble logs from all the site's servers in order to build a complete picture of site activity.

The second approach is to acquire data directly off the network at one or more points using a physically separate network monitor, shown in Figure 3.4. This approach uses one or more physically separate machines to monitor network traffic to and from the Web site directly on the wire at one or more locations on the network.

On-the-wire products typically listen for traffic at various points in your network and are therefore able to obviate some of the problems you might encounter due to caching or sessions being spread across Web servers. Both on-the-wire and server approaches can capture more accurate performance data than log analyzers and can even detect interrupted sessions, such as when the user hits the Stop button on their browser.

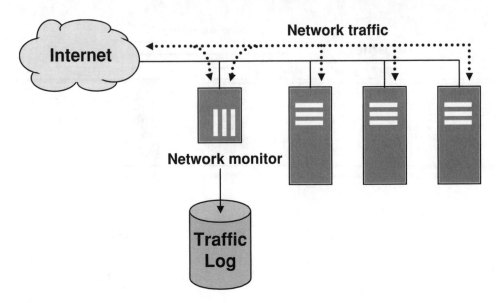

Figure 3.4 On-the-wire traffic monitoring.

One of the limitations of these products is their inability to deal with encrypted sessions. Because sessions using Secure Sockets Layer are encrypted, there is no easy way to access the contents of the data packets that make up a session. Some of the server-based products are capable of decrypting SSL connections, where the on-the-wire products can't. A limitation of the server-based products is that they are tied to specific platforms. The platform restriction may mean they will be incompatible with the platform used to run the Web servers. This means one must still rely on Web server logs for some portion of the data.

The log-based products have some differences as well. There are a few products that work by making use of client-based code, such as JavaScript functions embedded in the site's HTML pages. These functions transmit data to a server that logs the information sent. Some of these products are offered as a service rather than applications you run yourself.

Using embedded JavaScript in this way is a useful technique to know, because you may be able to employ it in your own site. One of the advantages is that most log information can be consolidated to a single log server that answers the requests from the embedded script. This simplifies the extract and load process for the warehouse.

We say "most log information" because it is possible for a user to disable scripting in his browser, thus preventing logging of information to the log server. The Web server will still log the page access, so the information may be picked up from that Web server's log. If a document request is a HEAD request then the page is not actually loaded, so the request will not be seen by the log server. Last, robots will typically not execute any embedded scripts so it is unlikely the log server will contain accesses from search engines indexing the site.

The big advantage to this technique is that most of the time it will work for most users, and if done properly it bypasses many of the problems with cache and proxy servers. The more complete session information that may be logged can greatly improve the quality of data in the warehouse.

Another significant difference between log-based products and network-based products is the ability to monitor current activities. With log-based products one may only analyze information after most events have occurred. Near real-time monitoring allows one to react quickly to events and provide up-to-the-minute reporting on site activities. The latter is most useful to site administrators. This kind of immediate information is usually not relevant to the more in-depth analysis performed by other types of clickstream data warehouse users.

Web Site Analysis Tools as a Data Source

It is possible to use the output of some of the site analysis tools as a data source for the clickstream warehouse. You can use the tool to process raw log files into a usable format for loading into the warehouse, or you can use the tool to provide site traffic summary information that can be loaded into summary tables in the data warehouse.

The latter, while appealing, is probably not a particularly good idea. This is due to the fact that a properly designed clickstream data warehouse will often supplement the Web server log data with log data from cache servers, proxy servers, and other log-based data sources. These additional data sources fill in many of the holes in raw Web server log data. This additional data makes it unlikely that one will be able to reconcile the summary data emitted from log file analysis tools with the more robust reports from a clickstream data warehouse.

It is much more likely that one may attempt to use the Web log file analysis tool to process the log files into a more usable format for input into the clickstream data warehouse. If the tool is capable of providing filtered and cleaned files as output then it may be used in place of custom-built or third party log file processing programs.

There are a number of criteria to use when examining a log analysis tool as a data source. Foremost is that it can output data at the log file record level, the lowest level of granularity. Most tools do not do this. Instead, they provide summary level exports, well above individual HTTP transaction detail. Most of the time this summary level will not be sufficient for the kinds of external data integration and complex analyses we want from the data warehouse.

Other criteria include the difficulty of exporting data from the tool, how much work it would be to integrate the tool versus writing software to process the data, whether the tool runs on the same platform as the warehouse server, whether the tool may be automated to run during the warehouse data extract cycle, the time it takes the tool to process the log file. Many log file analysis tools do not process the data fast enough to meet the warehouse data loading window. This is often because they calculate all of their statistics for reports while processing the file, rather than simply parsing and transforming the data for input.

Nevertheless, a common question remains: Why not use a Web log file analysis tool instead of building a clickstream warehouse?

Some of the obvious answers were discussed earlier, with the primary answer being that the use of only Web server log file data is insufficient to form a complete analytical picture of the business or its users. In general, it is impossible to support many functional departments without data from other internal—and possibly external—applications. Very few site analysis tools provide the ability to integrate this vital data, let alone view it through their interface. Instead, they focus mainly on summary-level statistics about Web site traffic and access patterns.

There are two other arguments against Web site analysis tools as an alternative to a clickstream data warehouse. The tools have evolved largely in isolation when compared to those of the larger business intelligence community. The end result has been tools with rudimentary user interfaces for delivering information. Few tools have the ability to go beyond static or parameter-driven reports to true online analysis or predictive modeling. Furthermore, most of the products are limited by their basic architecture and can't be easily extended by integrating with third party analysis and reporting tools.

When developing a data warehouse, end-user interface requirements drive a number of architecture and infrastructure decisions. The data requirements of business analysts often evolve over time, and they frequently need their data in specific formats. Without a variety of information delivery capabilities, many users will not receive what they need in a form that is suitable for use.

The last major argument against site analysis tools is their inability to deal with a variety of data quality problems present in Web server logs. The fault is not with the tools, because they can only provide information based on what is available within the log file. They must make predetermined assumptions about the input data in order to create many of the reports they provide. These assumptions may provide misleading results. A number of the more common data problems are listed in Table 3.5.

Table 3.5 Log Analysis Data Problems

DATA PROBLEM	DESCRIPTION
Underreporting site traffic	Log file analysis tools assume that the log is a precise record of the clickstream. This is unrealistic because of the various caching mechanisms in use on the Internet. Estimates by different sources are that anywhere from 20% to 50% of requests are served by some form of cache, meaning that the analysis tools can underreport traffic by these percentages.
Inability to count unique visitors	Unless the site analysis product makes use of its own user-tracking mechanism, or is capable of interpreting one that the Web site is using, the unique visitor counts can be overstated by an order of magnitude. A large portion of this problem is related to the dynamic IP addressing issues mentioned earlier.
Calculating page dwell time	The time a user spends on a page is calculated by subtracting the timestamp of the next request from the current request. It is possible for the user to do just about anything while on the page, from talking on the phone to taking a lunch break. The cache problem means that the user may access several pages between two page views in the log. Moreover, there is no way to tell how much time was spent on the last page because there is no reliable way to log the final exit from the site. Unfortunately for content sites, the last page view may be one of the most important because it is often information the user is most interested in, or indicates that the user could not find what they were looking for.
Calculating visit duration	The visit duration is usually calculated as the difference between the timestamps of the first and last page views. Since the actual dwell time on the last page is not generally known, calculating the visit duration using this formula will always shorten the actual visit duration by the dwell time of the last page.
Defining a session/visit and counting sessions/visits	A "visit" or "session" is the complete set of requests made by a user. The problem is that there is often no way to define the end of the session because the user simply leaves. One does not know when the user left because there is normally no indication in the log. Most tools assume a session has ended if there is no activity for some arbitrary period of time, most often 15 or 30 minutes.

(continued)

Table 3.5 (*Continued*)

DATA PROBLEM	DESCRIPTION
Calculating page view frequencies, average page views per session, etc.	Any of these calculations are potentially inaccurate because of the previously described data problems.

After considering this list of problems, one might conclude that Web log file analysis tools are worthless. This is true only if one believes the assumption that 20,000 reported hits a day means there were actually 20,000 people visiting the site, or if one believes the "least requested pages" report (a page with zero requests will never show up on this report!).

The truth is that these tools paint a useful, high-level picture of what is happening on the Web server. The more expensive and advanced products are capable of working around some problems to provide more accurate statistics, but they typically do not overcome the other user interface and data integration issues.

When constructing a clickstream data warehouse we need to be aware of all of these issues because we will face exactly the same data quality problems with log files. If the data is not handled properly, or if analyses are not properly constrained, end-users may incorrectly interpret the data they see.

A clickstream data warehouse has a number of advantages over the log analysis tools. Foremost is that we are not limited to log files as the only source of data. Any data source that is accessible may be incorporated so that we can fill out the gaps in the data. Where the problems may be out of our immediate control, as with caching, we can obtain log files from cache and proxy servers, systems at partner and affiliate sites, and third party providers to supplement the Web server log data. The remainder of this chapter discusses some of the data sources that frequently supplement the Web server log files.

Other Web Server–Related Systems

It is possible that the enterprise will be running cache servers, proxy servers, Web application servers, and other software as part of the technical infrastructure for the Web site. Any of these could provide log data to supplement the clickstream from the Web server. Sometime these applications are under the control of the Web site administrator, and sometimes a different group such as networking will manage the applications.

Firewalls and Proxy Servers

Starting with some of the basic networking infrastructure, two common applications are firewalls and proxy servers. Depending on the product, these may have log files that are in a format that can be parsed and used in the warehouse. Some have configurable log files, making the job of extraction and loading even simpler.

The reason one might want to use a firewall or proxy server log is that it typically monitors activity at the point where all traffic enters or leaves the enterprise network. This supplements the Web server logs with data about external ftp access, email access, and any other protocols that may be of interest and are not being logged elsewhere.

Cache Servers

Another common application in use by many Web sites to improve performance is cache servers. The idea behind using a cache server is that by moving content closer to the user, the amount of time spent traversing the network is reduced, and the cached document is already in memory and quicker to retrieve.

There are two ways that enterprises use caching and we should differentiate between them. The enterprise may install a proxy cache server for use internally. Web browsers in the enterprise are configured to use the proxy server, meaning that all requests from internal browsers first go to the proxy server. If the proxy server has the requested document in its cache then it will supply the document to the client, otherwise it will refer the request to the appropriate Web site.

This type of internal cache server is of limited value to the clickstream warehouse since it provides no data on external users, only what internal users are requesting. If one of the goals of the warehouse is to examine internal use of enterprise information, such as in web-based knowledge management systems, then this proxy server data may be of use.

The other way caching may be used by an enterprise is to improve site performance for external users. The enterprise may run a cache server in front of its Web servers in an attempt to improve site performance, although this is not often the case because the cache server is not really close enough to the end users, from a network topology point of view, to make much of a difference.

Regardless of the approach, if an enterprise uses a cache server then one should obtain the cache server log files for the warehouse. Cache server logs can be useful because they contain information about requests that did not reach the Web server, thus filling out some of the holes in the data. Cache servers are capable of logging the same kinds of data as Web servers, typically in something similar to Common Log Format, but with additional fields for cache server specific data.

There are a few cache products on the market that work in conjunction with user Web browsers and may create misleading data in the server cache or Web server logs. These products make the browser *prefetch* documents that are most often requested after the current page, loading these documents in the background while the user reads the current page. The effect is to make page loads look faster to the user since they will already be stored in the browser's cache. This behavior can create an inaccurate picture of user actions since the user may not request one of the prefetched documents. In addition to caching products, there are some browser-based products users can download for themselves that do the same thing.

Media Servers

As more businesses include multimedia presentations in Web sites, the importance of logs from streaming media servers will increase. Apart from media and online entertainment sites, businesses providing online training or support can make use of the media server log data to better understand their customers' needs.

There are many different formats and servers for streaming media, making this a difficult area to explore in detail. Since the RealPlayer software is popular we'll use some products from RealNetworks to provide a simple example of a streaming media log file.

As with several of their competitors, logging in the media and caching proxy server products is configurable. Rather than look at the details of configuration, we'll examine the contents of a single server log record. The lines below show a sample record from a RealProxy server log.

```
255.74.16.28 - - [20/Mar/2001:20:05:31 -0600]
 "GET /how_to_debug_logs.rm PNA/2.1" 200 15768000
 [WinNT_4.5_6.0.8.122_play32_PN04_EN_686]
 [00000000-0000-0000-0000-000000000000] - - 1320 88 14 [1100]
 20:05:42 255.33.37.244 0 15486 12 [Demand Cache Hit]
```

Table 3.6 explains each of the fields in the log record shown above. Most of the data shown in the log is similar to what we see from a Web server. Most of the additional fields are the kinds of data one would expect from a streaming media server. One very interesting field is the Global User ID (GUID).

When one installs the RealPlayer client software, the software generates a unique (per computer) identifier that may be used to track individual clients. It is possible that the client does not send this information, in which case it will be "UNKNOWN." The client software does have the option to suppress the GUID, in which case a GUID of all zeroes is sent.

Table 3.6 Log File Contents from a Streaming Media Server

FIELD CONTENTS	DESCRIPTION
255.74.16.28	Client IP address
– –	The next two fields are always dashes. The server does not record either of the standard Authuser or Ident fields.
[20/Mar/2001:20:05:31 -0600]	Timestamp of the request.
"GET /how_to_debug_logs.rm PNA/2.1"	The document request and the protocol and version. RealServer has two streaming protocols, and can use several transport types. A request for a bad file results in "UNKNOWN" instead of the GET request (not a very helpful message for server logs).
200	The HTTP status of the request.
15768000	The number of bytes sent to the client.
[WinNT_4.5_6.0.8.122_play32_PN04_EN_686]	This field is the equivalent of the User-agent field. The RealPlayer client software sends back the following information: the operating system platform and version, the player version, the player type, the distribution code, the language setting and the CPU type of the client machine. If this data is not sent then "UNKNOWN" appears between the brackets.
[00000000-0000-0000-0000-000000000000]	This field is the Global User ID (GUID) used to identify a specific user. Zeroes indicate the client has suppressed GUIDs in their client.
– –	According to the documentation these two fields would be the file size and file time, but are not recorded in the current version of the product.
1320	The length in seconds of the media clip sent.
88	The number of packets that were successfully re-sent to the client (resends are normally due to a transmission problem).
14	The number of re-sent packets that failed to reach the client in time to be used.

(continued)

Table 3.6 *(Continues)*

FIELD CONTENTS	DESCRIPTION
[1100]	A sort of bitmap to indicate the type of media sent. Each "1" represents the presence of the media, and "0" represents its absence. The fields are, in order: RealAudio, RealVideo, Event, RealImage.
20:05:42	Timestamp for when the media started playing.
255.33.37.244	The IP address of the server sending the media.
0	This field is always set to zero. It is supposed to be the average bit rate.
15486	The number of packets sent to the client.
12	The presentation ID field (used by the products, not important for our purposes).
[Demand Cache Hit]	This is proxy data, and indicates whether the media was on-demand or live, and whether it was in the cache or not. It is possible for this field to contain the value "UNKNOWN."

The interesting thing about this GUID is that Real Networks can link it to the software registration information the user fills out when installing the software. This provides a perfect example of how one can use a specific value to track a user over time. By using this value as a key, all of the log records can be tied to a specific user. With the GUID, one can look up the customer data in the registration system and build a user profile that extends beyond anonymous computer-related information.

In the log record example above we omitted three sets of data to make it more readable. If the server has statistics logging enabled, the RealPlayer client will send additional data about the connection once the player finishes showing a media clip. The first two sets of statistical data relate to RealAudio. This fairly technical data tells the server details about the connection between the client and server, such as bandwidth, bit rates, and the like.

The third set of statistics relates to viewer actions. This could be particularly useful information for the clickstream data warehouse. The data collected include whether the user paused, resumed, repositioned, or stopped the clip, and whether they clicked on an image map.

Streaming media is just an add-on for many Web sites. It is doubtful that there is much for the enterprise to learn from a visitor watching a clip of the annual shareholder meeting. For other businesses this extended data could be extremely valuable. If the enterprise provides online training it may find that many users pause or rewind at a particular spot. This would be an indicator of potential problems with the material. It may be that the content is confusing and the trainee needs to review it multiple times, or simply that the material is too long and the trainee wants to take a break.

With RealPlayer, the user may configure the software to not send statistics to the server, in much the same manner that the GUID can be blocked. Both this option and the GUID option are set by default, meaning the client software will send all information. As with many software companies, Real Networks probably banks on users not going to the trouble of changing these options, thus providing them with a useful source of data.

Web Application Servers

Web application servers are another potential source of data, though of a different nature. Web developers may choose to use Web-oriented application server software to construct the Web site and its transaction processing capabilities. In general, the Web application server creates its own logs for administrative purposes. These logs are usually not interesting as a data source for the clickstream warehouse.

However, many of the architectural components supplied by the application server vendors do provide the capability to do customized logging. For example, if the site uses e-commerce or personalization components built with the application server then it is likely that the server software can log transaction or personalization information. As an alternative to using an application log, one can always do a standard data extraction process from the back-end transaction database that typically supports the application server, assuming the schema of this database is open.

When working in a custom-built Web environment, it is important to determine how easy it is to do custom logging of data and events. Sometimes it can be as simple as changing some configuration options. Even if this is not the case, building the capability into the Web application may significantly enrich the data content in the clickstream warehouse. Sometimes it is more difficult to extract data about specific events out of the back-end database supporting the application than it is to add a logging function to the Web application.

Some vendors are starting to recognize the need for better intelligence from their products. For the most part, the solution has been to sell some form of analysis component as an add-on to the product suite. The difficulty one encounters with many of these add-on components is that they are narrow in scope and tricky to customize. It can be challenging, if not impossible, to extend the component's data content or functionality and develop it into a broader analytical solution.

Another common approach by application server vendors is to partner with other software vendors who provide products that fill in the gaps. An example of this is BEA Systems' partnership with Broadbase for customer behavior tracking functionality when using BEA's WebLogic Application Server. This approach can suffer from the same problems as providing a custom add-on. A further complication is that one now has another piece of software that is tightly integrated with the Web application.

Our belief is that it is better to separate true analytics into a data warehouse. Instead of trying to shoehorn software into roles for which it was not fully designed, it is better to build a data warehouse that provides a customizable and extensible information delivery infrastructure. Then one can layer various analytical and reporting applications on the warehouse in a simpler, faster, and more accurate manner.

This architecture cleanly separates analytical applications from software designed to support operations. The Web application developers can opt to use these server add-ons or third party software to provide transaction and operations-oriented services, and integrate that support directly into the Web site. Meanwhile, the analytics and the historical data reside in the data warehouse.

Business Applications

The actual business transaction data will be as important as the clickstream data for most enterprises. Unless the Web site is informational or based on an advertising-supported business model, business transactions are the main purpose for having a Web site. Without the detailed transaction data we can't augment the clickstream with simple facts such as the price of products, daily revenue, or the impact of online activities on product inventories.

The Web server logs tell us only what users were doing during their visit to the site. The logs do not tell us anything about underlying events or business transactions. By integrating the Web log data with the transaction data we can assemble much more interesting information, such as whether an online or email advertising campaign had an effect on site activity or sales.

When building a clickstream data warehouse we draw a distinction between two types of business transaction data sources: e-commerce systems and back-end operational systems. The differentiator between the two is somewhat arbitrary. E-commerce systems are designed specifically for online operations, while the other systems support the business day-to-day and likely predate the enterprise's online presence.

We differentiate between these systems for a number of reasons. The e-commerce systems are usually built with or integrated with the same Web technologies used in Web sites. They tend to run on a narrower set of operating systems, generally UNIX, Linux, or Windows NT, with UNIX being the most common. The systems tend to be designed with better mechanisms for integration than earlier stand-alone business systems. At the same time, it tends to be more difficult to extract data from these systems than their offline counterparts. Examples of these systems include purchasing systems from companies such as Ariba, business exchange and auction software from companies such as CommerceOne, and e-commerce platforms such as BEA Systems WebLogic Commerce or IBM's WebSphere.

Some of the commerce platforms provide event logging services that may prove to be a better primary data source for user actions than the Web server logs. In this case, the Web server logs are used to supplement the event logs provided by the commerce server. For example, the server could record when the user added to or removed items from their shopping basket. This data would be more difficult to identify from within the server logs than by taking the data from the commerce server log. Instead, we might use the Web server log data to fill in what the user looked at prior to and subsequent to the events.

In contrast, the back-end operational systems we refer to have generally been in place for a long time. They tend to run on platforms that are separate from those supporting the online systems. The also tend to be built using radically different technologies than their online counterparts. It is often difficult to integrate these systems with the Web site because they were designed for either a single purpose or the opposite, as a complete package for the enterprise. Examples that we would put into this class include order entry, finance, and Enterprise Resource Planning (ERP) systems.

Once the warehouse data requirements have been finalized it will be important to identify all the relevant business systems that contain useful data. These systems must then be analyzed to determine what business data is required to enhance the Web log data. We will explore this area further in Chapter 8 when we discuss data extraction. For now it is enough to know that there will be a number of other systems we need data from in order to build a comprehensive picture of the business.

Customer Contact Systems

The last of the internal systems that are used to supplement log data are the customer contact systems. Some of these systems are overlooked but they can be a rich source of information about customers. This is true whether the business is an online retailer or a business that sells to or supports other businesses.

Inbound Contact Data

The contact systems are of two general varieties. The inbound systems are those used by users actively searching out or contacting the enterprise. Outbound systems are used by the enterprise to contact customers or prospective clients. There can be a surprising number of applications managing the customer contact functions within an organization.

The inbound applications may include web-based user support, in which case much of the required information is likely to be in the resultant Web server logs. Web-based systems are often supplemented by applications as simple as inbound email management, or as complex as voice applications and computer-integrated telephony.

Most enterprises have manned call centers to handle customer support. In general, a call center makes use of automated call detection (ACD) and automated call routing (ACR) software to route inbound phone calls to the appropriate customer service representatives. The staff in these call centers typically have some sort of trouble ticket and problem resolution system for managing all of the calls. They will usually have access to the Web site, as well as specialized support applications for the Web site. The more sophisticated call centers are equipped with software that can also prioritize and route email, text-based chat, and support searchable knowledge bases for questions.

All of this user contact data is incredibly valuable if it can be assembled into a single picture of the user, whether the user is a business client or a consumer. For a clickstream warehouse, the contact information can be as useful as the transaction data because it provides insight into the state of any given customer relationship. The aggregated information can tell much about trends in products, marketing, service, and support.

Outbound Contact Data

Related to the inbound call center data is the outbound contact data. Outbound contacts are made in any number of ways and may be recorded in the same set of call center systems, or the data may be in independent systems. Data about outbound customer communications comes in many formats. It may be simple call detail records from outbound telemarketing, data from sales contact management applications, or newsletters mailed to customers and prospects.

Outbound messages are direct communication to customers or prospects and should to be managed for content and frequency of contact. This process is often not managed very well, resulting in overlapping communications. A clickstream warehouse can help to support the process by providing a historical record of dealings with all customers and prospects, but the warehouse should not be placed directly into the role of providing operational support.

As with inbound contact data, the two questions to answer are: What information do the end users want from the warehouse? and What data is it feasible to provide? In general it is feasible to provide data about the times and formats of customer contact. The content of the communications can be much more difficult to record and analyze in a meaningful way.

Apart from the usual telephony data, common contact mechanisms for online businesses include emails and newsletters. These can be interesting because it is possible to send both using HTML-formatted email. One can instrument these email messages to identify when a customer reads them using the Web bug technique mentioned earlier. Because the messages must be formatted and sent via computer, linking these messages back to log records can be done easily. We will talk more about the use of these techniques in Chapter 4.

There are some problems with call center data that can make it more of a challenge to obtain than other data. Call center systems are often not well understood as data sources. Most of the systems supply reports via their own reporting modules or third-party add-on software. None of this makes it easy to extract the contact data and transform it into meaningful information about the customer. A further complication is that much of the data is either not database-friendly, as with natural language trouble tickets and emails, or not recorded at all in the case of text-based chat or phone calls.

One area that tends to be problematic is finding a unique identifier to relate the various call-stream data with data in the Web server logs. Because multiple systems may be involved, each can have its own customer identifier. Unfortunately, it is quite common to have one customer number in the Web application, a separate identifier in the call center applications, and yet another in the transaction systems.

To extract data from the call center systems requires an understanding of what information your enterprise wants to learn about its users, what data is available within the systems, and what is practical given the constraints. Managing the end users' expectations of what is possible and how much effort it will take is an important part of the process.

External Data Sources

Even if we include all of the internal enterprise data, there will probably be some external sources of data that are needed to round out the information in the warehouse. Most of the time the data is external because the enterprise has either contracted out a task or outsourced some of the Web site's functions or infrastructure. Depending on the level of outsourcing, it is possible that most of the data, including Web server logs, would be sent from outside sources.

Content Caching Services

Earlier we mentioned cache servers as a potential internal source of log data. It is more likely that any caching done on behalf of the enterprise will be done either at a remote location or by an outsourced service, particularly for higher traffic sites. The most common outsourcers of caching services are collocation facilities, like Exodus and Digital Island, or content delivery services like Akamai.

In most cases you should be able to acquire the cache logs for your site from your service provider, but this is not always the case. Some of the providers charge for delivering log data, and some will not deliver the data. Most of the companies provide reporting on the performance of the cache service, but this is not a replacement for the detailed data.

Partners and Affiliates

If your enterprise has partnerships, linking agreements, or affiliate programs with other online enterprises then these enterprises may supply you with Web server log data. In some cases the contracts will require sharing of data in order to validate contractual information or payments. Sometimes the data is supplied in raw log format, and sometimes it is supplied via a summary report. Summary reports are usually not that useful for the data warehouse.

The type of contract will help you determine what, if any, data you can expect from the affiliated enterprise. A linking agreement is generally a simple statement that two enterprises agree to link to each others' sites and that they will abide by certain rules. Affiliate programs usually have a more formalized linking agreement and affiliate programs usually provide some form of incentive to the other enterprise in the agreement, whether it is monetary, increased exposure on the Web, or the halo effect from the association with your enterprise.

The norm with any of these contractual arrangements is to code the links on the other sites to track incoming referrals. When analyzing the Web server log data you should be able to identify the affiliate links and track them. The people in charge of these partnership programs analyze this data to manage the partnerships and measure their effectiveness.

Online Advertising Data

If your enterprise sells advertising space on your Web site then you will almost certainly be dealing with some form of advertising data from a third party. The same is true if your enterprise buys any online advertising of its own. The only difference between the two is in what data you will have available and what data the users will be interested in.

These days, few enterprises opt to sell and manage the advertising inventory on their own sites. Instead the job of displaying ads on one's site is done by advertising engine services like DoubleClick or Engage. These advertising services have a network of affiliated sites that agree to carry ads for the advertising engines, and the carrying sites are paid fees based on the number of ad views and clickthroughs. The enterprises who are advertising also contract with the service, paying for ads to be placed on the sites within the network.

The ads may be targeted to specific categories of Web sites within the ad network, set to run only at certain times of the day, or set to run based on a large number of other criteria. Likewise, payment for placement on your Web site varies based on information about your site and the display locations of the ads.

When an enterprise signs up to sell advertising space, the Web developers are given code or special instructions for placing the ad links on the Web site. These links are the mechanism by which the ad gets sent to the user and the ad is tracked. For example, the following HTML tags display a standard banner ad from DoubleClick on a Web site:

```
<A
REF="http://ad.doubleclick.net/jump/clickstreamconsulting.com/
homepage;abr=!ie;hmpge=index;ptile=1;sz=468x60">

<IMG SRC="http://ad.doubleclick.net/ad/clickstreamconsulting.com/
homepage;abr=!ie;hmpge=index;ptile=1;sz=468x60" border=0 height="60"
width="468">

</A>
```

You can see that this is a simple image link, and the only difference from other images on the site is that the image is served up by DoubleClick. The ad link also passes a number of parameters to tell DoubleClick what type of banner to display on the page.

Ads from advertising services are not limited to standard banner ads. They can also place what are termed *rich media* ads. These ads can include animation, sound, and video. The ads also do not have to be in the banner format. They can be any size, and they can also be sent as interstitial advertisements. An interstitial ad is an annoying device that creates a new window with the ad in it, and often pops up while the user is waiting for the Web page to load.

There is an important fact to note about ads that are placed on your site. The ad does not record a hit in the Web server log because the image is displayed from the advertising service Web server, not your Web site's server. Even if a user clicks on the ad there will not be a hit. This means you can know nothing about the ad, other than the fact that an ad was *probably* displayed when the page containing the ad was loaded. This is why you must rely on the service to provide you with data on the number of ads displayed and number of click-throughs.

As a seller of ad space you have limited access to this advertising data. This can be frustrating, particularly if users appear to be leaving your site at particular points where there are ads and not returning during that session. Fortunately, or unfortunately for sellers and agencies, clickthroughs are generally below 1 percent so seeing users leaving this way is not very likely.

As a buyer of ad space, you will have more clickstream data. While you will not know each time one of your ads is displayed on one of the advertising network sites, you will know each time someone clicks through the ad to your site. This information will be recorded in the referral field of the log record for the user's first hit. The advertising service will also provide you with data, typically in the form of reports.

The data delivery from advertising services can create some headaches for warehouse developers. This is because the services often sell clients based on their ability to provide reports of advertising activity, mitigating the need to send log data. Most services would prefer that you use their reports rather than sending you the log data related to your site.

Depending on the contract, you may have access to detailed data. If so, you should be able to build up a picture of all the sites where your ads were displayed, when the ads were displayed, how frequently they were displayed, and all of the data about the clickthroughs. If you get the detailed data you may also see cookie or query string data in the log. Most ad services set a cookie with every ad view so that they can track a user's ad views and try not to send them the same ads repeatedly. You may be able to link all of this data to your Web server logs, thus identifying specific users.

Syndicated Consumer or Business Data

The last external source of data to mention is data syndicators. These companies cull data from many sources and aggregate it into useful information about a particular individual, market, or subject area. It is common for marketing and product development departments to subscribe to one or more data syndication services, and for the IT department to have almost no knowledge of it. Yet combining this external information with that in the clickstream data warehouse provides a richer analytical environment.

There are two varieties of syndicated data that we are likely to want in a clickstream warehouse. One is market data. The market data provides an overall picture of the market and the enterprise's position in that market, sometimes providing detailed items such as market share by major competitors, sales numbers, and market forecasts. In the online world this data might include traffic data and top sites in a given category.

This market data is great for providing benchmarks to compare internal data to, and for evaluating the enterprise's position in the market. Depending on the data, it may be used during product development, forecasting, or when creating marketing campaigns.

The second variety of syndicated data that we often want to include in the warehouse is consumer information. There are many different types of consumer information, from simple mailing lists the enterprise might purchase for a marketing campaign to detailed demographic and psychographic data. It is possible to purchase detailed data about an individual's spending habits, buying and brand preferences, income, hobbies, cars, pet ownership, and reading habits.

The demographic and psychographic data is of particular interest to consumer-oriented businesses. Any data that provides more detail about individuals will help the business to better cater to those consumers. The finer the level of detail, the more that marketing and merchandising groups can segment customers, and the more likely the Web site can be customized to the preferred customers.

People have been worried about online privacy over the past few years because online applications can observe their behavior more closely than ever. The difficulty for most firms has been matching the online user to the offline data that one can purchase. Unfortunately, this focus on online privacy is misdirected. The scrutiny should be directed at the offline businesses selling personal data. Offline data syndicators are the companies that collect and sell massive amounts of personal information, with the explicit approval of banks, credit card companies, and even local and federal government agencies. We'll touch on privacy again in the next chapter. For the time being, expect that your business will want to track detailed information about users if it is a consumer-oriented business.

Summary

In this chapter we examined the clickstream data from Web server and media server logs as the primary source of information for the data warehouse, and we reviewed some of the common applications that provide supplemental data. We also looked at many of the problems inherent in the clickstream data.

We have not considered how this clickstream data may be used to reconstruct a user's actions during a session, nor how the Web site can track users over time. These topics require a more in-depth discussion of a number of Web technologies and methods. We will cover this information in Chapter 4.

Using Cookies and Other Mechanisms to Track User Identity

C lickstream data warehouses are the eyes and ears of the electronic enterprise. The clickstream history contained in the warehouse speaks volumes about the nature of user actions on a Web site. But without a mechanism to establish individual user identity, the analysis of user actions can only be done in aggregate, with all types of users lumped together and no way of following or accurately targeting the activities of a particular user or group of users.

By establishing user identity, clickstream business intelligence becomes richer and the focus of analysis can be dedicated to interpreting the actions of site visitors, whether they are consumers or business partners. This kind of analysis is usually termed electronic user Relationship Management, or eRM for short. A necessary condition for eRM is a user identity mechanism in order to determine which users performed what actions on a particular Web site.

This chapter discusses the mechanisms a Web site can use to manage user sessions and establish user identity. With this information in hand, we then look at the various types of users and online profiles we can create, and conclude with a discussion of personalization and privacy and their impacts on the data warehouse schema design.

Web Programming Techniques for Maintaining Application State

Chapters 2 and 3 discussed the nature of HTTP transactions and some of the problems of tracking application state from one request to the next. There are only three basic techniques available for tracking the state of an HTTP session. The first of these techniques is the use of cookies. The file format and data fields for a cookie were described in the previous chapter. This section will detail what a cookie is, how it is communicated between the Web browser and Web server, how cookies are used to manage session and user information, and how this information is recorded.

Cookies

The cookie protocol was developed by Netscape as a solution to the HTTP state problem described in Chapter 2, namely the problem of an application not knowing what happens during subsequent visits to different pages within a Web site. Simply put, a cookie is a variable stored in the browser by the Web server. It is the primary mechanism most Web sites use to keep track of client sessions.

As mentioned in Chapter 3, a cookie has a total of six parameters:

Name. The name used to reference the cookie.

Value. The value the Web site assigned to the cookie.

Domain. The Internet domain of the server(s) that have access to the cookie.

Path. The URL path within the domain for which the cookie is valid.

Expires. The expiration date of the cookie.

Secure. A flag set to indicate that a cookie is only used with a secure connection.

Cookies can be created in one of two ways: they can be sent from the Web server, or set from within client-side code. Most application servers and server-side scripting languages have built-in support for cookies. Below are several examples showing how a cookie can be created.

The first examples show some basic JavaScript code used to set a cookie from within the client browser. This code would be embedded in an HTML page and would be executed within the browser after the page has downloaded.

JavaScript uses an object called Document.cookie to support cookies. This object stores the cookies that are valid for the page the script is currently executing on. Creating a cookie can be as simple as embedding the following script:

```
<SCRIPT language=JavaScript>
document.cookie="myCookie=happy; expires=Sun,
   12-Jan-2002 00:00:00 GMT; path=/; domain=.mydomain.com";
</SCRIPT>
```

When values are set in the Document.cookie object a cookie is created. This script creates a cookie called "myCookie" with the value "happy" that will be sent each time a page is requested from any Web server in the domain "mydomain .com" until it expires on January 12 of 2002. Usually, the Web developer will write a generic script that takes the parameters and can be called from within other scripts programs on the page.

It can take a little more code to set cookies from the server side, but not much. For example, cookies could be set by a CGI program in PERL by directly writing the Cookie header and sending that header to the client. Server-side scripting languages can also be used to manipulate headers, although all of the major languages provide simpler facilities for setting and getting cookies. Some are simpler than others, as the following examples illustrate.

Using the server-side scripting language PHP, setting a cookie is very simple:

```php
<?php
    setcookie( "myCookie", "happy", mktime(0,0,0,1,12,2002), "/",
    ".mydomain.com", 0 );
?>
```

Setting cookies in Microsoft's Active Server Pages makes use of the Response .cookies object. This object contains parameters that match those needed to set a cookie. This is similar to the way in which a cookie is created in PHP, only it takes more code.

```
Response.Cookies("myCookie") = "happy"
Response.Cookies("myCookie").Expires = "January 12, 2002"
Response.Cookies("myCookie").Domain = ".mydomain.com"
Response.Cookies("myCookie").Path = "/"
Response.Cookies("myCookie").Secure = FALSE
```

As mentioned in Chapter 2, a set of headers is sent with every HTTP request or response. Once a cookie has been created it will be sent from the server to the browser as an HTTP header. When a cookie is sent from the server to the browser an additional line will be added to the HTTP headers, for example like that shown below.

```
HTTP/1.1 200 OK
Date: Thu, 08 Feb 2001 18:05:22 GMT
Server: Apache/1.3.9 (UNIX) PHP/4.0
Set-Cookie: myCookie=happy; expires=Sun, 12-Jan-2002 00:00:00 GMT;
  path=/; domain=.mydomain.com
Content-type: text/html
```

When the browser receives a Set-cookie header it will create the cookie with the values specified and store it in memory. Given the arbitrarily long time span a developer can choose for a given cookie duration, it is likely that the lifetime of a cookie will exceed the amount of time the browser is open. There-fore the browser saves all of its cookies to the hard drive.

The next time the browser is opened it will read all the cookies from disk and store them in memory again, making them available the next time the user visits a site. When cookies expire they are discarded from memory and no longer saved to disk.

When the browser contacts the server to request a page, the browser sends any cookies that are valid for that particular URL and domain. There is a slight change to the header when the browser requests a page from the Web site and sends a cookie to the Web server. The browser sends a Cookie header instead of the Set-Cookie header, and standard attributes are denoted with a prefixed dollar sign.

```
Cookie: $Version="1"; myCookie="happy"; $Max-age=10283756;
   $Path="/"; $Domain=".mydomain.com"
```

The Web site developers normally will not need to read the HTTP header to retrieve the cookies that the browser sends. Almost any Web development lan-guage or application server will process the header and make the cookies accessible. Cookies may also be read from within the browser.

For example, the way to retrieve cookies from within the browser using JavaScript is access the Document.cookie object mentioned early. This object contains the "name=value" pair for each cookie that is applicable to the page being displayed, with each pair separated by a semicolon. Because of the way these values are stored, most Web developers will write a function to retrieve a given cookie, as the following example demonstrates:

```
<SCRIPT language=JavaScript>
function getCookie( name ) {
  var cookie = " " + document.cookie;
  var searchStr = " " + name + "=";
  var cookieValue = null;
  var offset = 0;
  var end = 0;
  if ( cookie.length > 0 ) {
    offset = cookie.indexOf( searchStr );
    if (offset != -1) {
      offset += search.length;
      end = cookie.indexOf(";", offset)
      if (end == -1) {
        end = cookie.length;
      }
      cookieValue = unescape( cookie.substring( offset, end ) );
    }
  }
  return( cookieValue );
}
</SCRIPT>
```

Getting the value of "myCookie" that was set in an earlier example would be a simple call:

```
myCookieVariable = GetCookie( "myCookie" );
```

The value stored in "myCookieVariable" after this call would be "happy", which we set earlier.

On the Web application side, accessing cookies will depend on the environment and language used. With a PERL CGI program running under UNIX one method might be to use the environment variable HTTP_COOKIE. This variable stores the cookie values in a semicolon delimited string in exactly the same way as with JavaScript, so a Web developer would write a simple PERL routine to parse the string.

The process is even simpler using Active Server Pages. Instead of using the Response.cookies object described in the earlier ASP example to set a cookie, the Request.cookies object is used. Every cookie that is valid for the current document is stored in this object and can be retrieved with a single call:

```
myCookieVariable = Request.Cookies( "myCookie" )
```

PHP makes cookie access simpler still. When the Web server receives a request for a document the cookies are automatically processed into global variables with the same names as the cookies, thus eliminating the need for a function call to retrieve the data. For developers who do not like to use global variables, the cookies are also available in an associative array named $HTTP_COOKIE_VARS[]. For example, either of the following statements will print the value of the cookie:

```
<?php
  // This prints the contents of the cookie, i.e. "happy"
  echo $myCookie;

  // This also prints the contents of the cookie
  echo $HTTP_COOKIE_VARS["myCookie"];
?>
```

With the ability to set cookies for a client, send them back and forth between the Web server and browser, and access the cookies from programs on the server, the Web site now has the ability to record the state of user actions. This allows the Web site to manage a series of requests from a given user as a single session. It is possible to build relatively sophisticated session and user tracking systems by applying this simple mechanism, as we will see in a later section.

The definitive text describing what a cookie is and how it works is the Request for Comments (RFC) that defines the HTTP cookie protocol. The cookie RFC, along with all others, is available at http://www.ietf.org/rfc.html. Refer to the official document if you want all the gory details about how cookies are meant to function.

The HTTP Headers for a Simple Cookie Exchange

The following illustrates what passes back and forth in the HTTP headers during a simple session where a user goes online to by some junk food. Only basic HTTP and Cookie header information is shown to make this example easier to read.

There is one item in the current standard that can be confusing when looking at Cookie headers. When a server sets a cookie, the cookie name and value are always the first parameter in the list, followed by the cookie attributes. When a browser returns a cookie the positional notation is not used. Instead, all cookie attributes are prefixed by a dollar sign and the cookie name lacks the prefix.

1. The user goes to the site and receives a login page. No cookies are set at this time.

2. The user fills out an HTML form with a username and password and sends it to the Web server via an HTTP POST, resulting in the following in the header:

```
POST /hostess/login HTTP/1.1
```

3. The Web server sends back the shopping page and sets a cookie with the user's identity.

```
HTTP/1.1 200 OK
Set-Cookie: Customer="Mr_P"; Version="1"; Path="/hostess"
```

4. The user goes shopping and adds an item to their basket. This sends the form data on the product selection to the Web server. It also sends the cookie with the user identifier.

```
POST /hostess/pickitem HTTP/1.1
Cookie: $Version="1"; Customer="MR_P"; $Path="/hostess"
```

5. The server acknowledges the addition to the shopping cart and sets a cookie for the item selected when it sends back the next shopping page. The Web site now has information in the Web server log about the product the user selected.

```
HTTP/1.1 200 OK
Set-Cookie: SKU="Big Stuf Ding Dongs"; Version="1";
Path="/hostess"
```

6. The user enters the remaining purchasing information on the form to complete the order, resulting in another POST. This time both the user identifier cookie and the product SKU cookie are sent in the header. As before, these end up in the Web server log.

(continued)

The HTTP Headers for a Simple Cookie Exchange *(Continued)*

```
POST /hostess/shipping HTTP/1.1
Cookie: $Version="1";
Customer="MR_P"; $Path="/hostess";
SKU="Big Stuf Ding Dongs_0001"; $Path="/hostess"
```

7. **The server acknowledges the completion of the order. Since this is the last page, the server does not send back any Set-cookie: headers. If desired, the server could remove the cookies by sending a Set-cookie: header with null values and an expiration time that has already passed.**

```
HTTP/1.1 200 OK
```

The Query String and URL Rewriting

One of the big drawbacks to cookies is that it is possible for a proxy server to screen them out or for a browser to disable them. For this reason, many Web sites do not rely on cookies as the sole method to maintain application state or identify returning users. An alternative mechanism is to place the information to be passed back and forth into query strings. This technique is termed *URL Rewriting.*

Chapter 2 mentioned that when a form is submitted using the GET method, all the fields and values are encoded and appended to the URL to which the form is sent. Each field and value is put into the URL as a string of the form "field=value" with the field/value pairs separated by an ampersand (&).

The Web developer is not limited to forms when putting data into the query string. Any application that dynamically generates pages is capable of attaching a query string to any link on a page. This will work fine as long as the developer follows the rules for URL encoding.

The following HTML fragment shows an example of a link on a page. If a user clicks on the link, it sends the user—anonymously—to nextpage.html. The Web application knows nothing about that user.

```
<A HREF="nextpage.html"> Go to your new page </A>
```

Suppose that user was registered and had logged on with a user ID and password. Because the site dynamically generates its Web pages, the Web application that creates the pages can append to the user ID as part of the query string for every page it generates.

If the site wishes to track the user from one page to the next (assuming the user signed in somewhere) the developer can append the username as part of a query string on every link within the pages. If the user were to click on the link shown below instead of the link above, the Web server would receive the request and process it as normal, but the appended user ID and login status would now be available to the Web site.

```
<A HREF="nextpage.html?username=HAL&logged_in=true">Go to new page</A>
```

This simple technique can be applied to track a person's path through a Web site because the URL of each page the user visits is recorded in the server log, including the query string. This technique may be used for session management, although there are some drawbacks. One is that the query string is visible to the user in the browser's address window. In the above example, the following would show in the browser's address window after the user clicked the link:

```
http://www.yourdomain.com/nextpage.html?username=HAL&logged_in=true
```

The implication is that the user can see everything sent back and forth between the browser and server. This introduces the problem of leaking information about what the Web application on the receiving end expects as input. It's simple to change the contents of the query string in an attempt to break the Web application generating the pages. Even so, URL rewriting is a common method for passing user state from page to page.

Hidden Form Fields

The last technique for passing state information is to use hidden form fields. Hidden form fields allow the developer to place values into form fields that the user will not see on the Web page. These values will be sent back to the Web server whenever the user submits the form. The fields are passed to the server in exactly the same manner as any other form data.

The limitation with this technique is that it applies only to forms that are submitted, meaning the user hit one of the buttons on the form. If the user clicks on a link in the page rather than hitting a form button then the values in hidden fields will not be transmitted. Thus, the technique is normally used only for preserving values between specific sets of form pages.

Perhaps a bigger risk of using hidden form fields to retain state information is that it is embedded in the HTML text, so there is the possibility that it can be altered by the user. For example, imagine that a shopping cart application stores a customer's order data in hidden form fields. The data might include product data like the product ID, quantity, and price. A malicious user could modify the hidden field containing the price so that it is much lower, open the altered page in their browser, and then hit the Submit button. If the Web site uses the price in the hidden form field then the customer just received a personalized discount. The use of this technique has been documented many times, yet we still find Web sites storing unvalidated data in forms.

Managing Sessions and Tracking Users

Building on the mechanisms available for preserving session state between page requests, we can now move our discussion to the level of tracking a session throughout a user's visit to a Web site. The above techniques can be combined in a limited number of ways to manage sessions and track users, as we will see in the next section.

Using Cookies to Track Sessions

The first, and simplest, option for keeping track of a user session is to use the facilities that are available with the Web server. For example, Apache provides the "CookieTracking" and "CookieExpires" server directives.

If CookieTracking is turned on in the server configuration then the Web server will issue a unique cookie to each user who visits the Web site. The cookie has no default expiration date set, meaning the cookie will remain active in the user's browser only as long as the browser is running. This default can be changed using the CookieExpires directive, allowing the site to track the user across repeat visits over time.

When the user accesses the Web site for the first time the Web server will generate a unique cookie and set it with the document the user is accessing. For every subsequent access to any document on the Web site, the Web server will reset the cookie. The user's browser will send the cookie with every page request because the cookie is valid throughout the domain. Assuming the browser accepts cookies and the Web server is logging them, one can assemble every request the user made and recreate their session. The following is an example of what might appear in the server log if the same person were to access three different pages on the Web site.

```
255.108.216.122 - - [12/Jan/1997:00:00:00 -0800] "GET /index.html
   HTTP/1.0" 200 236 "-" "Mozilla/4.75 [en] (Win98; U)" "-"
255.108.216.122 - - [12/Jan/1997:00:00:00 -0800] "GET /page_one.html
   HTTP/1.0" 200 237 "-" "Mozilla/4.75 [en] (Win98; U)"
   "827645474623743846="
255.108.216.122 - - [12/Jan/1997:00:00:00 -0800] "GET /page_two.html
   HTTP/1.0" 200 246 "-" "Mozilla/4.75 [en] (Win98; U)"
   "827645474623743846="
```

The cookie value shows up in the last field in the log record. Note that the first record shows a dash for the cookie value. This is because one must set a cookie in the browser before it can be sent back to the server. This means the first record for a user's visit will not show a cookie value.

The obvious drawback to this technique is that it is anonymous. It only tells us that someone using a particular browser accessed the site and what pages were sent. Unless the CookieExpires directive is used, the user will be issued a new cookie and appear as a different user when they next turn on their browser and return to the site. Other drawbacks include problems with browser and server caching, which will be covered later in this chapter.

One advantage to this technique is that it will work with a Web site that has only static HTML pages—no programming is necessary to track the sessions. This technique is also fine if the goal is simply tracking what a given user views as they wander through the Web site.

There is one important factor to keep in mind when using cookies to track session state: browsers can be configured to stop accepting cookies. This can be a big hurdle when the goal is to identify all the pages associated with each visit. It means the first technique to learn with cookies is how to detect whether a given browser accepts them.

Some Web sites use a client-side language such as JavaScript to set a test cookie and then attempt to read it back. If the value for the test cookie is successfully read back then the cookie was accepted. If the read fails then the browser does not have cookies enabled. The script can then take some action to let the Web site know that cookies are not enabled. This works because client-side code like JavaScript can set and test cookies without interacting with the Web site.

Client-side code is not the best method to use because the browser may be running with JavaScript disabled, or a proxy server may be filtering the cookies. In either of these cases, the Web site will not know that cookies are disabled. Nevertheless, some sites make use of this mechanism.

A better way to detect if the browser is accepting cookies is to set a cookie on the initial request and check the value on the next request from that browser. This takes two HTTP requests—two page loads from the browser—in order to work. The most widely used solution to the problem of needing two requests is to set a test cookie and then redirect the browser back to the same page. A redirect is an HTTP header that tells the browser to stop loading the current page and start loading with a new page. Doing a test and redirect means the application does not need to wait for the second, possibly nonexistent, request.

This is possible in dynamic page generation environments (server-side scripting and most application servers). It works by sending a Set-cookie header followed by a Location header in response to the browser's page request. If cookies are enabled then the cookie will be sent to the server when the browser requests the page it was just redirected to. If cookies are not enabled then there will be no cookie.

At first glance this might not make sense, like calling a friend and leaving them a message to call you only if they don't get the message. If the browser is not accepting cookies then the server has no way of knowing this is the second page access and there was a prior attempt to set a cookie. The solution requires telling the server that this is the second page access by the client.

There are two ways to notify the Web application that this is the second page request. The first is to attempt to set a cookie and immediately redirect the browser to a second page that is identical to the first but has been programmed to expect a cookie. If no cookie is present then the Web application knows this and can act accordingly. This is not a particularly good solution but there are Web sites that actually do this.

The example below shows what the headers from the Web server look like when a user requests the page "index.html" for the first time.

```
HTTP/1.1 200 OK
Date: Thu, 08 Feb 2001 18:05:22 GMT
Server: Apache/1.3.9 (UNIX) PHP/4.0
Set-cookie: sessionid=testing; path=/; domain=.mydomain.com
Connection: close
Content-Type: text.html
Location: index2.html
```

When the server responds to the request for "index.html" it tries to set a cookie with a test value. The Location header tells the browser to load a different page called "index2.html". The server will receive the cookie from the browser for the index2.html request. If the cookie value is available in the header then cookies are enabled and functioning. If the cookie value is not available then cookies are disabled in the browser, or the browser is using a cookie-filtering program.

The more common method of notifying the server of the second request makes use of the query string. After setting a test cookie the server sends the browser *back to the same page* but appends a query string indicating that this is the result of a redirect. When the second request is received by the server, the application has available to it the query string. The application therefore recognizes that this is the request from a redirect and can use an alternate mechanism if there is no cookie present. The example below shows the headers the server would send the client for this technique.

```
HTTP/1.1 200 OK
Date: Thu, 08 Feb 2001 18:05:22 GMT
Server: Apache/1.3.9 (UNIX) PHP/4.0
Set-cookie: sessionid=new_session_id; path=/; domain=.mydomain.com
Connection: close
Content-Type: text.html
Location: index.html?test_for_cookie=True
```

These headers are nearly identical to the prior set, except that the Location header points back to the original page being accessed, in this case index.html. The sample PHP code shown below (sans error checking) uses this technique to check if cookies are enabled and functioning.

```
<?php
  // If nothing is set then this is the first visit to the server.
  if ( ($test_for_cookie != "True") and
       (empty($HTTP_COOKIE_VARS[sessionid])) ) {
    // Try to set a cookie with a 15 minute lifetime and
    // redirect the browser
    setcookie("sessionid", GetNewSessionID(), time() + 1800,
              "/", ".mydomain.com" );
    header( "Location:
http://www.mydomain.com/Index.html?test_for_cookie=True" );
  }
  // If test_for_cookie is set then we need to do the cookie test
  if ( $test_for_cookie == "True" ) {
    // Check the sessionid cookie to see if we received it
    if ( empty($HTTP_COOKIE_VARS[sessionid]) ) {
      // There is no sessionid so cookies are disabled. Figure out
      // how to track the session and move on.
      DecideWhatToDo();
    }
  }
  // If we reach this point then cookies are working so display
  // the page to the user.
?>
<HTML>
<HEAD>
<TITLE> Welcome to my nightmare </TITLE>
</HEAD>
<BODY>
Welcome to the first page of the rest of your visit.
</BODY>
</HTML>
```

The script is fairly simple and can be used on any page by changing the Location header. A smart programmer would write a generic cookie-testing script that runs on every page. This ensures that people linking into the site from elsewhere, such as via a search engine, will have their session tracked no matter what. If this test were only done on the home page then we would miss tracking a lot of users.

Note that if the Web site has an explicit entry point through which all users are funneled then the cookie check only needs to be done once on the entry page. This would apply to sites that require registration before access is granted, but it will not be true for a majority of Web sites. Even for sites that require registration, it would be desirable to track what enticing free content the unregistered visitors look at before deciding whether to register or leave.

Using URL Rewriting to Track Sessions

The prior example with cookies used the query string in a hybrid approach to communicate state information, specifically the data that the browser requested a page for the second time. The query string can be used as an alternative to cookies.

As with cookies, the first problem to overcome is that of identifying the initial request of a user's session. The first request from the browser accesses the Web page with no information supplied in the URL. In order to track the session, a session ID must be somehow placed on the URL for the current and all subsequent pages.

Unlike using cookies, there is no need to check if things are working before setting up some kind of session ID for tracking purposes. The same technique shown in the prior section to redirect the browser can be used to place a session identifier in the URL. When the page is first accessed there will be nothing in the query string, so a quick check for "sessionID" will turn up nothing. Not finding an ID, the server can issue a Location header with the original URL plus tracking data such as "?sessionID=08010C" as the query string. When the server receives the second redirected request, it will find the sessionID set. Now the server can display the page. This is virtually identical to using the *test_for_cookie* variable in the earlier PHP example.

The only additional work for the Web developer is to make sure that *every* link on *every* page has the same query string appended to it. This applies to all the links for the navigation bars, any links within the page text, and anything else that links internally within the Web site. If this is not done, then when a user clicks on a link to another page, that page will think this is the first page of the visit and set a new session identifier.

Using Hidden Fields to Track Sessions

As mentioned earlier, using hidden form fields to track sessions is not a common practice. The reason for this is that clicking on a link does not send form variables to the Web server. Only submitting a form sends the variables. Using hidden fields to track a session is something that would be done only on form pages, for example during an online purchase where each step in the process is a form submission that proceeds to the next step.

To pass data in hidden fields is very simple. It only requires that a field of type "hidden" be placed in the form, along with the value of that field. The user will not see this field on the form unless they view the page source. The following HTML code shows what a form with a hidden field looks like:

```
<HTML>
<HEAD>
<TITLE>Hidden Field Form</TITLE>
</HEAD>
<BODY>
<form action=buy_my_record.cfm method="POST">
<P>
Won't you please buy my record?
</P>
<input type="text" name="quantity" value="1">
<input type="hidden" name="sessionid" value="08010C">
<input type="hidden" name="real_quantity" value="200">
<input type="submit" value="Buy this many now!">
</BODY>
</HTML>
```

The form below doesn't display the hidden fields, but they're present and available to the Web application when the form is submitted. With this mechanism, the session data and state of a given transaction can be maintained throughout from one form to the next.

Session Management Design Techniques and Trade-offs

The techniques we reviewed demonstrate the basics for retaining information between page requests in a simple Web application. If the warehouse design goal is simply to keep track of which requests in the log file make up a given session then any of the above techniques is enough.

Our goal in a clickstream warehouse is to track every request and link it to a specific session and to an individual user so that we can derive more meaningful information and reconstruct important events. This means we need to look at how Web application environments make use of these techniques.

In order to do clickstream analysis well, a Web site must be designed to record the required analytical information, regardless of the session management and user tracking techniques in use. The reality for most Web sites is that multiple techniques are used for different purposes. The problem is that Web developers are usually tasked with implementing only site functionality, so clickstream analysis becomes an afterthought. Unless clickstream data collection is an explicit design goal, Web site designers will likely design a beautiful Web site that does not capture the necessary data—a big strategic business error.

For example, tracking users as they browse through a product catalog is not particularly important to the Web application. Selecting items to purchase and the checkout process are important. This may mean a session ID is not assigned until an item is selected for purchase. Ideally, we would want to capture everything the user looked at prior to the purchase, as well as the purchase information.

This design tension must be kept in mind if you are constructing the warehouse after the Web site is in production. It is likely that some important data will be exceedingly difficult to extract without a detailed understanding of how the site was constructed. In some cases the data may be unavailable unless changes are made to the Web application.

There are too many variations in the way higher-level tools manage sessions to cover them all here. Instead, we'll look at the most common techniques that many tools and products use.

One technique that a number of low-end "Web-site-in-a-box" products, as well as many of the older custom designed sites, use is setting all values related to a session into cookies. In an example of overeager use of a technique, everything from the session ID to the contents of a shopping basket is stored in cookies. This is great for the warehouse developer because all of the information associated with the user and session is available in the server log. However, there are many drawbacks to this technique for Web applications, so it will rarely be used on any of the larger commercial Web sites or in newer products.

The most common technique for session tracking is to set a single cookie with a unique session ID. All of the information about the session is tracked by the Web application on the server, frequently storing the data in a database. If the browser does not have cookies enabled then the application sends the session ID on the query string instead.

This is a much better technique since sending all the data back and forth is not necessary in most cases, and this technique is more secure. The drawback for the warehouse developer is that the only data available in the server log is a single session ID. All data about the user and much of the data about their actions is available only within the Web application running the site. A review of the Web application design and how it preserves a history of events will be vital in the data extraction process.

For sites implemented without a robust relational database and without Web developers who have a good understanding of database design, it may be impossible to reconstruct some user actions and events. For example, it may not be possible to map a session back to a user because there is no permanent storage of the session ID and the user associated with that session ID. Instead there is an impermanent session object holding all user and session information, and this object is lost once the session is closed. Many tools currently on the market and built on object databases make this mistake.

Most Web application servers and platforms provide built-in session management facilities so that the Web developer does not need to worry about the mechanics of the session. They need only decide what information to associate with a session. The product handles everything else, including passing the session ID back and forth. For example, Java Server Pages ties all session values to a single cookie and provides facilities for managing all session data. If cookies are not enabled then URL rewriting may be used instead, depending on the server, although support for URL rewriting is not mandated by the JSP specification. Microsoft's Active Server Pages provides similar session services.

With the higher-level session management facilities available to many developers, you may find that they do not know what underlying technique is used to track sessions. The only way to discover this is to read through the application software manuals and review what shows up in the Web server log. Where possible, you may want to talk with the developers about logging additional data. For example, when a session starts it would be nice to have a variable in the URL that says the given page request is the start of a user's session. Data extraction becomes much simpler with additional pieces of data like this.

Tracking Users

After learning about session tracking techniques, understanding how individual users are tracked is simple. The same techniques used to track sessions can be applied to identifying users. There are a few minor differences because tracking an individual user is not always the same as tracking a session.

Visitors

There is one case where tracking a session and tracking a user are the same: when the company doesn't need to identify individuals or doesn't need to build a profile of a user over time. Quite a few companies manage their Web sites using what we term "anonymous visitors." There is no identifying information to indicate that the user visiting the site now is the same user who visited the site yesterday.

In these cases, simply tracking a session from the point where a person first visits the site to when they last accessed the site will be enough. Each visitor is identified based on the session ID in the server log. Any of the session tracking techniques mentioned will work. Even the first—and simplest—technique of using a Web server's ability to set tracking cookies will suffice.

It is useful to differentiate between tracking this way as opposed to identifying repeat visitors. When the Web site is tracking in this manner we are really tracking and counting visits and not the users who come to the site.

Users

Since the most meaningful clickstream analysis is based on learning about user behavior over time, we really want to track repeat visits and assemble information about individual users. This means the Web site must uniquely identify each user and track each of their visits to the site.

User Identification Cookies

A simple technique to track a user is to set a cookie on their first visit using some specific parameters. The cookie value must be a unique identifier that is never reused and can always be associated with this user. The expiration date should be far enough in the future so that the cookie will remain valid from the current visit to at least the next likely visit. The domain and path should be set for the entire Web site so the user is identified no matter where they enter the site on their return visits. As a result, each time the user returns, all of the pages viewed during that visit will be associated with a specific individual. Further, prior visits by the same person may be linked to the current visit.

The user cookie approach is obviously not perfect. It suffers from the problems mentioned earlier with cookies, any one of which makes tracking the user across visits difficult or even impossible. It also requires that the Web developers create a single, centralized source of user identifiers to avoid problems with duplicate identifiers or multiple ID formats. Regrettably, other than making users log in, cookies are the only way to track a user over longer time periods. While imperfect, this is the single most common method for tracking repeat visitors.

A potential difficulty for the warehouse developer is that there are often two cookies associated with an individual. One cookie identifies the user and another cookie identifies the session. This is not always the case, as some Web sites use cookies only for user identification, relying on one of the other techniques for session management. Regardless, the result is that one must now link a user identifier with different session identifiers and the data in the server logs.

User ID Server

Creating a user ID server is a twist on the use of user identification cookies. This technique makes use of cookies and the ability to redirect a user's browser to another Web server. The advantage of a user ID server is that the Web site can issue unique user identifiers across multiple Web servers and different domains, providing a way for Web sites to profile users across Web servers and Web sites. The way this works is a fairly simple set of steps described below and shown in Figure 4.1.

1. Every Web page checks the user's request to make sure the user has a user identifier, either stored in a cookie or sent via URL rewriting.

2. When there is no identifier, the Web server redirects the user's browser to a separate user ID server. This is simply a Web server that generates a unique user identifier and attempts to set it in a cookie on the user's browser. It then redirects the browser back to the referring page with the user ID written into the URL. This means that the user ID server has effectively shared the contents of a cookie across domains because any Web server could call this server.

3. When the browser receives the redirect back to the original page it will have a cookie set from the user ID server's domain, and it will have this user ID encoded in the URL it is requesting from the original Web server.

4. The original Web server looks for a user ID and finds it in the URL. This Web server then sets a cookie with the user ID, thus creating a cookie for the Web site domain with the same contents as the cookie created by the user ID server.

In this sequence of steps the user visited the desired Web page briefly, was sent to the user ID server, and then sent back to the desired Web page. The user will not be aware of this series of events because nothing obvious is displayed in the Web browser to tell them they were redirected several times. In our round-trip above, the only indicator is that the final URL has the user ID written into it, something that was not there originally.

By setting up Web servers to redirect the user's browser in this way, one can issue unique user tracking cookies from multiple Web sites and be ensured that every Web site has the same user identifier. This can be very helpful when the company has multiple Web sites, or has outsourced or shared components of the Web site across domains.

User ID server redirection can be refined to make it a more underhanded way to track users across Web sites. The only indication of a redirect is that the URL of the link one clicked on is not the same as the link one has arrived at. This refinement makes use of yet another redirect. The Web server redirects the user to the same page one last time, but strips off the data written into the URL. Now the user has cookies from the user ID server and Web site, and never saw anything out of the ordinary. There is nothing visible in the page source of any Web pages either. The only item that gives this technique away is the identical user ID found in cookies from different domains. The interchange using the refined technique is shown in Figure 4.1.

What we found interesting is that the refined technique appears to be used by a number of prominent Web sites, including MSN.com, MSNBC.com, and Microsoft bCentral.com. We tested this by visiting these three sites after clearing all the cookies in the browser. Upon examination, each of the cookies had the exact same GUID. The only way to accomplish this across multiple domains and not to show anything in the URL is to use an ID server that works as we outlined above.

User Registration

Users may be encouraged or in some cases forced to register to access the Web site. Any combination of techniques may then be used to track users during visits because they identified themselves up front. This removes the dependence on any one technical approach to tracking users. Cookies may be used, and where they are not enabled, URL rewriting used instead.

Forcing user registration does not solve everything for the warehouse developer. Since the user logs in to the site, the warehouse must extract the Web site

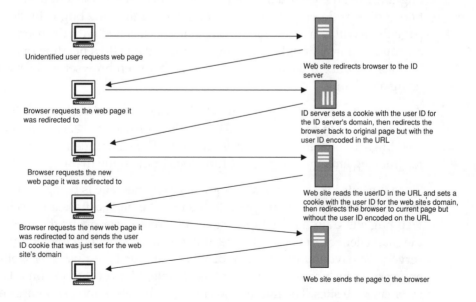

Unidentified user requests web page

Web site redirects browser to the ID server

Browser requests the web page it was redirected to

ID server sets a cookie with the user ID for the ID server's domain, then redirects the browser back to original page but with the user ID encoded in the URL

Browser requests the new web page it was redirected to

Web site reads the userID in the URL and sets a cookie with the user ID for the web site's domain, then redirects the browser to current page but without the user ID encoded on the URL

Browser requests the new web page it was redirected to and sends the user ID cookie that was just set for the web site's domain

Web site sends the page to the browser

Figure 4.1 Cross-domain User ID server.

login data and combine it with the information from the Web server logs in order to assemble visit data. We hope that the Web application provides enough data in the Web server logs to make the linking of users and log records possible.

Web Server Authentication

Native Web server authentication is an alternative to the more common application-based logins. This method is seldom used because it denies access to anyone who does not have a user name and password set up in advance, it requires administrator action to set up (although it can sometimes be automated), and the login shows up as a pop-up box over the Web page rather than being incorporated into the Web site design.

The advantage to the warehouse developer is that the user's name is logged into the Authuser field in all the standard log formats. Thus it will associate every request in the log with a valid user and will not require additional work to extract user names based on user IDs in the query string or cookies. Note that using this technique does not work for managing sessions, only for authenticating and tracking users.

Web Bugs

In Chapter 3 we discussed the use of web bugs, invisible images that allow the Web site to transmit data from a page view to another Web server. To use a web bug to track an individual user, one need only set a persistent user identification cookie as described earlier. Once set, each time the bug is loaded from a page there will be a record of the page view associated with the user, as well as any other information that one might transmit via URL encoding or additional cookies. Figure 4.2 shows the interactions between browser and server when using a web bug.

As we mentioned in Chapter 3, this technique will also work in email. Some of the companies that provide email marketing software or services regularly use web bugs to track the emails they send out. The technique is slightly different for tracking email messages, but functions in the same manner.

Since the enterprise knows to whom an email message is being sent, a unique identifier that is already mapped to the user's email address is encoded to the web bug's URL in the email message. When the user opens the message and the mail client retrieves the image, the information will be logged by the Web server. We have found evidence of this technique being used by well-known enterprises such as eToys, Barnes and Noble, Microsoft, and some U.S. government Web sites. The interactions between browser and server are shown in Figure 4.3.

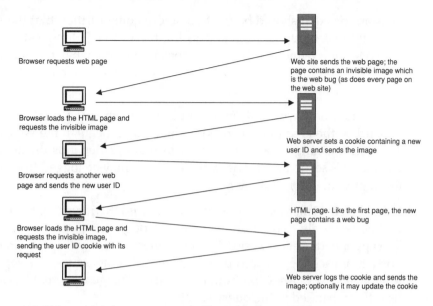

Figure 4.2 Using a web bug to set a user ID cookie from a Web page.

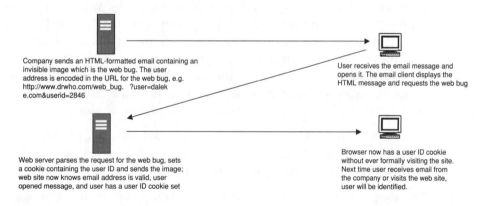

Figure 4.3 Using a web bug to set a user ID cookie from within an email message.

The ability to track the actions of users on the Web site, in addition to their receipt and viewing of email messages, means that web bugs will be with us for a long time. The information that online marketers can gather across these channels of communication is simply too attractive for most enterprises to ignore.

Logging Session and User Data

Armed with a general understanding of session and user tracking, we can now examine the implications for what is logged by the Web server. There are a few assumptions that should be verified before going further: that the Web server is configured to log cookies and to log the full HTTP request including the query string. Without this basic information and what is contained in the Extended Common Log Format, any further clickstream data warehouse work would be nearly impossible.

The assumptions you will make during the extraction phase of the project depend on the kind of user tracking data that appears in the Web server logs. The user tracking data that appears in the logs depends on the techniques used. In this section we'll briefly review what may be logged from some of the techniques mentioned earlier.

If the preferred method for tracking sessions is URL rewriting then the log data will be relatively easy to understand, although parsing is not always trivial. The appended user or session ID in the query string will appear in the request portion of each logged record. There are still some issues, like separating the first page view of a session from the "marked" page view that has a session or user ID embedded in the query string.

One item that may not be apparent when using query strings is the use of the Method attribute in the Form tag on form pages. As mentioned in an earlier chapter, the two methods of submitting form data are GET and POST. The primary difference as far as log records are concerned is that a GET places all form variables in the query string. A POST makes use of the HTTP header, meaning the data sent will not show up in the log. If the Web developer uses a POST and sends the session or user information on the form then there will be records in the log that can't be associated with a given user or session.

As with URL rewriting, when cookies are used each record in the log should contain the session or user ID cookie. Unlike URL rewriting, cookies can be disabled, resulting in data problems in the log file.

The simplest choice from a Web developer's perspective is to not track sessions or users if cookies are not enabled. This choice is supported by the fact that, according to recent estimates, only 5 percent of Web users are using cookie management software. Not tracking these sessions will create two disjoint sets of records in the Web server log. For the majority of users who have cookies enabled, the log file will contain enough data to associate records with the users who made the requests. All of the users without cookies will be logged with no cookie data. This unmarked data results in a set of records that must be treated separately in data extraction, either by lumping them under an anonymous label or dealing with them only at aggregate levels of detail.

Assuming that the site wants to track all users, it is likely that if cookies are not working, the Web application will resort to URL rewriting. This creates a more complex scenario when extracting log data because the cookies show up in log records in one field, while the query string shows up in a different field. This forces the warehouse developer to look in two different places to assemble the records that make up a session.

To make matters more complicated, cookies can be disabled in the middle of a session. If this happens then the log file will contain one set of records marked one way and a second set marked a different way, assuming the Web developer wrote the application to handle this case. More likely is that a new session will start when the cookies are disabled and it will appear as though the user had two immediately consecutive visits to the site. Each of these two apparent visits will be tracked in a different way.

The technique of using two variables, one for the session ID and one for user tracking, was mentioned earlier. The implication of this for log data is that different fields may contain the information to associate records with a session, and sessions with a user. Since some Web sites use a single user-tracking cookie, defining a rule for what constitutes a session is left to the clickstream warehouse developer.

Another Web application design option is to track user and session data during only certain processes on the site, like going to the checkout with purchases. In this case the only records in the log that will have a user or session ID are the records for pages associated with this process. The remainder of the records will be anonymous, leaving us a log with minimal session information except for certain key transactions.

Consider yourself lucky if the Web site forces users to log in to gain access, or only allows access from browsers with cookies enabled. The outlook from a warehouse developer's perspective is great because every record will be associated with a specific user and there will be no anonymous sessions to deal with.

No matter what techniques are used, there will always be some problems with the data in the Web server logs. Understanding how the Web application is managing sessions and tracking users will help resolve many of these issues. In Chapter 8, which covers data extraction and loading, we'll cover more information on anticipating and resolving some of these problems.

User Identification and User Profiles

With the mechanisms for tracking users in place and understood, we need to look at users and the user profiles that will be stored in the warehouse. As mentioned in Chapter 1, the term *user* refers to an individual who is visiting the Web site. The user's online identity is based on the information we have about them. This does not mean that we know who the actual person is; only that we know that this user is the same user who visited us before. Further, because of the anonymous nature of the Web and the ease of obtaining accounts with email addresses, a user likely has multiple online identities.

Classes of Online Users

From the individual user's perspective, there are really only two types of interaction they are involved in with a Web site. The person is either just surfing, visiting your Web site because there was something interesting to draw them, or they are trying to fulfill a specific task. The task might be as simple as looking up the times a movie is playing at a particular theater, or as complex as negotiating the terms of a contract for the purchase of specialty steel.

The users who are just surfing are usually content to be anonymous. If the user is on a mission then they typically want a Web site to remember who they are from prior visits. Having a Web site remember preferences or the particulars of their shipping and billing addresses is frequently viewed as more than just a convenience. In order to save any of this personalized information, the Web site requires a persistent user tracking mechanism like a persistent cookie or registered user ID.

The enterprise has a different perspective on users. A user can be any visitor coming to the Web site, regardless of whether that visitor is an individual, a search engine robot or an online marketplace agent. From the point of view of an enterprise there are three basic classes of user to consider: individuals, individuals acting on behalf of a collective entity, and automated agents. There may be a number of subgroups within each of these classes depending on the needs of the warehouse users.

Individuals

Consumer-oriented Web sites are most likely to consider different subgroups for individual users. The most common subgroups of individual users you are likely to be asked to track in the warehouse are listed below.

Anonymous visitor. These are visitors that have not been tracked yet. It is also possible that users who are not registered or are not customers are not tracked as part of the Web site's policies. Quite a few Web sites do not profile unregistered users and noncustomers.

Repeat visitor. This group only applies to Web sites that attempt to track unregistered users. The repeat visitors are those users who have previously visited the site but have not registered or otherwise patronized the site in a way that reveals their identity. These users are assigned a persistent user tracking mechanism to identify their visits. At least initially, it is likely that little additional information beyond the tracking identifier is known about their identity.

Registered user. The registered users are an important source of information to the enterprise because these people have voluntarily provided some indication that they are interested in what the Web site has to offer, and have possibly provided some personal information. In this case, they are no longer anonymous, although all we may know about them is some aspect of their online identity.

Customer. Assuming the Web site is involved in commerce, either through direct sales or by providing service for products sold offline, the customers will make up one of the more important groups used in analysis. Deciding which users are part of the customer group is not necessarily a simple task. For example, is a user who purchased a product and then cancelled the order or returned the product for a refund considered a customer? This area provides an endless source of mirth to the analyst designing the user dimension for the warehouse's end users. We will discuss the user dimension in more depth in Chapter 6.

Individuals Acting On Behalf of a Larger Entity

Knowing that individuals are acting on behalf of a larger entity is important to most enterprises, particularly those providing business products or services online. Tracking individual users tends to be easier for these sites because there is less likelihood that the users are anonymous. One of the important aspects of the user tracking mechanism used by the Web site will be its ability to associate the users with the enterprise they represent. The following three subgroups are a common way that enterprises look at this class of user. We use the term *proxy* to indicate that these users are agents of an organization:

Proxy Visitor. These visitors may be anonymous, or they may be required to provide some level of information before having access to the site. Many business sites, such as online marketplaces, ask anonymous visitors to provide the enterprise with some basic information in order to give the user access to the Web site. This is typically done so that they can have further contact with the user, for example by sending marketing materials or having a salesperson contact the visitor.

Proxy User. This group of users has provided enough information to the enterprise to accurately identify the user and the entity that they represent. The user and the entity they represent may not yet be a paying customer, but the Web site probably has some idea of what the user's role is.

Proxy Customer. The last group of users in this class is the customers. It is important to note that both the individual user and the business they represent must be tracked, since the business is the end customer. The user, as an agent of that organization, is equally important and should not be ignored. Determining which customers belong in this group can have the same set of problems as mentioned for customers in the individual user class. It is almost certain that departments within your organization will already have a number of ways they want to classify proxy customers.

Proxy visitors and proxy users make up the base of online prospects that the enterprise will want to market to. It is likely that the marketing and sales departments have particular information from the Web site that they already use to build lists of prospects. The role of the clickstream data warehouse is to provide cleaner and more detailed information to these departments and their operational systems. Ideally, much of the targeting and segmenting of prospects will be built into the warehouse so that everyone in the organization is working off the same set of models.

This second class of users can add significant complexity to the design of the data warehouse. This is because some departments will want to analyze data about individual users while other departments will want to analyze data after it has been aggregated to show only the entities the users represent. For example, staff in your sales organization will want to know who the first-time proxy visitors are, what sales geography these visitors are in, and how they should be ranked as prospects. The product development group may be more interested in what products or services the proxy customers are accessing, while the marketing staff will want to see how the product mix sold online relates to offline sales.

Many designers building clickstream warehouses for companies in the business market make the mistake of assuming that individual users are not important, and focus only on the information about the entities the users represent. Ignoring data about individual visitors can put unnecessary constraints on the analysis performed by many of the warehouse users.

Automated Agents

The last general class of users is the automated agents. There can be many types of agents accessing a Web site. Some of them, such as search engine robots indexing the Web site, are beneficial. There are also agents that act on behalf of marketplaces or related businesses, and may gather information or generate transactions. It is also possible that the agents are from a third party Web site that acts as a content aggregator or online comparison guide.

Regardless of the type of agent, someone within the enterprise will be interested in what kinds of agents are accessing the Web site and what they are doing when visiting. One of the common mistakes we see in the clickstream warehouse design is the filtering out of all agent-related data before loading the warehouse. Without this information it is impossible to determine what organizations are accessing the Web site and what they are doing. Analysis of agent data has led a number of organizations to redesign their Web sites to exclude some of the less desirable practices, such as third party *sniping* software for online auctions or deep linking (linking from one's Web site to pages inside another site, bypassing their navigation) from competing sites.

User Identification

The last section provided an initial method for classifying users, so the next step is to look at how we might identify those users. Identifying and classifying the Web site's users will be driven by the analytical needs of the warehouse users and is a topic we'll reserve for Chapter 6.

One item we need to reiterate at this point is the difference between tracking visitors and tracking users. When we talk about tracking a user we are talking about tracking a user's online identity across multiple visits. This implies that we are using a persistent tracking mechanism across visits. On the other hand, when tracking visitors we have no knowledge of who the visitors are from one visit to the next. The only clickstream history that can be assembled is a collection of log records that make up a particular visitor's session.

Because user tracking mechanisms like persistent cookies are readily available, users rarely go unmonitored, despite what they may think. Web sites can therefore distinguish returning users most of the time, even though the site may have no information about the user other than a user ID in a cookie and the clickstream history in the Web server logs.

The warehouse normally makes use of the persistent identifier in the log records to establish the online identity of a user, regardless of whether that identifier is in a cookie, stored as a variable in the URL, or in a hidden form field. In addition, it's possible to use other elements such as the session identifier, IP address, and, in the case of many automated agents, the User-agent field, although this data may be much less accurate for precisely identifying the user.

Dealing with Anonymous Visitors

The clickstream warehouse may see visitors as anonymous because the Web site has chosen not to use a persistent tracking mechanism or because users are blocking attempts by the Web site to track them across visits. Because of the inability to track a user across multiple visits, the data warehouse sees an anonymous visitor as a new visitor each time they come to the Web site. This means that the data warehouse will create a new user profile record for an anonymous visitor after every visit, resulting in multiple profile records for what is in reality the same user.

If we can uncover enough data about anonymous visitors then we may be able to identify repeat visits by these users in the clickstream warehouse. Identifying repeat visits by an anonymous user allows us to merge all of the redundant profile records for that visitor into a single profile. In essence we are creating an after-the-fact user tracking method for users who can't be tracked directly across visits by the Web site.

This after-the-fact tracking will not help the Web site to identify a user as a repeat visitor since session data is correlated offline in the data warehouse. These users cannot be tracked by the Web site because there is no way for the site to determine identity until after the warehouse has processed the data.

It is possible to discover quite a bit of technical information about a user if we want to try merging records, even if we do not have any tracking mechanisms available. Table 4.1 shows all of the information that we were able to assemble from a single page view to our Web site by one of the authors.

Much of the information shown in Table 4.1 is sent directly by the browser. The remainder must be assembled offline or via an application at the Web site. Given the amount of detail, you can see how it would be possible to develop a fuzzy matching algorithm to look through certain fields and attempt to merge anonymous visitor records when the warehouse is loaded. The matching rate and percentage of false matches will vary greatly depending on the Web site's user population and how well the matching algorithms are designed. These and other factors should be considered when deciding whether to attempt to track anonymous visitors across sessions.

Once an individual user has been assigned an ID for tracking, the job of managing their information becomes much simpler. When loading the warehouse we will be able to determine if they are a repeat visitor, a registered user, a customer, or in the case of business sites whether the user is a member of a particular organization. From this point the task of augmenting the user profile is straightforward.

Improving User Identification

Any user profile we create with artificial online identity information, like a userID or an email address, is still anonymous. Just because one knows that

Table 4.1 Information Transmitted by a Single Visit

DATA ELEMENT	VALUE	DESCRIPTION
Browser type and version	Mozilla/4.0 (compatible; MSIE 5.5; Windows 98)	This data comes from the User-agent field and tells us that the browser is Internet Explorer version.
Language	en-us	The Accept-language header sent by the browser tells the Web server what language the browser is set to, in this case U.S. English.
Last site visited	http://www.clickstream consulting.com	If linking from another page then the Referrer field is sent by the browser to tell us where the user came from.
Cookies enabled	Yes	The Web page did a cookie test using redirects to determine whether cookies were enabled.
Repeat visit	No	Because cookies were enabled, the site could tell that this was the first visit and not a repeat visit. If cookies were not enabled then the site would not be able to know this. Had this been a repeat visit then the cookie would tell the Web site the date and time of the last visit.
Java enabled	Yes	A simple Java applet on the page attempts to execute and send data back to the Web site about the browser and computer.
Javascript enabled	Yes	A simple piece of Javascript code tells us this, and is also able to set a cookie to communicate further data about the browser and computer.
VB script enabled	Yes	We can get the same data obtained from Javascript code, plus some nice extras.
CPU type	X86	The CPU type the browser is running on. Obtained via Javascript, VBscript.
Screen width	1280	The width of the computer's screen. Obtained via Javascript, VBscript.
Screen height	1024	The height of the computer's screen Obtained via Javascript, VBscript.
Screen color depth	16	The color depth setting from the computer's display properties. Obtained via Javascript.

(continued)

Table 4.1 *(Continued)*

DATA ELEMENT	VALUE	DESCRIPTION
Available screen width	1280	The width of the computer's screen available for use. Obtained via Javascript, VBscript.
Available screen height	828	The height of the computer's screen available for use. Obtained via Javascript, VBscript.
Date reported by browser	Mon May 21, 2001	Obtained via Javascript, VBscript.
Time reported by browser	20:31:36	Obtained via Javascript, VBscript.
Time zone reported by browser	Pacific Standard Time	Obtained via Javascript, VBscript.
Locally formatted date and time	Thursday, February 22, 2001 8:31:36 PM	Obtained via Javascript, VBscript.
Number of Web pages viewed in this browser window	8	We can see how many pages the user looked at, although we do not know what pages they were. Obtained via Javascript.
Browser plug-ins installed	ShockWave Flash, ShockWave Director, Windows Media Player, Adobe Acrobat Reader, MS Agent 1.5, MS Agent 2.0, MS DirectAnimation Control, Microsoft VRML 2.0 Viewer	This is a list of all the plug-ins installed in the browser. This list was made more legible, but the specific plug-in names and versions are also reported. Obtained via VBscript.
IP address	208.16.74.53	The client computer's IP address sent by the browser.
Network trace	255.2.248.1 255.232.26.18 255.232.2.181 255.232.8.37 255.232.25.247 255.232.9.218 255.81.116.198 255.181.49.32 255.16.74.53	This is a list of every hop through the network from the Web site to the client computer. We listed only the IP addresses, but the time taken for each hop and the server names along the way are also available. By looking at this data we know what networks (Sprint, a local ISP, another local ISP, and our network) were traversed. The trace is done on the server side based on the client IP address.

(continued)

114

Table 4.1 (Continued)

DATA ELEMENT	VALUE	DESCRIPTION
Hostname	7ip53.adninternet.com	The hostname assigned to the client computer. This is obtained by doing a reverse name lookup using the IP address reported by the browser.
Company owning the domain of the client	Ainternet, Inc. (AINTERNE T2-DOM) 225 SE 18th St Grants Pass, OR 97528 US Administrative Contact: Hal Clement Technical Contact: Hal Clement Billing Contact: Hal Clement Notify (NN888) nicnotify@RVI1.NET RVI1, Inc. 225 SE 18th St. Grants Pass, OR 97528 Phone: 541-555-0733 FAX: 541-555-9521	By querying the whois database we can find out what company or individual registered the domain name. This information often includes addresses, phone numbers, email addresses, and contacts.
Additional network information	Network ownership, name server hierarchy, technical information about the name server configuration, mail servers, mail exchanger records, administrative email address, etc.	Network information is available in great detail and can be produced almost in real time, telling us a lot about how a particular organization's computers and networks are configured.

someone is UserID=080200 or gabber@robots.com does not mean one knows anything meaningful, like a real name, address, or phone number. One of the primary goals of many e-commerce marketing departments is to determine the real offline identities of as many users as possible. Assuming we've established an online identity for a user and can now track their activities across visits, the next item to consider is whether to identify the real person behind the online identity. With most clickstream warehouses, building user profiles that include the user's real (offline) identity will be required.

In many cases obtaining real identities is not as difficult as one might think. First, we need to make sure that our user profiles uniquely identify each user. The Web site's persistent user tracking methods are the starting point, making it easy to know that a user on the site today is the same user who visited yesterday. The difficulty we face is our ability to associate the tracking mechanism with the user's profile at all times.

There are many reasons why the Web site may not be able to properly identify a returning user. The cookie we were using may have expired or the user may have deleted it from their system. It's possible the user forgot their login or password and simply signed up a second time and created a new login. There are so many potential problems with user identification that the Web site alone will not be able to handle all of them.

One option for increasing the accuracy of user identification is to improve internal tracking methods. The Web site might try to coax users into providing more personal information for additional services, a process called successive revelation. Some of this seemingly innocuous information can form the basis for accessing much more detailed information from other sources. We will cover this topic in more detail in the section discussing user profiles.

Another option is to contract with a third party user tracking service. These services offer the ability to track users and deliver prebuilt profiles for the site's visitors. User identification services are provided by a number of companies, including some online ad agencies that include user tracking as one of their offerings.

One might wonder how a third party can identify and profile users across Web sites. One possibility is for the third party tracking service to implement a user ID server as described earlier in this chapter. When using an ID server model, every Web site that joins the tracking service uses some form of web bug provided by that company. This means that each Web site affiliated with the service has its own cookie for its own Web site. However, the user ID stored in that cookie is identical across all of the subscribing Web sites. While each Web site sees a portion of the users—those users who visited their Web site—the user tracking service can see all users from all of the participating Web sites.

Depending on the contract, the Web sites may provide data such as a user's registration information to the user tracking service. This data is assembled by the service into a user profile. When a user already tracked by the service visits a Web site for the first time, the service provides that user's profile and ID to the Web site. In this way, it is possible for a Web site to very quickly build up a collection of reasonably detailed profiles on many of its users.

Banner ad networks such as DoubleClick have been tracking users across Web sites for quite a while. They work in a slightly different fashion than the user tracking services, but use similar techniques. The general process for how a user tracking service works is outlined below.

1. First, a Web site joins an advertising network. All pages that carry banner ads are configured to download banner ad image files from servers at the ad network (as described in Chapter 3).

2. The user visits a page at the Web site that contains a banner ad. By accessing the banner ad, the user provides all the data normally available in a Web server log. The banner ad network usually includes other data about the Web site and banner as parameters on the URL for the banner ad. When the ad server sends the image back to the user, it sets a cookie with a user ID in the browser.

3. The user then visits a page on another Web site, which is also a member of the ad network. The browser sends the user ID cookie to the ad server along with a request for the banner ad, and receives the banner image in return. The ad network now has a record of the Web pages the user visited at both Web sites, and what ads were received.

4. If the previous Web site had a data sharing agreement with the ad network, then the Web site may send user registration data as parameters in the banner ad URL. They may also have an agreement to share user data with the ad network separately via an online or batch update. Some user tracking services work this way as well.

5. When the user visits your Web site some time later, the same exchange occurs as in step 3. If your Web site also has a data sharing agreement then you will benefit by receiving a profile of this user from the ad network. The profile they provide is likely to be more detailed in certain areas than what your Web site has, thanks to the large number of participants involved in tracking the user.

Depending on what data is shared with the ad network or user tracking service, they might be able to identify the user's offline identity. This is particularly true when Web sites share data obtained from purchases. Then the user's address and phone number may become part of the profile. This information then allows anyone to assemble much more detailed data about the user's offline preferences and behavior.

Processing User Identity Data

When processing the user data we need to look through our list of users for duplicates. Assuming we have a user ID, we can associate log records with a user. If we do not find a matching user profile in the warehouse for the user ID shown in the log, it does not follow that we've never seen this user before.

An example of this problem is a user who visits the Web site from home and from work using two different computers. Without forcing users to register, we would not know that a visit from home and a visit from work were by the same user. Each computer would have a different user tracking cookie, and thus we would have two user profiles based on two cookies, and therefore two identities for the same user.

A related problem is sharing computers. Suppose a family of four shares a computer and uses the same browser. Unless a Web site forces users to register and log on, the site has no way of differentiating one family member from another. Even registration-enabled sites can be confused by the commonly used "remember my password" feature. With this feature enabled, any user will be automatically logged in under the original user's login.

Rather than take for granted the user data provided by the Web site, we must add facilities to better identify users and reduce duplicate entries. As a starting point, the clickstream warehouse must generate its own unique keys for user profiles. By generating user IDs in the data warehouse we can match user IDs from the Web site and merge the duplicates into a single user profile. Our criteria for a user ID are that the ID must be unique, must never be reused in the future and should be a simple computer-generated number with no *intelligence* built in. Intelligent keys are a constant source of problems because the rules and meanings of the related components of the key always change, creating inconsistencies that render the intelligence useless.

It's important to keep in mind that the Web site's user profiling will not be as accurate as the user profiling we do in the data warehouse. We have more facilities at our disposal for detecting duplicate users and filling in missing data. Whenever possible, you should create a process to repopulate the Web site's user profiles from the warehouse. This helps keep both systems synchronized and increases the accuracy of personalization and targeting done in the Web applications.

Using the "Real" Identity for User Identification

The most obvious data to use when looking for duplicate users is the elements related to the user's offline identity. If the user made a purchase online then we will have payment information such as a credit card number. With the payment information we have immediate access to as much offline data as we can afford. One problem with credit card or bank account numbers is the potential unauthorized access of that information. Because of the security and privacy issues, we recommend *not* storing credit card and bank account numbers in internal systems after a transaction has been completed.

Getting a name from a user might seem to be a great way to identify a user. The problem is that names are not unique, so the Web site can't count on the name to differentiate all of the users. Instead, the site will likely need to match the real name with a unique identifier and then use that identifier as a link to the user profile.

A real name is also helpful when linking the user's online and offline identities, although the name itself is not sufficient. What is interesting is that when you have the user's surname, a portion of the address will frequently be sufficient to identify the person behind the online identity. The surname and postal code are often all that is required to look up a full address and telephone number, uniquely identifying a user as well as their offline identity.

The other difficulty one encounters with names is that the many users will provide false names. The false name will hinder attempts to match addresses or households. If the site asks for a name as part of the user registration then the name will be highly suspect. If the user is purchasing products or services then the Web site is much more likely to have legitimate data because of the financial and shipping information required.

If the user made a purchase or had something shipped to their home or office then we have a physical address. This allows us to pull together multiple user profiles but we can't necessarily merge them. The problem is that an address is not a unique identifier since any number of people may live or work at the same address. It is a mechanism that can be effective at narrowing the possibilities.

When there are multiple user profiles with the same address, one can assign a household identifier to associate each of the profiles. This process is called householding, and there are many packages and third party services that will household name and address data for you.

Depending on the Web site, it may be possible to use the content accessed by the different members of the household or organization to profile those users. Based on this content profiling, it is possible to determine whether the members are distinct users or the same individual.

While it may seem that householding applies only to individual consumers, one should not discount householding data when working with users of business-oriented Web sites. Warehouse users often want to see what organization the users represent, and potentially their locations or departments as well. This is not really householding, but the principles behind it are the same.

Using Web-Based Information for User Identification

Regardless of the problems described above, offline identity data provides the best means of uniquely identifying users and merging user profiles. If we do not have any information about a user's offline identity then we must consider data the user supplied (if any), the data from the Web server logs, and items we can extrapolate based on that data.

Email Address

If a user provides your site with an email address, this can be used as a mechanism to track their online identity. The email address is better than many other methods because email is rarely shared and therefore maps to a single person, where some of the other methods can map to more than one individual.

Most users have multiple email addresses and can show up in the data warehouse as multiple identities. A good example of where this might happen is content sites that make free trial offers in an effort to draw more subscribers. The goal is to bring in paying users by offering free access for a period of time.

TheStreet.com is an example of a company that uses these types of promotions. If the promotion runs for a time period that is longer than that of the trial offer, users can sign up a second time. They simply provide a different email address when their trial offer expires. By doing this they can take advantage of the free offer repeatedly. The end result in the data warehouse is a collection of user profiles associated with different email addresses, all of which are the same person.

Simple Web site registrations where the user provides a pseudonym are another mechanism we can use to identify users. The Web site asks users to register to access site content. Rather than ask for a real name, the Web site allows a user to create their own unique login. This mechanism is anonymous for the user, but serves the site's need to track unique visitors with the added benefit that users can be tracked regardless of the computer they use.

Registered Pseudonym

Registered pseudonyms are used by many Web sites as a means to identify users. Any time a Web site can get users to log in for access it will be able to link all log records with that user. This is still not a perfect solution to the user identity problem because a user might have registered more than once.

This is often the case when a user forgets their login or password and doesn't want to go through the trouble of recovering it. Even Web sites that have a "remember my login" feature face this problem, especially when there is no real incentive for the user to use the same login from multiple locations. It does not matter to the user that they have two logins unless the Web site has features that make using a single login useful.

A good example of this problem can be found if we look at the AtomFilms.com site and compare it to the personalized MyYahoo! service offered by Yahoo .com. AtomFilms is a free site, and their incentive for users to register is that registered users can watch entire film clips, while unregistered users are only allowed previews of most clips. The site itself is well designed, but it does not have any special features that make a user care whether their login is the same from one visit to another.

The case is different with MyYahoo!. This site allows the user to customize the information they receive and remembers all of the customized settings between visits. One is likely to use the same login rather than registering several times from different locations. For Web sites like this, the registered pseudonym will probably be useful as an online identity mechanism.

IP Address

The IP address is another element we can use to identify a user. As we discussed in Chapter 3, this works if the user's computer has a fixed IP address. Since most people use a dialup connection, their address will be different each time they dial in. There is also the problem of some ISPs sending a different IP address for each HTTP request.

Since the IP address does not uniquely identify the user and may vary from one log record to the next, it is of limited value. It can provide us with some help in cleaning data. By building up a list of IP addresses used by a user we might then be able to use the addresses in conjunction with other data to merge duplicate user profiles.

For high traffic sites this approach will be ineffective because the likelihood of multiple users from the same ISP increases with the increased traffic volume. Therefore the IP addresses will have a significant overlap across users. Business sites may find more utility in the IP address than consumer sites. This is because the information about the organization the user represents is often as important as the individual user.

Browser Data

If we have gone through all of the above mechanisms and have not ruled out the possibility of the user being a duplicate then we can try to make use of browser information. If the Web site records some of the data listed in Table 4.1 then we can combine this with all of the other data we have and determine whether there are any further matches.

Some data is relatively common, like the browser type, version, and language settings. Computer-specific data such as CPU type, display height, and display width, when combined with the other browser information and IP addresses or the ISP can provide the needed elements to finalize a match. It is unlikely that a user profile we have winnowed to this point using other data will have exactly the same computer and browser characteristics as a second profile we believe to be a match.

Building User Profiles

The challenge for online businesses is to get the highest level of user identification possible without driving away potential users by asking for too much personal information. Once you've determined how the user identification and tracking methods will work, the next step is the task of constructing user profiles.

The user profile contains all of the information assembled about a user's online identity. The profile may contain data the user volunteers, data we collect from the Web site, data we deduce based on their behavior, and data brought in from outside sources. Some clickstream warehouses use profiles containing only the demographic categories or marketing segments that the users are placed in. Since our goal is to provide the most meaningful analysis possible, we will look at creating detailed user profiles.

Profile Structure and Content

The requirements gathering for the clickstream warehouse should have resulted in a set of analytical needs for the user dimension. In this section we'll focus on the structure and process for designing user profiles and look at data content and the database schema in more detail in Chapter 6.

If your Web site is built using a software package or framework, such as Art Technology Group's Dynamo application server, then chances are good that the Web site has some built-in user profiling abilities. The job of the warehouse designer is to review all of the information about the profiling capabilities of the Web site, what has been implemented, and how easy it will be to extract the profile data.

The profiles used by the Web site tend to differ from the profiles in a data warehouse. The reason for this is twofold. The Web site is using profiles to create personalized content, target messages, and execute transactions. The warehouse is using profiles to help the analytical process of end users. The kinds of information and level of detail required are usually different between the two profiles.

When reviewing the Web site profiles, a key question to ask is whether one profile should be the source of the other. There will be data in the Web site user profile that saves us from having to develop programs to extract that same data from Web logs or Web site databases. Likewise, there will be data we assemble in the warehouse that is not available in the Web site profile but which may be useful.

In most cases the best way to start building profiles in the data warehouse is to extract the Web site profiles, if available. These can then form the basis for profiles in the data warehouse. We mentioned in the last section the need to have a unique warehouse-generated key for user profiles that is not the same as that used in the Web site. This allows us to deal with duplicate profiles and provides some independence from the Web site. It also allows us to keep master profiles in the warehouse since the Web site's profiles are likely to contain a subset of the data we will need.

When looking at the content of the profile, a key decision is whether to create profiles that can track a user's offline identity or maintain profiles that track only the online identity and behavior of the users. In some cases, the only possibility is to create profiles that just track online identities. One must also be careful at this point about running afoul of the Web site's privacy policies. We will discuss privacy policies and the implications for data warehousing later in this chapter.

A profile for only the online identity will contain a subset of the information found in a full offline and online profile. One of the problems you may encounter with your Web site is that it only tracks customers or registered users. This may be due to limitations with user tracking in the Web application software or it may be a decision made when the Web site was built. The problem is that customers or registered users make up a small percentage of the total number of visitors to your site, and people will often visit a site several times before becoming a customer.

The implication for the data warehouse is that there will be a significant number of untracked visitors, putting more emphasis on the ability of the warehouse to determine whether two separate visits are from the same user and therefore belong to the same user profile. If the Web site does attempt to track every visitor then this problem is reduced significantly.

A different data management problem exists when warehouse users want to see offline identity information. It is unlikely that you will have all of the information needed when creating the initial profile for a user. This means some profiles will contain offline identities while others will not, creating difficulties for the query and analysis tools and the analysts using them. Care must be taken during the schema design to avoid the confusion and misleading query results that null data elements can cause.

The high probability of having some empty elements in a profile leads to another aspect of the profile creation process. Does one instantiate a user profile in the warehouse as soon as data is available, only after all profile data is available, or when certain key data elements are present? Any of these choices will impact both the design of the warehouse schema and the data loading or updating process.

If your Web site serves businesses rather than consumers then you must account for company data as well as individual data in the profiles. Since the users are acting as agents for a company, that company is your real customer. This means that the user profiles for all users representing a company must link to a company profile. When processing user data and updating user profiles, a second level of processing must take place so that new information can be updated in the company profile.

Obtaining Data for Profiles

The data elements in the user profile will be identified during the schema design process, when you determine the end-user analysis requirements, and what data is available from the Web site. We need to take a moment to look at where you obtain data for the user profiles. The process of obtaining data will be covered in Chapter 8 when we discuss data extraction, transformation, and loading.

Recall from Chapter 3 that the clickstream is one of several sources of data for the warehouse. A user-centric approach to marketing requires data from each interaction with the user, including email, calls to support centers, and purchases or transactions. Much of the initial profile data will come from the Web site, but these other user contact points should be considered.

There are five basic sources for obtaining user profile data: Web server logs, the Web site or Web applications, inferences based on the prior data, user contact data, and third party demographic or psychographic data providers. The simplest source is the data from the Web server logs. This covers everything from the Web site's ID used for tracking the user to the data elements listed in Table 4.1. Most of this data is readily available and can be loaded with minimal processing.

Directly observable data about a user is a source that is almost as easily extracted. This includes the data from the Web site and Web applications. Here we are looking at data from the Web site's user profiles, assuming the Web site has user profiles, and data provided by the user. This includes elements such as the user's pseudonym or login, email address, physical address, or even financial information such as credit card numbers. Data provided by a user is normally stored in the database that supports the operation of the Web site.

Thus far, the data we are accessing is either directly provided or accessible with minimal work. Based on the data we have from the Web server logs and Web site, we can infer further information and add it to the user's profile.

Some of this information is basic facts such as the user's ISP, duration of the user's visit, and the dwell time on each page. Some is more qualitative, like what the user was interested in based on dwell times or what the final purpose of their visit was based on the page they left from or the transactions executed.

User contact data can be used to supplement our user profiles. If a user calls the service center or sends an email to the customer support group, the information should be loaded into the warehouse. At an absolute minimum, contact data such as the user's email address or telephone number should be added to the user's profile.

Be aware that what is garnered via online sources is only the beginning of what many data warehouse users will need in the user profiles. The online and offline identities, purchases, or other business transactions are often not sufficient for analytic purposes. Many warehouse users want to know more details about users, and this detail comes in the form of demographic and psychographic data.

Demographic data is the facts about an individual such as the age, gender, income level, or occupation. Psychographic data is qualitative lifestyle information and might include the user's preferred types of music, movies, or other interests, as well as information on attitudes or values.

Both types of data are used for online marketing, but the psychographic data tends to be more useful when driving repeat visits and purchases. Fostering customer loyalty requires knowing something about user's prior activities, online behavior, life stage, and lifestyle. This information allows one to better differentiate users and make inferences about their behavior.

There are many ways to entice users to provide more detailed personal data that will lead to an offline identity. Many Web sites do not have the ability to directly determine a user's offline identity because they do not directly sell goods. Some of these sites coax users to reveal more information voluntarily over time through a process called *progressive revelation.*

One way of getting the offline identity of a user is to get the user to reveal small pieces of information one at a time. While many sites use some type of voluntary progressive revelation scheme to unveil user identity, one of the best examples is Yahoo!.

One need not be a registered user to access Yahoo!, and most of its services are free of charge. While Yahoo! sets a cookie for each user when they first visit the site, the cookie itself doesn't provide any clues as to the user's offline identity. When it is first set, the cookie can only be used to track the user across visits. But Yahoo! entices users to reveal a little more of their identity as they access different services, each time associating this with the user ID.

For example, in order to personalize Yahoo! information content with MyYahoo!, a user must establish a user ID of their choice and a password. In order to register the user ID and password, the user must give at least an email address and date of birth. Ostensibly, the reason for requiring the email address is to verify that the creator of the user ID actually exists, and so Yahoo! has some way to contact him if necessary. The user's age is required because some Yahoo! content may not be appropriate for children.

As we alluded to earlier, personal information can sometimes be purchased from a data syndicator that cross-references personal data by email addresses. The date of birth helps further verify user identity, assuming the user is honest when providing it. Even if the user isn't forthright about age, the syndicated information obtained via the email address may reveal the user's true date of birth.

Yahoo! email is free and accessible from any Web browser. To get a Yahoo! email account the user must provide a name, even if the user already has a registered Yahoo! user ID. The reason for this is unclear, but the user's real name can be used to look up identity information in syndicated psychographic databases.

Yahoo! has a mapping utility that many people use to find their way to unfamiliar destinations. The mapping utility also has a convenient proximity search for nearby businesses and points of interest from a given location. Some proximity search locations, like a user's home address or office address, get entered over and over as the user searches. In order to ease the difficulty of entering these kinds of addresses repeatedly, Yahoo! provides a way to enter favorite addresses in a drop down menu, identified by monikers like *home* or *office*. Once the user has entered his address under a name like *home*, Yahoo! can use it for reverse address lookups of user identity in syndicated databases.

Yahoo!'s shopping pages offer a myriad of goods, and Yahoo! provides a *wallet* mechanism to register a user's credit card, billing address, and shipping address. This eliminates retyping this information when shopping Yahoo! stores, but once this information is entered, the user's identity has been completely revealed from the credit card number.

Yahoo! also offers financial services, including electronic bill payment and financial portfolio management. In order to use electronic bill payment, the user must reveal a bank account number, which gives Yahoo! access to interesting information like the level of the user's account balance over time. If the user decides to use Yahoo! as the central point of access to a financial portfolio, account numbers of investments at various financial institutions must also be revealed. Obviously, Yahoo! can now see what kinds of investments the user has made and how much they are worth.

If you are a registered user at Yahoo!, it is interesting to look at your account info page, and see how it gets filled in over time as you slowly reveal your identity to them. By using progressive revelation to establish user identity, Yahoo! has created one of the largest and most complete databases of user psychodemographic information on the Web.

Successive revelation can be a highly effective means to generate more user data. Even so, most clickstream data warehouses will not be able to assemble significant demographic or psychographic information solely from the Web site. This is due in part to the Web site's desire to avoid scaring off prospective users by asking for too much information. It is also due to the poor quality of some user-provided data. For example, when asking for a user's age and income, it is likely that they will either leave the fields blank or provide incorrect information.

The linkage of online and offline identities is the holy grail of most advertisers and marketers because an enormous amount of personal data is available from offline sources. Knowing the real user behind the online identity means being able to enrich the user profile and gain more insight into customers.

One frequently asked question is, What kind of data is available? The answer is, Almost anything you can imagine. For example, you can obtain information for all the zip codes in your sample broken down by various consumer segments. This allows you to view your users along the lines of ethnic mix, income range, or age range. You can also use this data to fill in gaps in your user profiles, although the demographic data is provided in terms of percentages and ranges and is less accurate than individual data.

It is possible to get household data for the addresses or zip codes of your users and gain further details. This data contains more accurate income levels, ages, genders, and other information for the occupants of a household. From this point, it is only a small step to obtain psychographic data. Table 4.2 shows a sample of the kinds of psychographic data about an individual user one can purchase.

The best method to obtain demographic or psychographic data is through partnerships with the ad networks and user tracking services mentioned earlier, or via third-party data syndicators. In general, the data from online partners will contain more details about online behavior and interests, but less of the offline psychographic data. Some online firms will be able to provide the address data that is needed to identify a user's offline identity.

Detailed demographic and psychographic data can be easily obtained from commercial suppliers once you have a user's name and address. In addition, a few data syndicators have begun adding email addresses into their databases.

Table 4.2 Sample of Commercially Available Psychographic Data

PERSONAL DATA	DESCRIPTION
Full Name	First, middle, last name
Date of Birth	Birth date
Gender	Gender of the individual
Race	Race of the individual
Marital Status	Married, single, divorced; also links to spouse information
Children	Lists the age, gender of any children
Occupation	Current occupation
Income	Generally given as an annual salary range
Credit Cards	Whether the person has any credit cards; it is possible to obtain credit card types and numbers from some sources
Home Address	Primary mailing address
Telephone	Home phone, cell phone, work phone are all available
Vehicle Owner / Lessor	Indicates whether the individual owns or leases any cars, trucks, motorcycles
Vehicle Information	They will probably have the make, model, year, and license plate data for each vehicle owned
Homeowner / Renter	Indicates whether the person owns or rents their primary address
Length of Residence	How long the person has been at their primary address
Utilities	List of all utility companies servicing the individual; can include electric, gas, water, sewer, phone, cable TV
Nearest Neighbors	It is possible to obtain a list of neighbor's names and addresses from some services
Magazines	List of all magazines the person receives
Pets	Indicates whether the person owns pets, and may list the type and number of pets owned
Lifestyle Interests	List of any lifestyle interests known, e.g., hiking, fishing, knitting

The email address provides an even simpler way for a Web site to link a user profile to this offline information. Many data syndicators have been providing personal information to database marketers for years. Experian, Acxiom, and Lexis-Nexis are a just a few of the companies providing this data.

Enriching profiles is not something that applies only to individual users. Business sites must augment company profiles in much the same way. If your Web site serves businesses then you will probably have less interest in the demographic and psychographic data but will see more emphasis on corporate customer data.

The enrichment process works in the same manner as for individual users. You must first construct an individual user profile. The next step is to link this to a corporate profile that may at first contain nothing more than network information such as the user's—and therefore the company's—IP address. As we showed earlier, it is possible to use an IP address to identify the organization a user represents.

In this way, one can start to group employees by the enterprise they represent. The next step is to extend the information about these organizations so a company profile is built up. The data may be internal from order management systems, or it may be from external sources. Because much corporate data is less well structured, human intervention will probably be required to augment and clean up the information that is gathered. If your enterprise has the resources, it is possible to automate much of the data gathering for corporate profiles by integrating with third-party business data syndicators.

No matter how you profile users in the warehouse, obtaining profile data will be a multistep process. The tendency is to try to build detailed profiles when clickstream warehouses are first built. This may be unrealistic due to the amount of development required to extract, integrate, and clean the data. The pragmatic approach is to manage the directly observable data first, and then add processes to infer more information or integrate third-party data.

Web Site Personalization and User Profiles

Web sites have been attempting to offer personalized services for some time. The personalization comes in many guises, from simple greetings for repeat visitors to customized content. One of the reasons for personalization is to increase the chance that users will return to the Web site. It has been estimated that more than 95 percent of an e-commerce site's users are simply visiting. Of the few that become customers, many will not visit again.

Profiles in the Web site are used to improve site operations, either through customizing content or for on-site promotion and marketing. This means the user profiles in the Web site often need less information about the users than what we keep in the data warehouse. There is no reason to fill up a Web site profile with psychographic data unless that data is directly used. Most personalized features on a Web site use basic data or rely on information provided from offline processing.

Today it is much more likely that the detailed data in profiles will be used for analysis in the warehouse. Some of this analysis directly supports the Web site while the remainder supports other areas of the enterprise. The profiles in the clickstream warehouse should be designed specifically for analysis purposes. While profiles in the Web site contain the data required for personalized features on the Web site, the warehouse profiles should contain all available user information. Before going further, we need to look at some aspects of personalization in more detail.

Basic Personalization Methods

Most Web personalization software employs either inference-based or rule-based techniques to personalize products and services. Inference-based software requires profiles of users' interests and behavior on the Web site. One approach is to then match a user's profile against the profiles of other similar users and customize content according to the generalized matches that result.

Another inference-based approach attempts to build predictive models of user behavior so that the software can select appropriate content to display to a user based on their profile. This might lead to a model that says "Statistically speaking, customers who buy Sea Monkeys from the site are more likely to purchase handheld computers on impulse, so display a sidebar about the many uses of handhelds for Sea Monkey owners." This type of software is more adaptable than basic profile matching, but it can be much more difficult to implement and maintain. Often the models created are reduced to simple rules that guide content generation.

This leads to the rule-based techniques. Rule-based software is built around a set of hypotheses about user behavior on the Web site. These hypotheses are used to create rules or heuristics that drive the display of relevant content. The rules can be very simple and have nothing to do with a user profile. For example, a rule might say: If a customer puts a handheld into the cart, show a promotion for handheld cases. The rules may also be derived based on user behavior, so that content is displayed on the basis of information in the user profile.

The challenge with rule-based software is determining what the rules should be. Few packages are capable of providing anything more than templates for simple rules such as suggesting the user order chocolates when ordering flowers. These rules in these systems require constant maintenance or the results become highly predictable to the site's users and the goal of personalizing content is lost.

In almost all cases an analyst must research user data if the goal is to provide behavior-driven rules. The natural place for such analysis is the clickstream warehouse, providing an incentive to create good user profiles as well as business linkage from the warehouse back to the Web site.

Types of Personalization

Another way of looking at personalization is from the user's point of view. From this perspective there are two basic classes of personalized services. One class does something *for* the user, and the other class does something *to* the user. An example of "for" personalization is a news site that remembers the news categories a user visited in the past and then orders the display of current articles based on those categories. An example of "to" personalization is an advertising network deciding which banner ad to display based on a user's interests.

The distinction is useful because it helps to determine whether a feature is one a user desires, or one that the enterprise is trying to push forward onto a user. It also helps determine what types of data the personalized services may require.

"For" Personalization

As one might expect, there are fewer personalized services that do something on behalf of the user than do something on behalf of the Web site. Some of the more common services and profile data they use are described below.

Customization

Personalization has grown to encompass just about any features on the Web site that provide a departure from the standard page being displayed. Customization, once talked about as a topic separate from personalization, allows a user to set preferences for the interface or content on a Web site. This is most often used in personal interface setup like for content sites like news or financial services, such as the MyYahoo! service.

The main issue with this type of personalized interface is that it is often a rudimentary ability to change page layouts or organize content according to predefined categories. There is usually little ability for the user to make any changes outside the narrow categories provided by the Web site. All that is required in the user's profile is a list of the preferences they set. This preference data should be loaded into the warehouse profile, as it offers insight into a user's interests. At a minimum this data can be used to see what customizations are most popular on the Web site.

Recommendation Aids

Recommendation aids—not to be confused with cross-selling and up-selling—are features designed to display products or information to the user based on what the site knows about a user. These aids are either used to determine what is displayed to the user, or appear as recommendations to the user outside the primary content area in the Web page.

There are many different forms of recommendation aids. One of the more commonly discussed is passive collaborative filtering. With this technique, other users' interests are pooled and matched to interests from the user's profile to determine what related items may be of interest. When the software uses data about what a user was interested in during past visits, their prior purchases, and their interests, and closely matches other users' profiles, the technique can be very effective. Many sites such as Amazon.com use simple forms of collaborative filtering to recommend additional purchases. The suggestions show up on the page with captions like: "Users who purchased this also purchased . . ."

Active collaborative filtering directly involves users. This technique asks many users to express interest in topics or asks them to make a recommendation for others, frequently offering incentives for participation. The interest profiles and recommendations are then matched to the data in a user's profile and the results drive the content that is generated. Some sites are using this type of collaborative filtering to make gift recommendations. One problem with collaborative filtering is that often a product cannot be recommended until at least one person has purchased it.

These techniques require that a profile contain at least some data about a user's interests, either inferred from the pages they visit or provided explicitly via online interest surveys or preferences. Without a profile of interests the generated recommendations will be no better than a random display.

Localization

Localization is often tied to the topic of international Web sites and discussed as a separate topic. We view it as a form of personalization. Localization is really an attempt recognize a user's physical geography in the content displayed on the Web site. The most common example is the display of a Web site in different languages based on the nationality of users. Another example is a site like CNN.com, which tailors news to different regions of the U.S. and allows users to choose the regional version they want to see.

When you want to determine a user's locale implicitly, you can use a number of data elements that should be part of a user's profile. A browser's language settings can help locate a user, although the language is more useful when guiding users to a language-specific part of the Web site. The network location of a user will often tie to a specific geographic area, allowing you to update a user's profile with this information.

Service and Support

While service and support is not often thought of as a place for personalization, some Web sites offer personalized support based on the products or services purchased by a user or company. Your business can greatly improve customer service if the user profile contains information from both the Web site and other internal systems.

If the Web site and operational systems share the user profile then your business can provide highly customized online support. It will also be possible to identify postsale problems such as a late delivery or product problem requiring customer notification. Customer retention depends on personal service as well as personalized Web site content.

"To" Personalization

There are many types of service that allow a company to better target marketing and sales to users. These services are often categorized under personalization, although they really belong in a separate category of one-to-one marketing or database marketing services. Some of the most common personalized services that do something to, rather than for, a user are outlined below.

Advertising

Advertising is one of the services most often touted as personalized. The idea is that Web sites can display ads that users are interested in seeing. The way this works is that a company signs a contract with an online advertising network. The contracts generally require a specific number of views over certain period of time and at certain categories of Web site, preferably without a lot of repeat views by the same user. The ad network manages this by tracking users and rotating the ads it displays.

A contract for *targeted* ads means that the ad should be shown to viewers who fit certain criteria, whether than is age, income, or interests. The idea is that the users who fit these criteria are more likely to click through to the advertiser's Web site. Note that the advertiser pays for targeting. When the Direct Marketing Association says that they provide personalized ads to show users what they want to see they are being somewhat disingenuous. Advertising networks can usually charge significantly more money for targeted ads.

The profile data used by advertisers varies depending on their sophistication. Ad networks that do a good job of tracking users and collecting data will tend to have more accurate interest profiles. In general, the targeting criteria are based on categories of Web sites visited by the user and their prior click-throughs.

While not really personalization, detailed user profile data can be used to select advertising venues. For example, if many of the Web site's users live in urban areas and tend to be in certain parts of the country then the Web site can place online ads with regional sites and place radio ads in the markets where the users live.

Email Marketing

Some of the high traffic Web sites have turned to email marketing to make more money. Most email marketing programs involve sending messages to users based on the interests they show in their profiles. Many Web sites still use opt-out lists, meaning that a user must explicitly opt out of receiving messages. If the user does not opt out when registering on the site then they will receive email based on the interests listed in their profile.

The more ethical Web sites use an opt-in model. In this model, the user must explicitly state that they want to receive marketing messages, and often the categories they are interested in. When a user checks off these interests, the user's profile is updated with the information.

Noting that a good idea can be perverted, some companies have taken to resetting users' preferences so that they receive marketing email even though the users did not opt in. The America Online ISP has a policy of resetting opt-in preferences annually for all AOL subscribers. EBay sent messages to customers claiming that a bug left the preferences blank when the users signed up, so they reset these user's preferences to opt in for all categories. EBay received a lot of bad press when they did this because the message was sent out several times to different sets of customers who signed up in succeeding months.

These tactics cause problems for the clickstream warehouse because the data about interests in the user profiles is invalidated. By changing a user's preferences there is no way to know what a user's interests really are.

Cross-selling and Up-selling

Cross-selling is an attempt to sell items that are related to an item a user is currently purchasing. For example, when buying a bottle of herbal cold remedy online the Web site might suggest getting vitamin C as well. Up-selling is an attempt to sell a more expensive or more profitable product than the one the user has chosen. When the user selects the vitamin C, the Web site may provide an offer for the deluxe megasize bottle of vitamin C that is priced less per unit than the smaller bottle. Some overzealous Web sites carry this to extremes, asking if you would like to buy a house to go with the doorknob in your shopping cart.

Cross-selling and up-selling tend to make little use of individual profile data. Most approaches favor aggregate user behavior and product sales analysis over the interests in profiles of individual users.

Marketing

Personalized marketing is nothing more than targeting ads, promotions, or special offers to users based on their past activities, interests, and various events. Events fall into two classes: calendar events and lifetime events. Calendar events are those that happen regularly every year, like holidays or birthdays. Lifetime events happen once or periodically in someone's life, such as high school graduation or marriage.

Marketers take advantage of their knowledge of a person combined with knowledge of these events to build different types of semicustomized programs. For example, if a user made a purchase for Mother's Day last year then the Web site might send an email reminder of the upcoming event to the user this year. If user profiles have detailed information from data syndicators then the marketer can target similar reminders or promotions. For instance, with knowledge that the user has children the Web site might make special offers in advance of the children's birthdays.

Even without psychographic data, marketing can be tailored to groups of users. If the Web site has basic demographic data by zip code then users within specific zip codes can receive offers that are different from what is offered to users in another area. If the demographic data for a zip code shows mostly single-family dwellings then a financial site might promote mortgage refinancing offers, while promoting credit card offers in areas that are predominantly apartments.

Out of all of the personalization techniques discussed, those in the marketing area make the most use of detailed user profile data. This is the area that drives many of the user profile requirements in the warehouse.

Business Sites and Online Marketplaces

The personalization techniques we reviewed apply to business-oriented sites as well as consumer sites, but the emphasis is somewhat different. Demographic and psychographic data is not as useful because the users are representing an organization. Their decision-making and purchasing patterns will be different from individual consumers' patterns.

Many business sites are less personal and designed with more of a one size fits all model. Web site personalization tends to be geared to interface customization and marketing. The clickstream data warehouse is used to analyze both the usage patterns of individuals and the transaction patterns of organizations. Sometimes this data can generate information that is stored in user and corporate profiles. An example would be an industrial supplies marketplace that notes increased purchase patterns among certain customers when prices drop to a specific level regardless of the product quality specifications. This would indicate that the customers are price-sensitive, whereas other customers might be labeled quality-sensitive. Marketing efforts could then be targeted differently based on this profile information.

It is still necessary to build individual user profiles for business sites, but the individual profiles will probably be somewhat simpler than user profiles for consumer sites. The profiles of business users should be maintained separately from the profiles of the businesses they represent because both will be required. You need the individual profiles to provide the ability to analyze the patterns of individual purchasers as well as their organizations. There may be patterns at the individual level that lead to Web site modifications or improved marketing or training for less profitable customers.

Links Between Warehouse and Web Site Profiles

In general, the more in-depth your user profiles are, the better the analysis will be in the clickstream data warehouse. Analysis from the warehouse can create new information about users that ought to be stored in those profiles. This improved profile data should be provided to the Web site so that personalized services could be added or improved.

The difference between profile data and analytical results in the data warehouse can sometimes blur. For example, a user's purchasing pattern is more the result of data analysis than a profile component. However, the user's price sensitivity or product preferences might be useful in the profile, while the user's frequency of purchases might not be.

This implies that there are areas where the clickstream warehouse can be integrated with parts of the Web site to provide specific actionable information. In many respects, this is what third-party personalization products do. They collect and analyze Web site data, then use the results of the analysis to generate profiles and rules for creating personalized content. Clickstream data warehouses will be a much more effective source of analytical data for these products. With an appropriate architecture, a clickstream warehouse can augment both the Web site and third-party products. If the systems are not integrated then there will be much duplicated effort and data.

Privacy is an issue that should not be forgotten in this discussion of personalization. Because some practices use detailed personal data, there is growing opposition to data collection about individuals. This conflict between user information and user privacy is our next topic of discussion.

Implications of Privacy Policies for the Clickstream Data Warehouse

The conflict between privacy and Web sites' use of personal information has been building for several years. It was raised into the public eye by a number of highly publicized abuses by online companies. The debate today centers largely on whether public concerns about the privacy of personal information are legitimate, and if so, how they can be addressed.

Not all companies agree that privacy rights are universal, and many properly maintain that privacy is not officially defined in the same way that areas like contract law are. Their belief is that the information exchanged about a person is public information and comes as part of doing business. In addition, some users don't care that information about them is available and many will provide additional personal data in order to receive discounts, rebates, or access to additional online services.

According to privacy advocates, this willingness to provide personal data is due to the fact that users are never properly informed about the use of their data. Most users are not aware of the extent to which personal information is collected, bought, and sold. Anyone can easily obtain detailed information about an individual, regardless of whether his or her use is legitimate. It is hard to argue against the fact that easy access to personal data has led to increases in crimes such as identity theft. While users see benefits from e-business use of personal data, users also bear the risk of its misuse.

One of the consequences of this debate is Web sites' creation of privacy policies to head off future criticism or legal actions. The majority of commercial Web sites will have a privacy policy, though usually not in a prominent location. The content of these policies varies greatly from one site to another.

How often have you taken the time to locate and read the privacy policy on a Web site? If you are like most people, chances are not more than once. If you read these policies you will see a number of common statements and standard disclaimers. The wording in these policies often contains loopholes that allow the site to do many things with your data. The strength of the privacy policy is in all likelihood inversely related to the benefit the Web site gains from using your data.

In general, a privacy policy will contain statements about personal data the Web site collects, the security of this data, how it is used, and whom the Web site shares it with. They also state that by using the Web site you implicitly agree to the terms of the policy and any associated user agreements or terms and conditions. The various terms and conditions will often modify the stated privacy policy, changing or invalidating portions of it.

There are a number of common terms and phrases in these policies. For example, the statement that "changes can be made at any time" is one of the more common. It simply means that the Web site can, at any time, change or get rid of their privacy policy and do whatever they want with personal data. Most Web sites will include a statement that they will post the changes so users will be aware of them. Privacy advocates say that this is akin to offering a warranty on a car, with the ability to drop the warranty any time they choose.

The following quote from Yahoo!'s Web site is an example of the type of disclosure many Web sites make about sharing data.

> Yahoo! may send personally identifiable information about you to other companies or people when:
> - We have your consent to share the information;
> - We need to share your information to provide the product or service you have requested;
> - We need to send the information to companies who work on behalf of Yahoo! to provide a product or service to you. (Unless we tell you differently, these companies do not have any right to use the personally identifiable information we provide to them beyond what is necessary to assist us.);
> - We respond to subpoenas, court orders, or legal process; or
> - We find that your actions on our Web sites violate the Yahoo! Terms of Service, the
> - Yahoo! GeoCities Terms of Service, or any of our usage guidelines for specific products or services.

In essence, this quote says that they share personal data with all sorts of companies. The last item provides potential loopholes for their policies by referencing their terms of service and usage guidelines, although it does not say what they would do with your data under those circumstances.

The following quote from Barnes & Noble's Web site has an interesting twist to data-sharing clauses.

> We disclose this information to such companies under an agreement that requires that they obtain your consent first, usually under the membership or participation rules. If

you do not want us to disclose that information to the strategic partner, then you must contact them directly.

In other words, when Barnes & Noble wants to share data with a partner it will be up to you to learn this and tell that company not to use the data Barnes & Noble sends them.

A good privacy policy will spell out clearly what data is being collected about users, how long that data is kept, how it is used, how it is shared, and what type of policy it is. A good policy will also give users a say in how their data is used, via an opt-in or opt-out clause. An opt-in policy means that the Web site will not share your data with anyone unless you tell them it is okay by opting in to the program. Very few Web sites implement this type of policy, instead choosing opt-out policies. With an opt-out policy, the user must go out of their way to tell the Web site to not share any information.

An item that appears to be universally lacking from privacy policies is the mention of the use of Web bugs, either from the Web site or in email. Many Web sites justify this by saying that they mention the use of cookies as part of their policies. Another item that is frequently missing in privacy policies is what data Web sites collect indirectly through third parties such as data syndicators. Amazon.com is one of the few companies that take a more progressive approach by mentioning this data enrichment in their policy.

Unfortunately, Amazon.com was also at the center of one of the heavily publicized incidents when they weakened their privacy policy in the summer of 2000. The original version of the policy said that although they do not sell or share information about users with others, they might do so in the future, and they provided users the ability to opt out of this future action. The new policy removed the ability to opt out. A further weakening was the statement that the company will sell personal data if it sells parts of the company or faces bankruptcy.

A number of the more notable incidents involved the DoubleClick online advertising network. They weakened their privacy policy by removing the statement that they do not track the real identity of users. Their original policy said that they did not know any offline user information and therefore kept users anonymous. A related change said that they would identify users unless the user chose to opt out. Adding fuel to the fire, DoubleClick later planned on merging a complete set of consumer demographic data with their online user profiles. They backed down on this plan but the option still remains open for the future.

In an effort to avoid the public relations problems faced by companies like Amazon and DoubleClick, some Web sites participate in online privacy seal programs. TRUSTe and BBBOnline are two of the more prominent seals, and there are a number of others available. All of these programs have minimum standards the privacy policies must meet in order to show that they have the seal of approval. Generally, these standards cover the content of the policies but rarely prescribe specific practices that Web sites should or should not engage in.

There is a conflict of interest with most of these programs because the companies being monitored pay to be members. It is extremely rare for one of these programs to revoke their seal from a Web site. Because of this lack of enforcement against companies that violate the program's standards, the utility of these privacy seals has been tarnished.

Among the best-known incidents involved RealNetworks, a participant in the TRUSTe program. As mentioned in Chapter 3, RealNetworks' RealJukebox software creates a globally unique user identifier (GUID) when the software is installed and transmits that identifier back to RealNetworks when the software is used. The GUID, registration information, and usage data can be combined to profile users. RealNetwork's privacy policy did not disclose any of these practices. Yet TRUSTe did not revoke their seal after this incident. The reasoning was that RealJukeBox is downloaded software and therefore not covered by the Web site's privacy policy.

Microsoft had a similar experience with TRUSTe. A feature in Internet Explorer that notifies Web sites when a user bookmarks a page was publicized as an invasion of privacy, particularly since the user can't turn the feature off. Another involved software that would send user registration data and a GUID even if the user told the software not to send anything. Since TRUSTe does not have a statement covering installed software, Microsoft still displays the privacy seal.

Even in the case of a direct violation of a Web site's privacy policy, TRUSTe did not revoke their seal. An interesting case occurred with GeoCities, now a part of Yahoo!. In this incident, the FTC charged GeoCities with misrepresentation because the company stated that it would not share any user data with third parties, but shared detailed psychographic and demographic data with marketers. The company settled with the FTC and admitted no wrongdoing, but immediately changed its privacy policy to state they might share data without users' knowledge or consent.

A big part of the problem may be due to the conflict of interest. Organizations like TRUSTe can't afford to be too aggressive in enforcing their standards for fear that they will alienate their customers. Another aspect of the problem may be that there is no specific means of enforcement. Further, many of the privacy seals do not openly air the complaints filed against member companies. In the end, the result is that privacy seals are about as effective as a Web site's stated privacy policies.

Due to the abuses that have occurred with personal data, the lack of clear policies and enforcement, and also the newness of the Web as a medium for commerce, two things have happened. One is a call for government intervention in the form of online privacy laws. Many in the industry have fought against this, offering self-regulation as the alternative. Unfortunately, self-regulation is akin to letting the fox guard the henhouse. Issues such as those surrounding TRUSTe and the other privacy seals provide evidence that self-regulation is not working.

One item that makes the privacy issue more urgent is that ISPs can assemble massive amounts of data about users. Because an ISP is able to identify each user and sees all of the traffic generated by a given user, they are in the unique position to record and analyze every action a user makes online. User profiling by ISPs is one practice that is largely inappropriate. ISPs should not be selling data about where their customers go online or who they send email, a practice that is no different than telephone companies selling data about the content of your phone calls to third parties.

At the time of this writing we are aware of efforts by several of the largest ISPs to build more detailed profiles of user activities. With the notable exception of EarthLink, which explicitly does not track user behavior, these companies rarely have strong privacy policies covering their subscribers. So far the saving grace for users is that so much data is generated that the ISPs have difficulty doing even basic clickstream analysis.

Even if you approve of a Web site's privacy policy, there is no assurance that the Web site will actually comply with it. The burden of monitoring what a company does with the data is up to the users. All of these problems and mistrust have driven some users to take privacy into their own hands.

The most obvious way users attempt to protect their privacy is by deliberately providing incorrect information to Web sites that ask for personal data. This technique will not work if there is any commercial transaction since financial or shipping data usually reveals the user's real identity, which can then be linked to correct offline personal data.

The next step taken by some of the more technically knowledgeable users is to partially or completely disable cookies and the client-side scripting or Java capabilities of their browsers. The price one pays by doing this is a less than optimal experience on many Web sites. In some instances, the site will not function at all unless all of these are enabled.

The last line of defense is the use of various types of software that allow users to selectively block some information. There are free programs such as Guidescope and Internet Junkbusters that allow a user to selectively block cookies and banner ads. There are also *web anonymizers* that function as a proxy server between the user and Web sites, thereby making all interactions anonymous.

Users who use these kinds of identity-cloaking mechanisms become nearly impossible to track. A Web site will have a user profile only when a user voluntarily provides enough data to reveal their offline identity, and even then it will not include their overall Web surfing habits or transactions because tracking mechanisms have been disabled.

In response to these actions and to provide a better public relations spin, some advertising networks allow users to opt out of targeted advertisements and user profiling. If you visit the Web sites of these advertising networks you can ask them to provide an opt-out cookie that replaces the tracking cookie associated with their ads or web bugs. As long as this new cookie is present in the browser, that advertiser will not track you.

If a user employs the right privacy protection mechanisms it will not be possible to keep a user profile for more than a single user session. Even single session profiling may not be possible if cookies are completely disabled, for example. Further, any user-supplied data may be inaccurate unless there is a direct incentive to provide correct information like a mailing address or credit card number. Because of this, clickstream data warehouse designers should always be aware of which data is user-supplied and whether it is reasonable to assume that this data is of good quality.

Before building the clickstream warehouse you should carefully review your Web site's privacy policy. It is unlikely that the privacy policy will place restrictions on existing Web site services because the policy is likely to have been created after the Web site was designed. However, it's possible that the privacy policy will place constraints on either the design of the data warehouse or the uses of the information collected.

Policy-driven design constraints might include the exclusion of offline identity data from profiles, restrictions on how long the data is retained or leaving out some of the analytical capabilities your end users desire. Sometimes even simple business practices can be precluded.

For example, outsourcing is a common business practice. The data-sharing clause of the privacy policy may state that no personal data is shared with third parties without a user's consent. However, you may decide to use a name and address cleaning and householding service to clean data in the clickstream warehouse. The users' personal data will be shared with this company, even though they do not retain it once processing is complete. It is possible that this outsourcing is precluded by the Web site's policy.

The output of the clickstream warehouse may also be a source of contention. For example, collective demographic and user trend data is often shared with marketing partners. Sending this data from the warehouse to these partners could be violating the privacy policy. This is particularly true if you are sending data to online marketers with privacy policies of their own. They may have less restrictive policies, so that once the data leaves your enterprise and enters their domain, they can do things that your enterprise says it will not do. The biggest problem is that the user has no legal recourse against the third party, but may have against you.

The biggest conflict between user privacy and the Web site stems from the various uses of user profiles and data sharing. Since many Web sites are free to users, they support themselves by advertising. The way to make the most money to supply those free services is to sell targeted advertising whenever possible, and advertising can only be targeted if personal data is obtained by the site and then shared with the advertisers.

Personalization is much the same. In order to use personalized services, users provide some information about themselves. There is no conflict if that data is only used for personalization, but if the Web site shares this personal data with any third parties then there will be conflicting priorities. Users may want the convenience of personalization, but they may not want to pay the price of their privacy for this convenience.

Even simple profiling of users, such as where they link to your Web site from, can create problems. For example, if users visit medical sites before visiting your site, you may be able to infer something about the state of their health. The federal government has already subpoenaed information from some companies in order to examine the online trail left by potential criminals. This could lead to some frightening implications for both the Web site and its users.

Unintentional *data spills* are one last source of problems for both the Web site and the clickstream warehouse. A data spill occurs when a Web site inadvertently sends personal data to another party. The data is usually sent as a result of sloppy Web site coding, although there are cases where the transmission of data is intentional.

Often the data is transmitted via flawed URL rewriting, either in the URL of a banner ad or hyperlink or in the URL of the Web page itself. For example, several retail Web sites have been sending the SKUs of items users bought and Travelocity.com was sending the origin and destination of flight searches to advertising partners. Online advertising networks like DoubleClick have been the recipients of a lot of personal data in this way.

A look through the contents of the referring URL field in your Web site's log files may show a surprising amount of personal information about users, transmitted as parameters appended to the referring URLs. To extract the data, all you need to do is parse the parameters in the Referrer field. Many Web sites from Excite.com to FAO Schwarz have suffered from these types of unintentional data spills.

The same kinds of problems apply equally to nonconsumer Web sites. In some cases, the stakes are higher because improper transmission of an organization's data can involve service contracts, resulting in legal liability for your enterprise. Even though most business-oriented Web sites involve explicit contracts for service, most will still have privacy policies.

Most Web application and clickstream warehouse developers have never read the privacy policies of their own Web sites, and are unaware of any constraints on what they may develop. The bottom line for the clickstream data warehouse is that you should read your Web site's privacy policy and determine what, if any, restrictions you have *before* you start any design work.

Summary

We have covered a broad range of user-identity topics, ranging from the formidable problem of tracking users to the ethical use of user profile data. At this point you should have a good understanding of how user sessions are maintained and the various mechanisms to track users from one visit to the next. In addition, the review of user identification, profiling, and privacy topics gives you the basic knowledge you need to identify potential business, technical, and ethical considerations that will arise during the design of your clickstream data warehouse.

This chapter concludes the first half of the book. With a firm grasp of the underlying technologies and environment, the next step is to begin the process of building a clickstream data warehouse. The second half of the book discusses the important elements of clickstream data warehouse projects, from project planning through implementation. Chapter 5 discusses the structure of a typical project, the project plan, project staffing and our experiences managing some of these projects.

PART TWO

Building a Clickstream Data Warehouse, Step-by-Step

Planning, Managing, and Staffing a Clickstream Data Warehouse Project

This chapter marks the beginning of Part 2 of this book. In Part 1, we presented a detailed study of the Web site architectural components and data items that directly impact the design of a clickstream data warehouse. On top of this foundation of knowledge we can describe the process of building a clickstream data warehouse, step-by-step.

We begin this journey with an overview of the project life cycle of a clickstream data warehouse and basic information on starting, structuring, and managing the project. Our assumption is that the reader is familiar with general data warehouse project management tasks and techniques, and wants more information about the structure and flow of a clickstream-specific data warehouse project. We also assume basic knowledge about dimensional data modeling and data warehousing. If you are uncomfortable with any of these topics then we highly recommend reading *The Data Warehouse Lifecycle Toolkit*, by Ralph Kimball, et al., which covers these topics and many others in great detail and is a worthwhile addition to any data warehousing bookshelf.

This chapter is organized into two parts. The first part provides an overview of all the phases of a clickstream data warehouse project, summarizing the key tasks and providing a synopsis of valuable lessons that we have learned doing these projects. The second section covers project organization and staffing considerations.

Introduction to the Clickstream Data Warehouse Project Flow

Successful creation of a clickstream data warehouse begins with an understanding of the differences between building transaction processing systems and building data warehouses. Both require adequate planning and requirements definition, but gathering and analyzing the requirements for transactional systems is quite different than for a data warehouse. The data warehouse design process follows a different path requiring specialized techniques, and application development is of a different nature, requiring more flexibility for end users and easier extensibility for developers.

A key driver of the requirement for flexibility and extensibility is that data warehouse projects tend to evolve much more rapidly than transactional systems. Instead of automating a set of processes like a transaction-based system, a data warehouse provides a framework for answering business questions that evolves over time. Satisfying a set of initial business questions with a clickstream data warehouse results in a new awareness of additional business issues, creating new business questions that fuel further data warehouse development. These requirements for flexibility, extensibility, and evolution must be addressed in your approach to the project.

Figure 5.1 shows the five phases of a clickstream data warehouse project, along with the associated tasks and project tracks. Except for clickstream-specific wording, the project phases in Figure 5.1 are very similar to the general Business Dimensional Lifecycle that was originally presented in *The Data Warehouse Lifecycle Toolkit* by Ralph Kimball, et al.

Of the five phases of a clickstream data warehouse project, the first two phases, *project definition and planning* and *business requirements analysis,* are the most important because they set the direction for everything that follows. Once the first two phases are complete, the next phases, which comprise the bulk of the project, are the *design* and *implementation* phases. While the diagram shows the design tasks in phase 3 as concurrent, they are often done serially. For example, one usually completes the schema design prior to completing the other design tasks.

All but the smallest projects will have the three basic project tracks during design and implementation, namely, the *data source and database track*, the *applications track*, and the *architecture and infrastructure track*. The tasks in each track are relatively independent from one another, as are the staffing skills required to do the work. Although it is not explicitly shown in the figure, the development tasks conclude with systems integration testing and data validation.

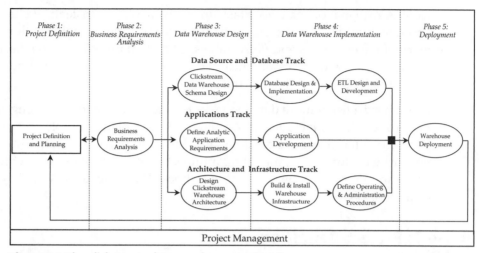

Figure 5.1 The clickstream data warehouse project flow.

The *deployment* phase, at the far right side of the figure, is often ignored. Improper planning for deployment can derail an otherwise successful project. Many of the system administration tasks and staff procedures should be finalized prior to deployment so that everything runs smoothly from the start.

Note that once the system has been deployed, the project cycle begins again. Clickstream warehouse development is a never-ending cycle of development. While most databases are intended to support the transaction processing requirements of a specific application, a clickstream data warehouse is meant to integrate data across systems and support evolving uses by many applications. End-user analysis from the data warehouse will lead to new business questions, which will, in turn, create new data warehouse information requirements. New data sources and new applications will continue to evolve to support the business as it changes. A properly designed data warehouse provides the infrastructure to anticipate and support these new needs.

The figure above shows the general structure of a clickstream data warehouse project and is useful for communicating information about the project at a high level. However, the project manager and development team need a more detailed picture of the project phases and associated tasks in order to implement a clickstream data warehouse. These details are explained in the sections that follow.

Managing the Project

This portion of the chapter is organized according to the phases of a clickstream data warehouse project shown in Figure 5.1. We won't go through a tedious explanation of every task in a given phase. Instead, we'll briefly describe what is done during a given phase, and then provide a short summary of the objectives and deliverables for that phase. We end the discussion of each phase with a Lessons Learned section that offers succinct advice on pivotal aspects of that phase of the project.

If you need a list of more detailed tasks for your own project planning, a sample project plan is included in Appendix A. The plan is usable as a starting point for determining the tasks involved in a clickstream warehouse project. For further information, including a project plan in Microsoft Project format, you can point your browser to our book Web site at www.wiley.com/compbooks/sweiger.

Phase 1: Project Definition and Planning

Whether building the system for the first time or adding new capabilities onto an existing warehouse, all clickstream data warehouse projects begin the same way: with planning. Most publications on clickstream data warehousing make it seem like you should bring in some staff, evaluate and buy some software, and start developing. This is precisely the wrong thing to do. A good clickstream data warehouse begins with foresight and planning.

The first step is to define the business goals of the project. The goals should not be defined in technical or functional terms like "integrating Web site data" or "providing Web site analysis capabilities." The goals should be couched in terms of business problems the system is meant to address.

The business goals provide half of the motivation for the project. The other half of the motivation is the project's return on investment (ROI) or some other business justification. Whatever the justification is, it should be clearly linked to the project's business goals. If it is not linked, or if it is unrealistic, then chances are good that the project sponsor will be disappointed when the project is delivered.

Assuming you have the business goals defined and the required business justification, then the scope of the project must be defined. Defining the scope of the project at this point can be difficult because the detailed requirements are not yet known. In general, the scope is bounded by the project goals but it will change as you gather and analyze requirements. Some new items may appear with higher priorities, or certain items may be too difficult to address in the first round of development, creating dependencies between the project definition and requirements analysis phases.

The initial project definition contains a short description of the business problems, what the project is and how it is expected to solve those problems. It also contains the initial scope, listing everything that will be included in the first round of development. There should also be a list of those items that are *not* in scope so that the project sponsors understand what is being deferred to another round of development.

Because most end users do not understand the details of data extraction and source systems, they will often assume that a given department's needs will be addressed in the initial scope, or that data for certain analyses will be present right out of the gate. Therefore, the out-of-scope list should include items that could be easily construed by those not directly involved with the project as being in-scope. In many cases, this will exclude certain subject areas, data that is not directly related to the core business problem, historical data beyond a certain point in time, or user groups or types of analyses that will not be addressed.

Completing the project scope is a key event. At this point, the project manager can take care of the activities required to initiate the project. Every organization does this differently. In general, one determines the project roles, assigns staff to the project, defines development procedures, and develops the initial project plan.

Summary of Project Definition Tasks and Objectives

The quality of the initial *project definition* plays a large part in determining whether a clickstream data warehouse project is a success or a failure. The initial scope sets expectations with the project sponsors and end users about the value of the project and what they will get individually and collectively. Once the goals, scope, and business justification are established, the project can be started.

At *project initiation*, the project manager assembles the core team, kicks off the project, and begins the planning for analysis and development. Key roles and responsibilities are defined, a general schedule is produced and the analysis phase is planned. The team should define all of the project development processes so that everything will be in place when development work starts. The high level tasks for this phase of the project are shown in Figure 5.2. The primary objectives for this phase are listed in Table 5.1.

Phase 1: Project Definition

Project Preparation

    Define initial project scope

    Determine project feasibility and justification

    Create project steering committee

Project Planning

    Assign project staff

    Prepare initial project plan

Project Initiation

    Conduct project kickoff meeting

    Develop training plan for project team

    Develop project communication plan

    Develop change management process

    Develop issue tracking process

    Define development process

        Define source code control procedures

        Define documentation standards

        Define coding standards (programs, scripts, SQL)

        Define data modeling standards

        Define quality control process

Ongoing Project Management

    Project communication

    Change management

    Issue tracking

    Project plan maintenance

Figure 5.2 Tasks for project definition and planning.

Table 5.1 Primary Objectives for Phase 1

PRIMARY OBJECTIVES
Determine exactly what the business objective is and define the motivation for doing the project in business terms.
Define the initial scope of the project jointly with both end users and IT, identifying which needs will be addressed, which needs won't be addressed, and what the general time frame will be.
Establish a collaborative relationship between the project sponsors, drivers, users, and the development team.
Set appropriate expectations with the project sponsors and drivers.
Create all of the necessary project processes and procedures to support the development team.
Create the high-level project plan.

Lessons Learned the Hard Way

Clickstream Data Warehouse Projects Are Different

These projects have more difficulties than many traditional data warehouse projects. Like any data warehouse, a clickstream data warehouse is highly cross-functional. The key clickstream-related difference is that the world of the database or warehouse developer is usually totally foreign to a Web developer. In order to bridge this gap, the data warehouse project team has to gain a detailed understanding of Web technologies and design to be able to implement an appropriate clickstream data warehouse. Conversely, the Web site developers must take warehouse analytical needs into consideration when constructing the Web site, such as creating appropriate user and session identifiers, and logging all the necessary data required by the clickstream data warehouse.

One thing that surprises many data warehouse developers the first time they encounter a clickstream data warehouse is the high rate of change incurred by the Web-based data sources. Unlike transaction processing systems, which change less often and in more predictable ways, Web sites are constantly undergoing revision. The changes can be as simple as the addition of new content, or as complex as a complete change-out of the underlying site technology. Expect at least one major change during the clickstream project and budget 20 percent more time for the ETL process than you anticipate.

The dynamic nature of the Web site means that the project team must foster a close working relationship with the Web development team. Otherwise, Web site changes can blindside the project. We've seen this happen a number of times, particularly when a third-party consulting group did the Web development. At one online content provider, the method of tracking users and the method of tagging pages both changed in the same week, requiring a complete design change for processing data extracted from the Web and application server logs.

Know Your Project Sponsor

This is something that should be apparent right at the start of the project. The sponsor is the business manager who believes in the goals, and sees the connection between those goals and your project. The sponsor isn't always the only person behind the project. Often the sponsor controls the budget, but another person is the real driver behind the effort. The driver works with the project manager to keep the project focused and moving.

A good sponsor or driver has a number of key traits: this person is a respected manager, this person is decisive, and this person has good political skills. There will be times when you need to have active involvement by the driver or sponsor to break up obstacles to progress. These obstacles can be as simple as obtaining a reluctant department's involvement or as difficult as convincing two divisions to cooperate when each has its own competing stake in the outcome.

Likewise, knowing the hot buttons for the project sponsors and drivers can help you avoid land mines that might come up during the project. Not surprisingly, the better your relationship with these people, the more likely the project is to succeed.

Choose Your Target Wisely

The clickstream data warehouse is really an infrastructure project to integrate and deliver information. That means it will have multiple uses, some of which you can't anticipate at the outset. In order to build this infrastructure you will need to start with a project that demonstrates enough value to ensure that future efforts build on the clickstream data warehouse rather than going their own way.

End users typically judge the value of the project, rather than the project team or IT. This is why you have to tie the project to business goals and make sure there is a clear justification. For example, don't deliver Web site traffic reports if the marketing department wants to measure how effective their promotion efforts are so they can reduce marketing expenses. Focus more specifically on those needs, and anticipate what will be required after those needs are met.

Our experience has been that clickstream data warehouse projects are often aimed too low. Rather than fulfill more valuable efforts, the project only meets basic needs. Then other projects are funded to support other requirements, resulting in multiple single-purpose applications that could have been put in place more effectively as a set of integrated applications on top of a single clickstream warehouse. We've lost count of the number of companies that spent a half-million dollars or more on a single product, only to start a new project to fulfill needs that the first product couldn't meet.

For example, a retailer with both traditional and online operations bought separate applications for Web site traffic analysis, personalization, segmenting and targeting customers, and promotion analysis. With each purchase, they spent an enormous sum implementing the packages, and each time ended up with software used by a single group of users because the applications were targeted to specific needs. These packages needed to extract data from the Web site, and in some cases they had to be integrated with each other. Properly measuring results across the business meant extracting data from all the packages—in essence building a clickstream warehouse. Imagine how much money, time, and effort could have been saved had the company chosen to build a clickstream warehouse to deliver data to the first package. Two of the subsequent point-product purchases could have been completely avoided, as well as the later nightmare of data integration.

Make Sure the Project Scope Is Clearly Defined

The definition of scope should be both tangible and manageable. You want to be able to point to the scope at the end of the project and say that the project completed everything defined as in-scope. Creating a manageable scope is tough because you must balance the project team's ability to deliver results within a realistic time frame against the usability of what you deliver.

We've seen projects with very narrowly defined scope, often as part of the "quick start" approach of some clickstream or CRM tool vendor. Following this approach creates two problems. It shortens the planning horizon to the completion of a small pilot, and it does little more than prove that you can deliver something that is barely usable in a short time.

We are not saying that you should create a colossal clickstream project. Rather, you should make sure to look at the organization's goals and create a plan that is linked to those goals. The first step still might be something as trivial as a software vendor's pilot implementation, however this will be only a small step along a path that leads to deliverables that are more in line with the business goals of the enterprise.

On the other hand, projects with a scope that is too large run into very different problems. These projects usually did not suffer from lack of long-term vision. Instead, they attempted to reach the final goal in one giant step. These projects get out of control due to an excessive and often fuzzy definition of scope. During the long time span required to deliver these mammoth projects, sponsors and drivers move to other positions or lose interest, or the project's original justification becomes irrelevant because the underlying business has changed. When faced with this situation, the solution is to break that larger vision into smaller pieces that deliver increments of business value along the way and allow for appropriate midcourse corrections in project direction.

Our assumption in the project definition effort is that there is strong motivation for doing the project. The motivation is not always couched in financial terms. The project might be part of a business initiative or it might be required in order to provide specific analytical capabilities. The best business case is backed up by a solid ROI. If a solid business case has not been developed, then the project definition process should include building the business case.

Set Appropriate User Expectations

The end users' expectations form the basis for what they believe the system should provide. If you don't meet those expectations then you are in trouble. The users will focus their frustration on the project team, and their managers will focus their frustration on you.

The problem of overpromising and underdelivering happens repeatedly in data warehouse projects. The sad fact is that most project teams are in a position to set appropriate expectations of their users. An unclear definition of scope mixed with poor communication from the project team is usually to blame for the missed expectations.

Once the project definition is complete, make sure you have the signed agreement of the key stakeholders in the project. This will go a long way toward setting their expectations appropriately.

The Project Scope Always Increases

Traditional database projects start with clear functional specifications. In contrast, data warehousing projects start with clear business requirements and minimal functional specifications. During requirements analysis both you and the end users will learn a lot that you did not know about the business and how it uses information. This will lead to changes in the goals and scope of the project. Data availability and quality problems uncovered during development will lead to further changes. The Web site will likely undergo at least one major change during the time the clickstream warehouse is being developed.

This means clickstream data warehouses have more stringent change management requirements than traditional systems. A good change management process is vital. The only way for the project manager to make proper trade-offs is to work in close collaboration with the project sponsors, drivers, and end users. The key word is trade-offs: If the users want an additional item then something must be given up. That something could be removing a different item from the development plan or pushing out the scheduled completion date.

Phase 2: Business Requirements Analysis

Once the goals and project scope are defined and signed off, the project team must gather the business requirements. Business requirements analysis forms the foundation for the entire project. Skimping on the requirements is a sure way to get the project into trouble. Many people use short-cycle iterative development as an excuse to avoid doing a thorough job of analysis. For a clickstream data warehouse project, this will lead to extensive rework and make the project longer rather than shorter.

The kinds of requirements needed for a data warehouse are different from those for transactional systems. Almost all the key information focuses on the decision-making process of the end users: which data, the frequency of different business questions, and how they do analysis. This is in contrast to transaction processing requirements, where the focus is on the function the employee performs. In transaction processing, each employee within a function always uses the same information in the same way. This is almost never true in a data warehouse environment.

Transaction processing systems treat users as interchangeable parts because they perform identical functions. This won't work for a data warehouse. Users of a data warehouse have different information requirements based on their particular tasks and knowledge. Traditional approaches to requirements and design don't do a good job of acknowledging these differences. You must use requirements gathering techniques specific to data warehouse construction and dimensional modeling if you hope to succeed.

The core of the clickstream data warehouse requirements methodology rests on business user interviews used to uncover specific information needed to design the appropriate dimensional data models. The requirements gathering techniques and process are explained in detail in books such as Ralph Kimball's *The Data Warehouse Toolkit* and *The Data Warehouse Lifecycle Toolkit*. In addition, the next chapter in this book describes the clickstream data warehouse metaschema, which is an important supplemental aid for clickstream-specific business requirements analysis and data modeling.

One might think that it is possible to skip these business interviews when building a system that just feeds data to another Web application, such as

Personify, for example. In this case, there are specific data requirements and no evident user requirements that are not met by the package. While we are certain that one can build a clickstream data warehouse to supply specific data to a software package, business users usually need more information, or more integrated information, than is available in a canned application. You won't be able to tell what users need unless you uncover those missed requirements by conducting business user interviews.

Summary of Business Requirements Analysis Tasks and Objectives

In this phase of the project, the team digs into the details of what types of information and analysis the end users require. The interviews with end users are followed by discussions with members of IT who control the applications that are data sources for the clickstream data warehouse.

The most important clickstream data sources are the Web server and Web application server log files, which were explained in detail in Chapter 3. The interview team must talk to the Web application developers, Web designers, and system administrators to understand exactly how the Web site functions and what data is or is not available. This analysis highlights what changes to the Web site may be required to log a complete set of clickstream information. One of the common operational changes is the creation of a method for tagging content so that end users can better analyze activity. Clickstream data analysis may also show that some of the requirements are not supportable due to gaps in the collected data. This usually has a direct impact on the scope of the project.

Once the requirements have been assembled into a document and approved by the end users, the next step is usually to revise the project scope and priorities with the project's sponsors. During business requirements analysis, one often discovers things that lead to changes in project priorities. The shifting priorities can expand or contract the scope of the project—something that requires approval from the project sponsors.

Since scope can shift until we complete this phase, detailed project planning for the design and development phase is delayed until the business requirements are well understood. At this stage, the project plan only has coarse time estimates for the subsequent phases.

The high level tasks for this phase of the project are shown in Figure 5.3 and the main objectives are listed in Table 5.2. These tasks and objectives are directly derived from the general data warehouse project requirements tasks and objectives originally presented in *The Data Warehouse Lifecycle Toolkit* by Ralph Kimball, et al.

Phase 2: Requirements Definition

Gather Business Requirements

    Create Interview Team

    Select End-user Interviewees

    Schedule Interviews

    Interview Preparation

    Conduct Interview Kickoff Meeting

    Conduct End-user Interviews

    Analyze Interview Findings

Gather Technical Requirements

    Conduct IT Interviews—Web Site

    Conduct IT Interviews—Other Systems

    Analyze Interview Findings

Document Requirements

    Document Interview Findings

    Publish Requirements Documents

    Provide Feedback to Web Site Group

    Revise Full Project Scope

    Define Initial Pilot Scope

    Update Project Plan

    Conduct User Signoff Meeting

Figure 5.3 Tasks for requirements definition.

Table 5.3 Primary Objectives for Phase 2

PRIMARY OBJECTIVES
Create a business requirements document that specifies key areas of opportunity, analytic and informational requirements, and the data sources.
Refine the scope of the project based on the more detailed understanding of both requirements and the data available (or not) to meet those requirements.
Document any changes that must be made to the Web site in order to support the users' information requirements.
Prioritize the project deliverables and make any necessary revisions to the project scope, budget, or timeline based on these priorities.
Develop the detailed project plan for the remainder of the project.

Lessons Learned the Hard Way

Use a Data Warehouse-Specific Methodology for Gathering Requirements

It is important that you use a methodology for gathering requirements that is specific to data warehousing. Standard system development methodologies will generally fail to uncover the information you need to properly build a useful system. This is because they so often focus on specific requirements, where our focus will lead us into areas that are vague because they are context-specific. People will often analyze information in different ways, even if they are doing the same job. Focusing just on the data, or just on the process—two things most development methodologies do—will not give you the proper perspective. To learn more about a data warehouse-specific approach, we suggest reading Chapter 4 of *The Data Warehouse Lifecycle Toolkit*, or the shorter section in Chapter 12 of *The Data Warehouse Toolkit*, and supplementing this with the clickstream data warehouse meta-schema described in the next chapter of this book.

Make Sure You Interview the Web Site Developers and Maintainers

While the principal focus of the requirements gathering phase is on business needs and the end users, it must be tempered by what can actually be delivered. This is done by interviewing technical staff in the IT department, particularly those who develop and support the Web site.

You want to interview these people after talking to a number of end users so you have an idea of what types of data you will need to support the users. As we mentioned in several of the earlier chapters, there are many ways to implement Web site features. Depending on what techniques were used to implement the Web site, the data that end users need may not be available. If you understand the high-level data problems in advance, then you can start to work with the Web site developers to make the necessary changes to the site design.

If changes are not possible or are resisted, these early technical interviews allow you to set user expectations at the beginning of the project. Informing the users early also moves the data availability problem from the technical realm to the business realm. When the sponsors and users realize that what they want is not available because of the Web site's implementation, they can take ownership of the problem and work with that part of the IT organization to correct it. Our experience is that 90 percent of the time the users want the data enough to find ways to get it. The only time they don't is when the development cost is too high to justify against the project's ROI.

Expect to Talk to 30 Percent More Users than You Planned to

One of the recurring comments we hear at the beginning of a project is, We know what the users are doing. Can't we cut back on the interviews and save a week or two in the schedule? The answer is a resounding No! Skimping on the requirements gathering only leads to misunderstandings and rework later in the project, when the work is more expensive to fix. Furthermore, after doing several interviews, we often hear project team members say, We never knew anything about those user requirements.

Gathering requirements through direct user interaction is critical. You must interview enough people to get a representative sample of users across the organization. Talk to people at different levels and interview a sufficient number so that you start to hear common themes from one interview to the next.

Understanding the day-to-day difficulties of getting and using information within an enterprise is valuable for more than the requirements. It helps you couch project communications in terms users will be more likely to understand and accept. It also allows you to set expectations with a large group of people. Many times the users will have an idea of what the project is but not whether it has any relevance to their jobs. The interview is a chance to guide their expectations to a more appropriate level, whether that is lower or higher.

What we find is that we always end up talking to more users than we originally planned. While talking to users, they will often suggest someone else who is more knowledgeable about a particular topic, or who has something interesting to contribute. Given this, you should always keep a number of unnamed interview slots built into the plan. The last thing you want to do is destroy your credibility this early in the project by exceeding the schedule.

Stay Focused on the Project Goals

During the end-user interviews, you will learn much more than you thought possible about how the organization uses information. The typical experience is to hear many stories about how information is used, and how "If I had this information I would have been able to solve the problem in hours instead of weeks."

After absorbing so much about the problems and opportunities available, you may consider more interviews and increasing the breadth of the project. This is normal, but remember not to stray too far afield chasing these opportunities. There may be some excellent problems that you can solve, but those problems may not be directly in line with the project's stated goals or they may already have been defined as out of scope. If this is the case, be sure to document the issues but do not expend too much effort expanding on them. There will be time after gathering requirements to reexamine the project scope and suggest changes.

Quick Study: How to Do Business User Interviews

To get the requirements right in a clickstream data warehouse project, we've mentioned that you must do the analysis somewhat differently, by interviewing business users. You need to learn what people do with the information provided by a system, rather than the mechanics of how that system is built. As we've mentioned before, this is not transaction automation, where the steps of transaction are defined. This is usage-centered design, where the focus is on what information is important to the business and how the users analyze it.

The primary goal for end-user interviews is to collect enough information to develop a comprehensive data warehouse schema that covers the areas of user interest. This means that if there is an area you think useful, but which is discounted by the users, don't waste time pursuing it.

At a minimum, you should leave each interview knowing answers to the following questions:

- What does this person do?
- What is important to them, and how important are they?
- What measurements are they interested in?
- What are the probable dimensions of the world according to them?
- Are they strategic, tactical, or operational in focus?
- What are they currently working on, and what business issue concerns them most?

Over the course of requirements analysis, the key things to look for are themes and repetition. Did people express the same or similar wish lists, metrics, and issues? If so, you've probably found the facts and the areas where the data warehouse will have an impact. The interviews tend to identify other issues related to data quality, availability, and granularity.

You should have prepared prior to the interviews and be able to talk in user-oriented terms. Remember that they may be naive about the development process and technical terms, but they are experts in the subjects you are trying to learn. If you can create an environment that recognizes their expertise and yours, you will have a successful interview. You also have an advantage that they don't—you are talking to people throughout their entire organization about these topics, and they are limited to a narrower view.

As you work through the interview process, you want to identify the full scope of information utilized by the business users. It is also important to identify areas where information is lacking, what is most important and least important, etc. Other goals are setting the appropriate expectations with the end user, and collecting information on their sophistication and understanding of their business. In a sense, you are selling the project to the users while getting requirements.

(continued)

Quick Study: How to Do Business User Interviews *(continued)*

After asking the basic questions about the user and their role in the organization, it is helpful to develop a framework that describes what they do. This will help you identify areas to focus on or to avoid, and tell you what information you will probably get. To develop this framework, ask interviewees about their positions, responsibilities, who reports to them, and who they report to.

You will probably start at a high level and sink into deeper levels until a particular topic has been explored fully. As a starting point, you should have some pre-planned questions prior to going into an interview. Ask open-ended questions, and try to avoid simple "yes-no" questions. A good approach is to ask what-if questions and what-then questions. For example, "What do you do if you notice lower than normal sales of a particular product?" or, "When you see this metric rise significantly what do you do? What do you do next?"

Approach each conversation with questions like, "What sorts of tasks you do on a typical day? When you do task X, is there any specific information or report you find helpful?" Instead of, "So tell me what metrics you use to do your job," ask, "I imagine there are a few key metrics that stand out in your mind as being most important." The first question style may limit the user's answer whereas the second, open-ended style may reveal more information about what is really important to the user and what information may currently be unavailable to the user. Another way to get at the key metrics is to use the dashboard metaphor. Ask the person, "Imagine that you could design a dashboard for your job, just like the dashboard for your car. What would you put on there to use as the three gauges and three warning lights?" This helps them conceptualize the information you're trying to uncover.

Identify the initial questions they ask themselves when doing their job and then move on to the questions that derive from these. Following the questions and answers in this way will reveal what business question they typically ask, what sources they go to for information, and what they consider key metrics. The sequence and types of questions they ask themselves helps you build a model of their decision-making process.

This process can be very useful when trying to determine how a user interface should be structured. If the application follows their thought process, then they will be able to relate to it. In general, user thought processes will change as they use the data warehouse and discover how to use it differently. This is one of the reasons we see several iterations of user interface on most projects.

It is important to cover the area of exceptions in user interviews. Often, routine work is not the most important focus of business analysis. It is the exceptions that cause them to take action, and what actions they take are critical factors. When they say "I do this," and describe some routine task they do on a frequent

(continued)

Quick Study: How to Do Business User Interviews (continued)

basis, one of your standard questions should be "Are there any exceptions that cause you to do something else?" There will often be exactly such an exception, and a whole new set of tasks associated with it. When uncovering things like this, consider how the data warehouse might help them by automating certain tasks, highlighting crucial areas, or providing information to make them proactive.

Identifying organizational issues is also an important aspect of user interviews. Use organizational questions to get a feel for the political landscape, and to generate more leads on other people to interview. During the interviews, ask yourself:

- Is there anyone who knows more about this particular topic?
- Is there any particular person who appears to be most or least efficient at their job?
- Is there value providing information in a new way?
- Who is for or against the spending money on this project?
- Which managers' areas will be most affected by this system?
- Which managers have the largest stake in the outcome?
- How does this person view the business?
- What questions is this person typically asked by others within this department or by his or her manager?

It is especially important to discover what information users don't have that would make their jobs easier. This is a difficult area to uncover, because you have to understand what they are doing in order to see the gaps in their decision-making process. Use your conversations with other people in the organization to provide insight into the current interview. If the interviewee seems content with what they have, and the project appears to be simply automating the information delivery process, press on the issue of what information may be missing.

As you can see, the focus of the interviews is broad and can go in many directions. The idea is to talk to as many people as is feasible given your time constraints. This allows you to slowly converge on the common problems and themes that keep cropping up. Once the information set converges, you are finished interviewing and can now use this information as the basis for the logical schema design of the clickstream data warehouse.

Always Get the Users and Sponsors to Sign Off on the Requirements Document

The most important reason for getting sign-off is to protect the interests of the project team. If the end users read the requirements and agree with the contents, then the project team has a strong basis for the project scope. That provides documented ammunition for excluding major changes down the road, should the need arise. Signing off also sets the expected outcomes of the project in the minds of the user community.

During the course of gathering business requirements, we always distribute the sections of the requirements document to the interested parties so that they can review what they said. Some people may make statements about business problems in private that they might not support publicly. If you simply publish the final document without review by the interested parties, you can find yourself in the middle of an argument, with various interviewees claiming that the requirements team didn't understand what they said.

It's a good idea to provide the final requirements document to every person you interviewed, as well as everyone on the project team. We normally do this a few days prior to an acceptance meeting. The team should invite the sponsors and primary users to that meeting and provide a presentation of the findings and what you will be doing next. This provides a great forum for setting expectations. Instead of basing their views on a single conversation during their interview, they can see the broader context of the project. We've found this technique extremely helpful as a way of letting people know where their needs fit into the overall project and why some departments have a higher development priority than others.

The last reason to get sign-off on the requirements document is rather obvious—it forces the team to document the requirements and put them into a form the users can understand. This increases end-user involvement and means the team can't be forced to treat requirements gathering as merely a technical exercise. Clickstream data warehousing projects require joint ownership between IT and the end users to succeed.

Phase 3: Data Warehouse Design

Up until now, the clickstream data warehouse project has gone forward with a relatively small project team to plan the project and determine the requirements. At the end of phase 2 the requirements were approved by the end users, the scope was settled and the project plan for the design phase was finalized. Now the project starts to get complicated.

Many things happen at the end of phase 2 and the beginning of phase 3, making the project manager's job more difficult. At this stage, it is important that the core project team be assembled. That means anyone who was not a part of the requirements gathering effort should read the requirements document before doing any work. The core team must have a detailed understanding of the goals and scope of the project, and exactly what the user requirements are.

The focus of this phase is design. A clickstream data warehouse is infrastructure that supports many different uses of information, from application data feeds to end-user analysis. It is essential that time be spent up front designing the database schema and defining the system architecture. This is not a simple development project that you can accrete piecemeal through a lot of design-build cycles, any more than you would trust a contractor to build your house one room at a time.

The most important design to get right is the database schema. The database schema forms the foundation for everything else that you build. If it is not done correctly then rework during the development phase will at least double the project schedule and cost.

As you are designing the database schema, you must also define the system architecture. Choosing the database vendor and a server to run the data warehouse is not sufficient. A clickstream data warehouse is not just another database. As described in Chapters 1 and 2, a clickstream data warehouse has many components as well as ties to other applications. You are really working on a complex systems integration project.

The system architecture defines the design principles behind the construction of the data warehouse. All of the major components must be identified and their interfaces defined. You also need to determine how you plan to integrate the warehouse with other systems. For example, what method will you use to extract data from a customer call center database? How will you send the clickstream data from a Web application server? You also need to specify the requirements and preferences for technology procurement. Would you rather build or buy a given component? What are your important criteria for evaluating products? In the end, you should be able to identify every major component of your clickstream warehouse in a single diagram and explain how they will be built and connected to other systems.

Summary of Design Tasks and Objectives

In this phase the project plan divides into the three concurrent development tracks shown in Figure 5.1:

1. The source data and database track.

2. The analytical applications track.

3. The data warehouse architecture and infrastructure track.

Whether the work is actually done in concurrent tracks with separate staff depends on the size and complexity of the project. Smaller projects often work on all three tasks with the same team members. On larger projects, a significant part of the project manager's job is to ensure constant and effective communication between staff working in each of these three areas.

The first step in the source data and database track is the design of the database schema. Intertwined with schema design is a great deal of source data analysis. In the project plan these tasks are separated because the bulk of the data analysis happens after the initial schema design work determines what data items are actually needed.

Differences between a clickstream warehouse project and a more traditional data warehouse project become apparent at this stage. Apart from some significant differences in the schema design, which are discussed in the next chapter, the analysis of Web site data adds a new level of complexity. We show this in the project plan below by breaking out Web data analysis from the data analysis you will do for other types of source data systems. You should estimate the time for these tasks separately. Chances are you will spend more time here than for any other individual source system.

To summarize, the logical schema design is the basis for almost all other design and development tasks. The content of this schema design is used to determine what source data will be required and what analysis is possible by end users. A proper dimensional model is the cornerstone of the clickstream data warehouse.

The applications track covers the design and development of all end-user applications from simple reporting to complex data analysis. One of the major tasks on the applications track is specifying all of the application-level requirements. All development required to deliver data from the warehouse is included in this track, whether for end-user reports or for data feeds to other applications such as Web site personalization engines.

The business requirements that were gathered at the beginning of the project drive the application development process. However, they are not in themselves sufficient as application specifications. At this point in the project there should be an understanding of who the different users of the system are, what data they look at, what problems they are trying to solve, and how they use information to solve those problems.

Part of the application specification is determining exactly what technology is needed to support the applications users desire. The technology requirements may include things like support for large data volumes, support for a large number of concurrent users, or advanced security features. If you do not already have query and reporting tools in-house then the single biggest item will be the specifications that drive selection of these products.

Often missing in application specifications is the usage models. Do users need reports, or ad-hoc queries, or OLAP analysis, or all of these things? Remember that this is not a transaction processing system, so a "one size fits all" approach to design will not work. The original business requirements also do not sufficiently specify detailed application features like exactly what parameters are used to constrain certain analyses or which calculations are used to derive certain measures. All of these things must be defined and placed into an application specification.

Downstream application data feeds, if any, also need to be specified. If the clickstream data warehouse is to supply data to other applications, for example an automated customer segmentation application, then the data content, format, and frequency of delivery all must be specified. Because of the myriad possible data sources and destinations, the data feed specification is a larger component of clickstream data warehouses than it is for other kinds of data warehouse projects.

The point at which the team starts defining the architecture and infrastructure varies from project to project. The tasks mostly involve understanding the existing environment and the requirements that drive your technology selection process. The architecture for your warehouse will depend on a number of factors: the existing computing infrastructure, the technology direction of the enterprise, and the business requirements gathered at the beginning of the project. At this stage in the project, the architect determines what technologies will be used and how they will be tied together. This may require evaluation and selection of a number of different software and hardware products. The time it takes to evaluate and procure these products is one of the most frequently underestimated tasks on clickstream warehouse projects.

The last step in this phase is a final review of the schema design, technical architecture, and application specifications. You should end up with a schema design document that specifies the logical schema, shows the mapping from source data to the schema, and defines how items like changing dimensions and data history will be handled. Many project managers combine the schema design document with the warehouse architecture specification. This architecture document contains all of the information mentioned earlier, showing the integration of the data, technical, and business components of the system.

The tasks for each track in phase 3 are listed in Figure 5.4. The primary objectives are listed in Table 5.3.

Phase 3: Data Warehouse Design

DATA SOURCE AND DATABASE TRACK

Data Warehouse Schema Design

> Determine dimensions
>
> Determine fact tables
>
> Determine base level fact granularity
>
> Define detailed facts and derived metrics
>
> Define dimension hierarchies and details
>
> Create initial schema design documentation
>
> Initial database sizing

Web Source Data Analysis

> Identify potential Web data sources
>
> Source data mapping
>
> Analyze format and types of logged data
>
> Meet with Web development team to discuss Web site design/logging issues
>
> Document data issues

Standard Source Data Analysis

> Identify data source systems
>
> Source data mapping
>
> Analyze and document source data issues
>
> Determine data retention needs
>
> Determine data security needs
>
> Determine approach for slowly changing dimensions
>
> Update schema design documentation
>
> User schema review and feedback

APPLICATION TRACK

Document High Level Application Requirements

> Define user interface needs
>
> Determine data access product categories required
>
> Determine data/application security requirements
>
> Identify initial reports/analysis applications
>
> Define user interface and application requirements
>
> Document initial application specifications
>
> Create application test plan

Figure 5.4 Tasks for design. *(continued)*

Phase 3: Data Warehouse Design *(Continued)*

ARCHITECTURE AND INFRASTRUCTURE TRACK

Develop Technology Architecture

      Review and document current technology environment

      Define data warehouse components and integration requirements

      Determine external system integration requirements

      Define project computing platform requirements

      Determine technology/product needs

      Determine build/buy approach for major system components

      Create project architecture and infrastructure plan

      Architecture review

Product Analysis and Selection

      Perform following tasks for each purchased component, e.g., an ETL tool, query tool, or data mining application

      Prepare product evaluation criteria

      Research available technology and identify suitable vendors

      Create short list of vendors

      Conduct detailed product evaluation

      Product evaluation

      Vendor evaluation

      Estimate hardware and software requirements

      Perform functionality test/prototype

      Prepare test environment for tool evaluation

      Select and build portion of data model for testing

      Obtain test data

      Build functionality test/prototype

      Conduct tests

      Document results

      Analyze results and make recommendation

      Purchase product

      Train developers

Figure 5.4 Tasks for design.

Table 5.3 Primary Objectives for Phase 3

PRIMARY OBJECTIVES
Do the dimensional modeling to create the clickstream data warehouse database schema and review it with the end users.
Analyze the source systems and source data to determine more detailed extract, transformation, and load needs, and identify and document data problems in detail.
Define the overall system architecture and review it with the core project team.
Identify, evaluate, and procure any products required to build the clickstream warehouse.
Document the high-level analytic application requirements and define a test plan for use during the development phase.

Lessons Learned the Hard Way

Don't Skimp on the Training

For most companies, building a clickstream warehouse involves a number of new technologies. If you don't have dimensional modeling skills on your core team then you should consider hiring consultants with this background to help. Regardless of who is doing the work, be sure to train everyone on the core team in the basics of dimensional modeling. It will save a lot of grief during development if the entire team understands the basics.

It's also essential to train the core project team in the fundamentals of Web technologies and Web data. If nothing else, have them read Chapters 1 through 4 of this book so they understand general Web architecture issues, user identity mechanisms, and problematic data elements.

In most clickstream data warehouses you will purchase at least one new product, and probably more than one. With almost every purchase you should add in the training costs for at least two members of the project team. By training two people you reduce the risk of a crisis should anything happen to one person. We've also found that sending staff in groups of two or more greatly increases the effectiveness of the training they receive, because of the mutual learning synergy.

Cutting corners on training is money that is almost never truly saved. The costs are added on in hidden ways, usually in the form of mistakes that require rework later in the project. Rework is the single biggest contributor to project delays. Besides, most team members will welcome the opportunity to improve their skills, and good morale makes team members more effective.

Know Your Web Technology Fundamentals

As mentioned above, project team data modelers must understand the Web technologies used in the Web site before designing the schema. Without that understanding, it is extremely difficult to identify problems or limitations with the site-generated data as it is mapped into the clickstream warehouse schema. We cover much of the necessary information in Chapters 1 through 4.

Schema Design Hints

Since the schema encapsulates answers to the questions users are asking, it forms the core of the clickstream data warehouse. While the next chapter describes a meta-schema that we use as a design template for all clickstream warehouse schemas, we have a number of additional design hints listed below:

- When creating the logical schema, imagine the perfect world and design for that. Then compromise with reality.

- Building a set of very rich attributes for each dimension is a good thing.

- Provide definitions for all of the data. It is very easy for users to interpret data in ways different than you anticipated. The term *sales* to one group will not necessarily mean the same thing to another group. Your published definitions will serve to highlight different interpretations between users. It is your job to facilitate the process of defining terms, but it is the end users who have to agree to the correct definition. If the definitional problems are not solved then the data warehouse will lose credibility when the first user misinterprets data.

- Prototype the schema design and play 20 questions with it. Show it to your users before it's finalized and see if there are questions they ask that you can't answer.

- The logical schema is not set in stone once it is completed. There will almost certainly be data problems that do not appear until you actually try to extract the data. The analysis tools will have special schema requirements for things like aggregates and OLAP analysis. Be prepared to support schema changes once the application developers start working in earnest.

- Creating only a data model is not enough. You must define how to handle dimension updates, fact table updates, changes to history, slowly changing dimensions, and how you will correct production data in the warehouse. If you leave this work until later, you may end up with major schema changes that disrupt application and ETL development.

Buyer Beware

A data warehouse project is, at its core, a complex systems integration project. While it is possible to buy off-the-shelf products to support different clickstream analysis tasks, there is no single product that will meet all of your needs. If you are building a clickstream data warehouse then you have chosen to build an information delivery infrastructure that can support many different analytic and Web application packages. This means that the architect must be familiar with many different tools, technologies, and design techniques. This is especially true when dealing with Web analytic and business intelligence software vendors, who will promise the world and then leave your neck in the noose.

Be wary of vendors trying to sell you the kitchen sink. Vendors of Web analytics who say they provide everything you need with their product—for example, personalization, promotion measurement, profiling, and reporting all in one—simply can't do it. The biggest problem with most of this software is that it is great at meeting a specific need like campaign management, customer segmentation, or identifying cross-selling opportunities. To make more money the vendor adds new modules. When they try to featurize the original product like this you inevitably run into problems. We like to say, "Pasting feathers on a chicken doesn't make it a peacock."

Even worse, many products are usually built with a closed data architecture that makes any use outside of the original features a nightmare. Some vendors like Personify and BroadVision embed database or OLAP engines directly into their products in the hopes that you will use them as a substitute for an enterprise clickstream data warehouse, which they are not. Others use a relational database like Oracle or DB2 but do not provide any documentation on the database design. Using these products as the base instead of doing your own schema design, or customizing them to meet your analytic needs, is often fruitless. Our experience has been that companies have the most success when they buy these products for their strength in a particular area, but don't use them as the database foundation for underlying analytics or data delivery.

In regard to ETL applications, it is important to closely examine their fit with your particular requirements. We've noticed that the current crop of data extract products have difficulty with Web log files. The vendors say they can process Web log files, but few do more than rudimentary file extraction. Inter-record processing is rare, yet this is one of the more important aspects of log extraction. Our experience on both non-Web and clickstream data warehouses is that many ETL products are available, yet most companies do their own ETL code because of the high cost of most products. Chapter 8 of this book covers clickstream ETL in great detail.

Don't Neglect the Architecture

Third-party software makes up components of the clickstream warehouse, but third-party software is not the system architecture. Instead, the data warehouse architect defines what services the warehouse will provide and how it will operate. The architectural design should avoid specifying vendor products early in the design cycle. The whole idea of a data warehouse architecture is that it is vendor-neutral so that you can properly evaluate your options for implementation. Once the *what* and *how* are defined, you have a framework for product selection within that architecture.

Clickstream data warehouses create new difficulties for the architect because the source data comes from a Web site built with unfamiliar technologies not used by more traditional business transaction systems that might also be connected to the warehouse. The architect must accommodate both the traditional database applications and the newer Web technologies in order to make everything work. Because of the added complexity more systems integration issues will crop up than you expect.

From an architectural perspective, the clickstream data warehouse is really a set of processing components. There are components that extract data from various sources, components that transform data, others that validate and load data, and more to deliver data. One important aspect that is often missed by inexperienced architects is the coordination of this processing.

Some processing is dependent on successful completion of other processing. For other parts of the system, there are no dependencies. If you have large data volumes or particularly complex processing, there may be competition for system resources at specific times. Some warehouses we've seen had terrific ETL designs and great query applications, but suffered outages several times a week because the architect did not put enough thought into a framework for handling interprocess dependencies and exception handling.

The lesson we've learned is that you have to pay attention to the architecture early in the project, and you have to involve the entire team when doing it. Data warehouse design is multidisciplinary. The project requires an architect with a broad knowledge base. But it also requires that other members of the core team contribute in their areas of expertise.

Design for Operation and Maintenance

Our last note about this phase is to design the system for smooth operation. If it takes specialized skills to resolve every problem that arises then neither you nor your users will be happy. The key to designing for smooth operation is twofold: Keep the system as simple as possible, and involve the people who will be administering the system.

Design simplicity should be a goal in all software development. Simplicity is often neglected with data warehouse projects because a set of off-the-shelf products is used. The trade-off made by the project manager and the architect in this case is usually development time and cost versus product price. The trouble is that maintenance costs are ignored in the product purchase decisions. Often it is simpler and easier to maintain a system that uses fewer software packages. Although many of these products are industrial strength, they can be so complex that only laboriously trained developers can work with them.

Many projects forget about the people who will be administering the system once development is complete. Administration tends to get lost in the flurry of activity to build the system. If you involve the system administrators, database administrators, and whoever will be the warehouse administrator during system design you will smooth the way during deployment. You will also find that most administrators have a lot of detailed knowledge that can save the project from serious trouble during development.

Phase 4: Data Warehouse Implementation

In the implementation phase, all the design work is translated it into a working clickstream data warehouse. During the design phase the project is relatively simple to manage because the number of people involved is still relatively low, but during implementation the project team will probably double in size. The developers will be working on concurrent development tracks, so each track remains manageable. However, many projects, particularly larger projects, run into trouble with communication between people working on the different implementation tracks.

Each track within the project has its own focus and deliverables. It is up to the project manager and architect to make sure that all components of the system line up when each track is completed. Managing a project at this stage is similar to managing any large systems integration project, so we won't belabor this point.

This phase will be the most time-consuming part of the project. Implementation makes up between 60 and 70 percent of a typical project schedule. One thing to note is that the more time you spend up front on the requirements and design, the less time you will spend in implementation. We saw this firsthand with two virtually identical projects in competing retailers. The first project took nine months to complete while the second took 16 months. The single biggest factor was the second company's philosophy. They believed that they could "save time by doing more programming and less documentation of stuff we're going to program anyway," which was a direct quote from the person negotiating the budget with the project manager.

We recommend forcing integration frequently as part of an iterative development cycle. This has the benefit of uncovering problems earlier, particularly when the integration is across project tracks. We also insist on a strict unit, system, and integration testing schedule during development.

Summary of Implementation Tasks and Objectives

The project plan for the data warehouse implementation phase in Figure 5.5 below shows each group of tasks for each track separately, and shows tasks in a linear order. The reality is that development of some items will not follow a linear flow from beginning to end. For example, when developing applications it will often be necessary to prototype reports or interfaces and cycle back and forth with the users before the final version is created.

One thing that is usually done first is setup of the development environment. The systems, database, and development software and any client software must be installed and tested. This often takes longer than expected, mostly due to drawn out purchasing negotiations and underestimating the time it takes to properly set up hardware. Once a working environment is present, everyone can split up and work on their individual tasks.

The next step is for the data modelers and the database administrator to translate the dimensional data model into a physical database design. Database sizing is calculated based on data storage, indexing, and optimization strategies and data aggregation requirements. You will usually have a number of databases for development so that different groups can avoid stepping on each other as they work.

Within this phase, the ETL tasks are typically the most time-consuming and resource intensive in the entire project. Assembling data from multiple systems that have little relation to one another and pulling it into a consistent view is a complex development task. The developers must map all of the data from the dimensional model back to the data sources and determine how to extract the data. Once the data is extracted there will be many processing steps to match and transform data elements, correct data quality problems, and load the cleansed data into the data warehouse. Since this is a task repeated on at least a daily level, the processes must be designed and built for easy automation.

Separating development tasks for dimension tables and fact tables as shown in Figure 5.5 may not be possible in a clickstream data warehouse environment.

While most traditional data warehouse extraction works in this fashion, a clickstream data warehouse adds an area of complexity. The clickstream data is normally in a single set of log files, yet it forms the basis of a number of fact and dimension tables. This means the ETL developers are often working on several different extracts from the same log files simultaneously. You'll need to consider this when creating your own project plan.

The reports or analytic applications usually can't be developed until a preliminary warehouse database is up and running. This database is often filled with sample data that was extracted during the design phase for data analysis purposes. While reports and applications are being developed, the person responsible for training should be documenting them. The creation of training materials and a training plan is also part of this phase.

The final steps in implementation are integration testing and data reconciliation. All parts of the system should have been running together during development, so integration tests ought to be a formality. The idea of "big bang" testing on a project with a long timeline is not something we recommend.

During data reconciliation, data modelers and application developers must make sure that what they are currently reporting matches any information the end users already receive by other means. If there are mismatches, it is important to determine the reason. More than half the time the data warehouse is correct, so be prepared to explain the differences, but be careful. Data reconciliation often creates conflicts in the organization. A lot of ego can be tied up in the old information and systems that provide it.

The tasks for phase 4 are listed in Figure 5.5, and the primary objectives are listed in Table 5.4.

Table 5.4 Primary Objectives for Phase 4

PRIMARY OBJECTIVES
Put the entire warehouse infrastructure—servers, software, and process management—in place.
Identify all of the major data problems and resolve them or alter the scope of data in the warehouse and document the problems for later resolution.
Build all of the back-end data warehouse components.
Develop all of the end-user applications.
Integrate and test the entire clickstream data warehouse.
Reconcile differences between information provided by other systems and the clickstream warehouse.

Phase 4: Data Warehouse Implementation

ARCHITECTURE AND INFRASTRUCTURE TRACK

Create Project Development Environment

Install & configure development hardware

Install & configure development software

Create development databases

Configure environment for developers

Design and Implement Process Automation Framework

Design and implement job scheduling and dependency mechanism

Design and implement problem notification and reporting mechanism

Integrate with ETL and client components where applicable

Design and Implement Backup and Restore Process

Determine backup/restore volume, frequency, retention, and growth requirements

Determine backup/restore approach

Select and acquire backup software and hardware

Install and configure backup software and hardware

DATA AND DATABASE TRACK

Physical Schema Design

Document database development standards

Determine partitioning strategy

Determine indexing strategy

Determine aggregation strategy

Determine database-level data security requirements

Review data access tool schema requirements

Update schema design document

Development Database Implementation

Configure development and test databases

Create warehouse schema

Assign physical names

Assign data types and sizes

Assign null options

Determine keys

Determine indexes

Determine partitioning

Identify and extract/create sample data for development use

Load sample data

Implement database-level security requirements

Figure 5.5 Tasks for system implementation.   *(continued)*

Phase 4: Data Warehouse Implementation *(Continued)*

High-level ETL Design

    Design and document architecture for extract, transformation, cleansing, staging, and loading data

    Define historical data needs and data retention requirements

    Define one-time history extract approach

    Define incremental extract and load approach

    Design program error and exceptional handling processes

    Prioritize dimension and fact table ETL development

    Create ETL test plan

    ETL design review

Dimension Table ETL Design and Development

    Perform following tasks for each dimension table, history extract may need to be separate set of tasks

    Document detailed source data mapping and transformations

    Develop data extraction routines

    Define source system interfaces

    Design extract process scheduling

    Design and develop extract programs

    Develop data transformation and cleansing routines

    Develop staging and loading routines

    Develop maintenance process for dimension

    Integrate into process automation framework

Fact Table ETL Design and Development

    Perform following tasks for each fact table, history extract may need to be separate set of tasks

    Document detailed source data mapping and transformations

    Develop data extraction routines

    Define source system interfaces

    Design extract process scheduling

    Design and develop extract programs

    Develop data transformation and cleansing routines

    Develop staging and loading routines

    Develop maintenance process for dimension

    Integrate into process automation framework

Data Administration

    Define warehouse data quality rules

    Design and build warehouse data QA routines

Figure 5.5 Tasks for system implementation.   *(continued)*

Phase 4: Data Warehouse Implementation (Continued)

Integrate with data load and process automation framework

Design and build data archival process

Create data reconciliation plan

Aggregate Design and Development

Design and develop aggregate creation process

Design and develop aggregate management process

Determine initial aggregate tables

APPLICATION TRACK

Application Design and Development

Prioritize initial reports/applications

Create detailed specifications for each report/application

Identify business measures, metrics, formulas

Determine standard formulas

Determine default summarization rules

Prototype report/application

Review specifications and prototypes with pilot users

Complete development of reports/applications

Validate report/application results

Performance testing and tuning

Application Management

Create user training materials

Create user training plan

Document application administration procedures

SYSTEM INTEGRATION

Integration Testing

Assemble all back-end product and custom ETL programs

Execute ETL test plan

Assemble all end-user/analytical applications

Execute application test plan

Run history data load

Execute data reconciliation plan for historical data

Run incremental data load

Execute data reconciliation plan for incremental data

Run entire data warehouse process from load to query

Validate results

Figure 5.5 Tasks for system implementation.

Lessons Learned the Hard Way

Pay Attention to Project Communication

One of the hardest activities to do well is communication. There are many things happening every day, and it may seem like people are talking to one another. Unfortunately, people may not be interacting with the right counterpart or may not be talking about the right things. The project manager and the architect both need to keep checking people's assumptions about their tasks and the implementation of their components.

One approach we've found effective is to circulate through the different areas of the project throughout the day and talk to people about details of the tasks they are working on. Moving from one person to another like this helps to build up a picture of the project and get a feel for how everything is going. Many times we find out that someone is having difficulty. In some cases the problem can easily be resolved by a quick conversation with the right people. Resolving problems this way avoids large team meetings to review progress and try to solve too many problems at one time.

That brings up project delays. Projects get to be six months late one day at a time. It's rare to have a single problem add six months to the schedule. It's common to have a problem that adds a few days to the project. It's also common to hear the project manager or developer say, "We can make that up pretty easily." Except that some other problem invariably adds a couple more days somewhere else. All those short delays eventually add up to one big problem. Getting out and talking to everyone for a few minutes per day can catch a lot of these things before they get out of control.

Frequent internal communication will also help you keep tabs on morale. When morale is low, there is often a cause. Many times the cause is simply poor communication. The worst example of this was a project in the insurance industry we worked on a few years ago.

We were called in because the project was behind schedule and there were technical problems. The first thing we noted was that the people working on the three different development tracks were each in a separate office, and the doors between them were always closed. After talking to the folks in each room we found that each group was behind on their tasks, they were having different unrelated problems and morale was terrible. After two weeks of informal conversations and long lunch discussions, the technical work and morale was far better. The core problem was effective communication between each of the groups. All that was required to get the project back on track was some work with the project manager and the architect on communication techniques and a change in how people shared offices. Not only did the project get back on track, it later won an industry Best Practices award for technical innovation!

The project team isn't the only focus of communication. You also need to make sure that there is a strong rapport with the Web development side of the house. Given the state of flux most Web sites are in, you have to pay attention to what those developers are doing and planning to do. You need advance warning of any impending Web site changes, whether technical or content. If you don't have that advance knowledge, your project can be totally derailed.

Beyond the development team, you need to keep everyone informed of project progress. In essence, you are marketing the project to the rest of the organization. Good marketing never hurts a project. Not only does the external communication serve to manage expectations, it also keeps people's egos in check.

More Little Milestones Are Better than Fewer Big Milestones

When building the project plan for the implementation phase, incorporate lots of milestones along the way. It's easier to look back and see progress when you can point to a number of accomplishments. The team's morale is better when they see a number of mileposts behind them. We help things along by celebrating the major milestones along the way. Socializing is a good way to keep people energized, with the nice side effect of improving team communication.

Our term for the milestones on projects that only have a few is "gravestones." It's hard to maintain morale and productivity when everyone has already been working for months on a milestone and there are still months to go before completion.

Use an Iterative Development Cycle

Reading through the chapter so far you may have gotten the impression that we don't believe in iterative development because we're so design heavy. That really isn't so—we just believe in knowing what we're building before we start work. The design phase doesn't spell everything out in gory detail. It provides the framework within which everyone has to develop. Detailed program design happens during development.

We've found that the best way to develop on these projects, particularly end-user applications, is to iterate. Users usually can't tell you exactly what they do want, but they can tell you what they don't want and what they like once you show them something. You should leverage this during application development. Design your application development approach to iterate not monthly, but as close to weekly as possible. This makes application development move forward much more smoothly and gives visibility to people outside the project.

While the application track is moving along, the heavy lifting on the back end is also underway. Iterative development applies equally to the data-processing tasks. There are so many complexities in this area that one of the easiest ways to address them is to use an iterative approach. The only thing to keep in mind is that iterative development doesn't replace architecture. You need a framework in place to provide the necessary structure within which development can cycle.

Not having the structure provided by an architecture gives the individual too much freedom and can leave developers feeling lost. Most people have an intrinsic need for some level of structure and discipline. Freedom for developers is important, but only within a larger framework. Set developers loose prior to having the architecture defined and you'll end up with a shantytown instead of that skyscraper you were supposed to build.

Expect Changes to the Design

Requirements gathering is never 100 percent accurate and no enterprise is static, so design is always working with some areas that are either missed or misunderstood. You may need to modify the schema, code that's already been written, or even the architecture. Don't resist making changes, even potentially severe ones. Flexibility is one of the values of iterative development.

Expect changes in your data. As we've mentioned many times, the clickstream is an unstable data source, changing as the Web site design and technology changes. Also, remember that data access tools affect the schema design. You should add time into the project plan for changes to the design that are forced upon you by the tools or applications you are using. For example, your original schema design may have been a standard star schema, but the tool you eventually selected requires a snowflake model instead. There's no way you could have anticipated this prior to the product selection.

Getting Historical Data Is Different

It is very unlikely that the clickstream data warehouse went live the same day its corresponding Web site went live. This means that there is a past history of Web log file data that needs to be loaded into the clickstream warehouse when the warehouse is created. Due to the extreme size of many historical data streams, extract and load processing for historical data is often quite different from routine daily ETL processing. In many cases the historical data will be archived, adding to extract and load complexity. Moreover, the format of the log file data sources may have changed over time or log data may be from systems built on completely different technology than the current Web platform.

That means the ETL developers probably need to build two separate ETL components, one for history and one for daily extracts and loads. Bear in mind that history extracts can sometimes be so complex they double the amount of time needed for ETL development.

Use Real Data to Develop End-User Applications

Whenever possible, load real data into the database used by your application developers. Sample data created by developers is always too optimistic. No matter how much source data analysis you do, there will be anomalies. The sooner you have real data in the application development database, the sooner you will find the data problems. The sooner you identify the data problems, the sooner you can pass that information over to the ETL developers.

If at all possible, try to work with a few end users who have some knowledge of the data and who are enthusiastic about the project. They will probably spot data problems even better than the developers. Just make sure they aren't abused—they have jobs they're trying to get done and are hoping your system will solve those problems. If you throw too much at them they may burn out, and that's the last thing you want to do to the users.

There Are Always Data Problems

Problems with the source data are a normal part of implementation. All data warehouse projects encounter them. There are several different types of problems and you'll doubtless encounter all of them. Nonexistent data is usually the first problem encountered.

In most cases, the majority of nonexistent data problems are highlighted during the schema design and data mapping tasks. What often trips people up is that data should be in a source system, but it takes the ETL work to uncover the fact that the transaction system isn't actually capturing the data described in that system's data model. Fortunately, nonexistent data problems are usually found during the first analysis of clickstream data, making it easier to resolve than many similar problems in business transaction systems.

Dirty data in all its innumerable forms is what most people imagine when they hear "data problems" mentioned. The one constant on all data warehouse projects is that you will find problems with source data. In some cases, the cause of the dirty data has been lingering for years. Problems with the relatively new clickstream data are also common. We mentioned some of these in Chapter 3 in the section titled "Realities of Log File Data." The book *Improving Data Warehouse and Business Information Quality* by Larry English is also a worthy read on the subject of data quality issues and resolution.

Validation of data as it is loaded into the warehouse is a normal part of the ETL process. This is true even if the source system is validating its own data. One of the primary rules of data quality is "Data is only as clean as its most rigorous use," which means that rarely used or unused data from some of your sources is almost guaranteed to be problematic.

Since every project runs into data quality problems, it is always a good idea to plan for some extra time on the ETL track. When it comes to timelines, this part of the project is the most frequently underestimated. A big reason is unfounded optimism regarding the quality of the data loaded into the clickstream data warehouse.

It is a good idea to put a data reconciliation task into the project plan after integration testing. We always reconcile data with that reported by other means because so many problems can sneak through the ETL process. When users get their first data from the clickstream warehouse they are likely to compare it to what they received in the past. Nothing makes them lose faith in the data warehouse faster than poor data integrity.

Phase 5: Deployment

The deployment phase is often neglected in our haste to get the clickstream data warehouse project out the door. Many projects assume that training users on the analytical applications and giving them access to the warehouse is sufficient. Unfortunately this only works well on paper, particularly if the users have not had much experience with online analysis.

The key to trouble-free deployment is planning. Prior to the actual deployment you must determine how client software will be delivered, how users will be trained on the data and applications, and how you will support those users when the system is put into production. Good user support processes created ahead of time can head off problems before they become serious. This will generate goodwill among your users, and happy users are a critical element in a successful project.

The technique we recommend for deploying a clickstream data warehouse is to do a pilot deployment first. This is normally done with a small number of users. The idea is to involve some users who are power users, some who are novices, and one or two critics of the project. A representative sample like this helps iron out training and support problems as well as technical issues. You might ask, Why a critic? Critics provide many complaints and make you look at what you are doing in a different light, even if you don't always agree with what they are saying. Sometimes the points they bring up can make a big difference in end-user acceptance.

On large projects, the approach to the pilot can be different. It's often wise to divide the entire project into parts, with each part delivering enough information to be usable to a single group of users. Then you can build and deploy each part of the project in turn. This provides valuable feedback before the entire system is set in stone and reduces risk. One of the problems of delivering a large project to users all at once is that everyone has been waiting for the system and building up their expectations. A single problem can alienate most of the user base very quickly.

Once the system is full deployed, there will still be a shakeout period where various data, application, and performance problems are corrected. When the end users incorporate the system into their daily routine, you know you've been successful. Then, based on their usage, new requirements will appear. When this happens it's time to loop back and start developing the next iteration of the project.

Summary of Deployment Tasks and Objectives

The system deployment phase starts with planning and documentation. If you want your warehouse to launch quickly and efficiently then diligent planning and documentation will help you get there.

Documentation efforts at this point are focused mostly on the care and feeding of the data warehouse and client applications. It's important that the system administrators, DBAs, warehouse administrators, and user-support staff have all of the required information assembled prior to the launch. Most of the time, the development team is doing the support and administration work at deployment. The problem with skipping this step comes after the system is live and people less familiar with the system take over system operations.

A big part of the work effort during deployment is installing and configuring all the hardware, software, and applications that make up the production system. Hopefully you were able to do most of the development on your production hardware, making this work a lot easier. If so, more time is spent taking development-related items off the existing production system than putting new items onto new production systems.

After everything is installed and configured, you have to load all of the data into the system. This process can take an afternoon or may take weeks. It depends on how complex the processing is and how much data history must be loaded. The final step in system installation is running through a full backup cycle. It's surprising how many times there are problems with backups. It is best to work through those problems prior to going live.

As we mentioned earlier, the deployment to end users really starts with a pilot deployment. This process might be as short as a week or as long as a month. It all depends on the complexity of the system and the number of users you have. During the pilot phase there is a lot of personal contact between the clickstream warehouse developers and the users to identify problems and help the users learn their applications.

After obtaining feedback from pilot users, the project team must decide how much will be changed and estimate how long the changes will take. While the modifications are made, the final scheduling for full-scale deployment can be done. The final task is to perform an acceptance test, although some organizations do not do this for in-house applications. We find it useful even in these situations because it marks a definite end to the development phase, although not to the project.

You must plan for a postdeployment phase where users will still require a lot of support. Once everyone is acclimated to the new system and has incorporated it into their work process they will start to come up with requests for new data or applications. A final part of the project is the definition of how the organization will incorporate requests for new applications or information, and setting up the maintenance staff for the system as it grows.

All of these tasks are outlined in Figure 5.6. In Table 5.5 you will find a list of the primary objectives for the deployment phase.

Lessons Learned the Hard Way

Don't Ignore Warehouse Operations

Clickstream data warehouse management issues are often given cursory attention because the focus of the project is on development of the system. There are a great many procedures that should be documented while development is under way.

Table 5.5 Primary Objectives for Phase 5

PRIMARY OBJECTIVES
Create written documentation for the clickstream warehouse management tasks and procedures.
Configure the final production environment and document the capacity planning that was done to accommodate growth.
Conduct a pilot deployment to find problems and obtain user feedback.
Deploy the system to all of the users.
Set up the processes and procedures for postdeployment maintenance and future development.

Phase 5: Deployment

Deployment Planning

    Create warehouse operation and administration manual

    Define problem user-support procedures

    Define performance management procedures

    Document system administration procedures

    Document database administration procedures

    Document application administration procedures

    Document user and application setup procedures

    Identify pilot users

    Identify all remaining production users

    Create pilot and full-scale deployment plan

    Review Plan

Create Production Environment

    Validate proposed hardware and software configuration

    Complete site plan and site preparation

    Install and configure production hardware

    Install and configure production software

    Install and configure custom software

    Determine database storage requirements

    Storage layout and configuration

    Create production database

    Document production system configuration

    Establish administrator and user access

    Configure production backups

    Create production process schedule

        Enter ETL batch schedule

        Enter aggregate management schedule

        Enter DBA batch schedule

        Enter backup schedule

Data Warehouse Creation and Validation

    Load all data

    Create indexes

    Create aggregates

    Validate data

    Run systems tests

Figure 5.6 Tasks for system deployment. *(continued)*

Phase 5: Deployment *(Continued)*

      Conduct volume and stress tests

      Test production backups

Pilot Deployment

    Install client software for pilot users

    Install client applications for pilot users

    Train pilot users

    Provide users with login/access

    Coaching/one-on-one training

    Obtain user feedback

    Make appropriate system modifications

      Data

      Applications

      Performance

Full-Scale Deployment

    Schedule access to client workstations for remaining users

    Install client software for remaining users

    Install client applications for pilot users

    Train users

    Provide users with login/access

    Coaching/one-on-one training

    Conduct system acceptance test

Postdeployment Activities

    Provide ongoing maintenance and support

    Adjust project steering committee

    Define postdeployment application development and release process

    Continue with new application development efforts

For example, the production system will need a backup plan. Given the amount of clickstream data generated, it is possible that system administrators and DBAs have never done backups of this size before. In some of the retail systems we've seen, a full clickstream data warehouse backup is equal in size to all of the backups for the other enterprise systems combined. The operators must learn a new set of backup procedures for the clickstream data warehouse.

Apart from the platform and database administration tasks, you must consider how to handle crises such as source system downtime that stops your production schedule or a user report of bad data. Handling these problems and questions can easily bog down developers when the warehouse goes live. Thinking about what might go wrong and setting up a process to deal with it ahead of time will go a long way toward ensuring smooth deployment.

Performance monitoring is another area that will require attention early in the deployment, particularly if the database is large. It sometimes takes the combined skills of a system administrator, DBA, and application developer to diagnose the trouble and arrive at the quickest solution. As users get familiar with the system their usage patterns will change. This means that system performance will continue to be an issue, so somebody should be assigned the responsibility of handling complaints and working on them. Very often this will fall to the DBA, which is why every clickstream data warehouse project should have a DBA directly involved in development tasks.

Train the Users One Step at a Time

Typically users are trained once on a particular analytical tool and then let loose on the system. This is one of the worst ways to deploy a data warehouse to end users. Training should be a three-step process.

1. First, train them on the data. The users should be familiar with what is in the warehouse, what is not in the warehouse, and where they can go for questions if they aren't sure about something. Most organizations will have to make some accommodations to the new data warehouse, particularly in the area of metrics and data definitions. People often get into trouble when they use metrics from a prior system, only to discover later that the formula for that metric has changed slightly. Training users on the data minimizes these difficulties.

2. The second step is to train the users on the basic mechanics of their particular tools. Since they already have a basic understanding of the data, they will be able to do basic analysis and reporting pretty quickly.

3. The third step in user training is more difficult and is often not done. Train the users on how to use the data provided to get their particular job done—that is, show the users how to analyze data in the warehouse that will solve one of their specific problems. Some people are not used to having a wealth of data to work from, and they get overwhelmed. Others don't know how to change the way they work, or don't want to. The business requirements document comes in handy at this point, because you can take business problems from there and show how to apply data from the clickstream warehouse to solve them. If you approach training in this way you will have a much more successful adoption.

A mistake that many projects make is training users too early. Hold off training until the client applications and the data are ready. It's much better to train on the real data rather than on a subset or manufactured data. We usually hold off training the users so there is no gap between the time they are trained and the time they start working with the system. One useful technique is to give access to users only after they've completed the training. This way, everyone is trained and the training can be put to use immediately.

Expect to train users more than once. It may take two or three times before it sinks in for some people. They also may have a better grasp of the context after they've struggled with it for a while. It often pays to schedule advanced training that demonstrates more complex features or data use after the system has been running for a few months. The more sophisticated users will be glad to receive advanced training and it maintains the interaction between the users and the data warehouse support staff.

Good Support Will Pay for Itself

Bad experiences early in the deployment will cause users to avoid the data warehouse. Incorrect data or application problems are frustrating and are an unproductive use of time. If users become too negative, they will find alternatives to using the clickstream data warehouse. If usage is difficult, end users often ask the data warehouse project team do their analyses, defeating the proper, user-based usage and discovery model of a clickstream data warehouse.

This can be avoided by testing as much as possible before deployment, then making sure that users know who to call for various types of problems. You don't want to call the DBA with an application question, for example, so think about who will be taking the calls. A quick response is another make-or-break item. The problem may not be resolved immediately, but getting back to the person with an acknowledgment can make a big difference.

Another technique is to provide a short period of coaching or one-on-one training to end users after they've been through the normal training and had a chance to try things out. This approach has the side effect of building a relationship between the support staff and end users. It may also help cut down on support calls because the user worked through tasks specific to their job rather than generic examples from a class. These users are also more likely to answer questions from their coworkers, saving the support staff from some of the easily answered questions that take up their time.

Plan for Growth

Just because the clickstream data warehouse is up and running doesn't mean development work is finished. Once people start using the system in earnest, they will discover new questions they can't answer with the existing data. This leads to a new round of requests for more development.

For example, a distributor we worked with put a sales margin analysis system in place. As they identified items that sold well online versus offline, they were able to adjust what was offered online and offline. A few months later this led to questions about the impact of out-of-stock conditions on the online and offline sales. Inventories were not part of the original scope, so new data and new applications were built onto the warehouse to handle these questions. As each business problem was solved, a new one popped up to replace it. This is the sign of a successful clickstream data warehouse project. The nature of analytic systems is that they are never done. If there are no new business questions then the business itself is stagnating.

This means that the project should prepare for new growth once the initial system is in place. As new development requests come in, they should be justified and balanced against other requests. After they've been prioritized, the project team starts with business requirements analysis and goes through all of the project phases again. The big difference is that now there is a complete data analysis infrastructure in place that makes new development much more rapid. You will still need some of the same staff, or equally skilled staff, to work on future development efforts. Disbanding the entire project team after the initial implementation is a mistake.

Project Staffing and Organization

Data warehouse projects require a wide variety of skills and experience. Different skills will be needed during different phases in the project. The rarity of finding a single person with the full range of skills makes staffing a challenge.

To be more effective when staffing the project, keep a few considerations in mind. The technology underlying the Web site will have an impact. If most of the clickstream data generated by the site can be extracted directly from Web server logs, your need of Web development skills on the team will be relatively low. If the Web site is built on special tools like an application server or e-commerce platform then there will be more complex data extraction issues requiring more detailed knowledge on the part of the ETL developers.

The skills and experience of the individual team members is not as important as getting the right mix of people and skills. If the team is working well together then people with the right skills for a task will be able to guide those who are less familiar. The best thing to look for is flexibility and a mix of technical knowledge, with some emphasis on database development. People who are more flexible and adaptable will fit better with this type of project, where requirements can't always be met in the way originally envisioned and odd problems crop up more often than with transaction-processing systems.

The most important aspect of these projects is focus on the business and user requirements. The project manager and the project lead should have a grasp of business problems and appreciate how nontechnical staff members accomplish their jobs. The business focus is an essential bridge between the needs of the end users and the system that is ultimately developed. The more business-oriented the project team is, the more likely the project will succeed.

To make staffing the project easier to understand, this section is organized into three parts. It starts with a discussion of the different *project roles* that must be filled by the project team, then discusses two potential *project organization* charts, and concludes with some advice on *project staffing*. Some of the information in this section is derived from material originally presented in *The Data Warehouse Lifecycle Toolkit* by Ralph Kimball, et al.

Project Roles

Since clickstream data warehouse projects are so complex, they have quite a few roles. Some of these roles are important at different phases, whereas others carry through the entire project from beginning to end. Don't worry about the large number of roles listed here. Each role does not translate into an individual on the project team. Rather, team members will fulfill a number of roles throughout the project. The idea is to give a flavor of the types of skills needed on the team and what knowledge is required by a given set of tasks.

Project Manager. The role of the project manager is almost always a full time role since it entails the day-to-day management of the project. The project manager is responsible for the coordination of all resources on the project, managing the schedule and budget, handling change control and issue resolution, as well as coordination with third-party partners.

The project manager also must have good writing skills. A data warehouse project produces more documentation than most other types of projects. Also, the documentation is usually aimed at the end users, unlike many of the more technical documents produced by other types of projects.

The ideal project manager has excellent communication skills and the ability to handle some of the political challenges the project will face. Apart from the normal range of project communications, the project manager is often involved in the requirements gathering effort. Working with the business analyst and supporting the requirements-gathering process will be required.

Project Sponsors. There are actually several varieties of project sponsor. The true sponsors are the business owners of the project and are usually the ones paying for the project. There are also *drivers*—people who work on the business side and have a more direct stake in the outcome of the project. It is typically they or their staff who will be using the output of the warehouse, and who have helped determine the project's business case. All of these people help define the project scope, prioritize work, and sell the use of the system to the organization. When problems arise that are partly or mostly business issues, such as forcing the adoption of key metrics and definitions, they will be the ones that make it happen.

Project sponsors are normally at a senior level within the organization and have the authority to get business staff, in particular the end users, involved with the project. The best sponsors have a vision of how the organization will make use of the information provided by the data warehouse so that everyone is working toward a clear goal.

Business User/Business Lead. This role represents the business users and works with the project manager as needed. In some organizations there will be an explicit business lead who meets with the project manager on a daily basis and participates in some of the project tasks. The business lead role is rarely a full-time role on the project. This is not to be confused with the many end users who will be interviewed as part of the requirements-gathering phase.

Business Analyst. This is the primary role during the requirements-gathering phase. The business analyst leads the effort and writes up the interview notes and the business requirements document. These projects typically involve interviewing a broad range of users in different departments and at many levels. Therefore, the role demands good interpersonal, verbal, and written communication skills. A technical person with a strong business background and some familiarity with dimensional modeling usually fills this role. Ideally, the business analyst has expertise in the business issues facing the company as well as more broadly within the industry.

Clickstream Warehouse Architect. The architect is responsible for the overall design of the system and supporting infrastructure. This includes ensuring that components of the system are developed according to design and performance specifications. In addition, the architect spearheads the resolution of all the technical issues that arise during the project. The person in this role must have experience and technical depth in database development, programming, and system design. Experience as a database or system administrator is very helpful due to the large size of most of these systems. Key personal attributes are assertiveness and flexibility, as this person will have to deal with developers who may want to stray from the design, or who may come up with better solutions than the architect originally envisioned. This role is often filled by an internal resource paired with a clickstream data warehouse consultant.

Data Modeler. The primary task for the data modeler is to create the logical schema for the clickstream warehouse. To do this the data modeler should have experience with database design and implementation, dimensional modeling, and familiarity with data warehousing techniques. On most projects, the overall data management strategy and the schema design for various extract, transformation, and loading processes will fall to the data modeler in combination with ETL developers. Many projects will combine this role with the database administrator.

Clickstream Warehouse Database Administrator. The DBA is responsible for installing the database, physical schema design, defining the aggregation strategy, and the maintenance of the database. Many of the physical database design decisions require the DBA to understand dimensional modeling almost as well as the data modeler. Without a grasp of why the logical schema is designed as it is, and how this schema design is used, the DBA will have a difficult time creating a physical schema design that works well. If the data modeler is not the same person as the DBA, then the DBA should be involved in the dimensional modeling. Early involvement will make the DBA's job much easier.

Data Extract Transform and Load (ETL) Developer. The ETL programmer is responsible for working with the architect on the ETL designs, and for creating the modules that process and load data into the warehouse database. This role is often filled by staff who are familiar with the source systems and platforms. They also require some knowledge of dimensional modeling in order to correctly process and load the data. If a data extract tool is used then the staff should either be specialists in that tool or receive training before the ETL design task starts. Very often the ETL developers are the first people to uncover data problems, so it is important for them to communicate regularly with other members of the project team.

Application Developer. This role is responsible for creating the various analytic applications for end users. If the organization is purchasing data access tools then they will be involved in this process as well. The application developer should not be a purely technical programmer. The best staff members for this role are those who support end users' information needs today or those who work on the business side as analysts. The role requires an understanding of how users interact with information, so user interface design is a plus, even though many data access tools limit how user interfaces can be created. If any specialized tools are used, like data-mining software for example, then training will likely be required. Many projects will use a mix of internal staff and the tool vendor's consultants during application development.

Source System Expert. The source system expert is a role potentially filled by several people during implementation, depending on the number of data sources involved. The role is responsible for helping with data extraction when it requires more knowledge about a source system than the ETL developer has. Although this is often a make-or-break role during ETL development, it is rarely a full-time role.

Webmaster or Web Application Designer. The Webmaster or Web application developer helps the ETL developers obtain Web data, whether that data is in Web server logs or scattered through several Web applications. This role is also necessary if any changes to the Web site are required, such as creating uniform user identifiers. This is a role that may be filled by a single person or a number of people, depending on how the Web engineering side of the organization is structured.

Trainer. The trainer handles all of the end-user data, tool and application training. Initially this involves assembling the training data, creating documentation on the data and applications, and putting a training plan together. The role requires good verbal and written communication skills. This role is often filled by one of the application developers.

System Administrator. Similar in role to the DBA, the system administrator is responsible for all of the system hardware. This entails sizing the system to meet estimated production workloads, handling procurement, installing, configuring, and maintaining the system. In many organizations, the system administrator during development may be different than the person filling the role when the system is in production. During the project, the system administrator must also work with the architect to define and document the various administrative procedures, and may be involved in some development activities, particularly in the area of process automation.

Clickstream Warehouse Administrator. This role is one that comes just prior to the deployment phase of the project when the system is nearing completion. The warehouse administrator is responsible for tracking the process schedules, handling problem reports, and the general management of the warehouse once it is in production. This role will often be combined with the production DBA's role since the DBA has operational responsibilities as well as involvement in development.

Data Administrator. The role of data administrator is new to many organizations, although those with existing data warehouses may already have a data administrator. On the project, this role is responsible for gaining agreement on the definitions of facts and attributes, managing metadata in the system and tools, and handling data quality issues once the system is in production. A major task after production is keeping track of source system maintenance, including the Web site, so that the ETL process does not run into problems when source systems change.

Project Organization

Equipped with an understanding of the roles, you need to determine how to organize the project team. Organizing the project team is intertwined with staffing issues, which we're saving for later. It will be easiest to start with a generic structure and then modify it based on the expertise and availability of staff for your project.

A generic organization chart for a medium-sized project is shown in Figure 5.7. You can see that there are only 12 positions for the 15 roles we defined. Given so many roles, you need to determine how they will collapse into positions on the project's organization chart. Role assignment depends on the skills of the people you put into these positions.

In this and all of the other organization charts, we show most of the project team reporting to the project manager. This is an administrative reporting relationship only. The project manager must handle the staff management responsibilities while the technical responsibilities fall to the project technical

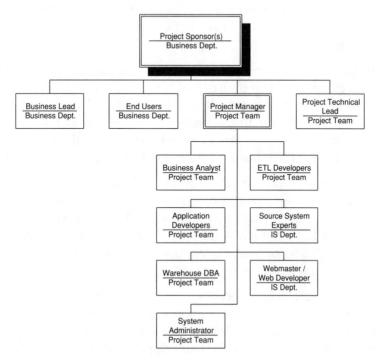

Figure 5.7 Organization chart for an average-sized project.

lead. Many external communication tasks, as well as anything affecting the project scope, budget, or schedule are the responsibility of the project manager. The project technical lead is in control of the design and implementation of the project. The lead typically takes on the role of project architect and is often the primary data modeler. This split in responsibility works well as long as the project manager is flexible when dealing with necessary design or programming changes.

The project manager needs to challenge the project lead if there are any design or programming changes that affect the scope, budget, or schedule. However, the project manager can't use these things as a club to force the project lead to meet unrealistic goals. In the end, the project lead should have the final word on design and implementation. At the same time, the project lead can't try to build the perfect system at the expense of the schedule or budget. This is why both positions report to the project sponsor, who acts as a tiebreaker if there are any major disagreements. We rarely see problems with this kind of reporting structure.

The DBA is the one position that frequently picks up multiple roles. The data administrator and warehouse administrator roles usually fall to the DBA, and sometimes the data modeling as well. As we mentioned before, end-user training is often handled by one of the application developers. Something that we've found works well is to pair the business analyst and application developer when training so that each brings different strengths to bear on the task.

In many smaller projects the business analyst role will be split between the project manager and project lead. On most average to larger-size projects we find that an external consultant fills the role of business analyst. Often a consultant will also be in the project lead position and work together with an internal resource who takes over when the consultant leaves at the end of the project. Figure 5.8 shows a common structure for large projects.

When a project has many data sources, or a large number of applications, the team can become unwieldy. In these cases, a response is to assign a lead developer for the resource intensive tracks in the project. This is shown in the organization chart when the ETL Lead and Application Lead positions have been inserted between the project manager and the developers. This helps the project manager in administration, and helps the project lead with technical management.

Once the project has successfully launched there will be a number of changes. Since a clickstream data warehouse project is really an infrastructure project, the foundation has been laid for building future applications. This means there will be less need for both ETL developers and application developers. A post-deployment organization chart is shown in Figure 5.9.

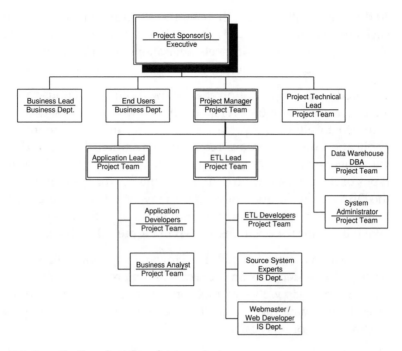

Figure 5.8 Organization chart for a large project.

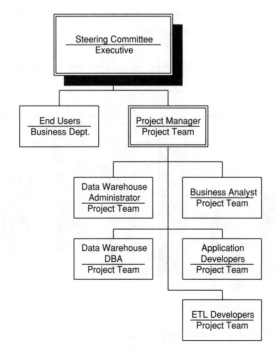

Figure 5.9 Organization chart when in production.

At this stage in the project, there will be a handful of technical staff running the clickstream data warehouse. The project sponsors are normally replaced with a steering committee that meets over a longer period of time, often quarterly, to discuss priorities for new enhancements or additions.

The production organization chart shows both a warehouse administrator and a DBA, as well as two developers. Often, the warehouse administrator role is assigned to either the project manager or, more commonly, the DBA. The application developers are required more often than ETL developers, since many new business requirements are related to new analyses more than new types of data. This can further reduce the size of the maintenance team since the DBA and application developers may be able to handle the ETL tasks. The maintenance team structure will be highly dependent on your organization, so take the number of positions shown in Figure 5.9 with a grain of salt.

One question that we hear a lot is, How many people will we need on the project team? This depends on the scope of the project as well as the project timeline. The projects we've worked on range in size from five or six people to projects involving more than 40 developers, with the most projects being on the lower end of this scale.

Many project managers also want to know when resources are assigned because this affects the lead time to staff the project, as well as the budget and rate at which money is spent. Figure 5.10 shows the staffing level at various phases in the project for our average project in Figure 5.7.

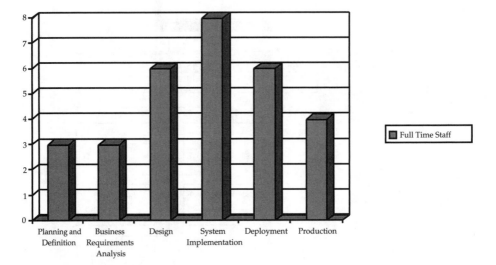

Figure 5.10 Average number of project staff by phase of project.

The chart shows only full-time core team members involved in the project. During the planning and requirements phases, this generally means only the project manager, technical lead, and business analyst are working full time. This chart excludes the part-time involvement of the many people in both IT and end-user departments who will be interviewed.

During the design phase, more resources are added because we often want to start training developers and include them in some of the key design activities, particularly product selection if any third-party software will be purchased.

When development is fully underway the number may be somewhat less than we show. This depends on how you divide some of the tasks, such as defining operational procedures. In some cases, the system administrator and DBA are only involved in a supporting role and work part time on the project. As we said, this is an average case for a midsized company. Many times we've seen the implementation phase have 10 or more people for less than a month, then drop to five or six for the rest of the project.

During deployment you still need most of the developers around to handle any problems or minor change requests. Once the system is in production, the staffing level drops significantly, often to no more than the warehouse administrator or DBA, one or two developers, and the project manager.

Project Staffing

With a general idea of how the project is organized, it makes sense to look at assigning people to the project. We mentioned a number of characteristics to look for when assigning the various roles to members of the project team, and most enterprises already have their own approach to staffing projects. We won't spend a lot of time going over this information, much of which can also be found in project management and team-building books. Instead, we'll close with a few suggestions on the initial positions, building the core team, and using consultants.

Initial Positions: The Project Manager, Project Technical Lead, and Business Analyst

The project manager has a great influence over the project team. A successful project requires a project manager who has a clear sense of the business, rather than a focus on the more technical elements of the project.

We were brought in to work on a project in the manufacturing industry that had floundered for nearly a year. The first thing the project sponsor said to us was, "I think the project manager is too technical. All I hear about is how the latest technology is going to solve the project's problems, and it changes every few months. This project was supposed to be done at year-end and I still don't have what I need." We worked with the project manager and convinced him to move over to the project lead position, giving up the day-to-day project management. It turned out that he was much happier with the new division of labor and he completed the project in only a few months.

This is not to say that technologists don't make good project managers. Rather, we're suggesting that the project manager focus on project management while the project lead focuses on the product and technology. Dividing the project roles and responsibilities between the project manager and project technical lead as we described earlier and putting them at an equal reporting level in the organization chart resolves many of these issues.

For the project technical lead, the requirements are similar. The lead must be able to look at the clickstream data warehouse from the users' perspective and see what will best fit their needs. This means a good mix of business and technical knowledge as well as experience with design of complex systems.

Our rule for the project lead is "The third time's the charm." It's a rare person who can do a good architecture and design when they have no experience with a class of technology. The most dangerous project lead is the one who has either been on only one project or designed only one system before. Speaking from experience, there will be so many good ideas filed away from the first system that the second is likely to be a Rube Goldberg contraption lacking the simplicity of a good design. The third time the project lead will have learned what went well and what went poorly. If your project lead has done zero or one data warehouse prior to this project, beware.

As we mentioned before, the role of the business analyst may be taken up by the project manager and project lead. This can work, but only if these people have a strong business sense and can set aside all of their technical leanings while gathering requirements. Otherwise, you are best off looking to a third person to fill the position. If focus is allowed to wander from the use of information by end users and uncovering business problems, trouble is guaranteed.

These important resources make up most of the project team during the first two phases of the project. Clearly defined roles and having the right people in them will make a big difference in the success of the project.

The Project Team: Finding the Talent

Apart from the positions mentioned above, who should be on the core project team? The next positions to fill are often the DBA, primary application developer, and primary ETL developer. The best members of the core team are people who understand both the business issues and technical challenges. They must be able to pick skills up quickly, and above all be flexible.

One way to identify a good DBA or ETL developer for the team is to ask lots of questions about data and see what names come up most often. These folks are often hard to come by because they are usually in valued roles in the IT organization. Externally, you should look at people with prior project experience in roles where they had to deal with users as well as the technology. Many people with the words "data warehousing" on their resume worked in isolation in the back room, or only wrote reports and were not involved in the heavy lifting to build the back end of the system. You want people who can work on both sides.

Good data access application developers are often technical people who provide information to end users and who like doing this work. They often have an interest in the business side of the house, but want to stay in a technical role. Analysts in end-user departments who spend their days obtaining and interpreting data also make excellent application developers.

Wherever possible, get the types of people we've mentioned involved in the project, even if they are available temporarily or on a part-time basis. Actively solicit extended team members and participants from other groups or departments. The best project manager will build a small, cohesive core team and borrow the rest of the people. This can be a key to delivering when there are internal staffing constraints.

Very seldom does an organization have all of the skills required to build a clickstream data warehouse. It's important that you allocate time before the project starts or in the project schedule to get everyone familiar with data warehousing concepts, development methodologies, and specific technical topics like dimensional modeling and available data access tools. There are many ways to do this, from customized training by a clickstream data warehousing firm to attending one of the many data warehouse conferences.

Using Outsourcers and Vendors

Never ever outsource the entire project, even if it is a huge, expensive project. Outsourcing a risky project only makes it riskier. You may outsource the development, but always have your own project manager, even if the outsourcer has his or her own project manager assigned. Don't fight having their project manager as well as your own. Two project managers might seem like overkill, but the outsourcer should have more than experience with what you want to build. It's a good way to develop the internal project manager's skills. If the outsourcer doesn't have more experience then your project manager will quickly become aware of this and be able to request a change or halt the project while you reevaluate the vendor. Your project manager should be learning from their project manager. If it goes the other way, you have a problem.

We believe in the mentoring model when working with new technologies. This means you should be sure that consultants in key roles are paired with your staff. You probably can't field the project architect in many cases, nor should you. Just make sure that your staff learns from the consultants in key roles. These roles are usually the project manager, project architect, business analyst, and dimensional modeler. Whoever fills those roles must teach your staff. Once the project is over you want to be able to continue development in-house. It can be very expensive to keep consultants on after deployment.

When hiring a vendor to lead an effort, listen carefully to the vendor. If they talk in terms of being prime or owning the project, make sure they are appropriate for the role. A company that provides an application is generally not the best one to have as prime. It is very likely that they will have a predefined technical architecture in mind that makes it easy to deploy their product (and future add-ons) at the expense of really fulfilling user requirements or allowing you to extend the system. That makes their design recommendations suspect. This applies to everyone from the smallest vendors like Kana to the largest, like IBM. On the other hand, if you are implementing using only one vendor's products, or if you have their infrastructure in place already, then go ahead and use that vendor.

If you are looking to a technology vendor to provide specific services, make sure they and the other consultants know this. We have been involved in several projects that almost failed because of infighting between different vendors who felt that they were best suited to provide the same component. Also, vendors will have their own baggage. Our worst experience was working in the automotive industry with technology vendors who approached the system design from opposite directions. One built from the top down, while the other built from the bottom up. Both were key to the success of the project, but their methodologies were incompatible. It takes a strong project architect to break the tie, and a strong project manager to make the vendors play nice.

If anyone tells you that the primary benefit of the product is that it solves your development troubles, show them the door. A clickstream data warehouse is business-driven, not technology-driven. A vendor's story about how their software will solve your development problems can be appealing, but it should not be the focus of your clickstream data warehouse architecture.

This is doubly true when the vendor sells to business managers who do not have a deep technical or project understanding, but know what they need. Vendors have entire departments to help couch a siren's song to the people who hold the purse strings. The message is presented well, in terms the user relates to. It also gives short shrift to the details of implementation, integration, and customization. This is why your project definition and requirements-gathering efforts must have a heavy business focus. You're competing with experts at convincing your users that their experts will solve the problems.

We know because we've worked for vendors. They can be helpful, supportive and they are definitely required for the project to succeed. If you get a vendor passed to you with a positive recommendation from a business department, listen closely. They may be allies but they can also be crafty, especially at the end of a financial quarter, so always remain skeptical.

Where and When Should Consultants Be Used?

There are consultants available who specialize in data warehousing. The best source for clickstream data warehouse consultants is firms that specialize in clickstream data warehousing or data warehousing for marketing automation. These types of firms are most likely to have the additional skills that go beyond what is needed for a standard data warehouse project.

When to use consultants is often not a choice. In some situations, the budget is not available to pay outside consultants to work on the project. In other situations, there may be no choice but to bring in consultants because the enterprise is understaffed. If there is a choice, it is a good idea to bring consultants in when none of the internal staff have worked on a clickstream data warehouse project before.

This brings up the question of where to use consultants on the project. As we said earlier, it's not a good idea to hand total responsibility for the project over to a vendor or outsourcer. The best model is a partnership where the consulting firm supplies key expertise and internal staff work with them on the project. The key requirement is that the consultants educate the staff while working with them. It's not a good idea to divide work so that consultants work on certain components while the staff work on others. Apart from paying for their work, you are paying for their expertise, so learn as much as you can from them.

The following are a few areas that are particularly well suited to the use of consultants.

Training. The value of training staff with an expert consultant can be tremendous. Several of the authors learned this business by first being trained by experts, followed by mentoring from those same consultants. Aside from the obvious value of teaching new skills to the project team, training is an investment in employees that pays off in areas like job satisfaction and retention.

Early project phases. Experienced consultants can speed the definition and scoping work along, and help set the project on a course to avoid some of the common pitfalls. The more experienced consultants have seen many similar projects and will be able to plan around many of the obstacles quickly. One of the goals of this book is to highlight the major pitfalls so you can avoid them, but there is no way to cover everything.

Another early part of the project where consultants can be very effective is requirements analysis and design. If they have a methodology for gathering clickstream data warehouse requirements and have done this work before, they will be able to do the work with you very quickly, and they will be able to teach you the skills you need. One of the areas where many organizations are weak is in business requirements definition for data warehouse systems.

One reason that consultants are often better at requirements gathering is that they don't carry with them the political baggage that an internal interviewer might. This allows the end-users to be more candid than they would normally be with someone working for the same company, particularly when the discussion might include the perceived performance of the person interviewing them. The consultants will also bring an outside perspective that allows them to see things that people within the organization might not otherwise perceive.

The same applies to design work. The lead designers should have both dimensional modeling experience and a detailed understanding of clickstream data or they will miss things that delay the project later, like what is *really* available in the clickstream and how accurate the data really is.

This experience and the talent to design and architect complex systems well is scarce. If you're spending a lot on the warehouse and you do not have in-house experience, spend the money on training, and bring in a consultant with both requirements-gathering and design skills. These two tasks go hand in hand. For these types of systems, it's rarely a good idea to gather business requirements and pass them off to a third-party data modeler or system designer.

The early phases of the project are where broad-based experience really pays. Just make sure that the project manager, business analyst, or architect you hire knows what he is doing and has referencable experience in all of these areas.

Product-specific help. Instead of learning as you go with various ETL or data access products, you can bring in a consultant who is already familiar with the particular product. This person will provide focused aid when working with the product. In particular, they can provide the developers with an overall framework for working with a given product or technology. Learning the design limits and how a product expects you to approach a problem are something that only comes from experience. This is a way to shorten that time, as well as getting work done quickly with an extra pair of hands. When this consultant leaves your developers should be experienced enough to continue working on their own on future enhancements to the warehouse.

Project validation. Bringing someone from outside the project team in at key points can help avoid problems down the line. Rather than incur the expense of having consultants do much of the work, you can bring them in at key points to provide advice on certain problems or validate an approach or technical solution. We've done this work a number of times ourselves, mostly validating the incorporation of clickstream data into an existing data warehouse.

A more common use of consultants is to examine a project after it has gotten into trouble. Many times an objective view is all that is needed to get a project back on track. We prefer the former use for validation to the latter because our bias is to prevent problems before they crop up. It's also more difficult because the validation can be interpreted by the project team as snooping or as a means by management to direct blame, particularly if there is some problem or delay on the project.

One point worth making about using consultants to find and fix project problems is that you need to understand how these consultants approach troubleshooting and validation work. They must be able to find problems and diagnose their root causes. The goal is not so much identifying the problem and fixing it, as identifying the real problem and how to avoid it in the future. This is the difference between treating the symptom and treating the cause.

This is very challenging work because identifying the real causes of problems is hard. There are many, many charlatans out there who will gladly charge a high price to tell how and why your project has a problem without telling you how to prevent that problem from coming back again a couple of months later.

We want to close with one last word of warning about using consultants: You should make use of their expertise and learn from them, but you should not become entirely dependent on them either. The best use of consultants is to solve specific problems or leverage specific skills rather than long-term staff augmentation. One of the few exceptions to this is when you can't keep certain skills in-house because they are either too expensive or not used frequently enough.

Summary

In this chapter, we provided an overview of the flow of work on a clickstream data warehouse project, and then went into more detail about the work performed during each phase of the project. Hopefully the advice-oriented approach helped you understand the nature of some of the tasks and the common problems faced on these projects.

With the understanding of the project phases and tasks, we moved on to project staffing and organization. The idea is to come away from this section with a sense of the roles people need to play in a project, how those roles fit into positions in an organization chart, and how you might go about staffing the project with internal and external resources.

Now that you know how a clickstream data warehouse project is organized and staffed, we can move into the specifics of building the data warehouse. We will start with the specifics of clickstream schema design, which are covered in the next chapter.

CHAPTER 6

The Clickstream Data Warehouse Meta-Schema

T his chapter explains one of the most important ideas in this book—the concept of the clickstream data warehouse meta-schema. Rather than starting from a blank slate, the meta-schema is a standardized template used as a starting point to create the logical schema design of any clickstream data warehouse. It ensures that all the important facts, dimensions, attributes, and aggregates of a clickstream data warehouse will be considered in the course of the logical schema design. This template can also be used as a vehicle to bridge the communication gap between business users and the schema designers.

This chapter assumes that the reader is already familiar with basic dimensional data warehouse design concepts. If you need more information on the logical design of star schemas, we suggest that you read Dr. Ralph Kimball's classic book on the topic, *The Data Warehouse Toolkit* (Wiley, 1996). For those of you who just need a quick refresher, see the sidebar on Dimensional Modeling Terminology.

While the meta-schema supports common types of clickstream analysis like site traffic statistics, it also enables more sophisticated analyses of both Web site activity and user behavior, including:

- Application-specific tracking of content and user actions related to that content.
- Analysis of individual user visits and behavior.
- Referring page analysis across user visits, including external referring pages and clickthroughs.
- Analysis of users' most common entry points to and exit points from the Web site.

A Quick Refresher on Dimensional Modeling Terminology

The following is a very brief review of the basic concepts of dimensional design:

- **Dimension.** A dimension table contains a related set of constraint attributes used to query against the transactional facts stored in the fact table. The constraint attributes correspond to natural business terms that are already familiar to the analytical users of the data warehouse. For example, when users analyze product sales information, they know which fiscal time periods they need to analyze, and these time periods should be represented in a natural way, like Fiscal Week, Month, Quarter, and Year, in a Fiscal Time dimension table.

- **Hierarchy.** Most dimensions store data in business-oriented hierarchies of information. For example, in a Sales Geography dimension table, the Los Angeles sales Office Location would be recorded as part of the Southern California sales District, which is in turn part of the larger Western sales Region. There would be columns for each of these three hierarchical attributes in the Sales Geography dimension table.

- **Fact.** A fact is a basic data element that is used in the decision-making process. Facts are what the user needs to know to make a decision. All facts related to a single event are stored in a fact table as a row. For example, the information related to a single insurance claim filed against a policy will typically be stored as a single row in a Claims fact table.

- **Granularity.** Every fact table has a uniform level of detail for each row stored in the table. The lowest data hierarchy level in the dimensions determines the grain of the fact table. For example, in a clickstream data warehouse, the grain of the fact table could be at the site-hit level, which would mean that the Content dimension needs to go down to the individual page component level because each site hit displays one component page content.

- **Aggregate.** An aggregate is a precalculated summarization of the rows in a fact table along one or more data hierarchies in one or more dimensions. The purpose of the aggregate is to reduce the number of rows that need to be processed to produce the result set of a query. For example, suppose a large retail sales data warehouse has 400 million rows in its sales transaction fact table. Furthermore, suppose a common user query is for Sales by District by product Category. This query can be satisfied by processing all 400 million rows each time the query is executed. But the database administrator could create a dimensional aggregate at the District and product Category levels and then this common user query would be executed against this much smaller aggregate. The aggregated fact table would certainly contain far fewer than 1 million rows, and maybe only a few thousand rows, depending on the sales transaction rate and the length of the data history spanned by the data warehouse.

For more information on dimensional schema design concepts, see Ralph Kimball's *The Data Warehouse Toolkit* (Wiley, 1996).

- Promotion analysis, including online ads, affiliated links, and search engines.
- Time-based tracking of users and their actions, including user-specific time zones, seasons, and holidays.
- Analysis for corporate reporting that is based on fiscal rather than calendar times.
- Analysis of the physical geography of user requests.

The meta-schema is applicable whether your site is a pure e-business or an electronic channel for a larger brick-and-mortar enterprise. Brick-and-mortar Web sites are just another type of e-business channel, and they have the same problems tracking and analyzing user behavior as a pure e-business. Without a clickstream data warehouse, the management of an e-business channel for a brick-and-mortar enterprise is flying just as blind as counterparts in the dot-com sector, and they are subject to the same sorts of business disasters. The old adage, "Know your customer," or in this case, "user," applies to any kind of e-business or e-business channel.

Evolving the Meta-Schema from a Sales Analysis Base

In this section, we develop the clickstream meta-schema, using a step-by-step approach. The best way to understand the meta-schema is by starting with a more familiar, nonclickstream data warehouse schema, the sales and marketing data warehouse schema, which is shown in Figure 6.1.

This familiar nonclickstream schema has a central *Sales* fact table with measures like sales price, product cost, time of the sales transaction, and number of items. The usual dimensions—*Time, Geography*, and *Product*—surround the sales fact table. To enhance this classic schema, we have added a *Promotion* dimension for tracking the effectiveness of any advertising or on-premises promotions. With such a schema, an enterprise can get answers to questions like, How do the sales by quarter for the top selling product in 2000 compare to the sales by quarter for the same product in 1999? or How much did the Christmas advertising promotion raise sales for its target products in the Eastern Region in the 4th fiscal quarter?

The CRM Customer Dimension

The sales and marketing data warehouse schema was destined to change with the arrival of the Customer Relationship Management (CRM) juggernaut in the late 1990s. Interestingly, in order to transform this sales and marketing data

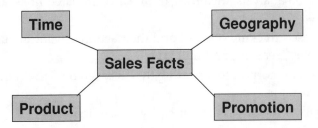

Figure 6.1 A typical sales and marketing oriented data warehouse schema.

warehouse schema into a CRM-oriented data warehouse schema, one need only add a single new dimension, the *Customer* dimension, as shown in Figure 6.2.

Adding a Customer dimension, the Sales and Marketing schema is much harder than it looks. Many sales transaction processing systems have only recently acquired the capability to identify which customer bought what products. For example, suppose you go into the grocery store and buy milk and pay with cash. The store has no way of knowing that the milk was sold to you, and that transaction cannot be tied to your recorded customer activity. But if the store has a loyalty card that you swipe through a card reader before you pay cash for the milk, then the sales transaction can be associated with your customer identity information, and the store may even give you a discount on the milk as a loyalty card reward. Without customer identity mechanisms like loyalty cards and sales force automation systems, it can be very difficult to tie sales transactions to the actual customer.

Because establishing customer identity in data warehouses is such new technology, CRM data warehouses are considered to be cutting edge systems in today's data warehouse environment. With a CRM-oriented data warehouse schema one can answer questions like, What customers responded to the Christmas promotion in the 4th fiscal quarter in the Eastern Region? or What was the difference in spending by customers who responded to the 4th quarter Christmas promotion, versus the 3rd quarter spending by those same customers, when the promotion was not in effect?

The User Activity/Site Hit Fact Table

The clickstream data warehouse meta-schema evolves naturally from the CRM-oriented data warehouse schema. The idea behind the clickstream meta-schema is that it tracks *user* activity, not just *customer* activity. On a Web site, all activities by all types of users are logged by the site's Web servers. The Web log files contain a complete record of the behavior of both customers and noncustomers.

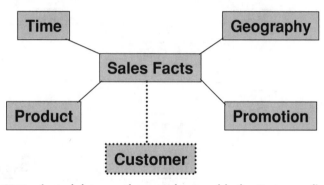

Figure 6.2 A CRM-oriented data warehouse schema adds the Customer dimension.

Unless your enterprise is a monopoly, most of the members of your market are *not* your customers, and it is likely that your enterprise spends much of its time trying to understand noncustomer behavior in an attempt to entice noncustomers to become customers. For brick-and-mortar businesses, much of this effort is based on intuition rather than facts, because they have no way to track the behavior of noncustomers. For example, suppose you go to a bookstore to buy a book, but after you get there you discover it is not on the shelves. You leave the store without anyone at the enterprise knowing that you came to look for the book. Your noncustomer behavior is invisible to the bookstore.

In contrast, suppose you shop for the same out-of-stock book at an online bookstore. The book is still out-of-stock, but the online Web site records your entire foray to find the book in its Web logs. Using the information in the clickstream, the online bookseller could offer to find the book for you or suggest an alternative book. At the very least, the bookseller knows that it is time to order the book, because there is market demand for it.

Since Web sites can track both customer and noncustomer activity, the CRM concept broadens to become User Relationship Management or, as it is more commonly called, electronic Relationship Management (eRM). Let's take a CRM data warehouse schema and transform it, step-by-step, into the clickstream data warehouse electronic Relationship Management (eRM) meta-schema.

CRM *Sales Facts* become *User Activity/Site Hit Facts* in the eRM environment, as shown in Figure 6.3 As we mentioned above, all user activity, not just sales events, can be recorded on the Web. Examples of additional types of user activity include casual browsing, registration on the Web site, directed shopping excursions, ad clickthroughs, exit from the site, and many other events. Through aggregation, user activity facts can be strung together into entire user visit histories, called *sessions,* which then can be classified by type of activity.

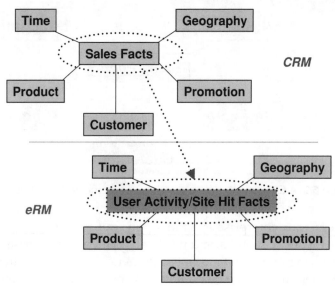

Figure 6.3 Sales Facts become User Activity/Site Hit Facts.

The User Dimension

The CRM-style *Customer* dimension becomes the eRM *User* dimension in the meta-schema, as shown in Figure 6.4. Users come in many different types, including customers, casual browsers, directed searchers, advertising click-throughs, and search engine robots. With a User dimension you can ask business questions that distinguish between the different types of users, resulting in much richer business intelligence than is possible with a more limited customer-only dimension.

The Fiscal and User Time Dimensions

The Time dimension splits into the *Fiscal Time* dimension and the *User Time* dimension in the eRM meta-schema, as shown in Figure 6.5. The enterprise-centric Fiscal Time dimension is analogous to the old corporate Time dimension used in most nonclickstream data warehouses. The new User Time dimension recognizes the worldwide nature of user access, which is definitely not done according to traditional corporate time rules. Internet users can be located in any time zone, and their seasons and holidays vary widely across their time zones and physical geographies. The User Time dimension makes it possible to analyze user activity by specific time zone and user-oriented seasonalities—something that is almost impossible using a "standard" time dimension.

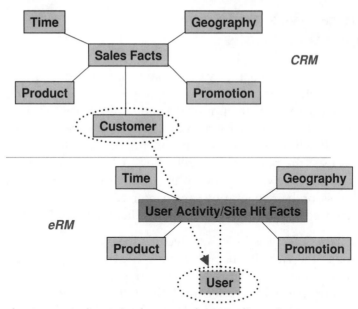

Figure 6.4 The Customer dimension becomes the User dimension.

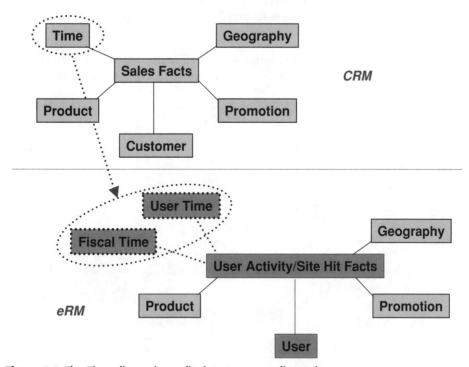

Figure 6.5 The Time dimension splits into two new dimensions.

The Physical, Web, and Site Geography Dimensions

The CRM-style Geography dimension splits into three new dimensions in the eRM environment, as shown in Figure 6.6. The first new dimension, *Physical Geography,* contains the physical location of the user, assuming it can be determined in the Web environment. Determining a user's physical location can be difficult, although there are a number of new products that attempt to do this to at least the postal code level using TCP/IP addresses. The user may also reveal their physical geography voluntarily, as when supplying a billing address, or their geography can be inferred using syndicated data that is cross-referenced by email address or some other identifier like a credit card number.

The *Web Geography* dimension records the user's path to the Web site and then through the Web site, using referring URL and page URL pairs to track a user visit as he enters the site and goes from page to page. This is possible because site entry pages have referring URLs that are external to the Web site, while internal pages have referring URLs that are located within the Web site. The URL pairs can be used to track advertising clickthroughs, search engine clickthroughs, affiliated links, internal site promotions, and any other activities involving links.

The *Site Geography* dimension describes all of the pages on the Web site, uniquely identifying each page. This dimension includes information on page size in

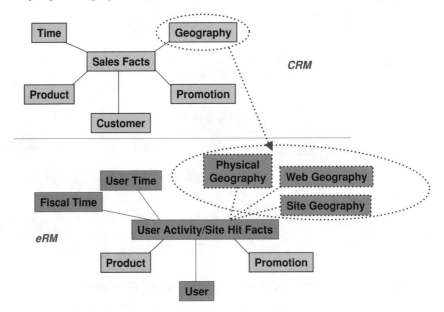

Figure 6.6 The Geography dimension splits into 3 new dimensions.

bytes, page version, linked pages, and rules that track how a page migrates as the site design is changed over time. The purpose of this dimension is to capture a picture of the primary structure of the Web site. It therefore consists mostly of entries for Web pages, since images and other elements do not normally affect the navigational structure of a Web site.

The Content and Activity Dimensions

The CRM Product dimension splits into the Content and Activity dimensions in the eRM meta-schema, as shown in Figure 6.7. Unlike brick-and-mortar businesses, Web sites are pure information entities. Web pages contain only content, while Web logs record both the pages and activities that one performs on that content. For example, if your e-business has a product-oriented site, then one class of content is your product catalog pages. You also have many other types of content on the Web site including registration forms, user feedback forms, business transaction forms, downloads, and advertising links.

The Activity dimension is the entity that truly differentiates the original CRM schema from the eRM schema, because this new dimension alters that nature of the data in the fact table. By adding the Activity dimension we are no longer storing only sales activity in the fact table, but are now storing every type of activity that can be tracked on the site.

Each type of content has a specific set of activities that correspond to it, and these activities reflect a user's behavior. Examples of activities include reading a page, a clickthrough on an ad, abandonment of a shopping cart, or a purchase transaction, to name a few.

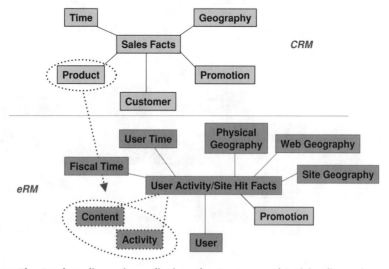

Figure 6.7 The Product dimension splits into the Content and Activity dimensions.

The Internal and External Promotion Dimensions

Finally, the Promotion dimension splits into the *Internal* and *External Promotion* dimensions in the new eRM meta-schema, as shown in Figure 6.8. In the Internet environment promotions can exist either internally within a site or externally outside a site. For example, a banner ad or affiliated link is an external promotional event, while an up-selling advertisement on the Web site is an internal promotional event.

It is useful to analyze each type of promotion separately, because the internal and external environments are so different. For example, because of the wide-ranging nature of advertising engines, banner ads can appear on sites all across the world—the equivalent of having billboards in Beijing, Prague, and San Francisco. Clickthroughs from these external sites need to be analyzed separately from the Internet Special promotions you do from within your own site.

This kind of analysis is not easily done with a single Promotion dimension that flags the two types of promotions instead. The data that one tracks for internal and external promotions tends to be different. It is also fairly common to have a combination of both internal and external promotions tied to a single row in the fact table—something that generally requires multiple dimensions or a specially designed dimension table.

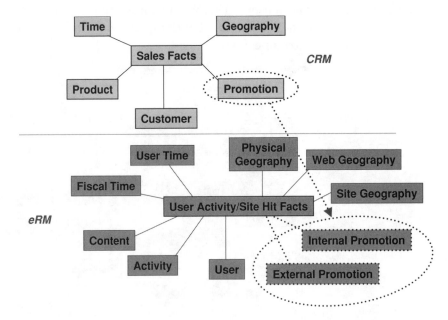

Figure 6.8 Promotion splits into Internal Promotion and External Promotion.

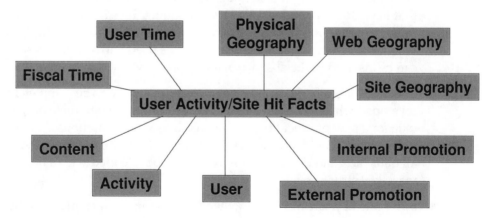

Figure 6.9 The site hit granularity meta-schema.

The User Activity/Site Hit Meta-Schema

Figure 6.9 is a table diagram of the completed User Activity/Site Hit clickstream data warehouse meta-schema. The meta-schema is designed to store data at the lowest level of granularity, the site hit.

Meta-Schema Attributes

We still need to discuss two very important, higher granularity meta-schema aggregates at the Page and Session levels. But before doing this, we need to present a detailed explanation of the column attributes of each of the tables in this base level of the meta-schema, starting with the ten dimensions. For each dimension, we identify each attribute and give either value range for the attribute or examples of potential values for the attribute.

We also identify the hierarchical level of each attribute in the *Level* column. Most attributes are at the top level (Level 1), but some dimensional hierarchies in the meta-schema are up to five levels deep.

Each dimension also has a primary surrogate key, which is shown as an attribute with a shaded background. Surrogate keys are completely synthetic, generated keys. They deliberately have no semantic relationship to the underlying fact or dimension data so we can avoid the data problems that semantic key relationships create. There are three common problems solved by surrogate keys:

- Sometimes data warehouse dimensions need to be populated with events that haven't happened yet, like the remaining days in the current month for month-over-month analysis, or records may have bad or duplicate keys for a variety of reasons. These records need surrogate keys so they can be inserted in the absence of a real primary key.

- The most carefully designed primary keys may need to be completely revamped when new sets of data, like a user list from another company, or data for a new product line, are merged into a data warehouse. Unless there is a surrogate key to deal with this problem, the entire database, including all of its facts and dimensions may have to be reloaded with a new primary key structure.

- Surrogate keys are also used to handle the issue of data and analytical needs that change over time. Clickstream data warehouses need to evolve to meet these changing requirements. Assuming one has done a proper job of dimensional design, the burden of such changes falls on the smaller dimension tables rather than the gigantic central fact table. Even so, dimension table attributes cannot change gracefully unless there is a synthetic surrogate key to use while the underlying table is restructured. For example, suppose you wanted to start using nine-digit zip codes in a Physical Geography dimension that only supported five-digit codes previously. If the five-digit code were the primary key of the table, then all the data would have to be reloaded with the new, longer key. Instead, with a surrogate key, new nine-digit zip codes can be loaded beside the older five digit zip codes, and the original records automatically acquire null values for the four-digit extension when the new column is created. Because of surrogate keys, the table does not have to be reloaded to accomplish this change.

Fiscal Time Attributes

Efficient representation of the multitude of time values over the several year time history of a clickstream data warehouse requires that the *Fiscal Time* dimension be split into two different tables. These tables, the *Fiscal Date* and *Fiscal Time-of-Day*, are shown in Tables 6.1 and 6.2.

The Fiscal Time dimension is split into separate Fiscal Date and Time-of-Day tables to prevent a single Fiscal Time dimension table from becoming too large. For example, if one had a single Fiscal Time dimension covering the entire three-year rolling time window of a typical clickstream data warehouse, there would be 94,608,000 rows in that consolidated dimension. Since almost all useful queries are constrained by time, this giant dimension would incur huge join overhead for most queries. By splitting the dimension into

Table 6.1 Fiscal Date Dimension Attributes and Values

LEVEL	FISCAL DATE ATTRIBUTES	EXAMPLE VALUES
1	Surrogate Fiscal Date Key	Unique Integer Identifier
1	Date Type	In-range, out-of-range, bad, duplicate, null, etc.
1	Season	Summer, winter, spring, fall, Christmas, etc.
1	SQL Date Timestamp	The date stored in the native date format of the database
1	Fiscal Year	The fiscal year
2	Fiscal Quarter	The fiscal quarter for this date
3	Fiscal Month	(1..12)
3	Month Type	4-week or 5-week month
4	Fiscal Week	(1..53)
4	Week Type	quarter-end week, etc.
5	Fiscal Day Number	(1..366)
5	Day Name	Monday, Tuesday, etc.
5	Day in Week Number	(1..7)
5	Day in Month Number	(1..31)
5	Day Type	workday, weekend, holiday name, etc.

Table 6.2 Fiscal Time-of-Day Dimension Attributes and Values

LEVEL	FISCAL TIME-OF-DAY ATTRIBUTES	EXAMPLE VALUES
1	Surrogate Fiscal Time-of-Day Key	Unique Integer Identifier
1	Time Type	in-day, bad, duplicate, null
1	Period in Day	Morning, afternoon, evening, day shift, graveyard shift, etc.
1	SQL Time Timestamp	The timestamp in native database format
1	GMT Hour	(0..23)
2	GMT Minute	(0..59)
3	GMT Second	(0..59)

two tables, the cardinality for a three-year rolling time window goes down to 1,096 days, assuming one leap year in the window. The cardinality of the Time-of-Day dimension shrinks to the number of seconds in a day, which is 86,400.

Furthermore, analytical user query paths are usually either by date or by time of day, but not both. Therefore, join paths will use one small dimension or the other, greatly improving join efficiency over one huge dimension.

As a practical matter, the Fiscal Date dimension can be extended with a separate Gregorian calendar date hierarchy, since day, week, and month numbers can vary between the Fiscal and Gregorian calendars, and users may wish to do both fiscal and calendar analyses off the same Fiscal Date dimension.

The fiscal date dimension contains one row for every day within the time period spanned by the data warehouse. Each row contains all of the attributes relevent to that date, as with the "standard" time dimension used in nonclickstream data warehouses.

User Time Attributes

The *User Time* dimension has a date/time-of-day table split similar to Fiscal Time. In this instance the dimension is turned into the *User Date* and *User Time-of-Day* tables shown in Tables 6.3 and 6.4.

The User Date and User Time-of-day tables are used to analyze user behavior from the user's perspective, not the organization's perspective. User Date and User Time-of-Day are based on a particular user calendar, which can be the Western Gregorian calendar, but can also be the Chinese, Islamic, or South

Table 6.3 User Date Dimension Attributes and Values

LEVEL	USER DATE ATTRIBUTES	EXAMPLE VALUES
1	Surrogate User Date Key	Unique Integer Identifier
1	Date Type	In-range, out-of-range, bad, duplicate, null, etc.
1	User Season of Date	summer, winter, spring, fall, Christmas, Rosh Hashanah, Diwali, Chinese New Year, etc.
1	Calendar Type	Gregorian, Japanese, Chinese, Islamic, South Indian, etc.
1	SQL Date Timestamp	yyyy/mm/dd
1	Calendar Year	2002, 2003, etc.
2	Calendar Quarter	1=January-March, 2=April-June, 3=July-September, 4=October-December
3	Calendar Month	(1..12)
3	Calendar Month Name	January, Tishri, Pus, Ramadan, etc.
4	Calendar Day Name	Monday, Tuesday, etc.
4	Day Number in Calendar	(1..366)
4	Day in Week Number	(1..7)
4	Day in Month Number	(1..31)
4	Day Type	workday, weekend, holiday name, etc.

Table 6.4 User Time-of-Day Dimension Attributes and Values

LEVEL	USER TIME-OF-DAY ATTRIBUTES	EXAMPLE VALUES
1	Surrogate Fiscal Time-of-Day Key	Unique Integer Identifier
1	Time Type	in-day, bad, duplicate, null
1	Period in Day	Morning, afternoon, evening, work time, after work, night, etc.
1	User Time Zone GMT Offset	(-12..+11)
1	SQL Time Timestamp	hh:mm:ss
1	User Hour	(0..23)
2	User Minute	(0..59)
3	User Second	(0..59)

Indian calendar. Each calendar has its own set of holidays, workdays, and weekend days. Because of the instantaneous, worldwide reach of the Web, usage patterns are affected by a given user's calendar as well as time zone. The time zone is indicated by the *User Time Zone GMT Offset* in the User Time-of Day table.

Determining which calendar is adopted by a user can be difficult, but the locale attributes in the Physical Geography dimension can help identify particular local calendars. In cases where calendar determination is not possible, a default calendar may be chosen. The user's GMT Offset can be obtained using JavaScript to send the local time from their browser back to the Web server when a page is accessed.

Physical Geography Attributes

Now, let's develop the three Geography dimensions, starting with *Physical Geography,* shown in Table 6.5.

Physical Geography is used to store the physical location of the user generating a site hit, to the extent that the location is known. Whether the physical location of a site hit can be determined down to the degree of detail shown in the meta-schema table depends on the particular situation. There are several new products that resolve host IP addresses to either U.S. Postal Zip Codes or global Country/State or Province/City location names. Further physical location resolution down to the Street Number, Address1, and Address2 attributes may depend on specific information voluntarily revealed by the user during registration. For example, the Web site might record a billing address for an online purchase, or perform a reverse lookup in an email

Table 6.5 Physical Geography Dimension Attributes and Values

LEVEL	PHYSICAL GEOGRAPHY ATTRIBUTES	EXAMPLE VALUES
1	Surrogate Physical Geography Key	Unique Integer Identifier
1	Country	USA, Canada, UK, France, Germany, Japan, China, etc.
2	State or Province	California, Ontario, Bavaria
3	County or Township	Santa Clara, DuPage, King, etc.
4	City	San Jose, Medford, etc.
5	Street Number	3814, 12668, etc.
5	Address 1	Shasta Ave., W. Flagler Road, NE Flanders, etc.
5	Address 2	Suite 100, Apt. 3B, etc.
1	Zip or Postal Code	95126, 2G24R, etc.
2	Zip or Postal Code Extension	2314, etc.
1	Region	Physical region like eastern, western, Europe, etc.
1	Type of Location	Home, Apartment, Business, Government office, etc.

address database. If the email address is not known, it can usually be collected and passed back to the Web site by using a JavaScript routine or ActiveX control.

In some cases, physical location analysis may not be important to the business model, which does not value where a user is physically located. In these cases, this dimension can be dropped from the actual data warehouse schema. Remember, the meta-schema is only a template, not necessarily the actual clickstream data warehouse schema.

Web Geography Attributes

Like the Fiscal and User Time dimensions, the Web Geography dimension splits into two physical meta-schema tables, *Host Geography* and *Referrer Geography*.

Host Geography identifies which remote host site caused the site hit via the IP address that is logged with every hit. The actual *Host Name* can be determined by using Domain Name Service (DNS) to resolve the IP address. The host could be an ISP like AOL or Earthlink, or a user from a corporate domain looking at your site. Identifying these hosts can tell you a lot about the origin of traffic to your Web site, and what kinds of domains have a user audience for your content.

Table 6.6 Host Geography Dimension Attributes and Values

LEVEL	HOST GEOGRAPHY ATTRIBUTES	EXAMPLE VALUES
1	Surrogate Host Geography Key	Unique Integer Identifier
1	Host 32-bit v4 IP address string	138.205.16.1
2	Byte 1 of IP address	138
2	Byte 2 of IP address	205
2	Byte 3 of IP address	16
2	Byte 4 of IP address	1
1	Host 128 bit IPv6 address	For the future v6 IP address format (8 two-byte fields)
1	Host Name	Fully resolved hostname, e.g., data33.coremetrics.com, or unknown (if not resolvable using DNS)
1	Domain Name	Just the domain portion of the remote hostname, e.g., aol.com, earthlink.net, ncr.com, oracle.com, unknown (if not resolvable using DNS)
1	Host Country	USA, Singapore, etc.
2	Host State or Province	California, Ontario, etc.
3	Host City	Los Angeles, Bangalore, Frankfurt, etc.

As of this writing hostnames are logged as 32 bit addresses consisting of four one-byte fields. As more devices such as cell phones and PDAs get IP addresses, the IP address field in version 6 of the Internet Protocol will expand to 128 bits consisting of eight two-byte fields. We reserve an attribute in this dimension for future 128-bit v6 IP addresses.

We also include the *Host Country, Host State or Province,* and *Host City* attributes in the Host Geography dimension. This information is used to determine the general physical location of the users generating site traffic. As we mentioned earlier, there are a number of new services that can map the remote IP address to a corresponding city, state, and country of origin. The information can then be included in this dimension or in the Physical Geography dimension we previously described.

The *Referrer Geography* portion of the Web Geography dimension contains the *Referring* and *Referred URLs* attributes. These URL pairs record the reference patterns between the content components that make up the site hits. The *Referring URL* information has an *External/Internal Flag* that is used to indicate whether a referring URL is external to the site. Like remote host names, external referring URLs are very important in determining which external sites drive traffic to your Web site, and determining which site pages are the top entry pages. You

Table 6.7 Referrer Dimension Attributes and Values

LEVEL	REFERRER ATTRIBUTES	EXAMPLE VALUES
1	Surrogate Referrer Key	Unique Integer Identifier
1	Referring URL	http://www.search.google.com
1	Referring Page ID	Unique referring page identifier for dynamic pages
1	Query String	?search=clickstream+data+warehousing
1	Referring Domain	google.com
1	External/Internal Flag	Indicates whether the referring page is internal or external to the site
1	Referred URL	www.mysite.com/index.html
1	Referred Page ID	Unique referred page identifier for dynamic pages

may also want to seed high traffic external referring URL sites with extra advertising, affiliated links, or special offers, to drive even more traffic to your Web site.

By having separate *Host Geography* and *Referrer Geography* dimension tables, a single query can determine, for example, the top 10 host domains for each *external* referring site. This query allows the analyst to determine if the actual user demographics of these top host domains fit the site's desired user demographic profile. If not, measures must be taken to attract a different clientele. If the Host and Referrer information were in the same Web Geography dimension table, this type of query would not be possible without convoluted, multi-statement SQL.

Site Geography Attributes

The Site Geography dimension records the structure of the Web site itself, including the URL of each page, the Parent URL of each page ("/" for the root home page parent), and other attributes like the number of bytes in the page, the version of the page, and the purpose of the page. For static sites, this dimension fully defines the structure of the pages on the site. Using this information, analysts can aggregate site hit information by page and do page-oriented traffic analysis. The dimension should also store the history of changes to the Web site, allowing end users to analyze aspects of user behavior before and after changes were made.

Unfortunately, sites that use dynamically generated Web pages usually have no fixed page URLs other than that of the home page. All other site pages have dynamically generated content and URLs that are meaningless outside the Web application server. As we discussed earlier in this book, some mechanism must be created to log meaningful dynamic page identifiers, referring

Table 6.8 Site Geography Dimension Attributes and Values

LEVEL	SITE GEOGRAPHY ATTRIBUTES	EXAMPLE VALUES
1	Surrogate Site Geography Key	Unique Integer Identifier
1	Page URL	www.mysite.com/articles2.html
1	Page Identifier	A unique page identifier. Many dynamic pages have meaningless URLs, so they need a separate page identifier that is associated with the page by the Web application.
1	Parent URL	www.mysite.com/index.html
1	Total Page Size	Size in bytes of the page, including all component items such as images or scripts that are loaded with the page
1	Page Version	The version of the Web page, e.g., 2.1
1	Date of Last Revision	04/03/2002 (MM/DD/YYYY)
1	Primary Page Purpose	Home page, search, information, shopping basket, product description, download, etc.

page identifiers, page content indicators, and user-event indicators, or analysis of user activity/site hits below the home page of these sites will be impossible.

One way to record this information from an application server is by encoding these identifiers in the query string of the generated pages, but this creates a custom-code maintenance environment that can defeat much of the speed and flexibility of dynamically generated pages. Because almost all dynamic application servers lack a centralized logging mechanism that could record this information without custom code, many dynamic Web sites cannot to do meaningful clickstream analysis, which is a prescription for business disaster. We do not recommend using dynamic Web site application servers unless they have a centralized logging mechanism for all events and content. Check first, before you buy one of these products.

A small window into the nature of dynamic site user activity can be obtained using static hallway and doorway pages that partially mirror site structure and content. Hallway and doorway pages are often created to support the indexing of dynamic site content by search engines. These static pages do get logged in a meaningful way, just like any other static page. For hits that are the result of search engine matches on hallway and doorway pages, user activity can be tracked. But if a user comes into the site by any other means than the hallway or doorway pages, then all of his pages will be generated dynamically, making clickstream analysis problematic.

In the Site Geography dimension, we deal with this problem by having a unique Page Identifier attribute, in addition to the potentially meaningless URL. It is up to the clickstream data warehouse design team to work with the

Web implementation team to create the right set of page identifiers so that user behavior can be recorded and analyzed.

User Dimension Attributes

The User dimension contains all the attributes required to identify a site visit by a user. As we discussed in Chapter 4, establishing user identity is difficult, and doing a good job requires a joint effort between the Web site implementation team and the data warehouse design and implementation team.

The only easily obtained user identity information is the user-agent information, which we break out into two attributes, *User Agent Type,* and *User Agent Name.* User Agent Type indicates whether the corresponding site hit was done by a real user or an indexing robot. The additional User Agent Name attribute gives the name and version number of the user's browser or the indexing

Table 6.9 User Dimension Attributes and Values

LEVEL	USER ATTRIBUTES	EXAMPLE VALUES
1	Surrogate User Key	Unique Integer Identifier
1	User Identifier	Unique natural key, with a special user value for *unidentified* users
1	User Agent Type	Browser, indexing robot
1	User Agent Name	MSIE 5.01, Netscape 4.75, Googlebot 2.1, etc.
1	User Type	Type of user (visitor, shopper, business agent, etc.)
1	Gender	Male, female, unknown
1	Registered Username	Registered user name, if any
1	Email Address	Email address, if any
1	Email Domain	Email domain, if any
1	Market Segment	Market segment fields, if any
1	Demographic Information	Demographic information, if any
1	Timestamp of Last Purchase	SQL timestamp of last purchase, if any
1	Credit Profile	Credit score fields, if any
1	Daytime Telephone Number	Daytime telephone number, if any
1	Evening Telephone Number	Evening telephone, if any
1	Home Telephone Number	Home telephone, if any
1	Work Telephone Number	Work telephone, if any
1	Billing Address	Billing address, if any
1	Shipping Address	Shipping address, if any

robot. These fields are shown in the schema as columns, although the physical table design might be quite different because one user can have more than one browser or computer.

All the subsequent User dimension attributes are optional, and exist only if provisions have been made in the Web site application to capture this information. *User Type* and *Gender* may be known based on session behavior or user registration events. *Registered Usernames* are captured by voluntary user registration events, and *Email Addresses* can be provided voluntarily by request or, occasionally, involuntarily via a client-side script. *Market Segment* and *Demographic Information* can consist of many fields describing the user, and these may come from a third-party syndicated data provider. If the site supports purchases, user attributes like *Timestamp of Last Purchase, Credit Profile, Telephone Address,* and *Shipping Address* can be obtained from checkout information and credit card providers.

Similar to the unique Page Identifier, reliable user identification requires a unique *User Identifier* that includes special values for unidentified users. It should be an e-business goal to entice the user to progressively reveal his identity with each continued use of the Web site. This additional identity information can then be filled in at each data warehouse load.

Content Dimension Attributes

For all practical purposes, every site hit displays some component of page content. Each component of content has a *Content URL,* and because of dynamically generated pages, a unique *Content Identifier.* Content components have a *Content Type.* The *Content Group* identifies the grouping this object belongs to, as defined by your end users. The *Content Purpose* simply states what user-oriented task this object was meant to perform. In some cases there really isn't a purpose, whereas for Web pages there is always some purpose, even if it is simply display of information.

The Content dimension describes all of the objects on the Web site, uniquely identifying every object the clickstream data warehouse is expected to recognize. In essence, this is the dimension that contains every object a user has ever accessed. The dimension includes information on page size in bytes, page version, linked pages, and is loaded in a way that allows one to track how an object migrates as the site design is changed over time.

Activity Dimension Attributes

Each site hit is the result of one or more user activities on a piece of content. Activities have a unique *Activity/Event identifier* similar to a Content or Page

Table 6.10 Content Dimension Attributes and Valuess

LEVEL	CONTENT ATTRIBUTES	EXAMPLE VALUES
1	Surrogate Content Key	Unique Integer Identifier
1	Content Identifier	Unique identifier for the content component
1	Content URL	URL of the content component, e.g., www.mysite.com/InternalAdImage21.gif
1	Content Type	Web page, image, media clip, java applet
1	Content Group	Product information, external article link, search results
1	Content Purpose	Home page, registration, navigation, ordering, content display
1	Associated Page	The content identifier of the user-displayable Web page this object is associated with
1	Content Size	Size in bytes of the page or object
1	Content Version	Version number, if applicable, e.g., HTML 4.0
1	Date Created	04/01/2002 (MM/DD/YYYY)
1	Date of Last Revision	04/02/2002 (MM/DD/YYYY)
1	Last Modified By	Person who last modified this object
1	Date Removed From Site	04/03/2002 (MM/DD/YYYY)

Identifier. *Activity Types* group into named *Activity Groups.* Activities do not have an URL, because they are not content. Rather, activities reflect the users' interactions with that content.

This dimension provides a useful mechanism for aggregating behavior into types or groups that can be used for more meaningful analysis. For example, end users are often interested in the amount of time visitors spend performing different activities. This dimension provides the handle to easily pull out that information.

Table 6.11 Activity Dimension Attributes and Values

LEVEL	ACTIVITIES ATTRIBUTES	EXAMPLE VALUES
1	Surrogate Activity Key	Unique Integer Identifier
1	Activity/Event Identifier	Unique identifier of an activity or event
1	Activity Type	Ad clickthrough, add-to-basket, buy, pack, ship, approve credit card transaction, session start, session end, login, download article, register user name, etc.
1	Activity Group	Advertising, Shopping, Purchase, Downloads, Registration, etc.

Table 6.12 Internal Promotion Dimension Attributes and Values

LEVEL	INTERNAL PROMOTION ATTRIBUTES	EXAMPLE VALUES
1	Surrogate Internal Promotion	Unique Integer Identifier
1	Internal Promotion URL	www.AffiliatedLink.com/index.html, www.mysite.com/InternetSpecial4.html, etc.
1	Internal Promotion Identifier	Unique integer identifier
1	Clickthrough URL	www.mysite.com/CampingStoveSale.html, etc.
1	Internal Promotion Type	Internal ad, affiliated link, external article link, sale, etc.
1	Internal Promotion Version	1..n
1	Internal Promoted Product or Service	SKU or service code
2	Internal Promoted Brand	Coleman, etc.
3	Internal Promoted Category	Camp stoves, etc.

Internal Promotion Attributes

Internal promotions are promotions that are local to the site. Like other types of content, these promotions have an Internal Promotion URL and an Internal Promotion ID. Dynamically generated content may have a URL that varies, so the identification of promotions will be important. There is an Internal Promotion Version number attribute so different versions of an internal promotion can be analyzed for effectiveness. If a particular product or service is promoted, the product SKU or service code, brand name, and category are also recorded in this dimension.

External Promotion Attributes

External promotions are clickthroughs from external advertising mechanisms like banner ads, affiliated links, or interstitial advertisements in separate pop-up windows on other sites. The External Promotion dimension has the expected External Promotion Identifier, with the URL being the referring URL from the clickthrough.

External promotion clickthroughs usually come through an external promotion engine or sponsor, like the DoubleClick ad network or an affiliated link sponsor. The promotion usually has a standard format like a particular size of banner ad or vertical skyscraper ad. Just like the Internal Promotion dimension, there is likely a Promoted Product or Service, which has a certain Promoted Brand, that is part of a certain Promoted Category of product or service.

Table 6.13 External Promotion Dimension Attributes and Values

LEVEL	EXTERNAL PROMOTION ATTRIBUTES	EXAMPLE VALUES
1	Surrogate External Promotion Key	Unique Integer Identifier
1	External Promotion URL (referring URL)	Full text of URL including query string
1	External Promotion Identifier	Unique integer identifier
1	External Promotion Engine/Sponsor	DoubleClick DART, 24/7 Media, affiliated link sponsor, etc.
1	External Promotion Format	Banner, skyscraper, interstitial,etc.
1	External Promotion Version	1..n
1	External Promoted Product or Service	SKU or service code
2	External Promoted Brand	Brand code, e.g., Tide
3	External Promoted Category	Category name, e.g., Detergents, etc.

Further information about the promotion might be recorded in this dimension as well. For example, it might be useful to have the promotion cost (if available in a per-unit form) in the dimension. With this cost, one could calculate the costs of a promotion relative to its impact on traffic or revenues. Other information that might be useful is the company information for affiliated links.

User Activity/Site Hit Fact Table Attributes

At last we arrive at the attribute definition of the User Activity/Site Hit fact table, at the site hit level of granularity. The first 13 shaded fields are the foreign keys used to join the fact table to its 13 dimension tables. Taken together they are the unique composite key for each fact table row. Beneath the composite key, there are several measures: the *Site Hit Load Time,* the time the hit was *received,* the time the hit was *completed,* the *number of bytes transferred* in the hit, and the hit's HTTP transaction *status code.* The User Activity fact table is not too wide with 12 composite key columns and five fact measure attributes. But the fact table will have a very large number of rows, since each page view typically generates many site hits.

Of course, the User Activity/Site Hit fact table could have additional measures specific to the purpose of the Web site. For example, if the site involved purchasing goods that were for sale, the *Cost of an Item* and the *Total Purchase Amount* could be recorded for each site hit related to a purchase event, as tracked by the Activity dimension. For many hits, the cost and purchase amounts would be zero because the particular hit's content wouldn't have

Table 6.14 User Activity/Site Hit Fact Table Attributes and Values

LEVEL	USER ACTIVITY/SITE HIT FACT ATTRIBUTES	EXAMPLE VALUES
1	User Surrogate Key	Unique integer identifier
1	Fiscal Date Surrogate Key	Unique integer identifier
1	Fiscal Time-of-Day Surrogate Key	Unique integer identifier
1	User Date Surrogate Key	Unique integer identifier
1	User Time-of-Day Surrogate Key	Unique integer identifier
1	Physical Geography Surrogate Key	Unique integer identifier
1	Host Geography Surrogate Key	Unique integer identifier
1	Referrer Geography Surrogate Key	Unique integer identifier
1	Site Geography Surrogate Key	Unique integer identifier
1	Content Surrogate Key	Unique integer identifier
1	Activity Surrogate Key	Unique integer identifier
1	Internal Promotion Surrogate Key	Unique integer identifier
1	External Promotion Surrogate Key	Unique integer identifier
1	Site Hit Load Time	In seconds
1	Time Hit Received	timestamp
1	Time Hit Completed	timestamp
1	Bytes Transferred In Hit	0..n
1	Site Hit HTTP status code	200-600

anything to do with a purchase. But for shopping basket or purchase order site content, the cost of each item could be recorded as it was put into the basket or purchase order, and if the user made it through checkout, the Total Purchase Amount could be recorded for the hit that corresponded to that transaction.

The "Business Questions that Can Be Answered Using the Meta-Schema" sidebar gives some examples of the business questions that can be answered using the meta-schema.

The "Sizing Meta-Schema Fact and Dimension Tables" sidebar gives some guidelines on sizing meta-schema fact and dimension tables. Although the meta-schema is used to do logical schema design, it is always a good idea to scope out the physical size of the underlying data early in the design process. That way, awareness of "deal-killer" physical infrastructure size issues, like the total size of disk farms, the size of database backups, the size of database memory cache, and the size of extract, transformation, and load data staging structures can be addressed as early in the design phase as possible.

Business Questions that Can Be Answered Using the Meta-Schema

It isn't always easy to see what business questions might be answered when looking at the meta-schema design. The goal is to answer any clickstream-related questions that might be asked. The following types of business questions can be answered using the meta-schema as it stands:

- Which external sites drive the most traffic to our site?
- Which external advertising campaigns were the most effective?
- What search terms are users using to find our site?
- What are the most popular site entry pages?
- What are the most popular site exit pages?
- On what pages or content do the users abandon the site and why?
- What are the demographics of the site's most frequent returning users?
- What physical geographies are generating the most site traffic?
- Which remote hosts (ISPs and corporate hosts) are generating the most user traffic?
- What are the trends in user access for various types of content?
- How do my internal promotion conversion rates compare with my external promotion conversion rates?
- What are the most popular/least popular user activities on my site?

If the meta-schema were augmented to record transaction information for an e-business site, one could also ask the following business questions:

- What is the click-to-basket ratio by user market segment by physical geography?
- What is the basket-to-buy ratio by ad type by referring URL?
- What is the click-to-buy ratio by time spent on the URL by day of week?
- What is the site abandonment rate by referring advertisement?
- What is the average transaction value?
- What is the average number of clicks to buy?
- What percentage of users make up the bulk of revenues? Of margins?
- What products are most or least profitable?
- Where are our best customers located?
- How do revenues online compare to offline, and what user segments are most profitable?

Sizing Meta-Schema Fact and Dimension Tables

One outcome of logical schema design is an estimate of the size of the underlying clickstream data warehouse database. The rule of thumb for estimating the size of any dimensional schema table is as follows:

1. Total the actual size in bytes of all the attribute columns in the table, producing the *table width*. Integers are usually at least four bytes in size, and special data types like timestamps may have their own special format that spans eight or more bytes. Character strings are usually one byte per character, unless special character sets are in use. This provides a worst-case string sizing since most strings are usually stored in variable-lengh format. URLs and query strings can be quite long, and HTTP does not set any limit on their length. It is best to reserve at least 256 bytes for the URI portion of the URL and at least 2048 bytes for the query string.

2. Multiply the *table width* times the *expected number of rows* in the table. This gives the *nominal table size*.

3. Multiply the *nominal table size* times 3 to get the *total size* of the table, all of its indexes, and overhead associated with storing these data structures.

Table 6.15 Byte Widths of the Meta-Schema Tables

TABLE NAME	TABLE WIDTH IN BYTES	COMMENTS
Fiscal Date	100	
Fiscal Time-of-Day	50	
User Date	100	
User Time-of-Day	50	
Physical Geography	600	Numerous address strings add to length
Host Geography	500	
Referrer Geography	2700	URLs and Query strings add to length
Site Geography	800	URLs add to length
User	2,200	Demographic information and address fields add to length
Content	300	
Activity	20	
Internal Promotion	2,800	URLs add to length
External Promotion	2,500	URLs add to length
User Activity/Site Hit Fact	100	Skinny—only integers and timestamps

(continued)

(Continued)

Keep in mind that this is a rule of thumb, and is not meant to be a precise sizing calculation. Using the meta-schema attribute definitions we arrive at the table widths found in Table 6.15.

Next, we need to estimate the expected number of rows for each table. The exact number of rows is specific to your situation but we can provide the sizing rules shown in Table 6.16.

Table 6.16 Rules for the Expected Number of Rows for Each Table in the Meta-Schema

TABLE NAME	RULE FOR THE EXPECTED NUMBER OF ROWS
Fiscal Date	Number of years of history * 365
Fiscal Time-of-Day	86,400
User Date	Number of years of history * 365
User Time-of-Day	86,400
Physical Geography	Potentially as many as the number of users, but far less if Physical Geography is kept only to the city level, for example
Host Geography	The number of unique hosts is some small fraction of the number of site hits
Referrer Geography	Referred/Referrer pairs are limited to the number of pages on the site plus the number of external references, which is related to the site hit rate
Site Geography	Number of pages on your site
User	Could be millions, could be much less. It depends on your user population.
Content	Number of content components on your site
Activity	Probably less than 100 rows
Internal Promotion	The lower bound is the number of internal promotions; the upper bound is closely related to the number of internal promotion clickthroughs during the historical period
External Promotion	The lower bound is the number of external promotions; the upper bound is closely related to the number of external promotion clickthroughs during the historical period
User Activity/Site Hit Fact	Can be enormous since it is directly related to the amount of site traffic. Equal to the total number of site hits for the historical period.

(continued)

(Continued)

Dynamically generated Web sites and their dynamically generated URLs can cause the Site Geography, Web Geography, and Content dimensions to continually grow in size unless one devises a page tagging and content coding strategy that can recognize when the same pages and content components are seen more than once.

By multiplying the estimated expected number of rows in a table times it's table width, you get the estimated nominal size of the table in bytes. Don't forget to multiply the estimated nominal size times 3 to get the estimated total size, which allows for indexes, aggregates, and other table overhead.

The Page Activity and Session Activity Aggregates

Obviously, the User Activity/Site Hit fact table and the dimensions described in the previous section are at the lowest level of granularity—the site hit. Analyzing activity at this level is quite useful for generating site traffic statistics and calculating many different metrics associated with site administration. But most business users analyze user activity from a page or session perspective, requiring two new aggregate tables at the Page Activity and Session Activity levels. Let's start with the Page Activity Aggregate, which is shown in Figure 6.10.

The Page Activity aggregate rolls up site hit information from the User Activity/Site Hit fact table into the Page Activity fact table, whose attributes are shown in Table 6.17.

The Time Hit Received and Time Hit Completed attributes at the hit level are used to calculate the overall *Page Dwell Time* for a page, and the first Time Hit Received field for a page becomes the *Page Start Time* in the Page Activity table. This and other calculations will be discussed in the data extraction examples in Chapter 8.

By totaling the number of bytes transferred for all the hits that comprise a particular page, the total *Page Bytes Transferred* is calculated. Finally, the overall status code, either 200 if all the hits that comprise a page were successful, or the error code if some hit was not successful, is recorded as the *Page HTTP Status Code.*

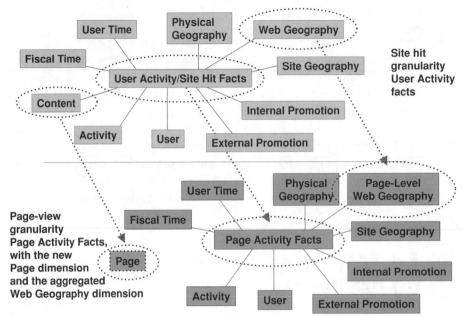

Figure 6.10 The Page Activity aggregate.

Table 6.17 Page Activity Fact Table Attributes and Values

LEVEL	PAGE ACTIVITY FACT ATTRIBUTES	EXAMPLE VALUES
1	User Surrogate Key	Unique integer identifier
1	Fiscal Date Surrogate Key	Unique integer identifier
1	Fiscal Time-of-Day Surrogate Key	Unique integer identifier
1	User Date Surrogate Key	Unique integer identifier
1	User Time-of-Day Surrogate Key	Unique integer identifier
1	Physical Geography Surrogate Key	Unique integer identifier
1	Host Geography Surrogate Key	Unique integer identifier
1	Page Referrer Geography Surrogate Key	Unique integer identifier
1	Site Geography Surrogate Key	Unique integer identifier
1	Activity Surrogate Key	Unique integer identifier
1	Internal Promotion Surrogate Key	Unique integer identifier
1	External Promotion Surrogate Key	Unique integer identifier
1	Page Surrogate Key	Unique integer identifier
1	Page Start Time	Timestamp
1	Page End Time	Timestamp
1	Page Dwell Time	In seconds
1	Page Bytes Transferred	0..n
1	Page HTTP Status Code	200-600

The Page Dimension

The Page Activity aggregate contains two aggregated dimensions from the site hit level and one new dimension. The first aggregated dimension is the Page dimension, which is shown in Table 6.18.

The Page dimension replaces the User Activity/Site Hit *Content* dimension at the page level. All we are really doing is rolling all of the various items that create hits up to the actual object that is displayed to the user. It contains the Page URL and unique Page Identifier for dynamically generated Web pages. It also has a Page Type field to distinguish between static and dynamic pages.

One new attribute of the Page dimension, *Total Page Size,* is also stored in the Site Geography dimension. This is the total number of bytes of all elements that make up the final page. We include this so that it is possible to identify in the fact table those Web pages with incomplete transfers.

The User Activity/Site Hit Web Geography dimension aggregates up to the *Page-Referrer* Web Geography dimension, as shown in Figure 6.10 and in Table 6.19. The original *Referrer* dimension is at the site hit level of granularity, and each referrer/referred pair is for site hit referral pairs. These get aggregated up

Table 6.18 Page Dimension Attributes and Values

LEVEL	PAGE ATTRIBUTES	EXAMPLE VALUES
1	Page Surrogate Key	Unique integer identifier
1	Page URL	URL
1	Page Identifier	Calculated unique page identifier. Many dynamically generated pages have meaningless URLs, so they need a separate page identifier.
1	Page Type	Static, dynamically generated
1	Page Content	Product information, external article link, search results, etc.
1	Page Purpose	Home page, registration, navigation, ordering, content display, etc.
1	Page Size	Actual size in bytes of the HTML page
1	Total Page Size	Size in bytes of the HTML page plus all content that is be loaded with the page
1	Page Version	Version number of the Web page, if applicable
1	Date Created	04/01/2002 (MM/DD/YYYY)
1	Date of Last Revision	04/14/2002 (MM/DD/YYYY)
1	Last Modified By	Person who last modified this page
1	Date Removed from Site	08/03/2002 (MM/DD/YYYY)

Table 6.19 Page-Referrer Geography Dimension Attributes and Values

LEVEL	PAGE-REFERRER GEOGRAPHY ATTIBUTES	EXAMPLE VALUES
1	Surrogate Page-Referrer Key	Unique integer identifier
1	Referring URL	http://www.search.google.com
1	Referring Page ID	Unique referring page identifier for dynamic pages
1	Query String	?search=clickstream+data+warehousing
1	Referring Domain	google.com
1	External/Internal Flag	Indicates whether the referring page is internal or external to the site
1	Referred URL	www.mysite.com/index.html
1	Referred Page ID	Unique referred page identifier for dynamic pages

to the page level in the *Page-Referrer Geography* dimension, so the last site hit in a series of hits for a page is listed as the Referring URL for the next page, which is the Referred URL. There are no new attributes in this pure dimensional aggregate.

The Session Dimension

The other new dimension at the Page Level of aggregation is the *Session* dimension, which is shown in Figure 6.11.

Assuming that the Web site creates a Session Identifier, page activity during user sessions can be tracked using the Session dimension shown below.

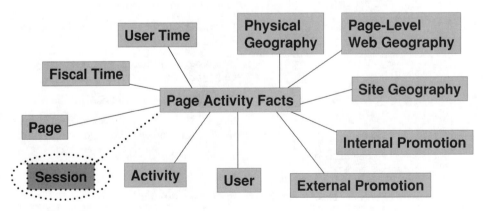

Figure 6.11 The Session dimension.

Table 6.20 Session Dimension Attributes and Values

LEVEL	SESSION DIMENSION ATTRIBUTES	EXAMPLE VALUES
1	Page Surrogate Key	Unique integer identifier
1	Session Identifier	Unique Session Identifier
1	User Identifier	Foreign Key that Identifies the Session User
1	Session Type	Clickthrough, Shopping Cart, Purchase, Information Search, etc.
1	Session Status	Success, Abandoned, Error

Even if the Web site does not perform any session management, it may be possible to infer the session based on timestamp and referral data in the Web logs. This topic is discussed in more detail in Chapter 8.

The Session dimension contains the identifiers, *Session Cookie Variable Name, Session Cookie Value, Session Identifier* to identify the session, and a *User Identifier* foreign key to indicate which user the session belongs to. The *Session Type* indicates what kind of session it was, and the *Session Status* indicates whether the session was successful, voluntarily abandoned, or had an error. Obviously, the Session Type and Session Status information needs to be inferred from the session's pages as log data is processed.

It is interesting to note that because sessions are higher-level dimensional construct that include both pages *and the site hits that comprise a page*, the Session dimension can also be added as an additional dimension to the User Activity/Site Hit base granularity meta-schema, not just to the Page Activity aggregate.

The Session Aggregate

Another way to handle sessions is to aggregate up one more time from the Page Level to the Session Level. Creating the Session Level aggregation is not as straightforward as the Page Level aggregation, but this highly summarized level is very useful for business analyses. Aggregating from the Page Activity level aggregate to the Session Activity level aggregate is depicted in Figure 6.12.

As shown in Figure 6.12, the Page and Site Geography dimensions aggregate out completely in the Session Activity schema. Session level analysis does not include any intrasession pages, so these dimensions disappear completely.

For the same reason, the *Page-Referrer* Web Geography dimension aggregates up to external-only referring URLs, with all the intrasession page pairs deleted. The *External Referrer Geography* dimension is shown in Table 6.21.

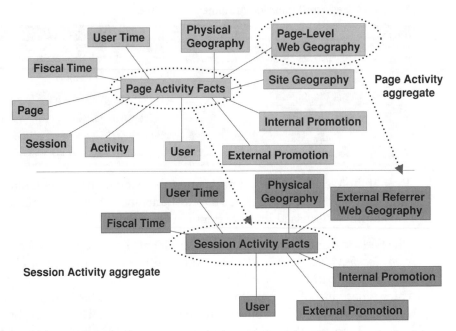

Figure 6.12 The Session Activity aggregate. The Page, Activity, Site Geography, and, interestingly, the Session dimensions aggregate-out at the Session Activity level of granularity.

In this aggregate, the Session Dimension disappears because it becomes a degenerate dimension, that is, a dimension in which all of its attributes and values are also in the corresponding fact table.

The Session fact table is shown in Table 6.22. The *Session Identifier, Session Type,* and *Session Status* are the same as they were in the Session Dimension. Additional measures include the *Session Start Time, Session End Time, Session Length, Entry Page URL, Entry Page Identifier, Exit Page URL, Exit Page Identifier, Number of Pages Visited,* and *Total Bytes Transferred.*

Table 6.21 External Referrer Geography Dimension Attributes and Values

LEVEL	EXTERNAL REFERRER GEOGRAPHY ATTRIBUTES	EXAMPLE VALUES
1	Surrogate External Referrer Key	Unique integer identifier
1	External Referring URL	http://www.search.google.com
1	External Referring Page ID	Unique referring page identifier for dynamic pages
1	External Query String	?search=clickstream+data+warehousing
1	External Referring Domain	google.com
1	Entry Page URL	www.mysite.com/index.html
1	Entry Page ID	Unique referred page identifier for dynamic pages

Table 6.22 Session Activity Fact Table Attributes and Values

LEVEL	SESSION ACTIVITY FACT ATTRIBUTES	EXAMPLE VALUES
1	User Surrogate Key	Unique integer identifier
1	Fiscal Date Surrogate Key	Unique integer identifier
1	Fiscal Time-of-Day Surrogate Key	Unique integer identifier
1	User Date Surrogate Key	Unique integer identifier
1	User Time-of-Day Surrogate Key	Unique integer identifier
1	Physical Geography Surrogate Key	Unique integer identifier
1	Host Geography Surrogate Key	Unique integer identifier
1	External Geography Surrogate Key	Unique integer identifier
1	Internal Promotion Surrogate Key	Unique integer identifier
1	External Promotion Surrogate Key	Unique integer identifier
1	Session Identifier	Unique Session Identifier
1	Session Start Time	timestamp
1	Session End Time	timestamp
1	Session Length	In seconds
1	Entry Page URL	URL of the entry page
1	Entry Page Identifier	Unique entry page identifier
1	Exit Page URL	URL of the exit page
1	Exit Page Identifier	Unique exit page identifier
1	Number of Pages Visited in Session	1..n
1	Total Bytes Transferred	0..n
1	Session Type	Shopping basket, registration, purchase, search, informational, unknown, etc.
1	Session Status	Success, abandoned, error code, etc.

This concludes the definition of the clickstream data warehouse meta-schema and its aggregates. In the next section we discuss three applied variations of the meta-schema.

Variation 1: B2B Applications of the Meta-Schema

The meta-schema and its aggregates are good starting templates for the logical schema design effort of any clickstream data warehouse. Every type of business will require its own variations on the meta-schema; we discuss three in the sections that follow.

The first variation is a business-to-business (B2B) meta-schema. Rather than selling to individual consumers, most B2B sites are trying to sell something to other businesses. There are many different types of B2B sites, from online marketplaces to traditional businesses that sell equipment or services to other businesses. First, we will cover the major modification to the meta-schema that applies to all B2B models.

Adjusting the User Dimension for Business Use

Since the actual Web site user is a business in the B2B case, the User dimension becomes more complex. Businesses usually have multiple employees acting on behalf of the company, purchasing agents, for example. This causes the generic meta-schema User dimension to split into a *Company* dimension, containing the attributes of the organization that is the end customer, and the *Corporate User* dimension, describing the attributes of the employee acting on behalf of the business.

A diagram of the modified schema is shown in Figure 6.13. This diagram shows the meta-schema at the page level of granularity, but the meta-schema could be at the hit or session level as well. The change to the User dimension applies across all of these levels.

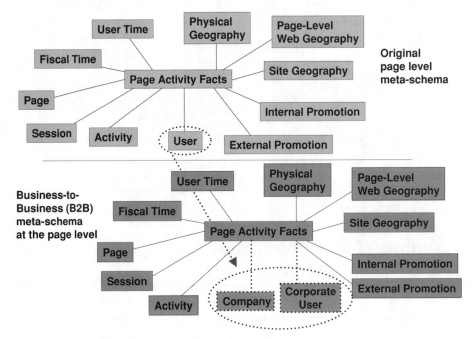

Figure 6.13 The B2B meta-schema.

The Company dimension and Corporate User dimension attributes are shown in Tables 6.21 and 6.22. Many B2B sites require more intensive user tracking, including user registration with specific information about the user's organization. The registration usually includes attributes like the company name and address, the business telephone number, the fax number, and the type of business. Examples of these attributes are included in the Company dimension shown below.

Table 6.23 Company Dimension Attributes and Values

LEVEL	COMPANY ATTRIBUTES	EXAMPLE VALUES
1	Surrogate Company Key	Unique integer identifier
1	Company Identifier	Unique business identifier
1	Domain Name	The company's Internet domain name
1	IP address range	The known IP addresses or address range of the company (helps in user identification)
1	Company Name	Standardized business name
1	Country	USA, Canada, UK, France, Germany, Japan, etc.
2	State or Province	California, Ontario, Bavaria, etc.
3	County or Township	Santa Clara, DuPage, King, etc.
4	City	San Jose, Medford, etc.
5	Street Number	3800, etc.
5	Address	Shasta Ave., W. Flagler Road, NE Flanders, etc.
5	Address 2	Suite 100, Building 10, etc.
1	Postal Code	95126, 2G24R, etc.
2	Postal Code Extension	2314, etc.
1	Type of Location	Main office, New Jersey factory, warehouse, invoice department, etc.
1	Business Telephone Number	Telephone number
1	Fax Number	Fax number
1	Business Type	Manufacturer, software, computers, telco, etc.
1	SIC Code	The Standard Industry Classification code for this company
1	Market Segment	Market segment fields, if any
1	Timestamp of last Purchase by Business	SQL timestamp of last purchase, if any
1	Business Credit Profile	Credit score fields, if any

The Company dimension is one that can easily be enriched with third-party data. For example, the data warehouse might import more company attributes from one of the syndicated business databases like Dun and Bradstreet. These databases can supply information on all of the business's locations, as well as specific details like credit history or debt load that one might be interested in.

State-of-the-art clickstream data warehouses take this dimension a step further, using it as a mechanism for organizing and searching textual or other media. As the organization collects information from Web sites, clipping services, or other means, the information can be tagged through this dimension. With a Web-enabled reporting and analysis product, this supplemental information can be viewed within the end-user's environment to further aid in decision making.

The Corporate User dimension enhances the original User dimension by adding business-specific attributes associated with a corporate user. During registration, many B2B Web sites require employee profile information, including elements like the employee's title, email address, and office address. These values are stored in the Corporate User dimension shown in Table 6.24.

Other than two new surrogate keys for each dimension, there is no change to any of the fact tables in the original meta-schema.

Variation 2: Adding Clickstream Characteristics to Existing Business-Oriented Schemas

Since many organizations that sell to businesses already have data warehouses that cover offline sales operations, building a pure, stand-alone clickstream data warehouse may not make sense. Instead, the goal should be to integrate the original data warehouse with the new clickstream data. How the existing data warehouse is enhanced depends on the type of business and the design. We will walk through a number of modifications that make sense for most businesses.

The first step is building the clickstream portion of the data warehouse as described in the previous section. Because much of the user behavior being tracked occurs prior to or is associated with a sale, the meta-schema is something that is "in front" of the traditional schema. The fact tables containing hits, page views, and sessions and the associated dimension changes outlined above allow for complex analysis of corporate buyer behavior that is otherwise not visible, in much the same way that consumer behavior becomes visible on a consumer-oriented e-commerce site.

Table 6.24 Corporate User Dimension Attributes and Values

LEVEL	CORPORATE USER ATTRIBUTES	EXAMPLE VALUES
1	Surrogate Corporate User Key	Unique integer identifier
1	Corporate User Identifier	Unique employee identifier
1	Company Identifier	Foreign key that identifies the business that employs the user
1	Registered Username	Registered user name, if the Web site uses registration names
1	User Name	Employee name, if any
1	User Title	Purchasing agent, accounts payable, purchasing manager, etc.
1	User email Address	Email address, if any
1	User email Domain	Email domain, if any
1	Business Type	Manufacturer, software, computers, telco, etc.
1	SIC Code	The Standard Industry Classification code for this company
1	Market Segment	Market segment fields, if any
1	Timestamp of Last Purchase by Employee	SQL timestamp of last purchase, if any
1	Business Credit Profile	Credit score fields, if any
1	User Telephone Number	Employee telephone, if any
1	User Fax Number	Employee fax number
1	User Billing Address	Billing address used by employee, if any
1	User Shipping Address	Shipping address used by employee, if any

Since we've already built the clickstream analysis portion of the schema, the next step is to incorporate some of the clickstream dimensions and attributes into the structure of the existing data warehouse. Going back to the discussion at the beginning of the chapter, most businesses have a variation of the standard sales and marketing or CRM schema shown in Figure 6.2. To this schema we need to add several new dimensions, shown in Figure 6.14.

Given that most business-oriented schemas already have a *Company* dimension that tracks the companies that make up the firm's customer base, the first modification to that schema is to extend the Company dimension to include the Web-oriented data. We also need to add the Corporate User dimension that was described in the previous section.

One problem with adding the Corporate User dimension is that all of the original fact rows will not have an associated row in this dimension. We must add

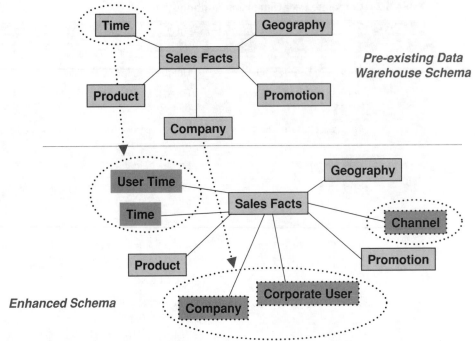

Figure 6.14 New dimensions for the preexisting warehouse schema.

an "unknown" or "not Web customer" row as the catch-all for product Sales that do not move through the Web site. In this way we can extend the dimensionality to cover both online and offline transactions.

One additional dimension that may not be present in the preexisting data warehouse is the *Channel* dimension. The purpose of this dimension is simply to differentiate the channels through which a product or service is delivered. In the simplest case, there would be two rows containing "traditional sales force" or "Web site."

It is possible that Channel information may already be incorporated in the sales-oriented Geography dimension in the existing data warehouse. Many manufacturing and distribution data warehouses include channel data already. In this case, we would simply add one more type of sales channel— the Web channel—to the Sales Geography dimension.

The original time dimension must be modified to reflect the new clickstream requirements—namely, the addition of the User Time dimension and, in the case of the original time dimension, addition of the Time-of-Day table. Again, the original, non-Web sales transactions will not typically have user times or time of day associated with them. When rekeying the original fact rows, keep in mind that these rows must be linked with the new time dimensions in some way. Most often, an arbitrary time like "12:00:00" will be associated with non-Web transactions.

After adding the dimension, the last remaining step is to incorporate the sales fact rows from the Web site into the preexisting Sales fact table. This may be a simple data extraction job, or it may be very complex. If the Web site has its own order processing system then this work is likely to be more than a simple transfer of data.

Many times, the requirements driving a clickstream warehouse focus on the Web analytics rather than more traditional analysis like channel contention or cannibalization. Therefore, one might question the need to include the clickstream data in the original data warehouse since the sets of analysis are discrete.

It is for this reason that we suggest starting with the clickstream meta-schema to support analysis of all the Web site information, before extending the data into the existing data warehouse. However, we strongly believe that the two sets of information must be brought together for maximum business impact.

By incorporating clickstream analysis as part of the channel through which products or services are moved, new possibilities are opened up. For example, one machinery supplier realized that a large number of companies buying through the Web site were located in a region where there was no direct sales force. They were able to examine the costs and benefits of the Web site versus the traditional sales force, and decided to open a small office to increase their penetration in that market. This discovery was made when comparing sales in different channels by the geography of the customers.

Another benefit of marrying the clickstream user behavior information to traditional sales data is a much better understanding of customer behavior, which may enhance the performance of the Web channel. Often, corporate users purchasing online are on a mission—they want to get in, get the product or service, and go back to other work. Unlike many types of Web sites, maximizing time spent on a B2B Web site can be detrimental to the business. Clickstream analysis can suggest places where the process might be streamlined to make the customer's job easier and faster.

The examples we just reviewed are probably simpler than real-life data warehouse situations. For example, most business-oriented data warehouses have fact tables for Orders, Shipments, and Inventory as well as for Sales or Revenue analysis. The clickstream schema modifications would need to be extended to each of these different fact tables.

In spite of this, these examples show how easily the meta-schema can be extended to meet the needs of both pure-play e-commerce and traditional companies, and how resilient the meta-schema is under different business models.

Variation 3: Supporting a Large Site with Multiple Replicated Web Servers

Many larger Web sites have replicated Web servers in order to meet the high traffic demands of large user populations. The meta-schema puts all this activity into one site-hit fact table, and it can be difficult to see what traffic goes through different servers. It is also difficult to determine which servers are experiencing errors, and which servers are suffering from performance problems.

This can be solved by adding a *Server* dimension to the User Activity/Site Hit meta-schema. The Server dimension identifies the location site traffic is served from, as shown in Figure 6.15.

The new Server dimension has the attributes shown in Table 6.25. We include both a server name and a hostname because it's possible to link multiple IP addresses to the same server, as well as linking multiple hostnames to the same IP address. Without allowing for storage of all these attributes, it would be difficult to differentiate traffic loads on multiple Web servers running on the same machine, and it would be harder to roll traffic loads from multiple virtual Web servers up to the actual machine running those Web servers.

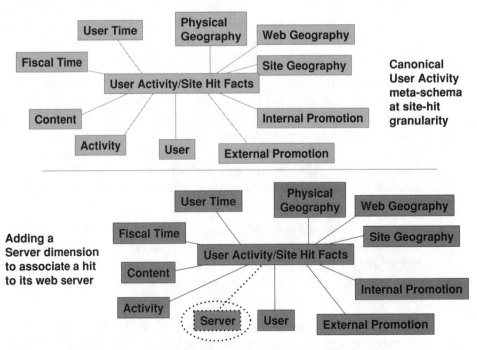

Figure 6.15 Adding a Server dimension to track activity on specific servers.

Table 6.25 Server Dimension Attributes and Values

LEVEL	SERVER ATTRIBUTES	EXAMPLE VALUES
1	Surrogate Server Key	Unique integer identifier
1	Server Name	The name of the physical server hosting the Web server or application
1	Hostname	The fully qualified hostname of the server
1	Server IP Address	The IP address associated with the individual server
1	Server Type	Replicated Web server, application server, SSL server, cache server
1	Software	Apache, Microsoft IIS, ATG Dynamo, etc.
1	Software Version	3.5, 5.0, etc.

This dimension also contains other attributes relevant to the administrator doing analysis of the site's infrastructure. You may wish to add other descriptive attributes, such as the amount of memory in the server or the CPU speed, to better analyze resource usage or performance.

Summary

In this chapter we presented one of the central ideas of this book—the clickstream data warehouse meta-schema. This meta-schema is intended to be used as a universal template for the logical design of a clickstream data warehouse. The dimensional models for the meta-schema were presented at different levels of aggregation, including the base level of site hits, the page level, and the level of user sessions, with all the details about the corresponding fact tables and dimension tables, and their attributes. We also included three variations on the schema, one for business-to-business models, and one that supports Web site administration for large sites with many Web servers.

After doing the logical schema design using the meta-schema, the next step is to decide on the appropriate physical design for the database and choose the technology infrastructure to run it. This difficult topic, which is missing from most books on data warehousing, is the subject of the next chapter.

Site Traffic Statistics Generated by the Meta-Schema

The meta-schema can be used to generate the following site administration and traffic statistics:

- The number of hits for any time quantum.
- The most popular site content components.
- The least popular site content components.
- Time-of-day analysis of site traffic.
- What site traffic comes from which external sites (referring site report).
- The most popular internal referring pages (referring page report).
- The number of unique users for any time quantum.
- Average page views per unique user.
- The amount of traffic generated by different user profiles.
- Data transfer rates by any time quantum.
- What traffic comes from which physical geographies.
- The most common domains hosting user requests (like aol.com, yahoo.com, etc.).
- User agent analysis, including browsers and indexing robots.
- Error analysis by individual content component.
- Site performance analysis, including component load times.
- Which server has the slowest page load times.
- Which servers handle the most site traffic.

All of the above can also be compared in a historical fashion by any time quantum, including second, minute, hour, day-over-day, week-over-week, month-over-month, and year-over-year. Site administrators can also do historical trending on any of the above statistics over any period in the clickstream data warehouse data history.

CHAPTER 7

Implementing the Appropriate Clickstream Data Warehouse Technology Infrastructure

In the last chapter, we showed how the meta-schema is used as a tool for the logical design of a clickstream data warehouse schema. Once the logical design of a clickstream data warehouse is complete, the next challenge is to implement the physical design of the data warehouse. This includes everything from extract, transformation, and load, to the physical layout of the tables, aggregates, and indexes that comprise the resultant data warehouse.

A successful physical implementation of a clickstream data warehouse is highly dependent on the quality of the underlying clickstream data warehouse technology infrastructure. This infrastructure consists of software, hardware, and network components, and all of them have to work in harmony to produce the optimal clickstream analysis environment. The authors of this book find that many sites fail to implement an appropriate clickstream data warehouse technology infrastructure, and these bad choices haunt the data warehouse throughout its lifecycle. Furthermore, the overhyped marketing environment that surrounds many of these technology components creates a void in which implementers are starved for accurate information, leading to suboptimal implementations based more on myth and ignorance than on the facts.

In this chapter we review the clickstream data warehouse functionality of major infrastructure technology components. This includes a detailed review of relational database support for a clickstream data warehouse environment, including important topics like partitioning, indexing, dimensional aggregates, and dimensionally aware join algorithms. We explain all of the important Relational Database Management System (RDBMS) features and show what makes sense in a clickstream data warehouse environment, using Oracle functionality and syntax for examples unless otherwise specified. On the hardware side, we explain the tricky process of mapping database objects onto disk drives, including a detailed discussion of logical volume management functionality. We conclude with a discussion of the relative merits of commercially available database software products for clickstream data warehouse implementations.

Database Support for Clickstream Data Warehouses

The two primary load-time goals of a clickstream data warehouse are:

- The successful extraction and load of the next increment of clickstream history into the data warehouse within the required load time window.

- The construction of the necessary supporting query optimization structures, such as indexes and aggregates, also within the same load time window.

Because clickstream data can be so voluminous, just extracting and loading it into the data warehouse can stress the software, hardware, and network resources of the underlying infrastructure to its limits. Adding query response time optimization structures like indexes and aggregates can blow the whole process out if its time window. Once everything is loaded, the query optimizer needs to make appropriate use of the database infrastructure, using parallelism, partitioning, indexes, and aggregates to give the quickest possible query response time.

RDBMS systems have developed sophisticated data structures and algorithms designed to speed these operations. As the volume of data and the load frequency increases, the analytical requirements become more complex; and as the batch load window shortens, it becomes more important to select an RDBMS engine that provides the richest set of supporting functionality.

These crucial functionalities separate into the following seven categories:

Bulk/Batch Load. Parallel bulk load programs can efficiently load base dimension and fact tables, leaving more time in the load window to build necessary indexes and aggregates.

Partitioning. Partitioning can make huge clickstream data warehouse tables and indexes much easier to manage during extract, transformation, and load. Partitioning also provides the basis for many parallel query algorithms.

Indexing. Indexes are one of the keys to improving query performance, and new types of indexes like bitmap indexes and partitioned local indexes can greatly improve the clickstream data warehouse analytical environment.

Specialized Joins. Dimensional clickstream data warehouse schemas do a lot of joins, and important new join algorithms have been created specifically to support dimensional schemas.

Dimensional Aggregate Management and Awareness. Creating dimensional aggregates is one of the most time-consuming load-time operations, but once they are created, it has always been a challenge to get user queries to properly utilize them. New aggregate aware optimizer algorithms allow the database to automatically translate user queries to use the best possible aggregate, greatly reducing query response times.

Parallelism. It is safe to say that without parallel database operations, large clickstream data warehouses would simply not be possible. We explain how to make the best use of parallelism in a clickstream data warehouse environment.

SQL Extensions. SQL has had many deficiencies that have made analysis of a clickstream data warehouse unnecessarily difficult. Many of these problems have been resolved, and we review the new functionality.

We will now explore each of these categories in more detail.

Bulk/Batch RDBMS Loaders

One of the quickest ways to load data into a clickstream data warehouse is via a bulk loader utility provided by the RDBMS, like the SQL*Loader for Oracle. The loader utility is invoked from the command line or through a GUI, and takes as input the data file to load along with a control file that specifies the destination database table, the input file format, and any special instructions for the utility.

To achieve optimum load performance, it is best to minimize the amount of additional work that the loader utility must perform beyond reading the data from the input file and writing it to the database table. Generally, the less logic applied to the input file during the data load—like data type conversions, combining multiple physical records into a logical record, conditional logic on input data, applying SQL operators on input data—the better the performance of the loading process. It is often more efficient to perform these operations after the load process, when the data is already in a database table and SQL operators can be used to efficiently transform the data.

It's also desirable to minimize the maintenance tasks that must be performed on ancillary table data structures during the load. For instance, database triggers, constraints, and indexes can be dropped or disabled before the load and rebuilt after the load completes. Disabling and rebuilding these features makes sense only if the load impacts a significant portion of the data in the target table. By instrumenting the load processes to see how long each individual step takes, one can determine whether a load performance threshold has been crossed, making it faster to drop and recreate an index than update it in place, for example.

Finally, data stored in fixed length fields will load much faster than variable length or delimited fields. Fixed field formatting is a good practice if the input fields can be in a fixed length format before they reach the database, and if the data load volumes are immense.

The largest tables in a clickstream data warehouse are the fact tables. In general, fact tables that are significantly updated during a data load should have indexes, constraints, and triggers dropped or disabled during the data load process. Then the fastest available method for loading the data into the table is used, depending on the table structure (e.g., partitioned versus nonpartitioned) and the available resources (processors, memory, I/O capacity). Finally, the indexes are rebuilt, usually in parallel, and the constraints and triggers are reenabled.

The next two sections describe the mechanisms for bulk loading data using Oracle's SQL*Loader utility.

Conventional Path Load

The conventional path load is the simplest method for data loading that fully maintains the integrity of the database table. The input data is loaded, by field, into a bind array, which is subsequently inserted into the destination database table using a SQL INSERT statement. After each row is inserted into the destination table, the associated indexes are updated, and the constraints and triggers are enforced. This approach should be used for all relatively small tables and those very large tables that have a small number of new rows inserted during the load.

Conventional loads can execute concurrently, even on the same database object, by issuing multiple SQL*Loader commands, each with its own input file. However, the loader processes will compete with each other for system resources, like disk devices, during the load process. With this type of parallelism, the administrator is responsible for dividing the input files appropriately so that each loader process has approximately the same amount of work.

The loader utility can also load a partition of a partitioned table. For this approach, the input file should only contain data that belongs in the partition being loaded since record rejects will impact load performance. A parallel load of a partitioned table can be performed by issuing an SQL*Loader command for each partition of a partitioned table. Again, the administrator must appropriately construct the input files to make this approach feasible.

Direct Path Load

The direct path load in Oracle's SQL*Loader gives improved performance over the conventional load at the cost of some of the flexibility allowed with the conventional load process. In a direct path load, input records are parsed and converted into database block format; then the database blocks are written directly to the database datafiles, bypassing most RDBMS processing. The load process doesn't compete with other database users for system resources and can take advantage of operating system asynchronous I/O to overlap buffer fill and write processes.

SQL functions are not allowed on the data fields in a direct path load since the normal logic of the INSERT statement in the conventional load is bypassed. However, these functions can be applied to the database table after the load has completed. In the direct path load, referential and data integrity constraints are disabled before the load. Therefore, you need to handle referential and data integrity programmatically as part of your data staging tasks prior to loading, which we discuss in the next chapter on extraction, transformation, and load. Otherwise, you risk the introduction of data quality issues that require significant manual intervention to find and correct. Direct path loads can be manually parallelized in the same way as conventional path loads, by issuing multiple load processes concurrently on separate input files.

Partitioning

Partitioning is used to support very large tables and indexes by decomposing them into smaller, more manageable pieces or partitions. Tables and indexes can be partitioned using one of several methods described below. A partitioned table is treated as a single object from the perspective of a user query, but the individual partitions are managed as separate objects by the database. Having the table subdivided in this manner improves the manageability, availability, and query performance against large volumes of data.

Table maintenance operations benefit greatly from partitioning, since operations can be invoked on a partition of a table at a time without impacting the other partitions in the table. The ability to individually maintain partitions increases the availability of the data for query applications, because they can use the partitions that are not being modified. The availability of the data is also increased during failures. If a failure only impacts only a subset of the partitions of a table, the unaffected partitions continue to be available to query applications.

Partitioning enhances query performance. With partitioning, the RDBMS query optimizer can specify efficient query processing algorithms like query partition elimination, partition-wise joins, and parallel SQL data manipulation language (DML). In *partition elimination*, also called *partition pruning*, the query optimizer directs queries to use only certain partitions during table accesses. The optimizer determines which partitions can be eliminated from consideration based on the query constraints, determined from the WHERE clause of the query. *Partition-wise joins* allow a large join operation, in which at least one of the tables is partitioned, to be separated into several smaller join operations on the underlying partitions. The smaller joins may be executed serially or in parallel, but the end result is usually much improved join performance. Parallel SQL also allows the query execution plan to take advantage of partitions to parallelize INSERT, UPDATE, and DELETE SQL operations across all the partitions in a table.

Finally, partitioning gives the database architect another layer of abstraction in configuring the database objects. The storage hierarchy for non-partitioned tables versus partitioned tables is shown in Figure 7.1. Note that partitions sit between tables and tablespaces, with a many to one relationship between both. We assume that volume management software is utilized so that datafiles can map to multiple physical devices. Partitioning provides even more control over the placement of database objects within the physical disk layout.

The sheer volume of User Activity fact table data means partitioning must be used to get the best query performance and most flexible database management functionality out of your clickstream data warehouse. Other likely partitioning candidates include the largest meta-schema base dimensions, such as the User and Referrer Geography dimensions.

The methods of partitioning supported by Oracle include range partitioning, hash partitioning, and composite partitioning, and these are discussed in the sections below. We then discuss how the database optimizer invokes partition elimination to reduce the amount of data in the scope of query execution in order to improve query performance. The discussion on partition-wise joins is deferred to the section on Specialized Joins, which comes later in this chapter.

Range Partitioning

Range partitioning divides the data in a table according to a range of values defined over one or more columns in the table. The most common use of range partitioning is to partition a large fact table by its time-based key column(s).

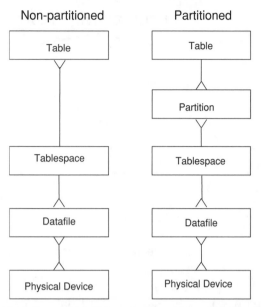

Figure 7.1 Non-partitioned versus partitioned storage hierarchies for a table.

Consider a time-based fact table that contains a rolling window of 13 months of data. The 13-month historical time window supports reporting for the prior 12 months, as well as the ability to compare the current month to the same month in the prior year, i.e., the thirteenth month. The oldest month's data is archived and then removed from the fact table at the end of each month, and a new month is added to the fact table. Which columns in the fact table are used to do time partitioning depends on how the date key of a site hit is represented in the fact table. The fact table is typically partitioned on the surrogate key range corresponding to the equivalent foreign keys in the Fiscal or User Time dimensions. It could be partitioned according to the year, month, and day fields in the SQL Date Timestamp column, or as a composite key using the separate Year/Month/Day time hierarchy columns. In Figure 7.2, we show the User Activity fact table is separated into 13 partitions based on YYYY-MM-DD, with each partition holding one month's data for the period from January 2000 to January 2001.

The boundaries of the partitions are defined by specifying the upper bound for each partition in the "VALUES LESS THAN" specification. For example, a query that compares site hit information for January 2000 to site hits for January 2001 only needs to access partitions 1 and 13. Because the query is constrained to only two months, partitions 2 through 12 are eliminated from consideration by the optimizer, saving a tremendous amount of I/O and processing activity.

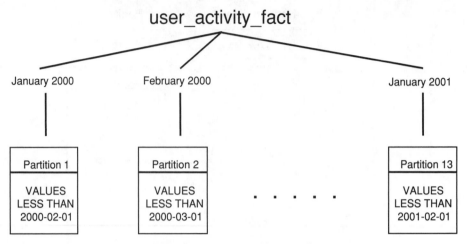

Figure 7.2 User Activity fact table range partitioned by month.

To add February 2001 data to the fact table while maintaining the rolling 13-month time window, the February 2001 data is loaded, cleansed, and indexed into a separate empty staging area table with the same partitioned column format as the target partitioned table. Then the ADD PARTITION and the EXCHANGE PARTITION commands are used to create a new partition in the fact table and add the data from the staged table to the new partition. Finally, a DROP PARTITION command is used to drop the oldest partition for January 2000.

When using range partitioning, the number of rows in each partition should be approximately the same in order to achieve the best query performance. Since the cardinality of the partition key is application dependent, the database administrator has to be careful to choose a partition key that ensures an even data distribution. With an even data distribution, each individual parallel operation across the set of partitions participating in a query will finish in approximately the same amount of processing time, giving the fastest possible parallel query execution path. Time-based partitioning may be best for the User Activity fact table, but different key partitioning schemes may be required for partitioned dimension tables.

Range partitions are managed independently, which eases the burden of incremental loading on the database and simplifies backup and restore. For example, backup becomes simpler in a time-partitioned fact table, because the data in the partitions from earlier months does not change over time, meaning that backups can be confined to new partition data only. In a similar way restore is simplified because it can be confined to the effected range partition, not the entire table or database.

Hash Partitioning

Range partitioning relies on the underlying assumption that the partitioned table has a key that will range partition the data into uniformly sized segments. In many cases there isn't any range partitioning key that will give a uniform data distribution—a condition known as *data skew*. In situations where data skew is an issue, hash partitioning is a good alternative. Hash partitioning uses a synthetic randomization function, called the hash function, to take the data skewed key values as input and produce uniformly distributed hash partition numbers for the corresponding rows as output. Unlike the key values in range partitioning, the hash keys in hash partitioning have no logical meaning to end users. That is, the fact that a row is in hash partition 99 says nothing about the time-of-day in its timestamp, the type of user, or any other logical property associated with the original input key values.

The database engine usually supplies the hashing function, although some engines allow users to specify their own hash function. Hash functions take the hash key column values of a row as input and output the partition number where the row is then stored. In the case of Oracle, the number of partitions specified should be a power of 2 (2, 4, 8, 16, etc.) for the hashing algorithm to obtain the most uniform data distribution. Figure 7.3 shows a User dimension table hash partitioned into four partitions based on the user_id column in the User dimension.

Partition elimination can occur in hash partitioning, although it does not occur as often as it does in range partitioning. Suppose an analyst is doing a drill down query from site hits in a User Activity report on a set of hits for a particular group

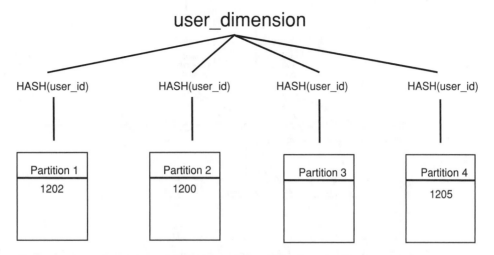

Figure 7.3 User dimension table hash partitioned into four partitions.

of three users. If the drill down query retrieves User dimension information for three particular users by constraining the query with a "WHERE User_id IN (1200, 1202, 1205)" clause, then partition elimination will occur. Since the table has four partitions and the constraint has three users spread over three partitions, one of the partitions, Hash Partition 3, will be eliminated from the query by the optimizer.

Composite Partitioning

Recent versions of Oracle support composite partitioning, which combines the advantages of range partitioning and hash partitioning. In composite partitioning, a table is partitioned first using range partitioning, and then each range partition is further subpartitioned using hash partitioning.

Our example of composite partitioning builds on the above range partitioning example by hash partitioning each month's data into subpartitions by user_id. The details of the subpartitions for January 2000 are illustrated in Figure 7.4. The total number of subpartitions necessary to store the table is 13 range partitions times 4 hash partitions for each range partition, or 52 physical table partitions. Partition elimination, parallel SQL, and partition-wise joins are all possible under composite partitioning.

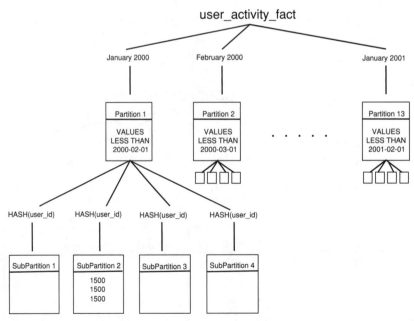

Figure 7.4 User activity fact table composite partitioned by month with four subpartitions per month.

For example, a query parse tree that returns the site hits for January 2000 where user_id=1500 is pruned using composite partition elimination to access only User Activity fact table Range Partition 1, based on the time constraint of January 2000, and further pruned to access just User dimension Subpartition 2, based on the user_id=1500 constraint. The query execution plan for parallel queries executed against tables with composite partitioning allows parallel processes to operate all the way down to the subpartition level, with intra-partition parallelism on range partitions.

Range partitioning by month obviously has logical meaning to analytical users since the data is mapped into partitions based on the same Date Timestamp column value ranges entered by the users for their query constraints. The division of data within a hash partition has no logical meaning to users since it is based on the randomization of keys by the hash function. It is important to remember that *no data* is stored at the top partition level in composite partitioning; the physical data is stored only at the subpartition level.

Partition Elimination

The query optimizer utilizes partition elimination to remove unnecessary index and table partitions or subpartitions from consideration based on the constraints specified in a query. By removing partitions from the query execution path, many optimizations are possible, including reduced temporary table sizes for sorts and joins, improved system resource utilization, and, of course, faster query response times. This section summarizes the situations where partition elimination occurs.

For range partitioned tables and indexes, partition elimination is possible only with range (e.g., attribute BETWEEN value AND value), set membership (e.g., attribute IN(value, value, value)), and equality (e.g., attribute = value) predicates in the WHERE clause of a query. The attributes in the WHERE clause must result in a set of candidate surrogate keys that match those in the partitioning key range for partition elimination to be applicable. For hash partitioned tables and indexes, partition elimination is only possible with set membership (e.g., attribute IN(value, value, value)) and equality (e.g., attribute = value) predicates in the WHERE clause of a query. The attributes in the WHERE clause must result in a set of candidate surrogate keys that, when the hash function is applied, match those in the hash key range for partition elimination to be applicable. For composite partitioned tables, partition elimination is applied successively on both the range and hash partitioning levels as described above. For more details on index partition elimination, see the next section on Indexing.

Indexing

Without indexes, searching for particular rows in a table would be like searching for a needle in a haystack. In a haystack, in order to find the needle, one has to pick up pieces of straw until one finds the needle, searching through $N/2$ pieces of straw on average, assuming the haystack contains N pieces. If the haystack were small, this would not be a problem. But if the haystack were very large, like a clickstream data warehouse fact table with millions of rows, repeatedly searching through all that hay for the next needle would become very burdensome. The same is true of tables without indexes. If one wants to find a particular row, one starts searching at the beginning and searches until he finds the row, going through $N/2$ database pages on average before finding the target row, assuming the table is spread over N pages.

Indexes are an additional data structure that is created on one or more key columns for the target table. The index data structure is designed to make the data access overhead to find any row in the table small and uniform. For example, using an index on a particular clickstream data warehouse fact table, one might be able to guarantee that it took only, say, three page I/Os to get to any row in the table, instead of $N/2$ page I/Os. As N grows large, indexes provide significant performance advantages.

Indexed table access is always faster in cases where the query selects a small percentage of the rows in the table. But a full table scan provides better performance for queries that require a large percentage of rows from the table. It is pretty easy to see why this is true. Suppose it takes three page I/Os to get a particular row in a fact table using an index. If one was trying to average some measure in a fact table over its entire history, one needs to read every row, which is a full table scan. If one were to use the index to do the full table scan, one would have to do three index I/Os for every row read in addition to reading all the database pages containing the rows. It would be much faster to just read the rows directly on the database pages, bypassing the index.

In a clickstream data warehouse environment, indexes are created and modified at extract and load time. Any index activity must fit into the batch load window of time. If a database administrator creates too many indexes or fails to use techniques like table and index partitioning, which significantly decrease the amount of index maintenance overhead, index maintenance operations can exceed the time allotted by the batch window. It is also very important to exploit parallelism during index maintenance to ensure that the batch load window is not breached.

In this section, we discuss the index types that are useful in clickstream data warehouse environments, including single-valued and composite B-tree indexes, bitmap indexes, and function-based indexes. We conclude with a discussion about indexing on partitioned tables.

B-tree Indexes

Binary tree, or B-tree, index structures are the most commonly used mechanism to improve query performance. By providing a balanced branch and leaf mechanism to enable direct access to any row in a given table with equal speed, the B-tree index structure is an important component used by the database optimizer when it constructs the most efficient query execution plan. The flatter the B-tree, the quicker the access since descending each branch level typically involves an additional I/O to disk where the index is stored.

A B-tree index stores the mapping between pairs of table key column values and table rowIDs in a B-tree data structure. The initial step in building a B-tree index is to sort the data in the table based on the column(s) to be indexed. Then, the B-tree index structure is loaded with the column value(s) plus the corresponding rowIDs in this sorted order. During indexed access to the table, the index structure is searched to locate the rowIDs of the desired table rows. Then the data is retrieved from the table based on the rowID.

Building the optimal set of indexes for the fact tables and the largest dimension tables is a balancing act between creating the most extensive set of indexes for the best possible query performance, while limiting all the index creation overhead to fit within the extract and load time window. The optimal set of indexes for query performance is based on which columns are accessed most frequently by user queries. The constraints on WHERE clauses and most frequent dimension table join conditions identify the best candidate columns for indexes. A B-tree index will perform best if the index key column(s) have mostly unique values. Key columns that have lots of repetitive values are better candidates for bitmap-structured indexes, which are discussed below.

An index structure that references only one key column is a *single-column* index. A *composite*, or *concatenated* index includes multiple key columns in the index definition. Again, for composite indexes, the composite key should have mostly unique values for the best query performance results. If multiple queries frequently use a few combinations of columns, consider a composite index that is the set union of those columns.

As we will see in the discussion of specialized joins, the order of the columns in the index definition is important to ensure that the cost-based optimizer actually uses the index. The optimizer chooses the index for a query based on the leading columns in the index, so it is important to order the key columns with the most frequently used ones first. For column values that have an equal chance of appearing in queries, put the one with more unique values first. Placing the columns with the most unique values first in the index will result in a flatter, better-performing B-tree structure.

If a query only uses the key columns in an index to produce its result set, the underlying table will never be accessed since the index itself satisfies the query. By indexing the more frequently requested columns in a dimension table, like the dimensional hierarchies, while excluding less frequently requested informational columns, many queries can be satisfied by the index only, saving a lot of processing time.

Fact tables are typically indexed on a composite key that consists of the surrogate foreign key columns for the dimension tables. If you find yourself creating indexes on the non-foreign-key measure columns in a fact table to improve query performance, you should reexamine your fact table design. A fact table should consist of just surrogate foreign keys and additive measures, and the metric columns should never function as key values in queries. If they do, that probably means you have defined a measure that is really a key or, more likely, an attribute of a dimension, and the clickstream data warehouse schema needs more refinement.

Bitmap Indexes

A bitmap index structure can be thought of as a matrix with one row in the matrix for each row in the indexed table and one column in the matrix for each possible column *value* in the column being indexed. For each row in the table, a bit is set in the bitmap structure that identifies which *column value* that *row* contains. Note that the bitmap values are mutually exclusive within each row of a table, which means that any one row in the table can contain one and only one value for the column. A mapping function returns the rowID of the actual row(s) based on the bit position of the column value in the bitmap. A bitmap index is ideal for columns in which the number of distinct values is small relative to the number of rows in the table. Creating a bitmap index on a unique column implies that the index structure will have the same number of rows and columns as the table (i.e., N x N matrix structure), which is highly undesirable. As mentioned in the previous section, one should use a B-tree index for key columns with large numbers of unique values relative to the number of rows in the table.

Consider the Gender column in the User dimension table that is commonly used when performing user demographics analyses. This column is an ideal candidate for a bitmap index since it typically only has three distinct values—Male,

Female, and Unknown. In our example, if rows 1, 4, and 5 are Male, rows 2 and 6 are Female, and row 3 are Unknown, the Gender column would look like this:

ROWID	GENDER
1	Male
2	Female
3	Unknown
4	Male
5	Male
6	Female

In order to represent the Gender value for each row in the table, the bitmap index structure would be constructed as follows:

ROWID	GENDER = 'Male'	GENDER = 'Female'	GENDER = 'Unknown'
1	1	0	0
2	0	1	0
3	0	0	1
4	1	0	0
5	1	0	0
6	0	1	0

The first row in the table (rowID 1) has a gender of Male, so the bit in the column labeled "Male" is set to 1 and the remaining columns are set to 0. The second row (rowID 2) has a gender of Female, with the bit in the column labeled "Female" set to 1. The rest of the structure is similarly populated to set the correct Gender bit for every row in the table. The rowIDs in the index are actually derived using a mapping function, rather than being stored directly in the index structure. Bitmap indexes can be utilized in combination with other access methods like full table scans and B-tree indexes, for performing table joins and the resolution of WHERE clauses. In particular, if there are bitmapped indexes on columns involved in a WHERE clause, the result set can be easily calculated by performing the corresponding Boolean operations directly on the corresponding bitmaps, and then converting the resultant bitmap into the rowIDs of the result set. Consider the above index on the Gender column in the following query:

```
SELECT COUNT(*) FROM USER_DIMENSION WHERE GENDER = 'Male'
    OR GENDER = 'Unknown';
```

The rows in the sample table can be identified by performing a logical OR of the columns with bit value set to 1 for Male and Unknown in the bitmap index structure. After the OR operation, the rows with rowIDs of 1, 3, 4, and 5 satisfy the constraint.

One of the problems with bitmap indexes is their sparsity. All but one of the bit values for a given index row are zero, since only one column value can be set for each row. Oracle solves this problem by compressing the bitmaps when the index is created. As a result, a bitmap index can occupy as little as 5 to 10 percent of the space required for a B-tree index. However, when a column value that is indexed with a bitmap index is modified during extract and load, the compressed bitmap must be uncompressed, modified, and compressed again for storage in the index structure. The large storage overhead associated with this uncompression/compression procedure makes it difficult to use bitmaps on fact tables that have bitmapped indexes left in place and updated during the load, because they have to be expanded and updated every time the load takes place. This is not an issue if the bitmap indexes are dropped before a load and then rebuilt, because the compression is done essentially in place on a clean build.

The largest tables in the clickstream data warehouse—the large fact tables, dimension tables, and aggregate tables—benefit the most from bitmap indexes. As we will see in the discussion on Specialized Joins below, bitmap indexes are a key component in a new, very efficient, index lookup and join mechanism called the star transformation, which is used to process highly selective queries against a dimensional clickstream data warehouse schema.

Function-Based Indexes

Normally, when a function is used in the WHERE clause of a SELECT or DELETE statement, the function defeats the use of an existing index on the underlying column(s), resulting in a less efficient query execution plan and longer query run times. If a function that involves one or more table columns is used regularly in queries on the data, a specialized index, called a function-based index, can be constructed that precomputes the value of the function for the table column(s) and stores the result in an index structure. The function can be an arithmetic expression, Oracle PL/SQL function, package function, C callout, or SQL function. A function-based index can be created as either a B-tree or a bitmap index.

A simple example is to consider the zip_code column of the Physical Geography dimension table and assume that we store nine digit zip codes as a character data type. If users run queries that searched for a specific five-digit zip code, query performance would be improved by building an index on zip_code with the SQL substring function SUBSTR applied as follows:

```
CREATE INDEX phys_geog_5_digit_zip_ix1 ON physical_geography_dim
    (SUBSTR(zip_code,1,5));
```

SELECT and DELETE statements with the clause "WHERE SUBSTR(zip_code,1,5) = '06405' " will use this function-based index to identify the appropriate rows in the Physical Geography dimension table. The more complex the function definition gets, the more query performance typically improves.

As the cost for disk storage continues to drop, the case for function-based indexes has become less compelling. Database administrators should consider altering tables with function-based indexes to add a new column with the function result, instead of building the index. For instance, as we recommend in the meta-schema, the column, zip_code_5_digit, could be added to the Physical Geography dimension to store the results of the SUBSTR function applied to the 9-digit zip_code column. Then the column will be available to all users through the table definition and the function is precomputed. This approach does not require the use of a function-based index, and instead could use a more traditional B-tree index or bitmap index, depending upon the resulting cardinality. Function-based indexes are more of a stopgap measure to provide the benefits of using an index based on a function, until such time that the administrator can alter the corresponding table structure and load the instantiated results of the function into a new column.

Indexing Partitioned Tables

Like tables, indexes can grow very large. Indexes on fact tables can become enormous. Just as a large table can be partitioned to make table extract and load maintenance easier, indexes can be similarly partitioned to avoid global index rebuilds during load time. Partitioned indexes also speed query execution through partition elimination by the query optimizer.

Oracle has two types of partitioned indexes, *local* and *global*. Suppose the User Activity fact table in a clickstream data warehouse is partitioned by fiscal_month. A local index would be one that partitions itself with the same partitioning column, fiscal_month, as the partitioning column of the underlying table. In a local index, *rowID references within an index partition never cross the identical partition boundaries in the underlying table*. A local index inherits the partitioning attributes of its corresponding table, whether the table is range, hash, or composite partitioned. All the rows in each table partition have a corresponding index entry in each corresponding index partition. The index is equi-partitioned with underlying table, meaning the table and its index have the same partitioning method, number of partitions, and boundaries for range partitions.

A *global partitioned index* has keys in one index partition that refer to rows stored in more than one underlying table partition. A global partitioned index can be defined on any type of underlying partitioned table, like hash, range, or composite, but the index itself must be range partitioned. Each index partition is associated with multiple table partitions and the maintenance advantages of equi-partitioned local indexes do not exist with global indexes. Modifications to a table partition typically affect many global index partitions. In the case of a data load to one table partition, multiple index partitions will be affected and the global index will have to be completely reconstructed. Rebuilding global indexes during periodic load processing requires additional system resources and may impact the load time window. Because of these problems, global partitioned indexes should be carefully considered before they are defined on partitioned tables.

Let's look at some examples of local and global partitioned indexes, starting with local partitioned indexes. Suppose we have the following User Activity fact table partitioned by fiscal_month, with an equi-partitioned local index called uaf_local_ix1, as shown in Figure 7.5.

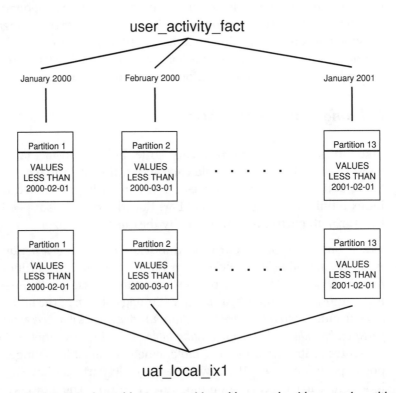

Figure 7.5 User Activity fact table range partitioned by month with an equi-partitioned local index.

The partitioning scheme defines a 13-month rolling time window so the current month can be compared year-over-year.

It is extremely important to realize that the partitioning key of a partitioned index is not necessarily a member of the columns being indexed. It is perfectly all right to have the index columns be *content* and *activity*, while the partition key is *fiscal_time*.

If the partition key is a member of the index columns, specifically the leftmost columns of the index, the index is said to be *prefixed*. In the example, the partitioning key is the fiscal_time key for the User Activity Fact table and also for the index since the index is local. For the index to be prefixed, the first column in the index definition must be the fiscal_time key. For example, if the index uaf_local_ ix1 is defined on the fiscal_time and content columns, then the index is prefixed.

Partition elimination for index partitions has many of the same characteristics as partition elimination for partitioned tables described in the previous section. The query optimizer considers both the index and table partitioning schemes in order to determine which index partitions, if any, are accessed to satisfy a query. By using the local prefixed index, uaf_local_ix1, above, queries that constrain on fiscal_time "WHERE fiscal_time < 2000/03/01" are pruned to access only the relevant partitions of the index.

If the partitioning key of the index is not a leftmost member of the columns that are indexed, then the index is not prefixed. For example, if uaf_local_ix1 is defined on the columns content and activity, then the index is nonprefixed. This local nonprefixed index is useful for queries that return user activity by content type over the entire 13-month history in the fact table. Index partition elimination would not occur for these queries, since there are no constraints on the fiscal_time partitioning key. In other words, all index partitions must be accessed to satisfy the query. However, the index partitions in these queries can be scanned in parallel by range queries using the IN operator on the indexed columns.

Local partitioned indexes should be used whenever possible to streamline extract and load processing. By having equi-partitioned local indexes, table and index modifications can be confined to the last partition of each structure during the load, significantly reducing extract and load overhead. Utilizing local indexes also reduces the amount of data that is unavailable during partition maintenance or tablespace recovery operations, because only the affected partitions are offline. And unaffected partitions in the User Activity fact table can be accessed while the archiving operation executes. Finally, with local partitioned indexes, the database engine maintains the index partitioning automatically as old partitions are dropped and new ones added to the underlying partitioned table.

Now let's turn our attention to global indexes. As mentioned above, a global partitioned index is partitioned on a different key than the underlying partitioned table. This means that the keys in one index partition refer to rows stored in more than one underlying table partition. A global partitioned index can be defined on any type of partitioned table, like hash, range, or composite, but the organization of the index itself must be range partitioned.

In Figure 7.6, we have added a global index, uaf_global_ix1, to the User Activity fact table, organized into 10 index partitions, using range partitioning on the User column, which we have named user_id for the purposes of discussion in this chapter. The columns in a global index must be prefixed by the index partitioning column(s), because they don't relate to the partitioning key of the underlying table. In this example, the only column in the global index is user_id, which obviously satisfies this constraint since it is also the partitioning key for the global index. This global index aids our example because the User *dimension* table is also identically range partitioned on user_id, with 10 table partitions containing 1 million User records per partition. By using the global index, joins on user_id between the User dimension and the User Activity Fact table can be processed very efficiently in parallel.

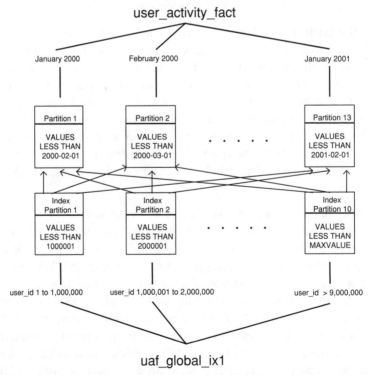

Figure 7.6 User Activity fact table range partitioned by month, with a global index partitioned by user_id.

Each global index range partition should have approximately the same number of key values, or the partitions will become unbalanced. In the example, the global index structure maps to a rowID in a particular User Activity Fact partition if the user hit the site during the month covered by the partition. If the frequency of site hits is such that every user hits the site about 10 times each month, then the index partitions will contain about the same number of rowIDs for each user_id range partition.

Non-partitioned indexes are a special case of global indexes. Non-partitioned indexes can always be built on a partitioned table. From an optimizer perspective, non-partitioned indexes behave like global partitioned indexes because the index entries map onto multiple underlying table partitions.

Specialized Joins

Analytical users of a clickstream data warehouse are very performance conscious. They want the fastest possible query response times, and IT also wants the collective concurrent query throughput to be as large as possible. At the center of this performance spotlight is the database query optimizer, which must generate the most efficient query execution plans that result in the greatest concurrent query throughput, while providing the best possible individual query response times.

Making the query optimizer live up to its name is tricky business. The data warehouse implementation team must follow all of the appropriate logical and physical data modeling rules, implement the right combination of partitioning and indexing structures, and configure database engine parameters correctly.

In this section we will review three specialized joins that are specific to optimizing clickstream data warehouse query performance and throughput—star queries, star transformations, and partition-wise joins.

Star Queries

The Oracle cost-based optimizer recognizes the special nature of multidimensional star schemas and attempts to choose the most efficient query execution plan for these schemas. The optimizer's decisions can be influenced through query hints as described below. These hints are useful during tuning exercises to ensure that the optimizer is choosing the best execution path for queries.

A star join is a primary key to foreign key join between a dimension table and the fact table in a star schema. A star join example, using our canonical clickstream data warehouse meta-schema is shown in Figure 7.7. Unlike the earlier examples in this chapter, which use the base-level granularity User Activity fact table and dimensions, this example, and the examples that follow it, are based on the page-level granularity Page Activity fact table aggregate, described in Chapter 6. This example also extends the data model to serve a hypothetical electronic commerce site that advertises online and sells these products through online ad clickthroughs. As such, the Page Activity fact table contains the following measures:

number_clickthroughs. If the page is an ad clickthrough page, then the measure value is 1, otherwise 0.

number_baskets. If the page is a put-the-item-in-the-basket page, then the measure value is 1, otherwise 0.

number_buys. If the page is a buy-the-item page, then the measure value is 1, otherwise 0.

number_errors. If the page caused an error, the value is 1, otherwise 0.

status_code. The HTTP status code returned for the page.

dwell_time. The number of seconds the user spent on the page.

number_bytes_served. The actual number of bytes of the page served to the user. It may be less than the actual page size if the user abandons the page before it is completely delivered.

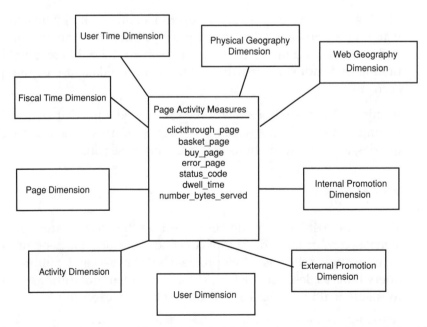

Figure 7.7 Page Activity fact table and associated dimensions used in the specialized join and aggregation examples.

Only one of number_clickthroughs, number_baskets, number_buys can be set because a page can only serve one function, as the clickthrough destination, as the add-to-shopping-basket page, or as the final-buy page. Any page can be an error page, and, if so, the status_code would indicate the HTTP error. The page dwell time in seconds is also recorded, as is the number_bytes_served, which may be different than the number of bytes in the actual page if the user abandons the page before it is completely rendered or if an error occurs.

In the following example, the User Time, Physical Geography, and External Promotion dimensions are joined to the Page Activity Fact table by the primary key of each of the dimension tables. The query returns the number of ad clickthroughs delivered by DoubleClick (using the External Promotion dimension) for users in the European Region (using the Physical Geography dimension) in January 2001 (using the User Time dimension).

```
SELECT ut.month, ut.year, pg.region, ep.ad_engine,
SUM(paf.number_clickthroughs)
FROM user_time_dimension ut,
     physical_geography_dimension pg,
     external_promotion_dimension ep,
     page_activity_fact paf
WHERE ut.month = 'January' AND
      ut.year = '2001' AND
      pg.region = 'European' AND
      ep.ad_engine = 'DoubleClick' AND
      ut.user_time_key = paf.user_time_key AND
      pg.physical_geography_key = paf.physical_geography_key AND
      ep.external_promotion_key = paf.external_promotion_key
GROUP BY ut.month, ut.year, pg.region, ep.ad_engine;
```

In order to build the star query execution plan, the query optimizer gathers all the dimension table information. The optimizer identifies the join key values, namely "January 2001" for the User Time dimension, the "European" Region for the Physical Geography dimension, and the "DoubleClick" ad engine for the External Promotion dimension. Then, using these keys, the specified dimension columns are returned and the associated number of clickthroughs from the Page Activity fact table is summed.

The cost-based optimizer will execute the star query execution plan if:

- Statistics already exist for the tables used by the query. They are created via the Analyze Table command.
- The Page Activity fact table must have a concatenated-key B-tree index on the columns user_time_key, physical_geography_key, and external_promotion_key. For the purposes of this example we call this index paf_concat_ix1.

- The dimension join keys specified in the query must be the first three keys of the index, which is obviously true in this case.

Let's execute the star join. First in the join order are the dimension tables, user_time, physical_geography, and external_promotion, which are joined together using the key value constraints specified by the query (e.g., "January 2001," "European," "DoubleClick") to produce the output table columns month, year, region, and ad_engine. This step of the star join produces a Cartesian product of the dimension tables since there are no common joinable keys between the dimensions (for example, the user_time_key appears in only the user_time and not in physical_geography or external_promotion). This is the desired behavior, since the small dimension tables can support the overhead of a Cartesian product join, as opposed to one done against the giant fact table.

The next step in the join order is to complete the join against the data in the Page Activity fact table using the concatenated-key Page Activity fact table index, paf_concat_ix1, and nested loops. A nested loop join is executed as follows:

> For each row in the driving table, find all rows in the inner table that satisfy the join condition.

In our case, the driving table in the join is really not a table but the Cartesian product of the dimensions. The inner table is the Page Activity fact table. The nested loop executes as follows: For each row entry in the Cartesian product that matches our query constraint key values (e.g. "January 2001," "European," "DoubleClick"), retrieve and SUM the number_clickthroughs column from the Page Activity fact table. In this fashion, we probe the fact table through the concatenated-key index, paf_concat_ix1, avoiding a full table scan of the fact table. Finally, the number_clickthroughs column for each row returned is combined with the associated header information (e.g., month, year, region, ad engine name) to produce the query results.

Oracle allows query designers to force specific query execution paths using a mechanism called *hints*. To guarantee that the optimizer uses the star join execution path explained above, one must first order the tables in the FROM clause in the order of the keys in the concatenated index with the fact table last (e.g., user_time_dimension, physical_geography_dimension, external_promotion_dimension, page_activity_fact), and then add the following hint to the query as shown below:

```
SELECT /*+ ORDERED USE_NL(page_activity_fact)
           INDEX(page_activity_fact paf_concat_ix1) */
        ut.month,...
```

This hint specifies that the join order of the query should match the order of the tables in the FROM clause (i.e., ORDERED), that a nested loop join should be used with the page_activity_fact as the inner table (i.e., USE_NL), and that the concatenated index should be utilized to probe the user_activity_fact table (i.e., INDEX).

As an alternative, the more general STAR hint could be used to remind the optimizer that this query is being done against a star schema, and it should search for execution plans that properly utilize the dimensional model. This type of hint is specified as:

```
SELECT /*+ STAR */ ut.month, ...
```

Some dimensional schemas, notably those created for the MicroStrategy analytical tool, separate dimensional hierarchies into distinct referentially related tables, which can make the star schema look more like a multilevel snowflake when depicted on paper. For example, the meta-schema's Physical Geography dimension can be normalized into a hierarchy of dimension tables: the Zip Code, City, State, and Country tables.

But multilevel snowflake schemas can confuse the query optimizer when it tries to execute a star join. Oracle recommends that one instead create a denormalized view that collapses the entire hierarchy of snowflaked dimension tables back down to a single logical dimension table. The example of such a denormalized view is shown in Figure 7.8.

```
CREATE VIEW physical_geography_dimension AS
SELECT /*+ NO_MERGE */
    *
    FROM zip_code_dimension zcd,
         city_dimension cid,
         state_dimension std,
         country_dimension cod
    WHERE zcd.city_key = cid.city_key AND
          cid.state_key = std.state_key AND
          std.country_key = cod.country_key;
```

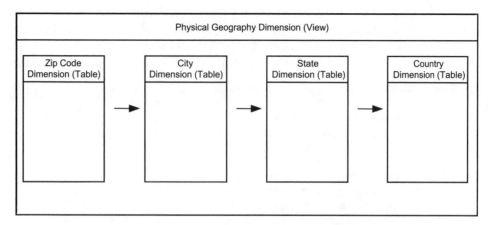

Figure 7.8 Denormalized view for snowflaked dimension tables.

This denormalized dimension definition (view) serves two purposes. Since the four dimension tables are grouped together under the view definition, the number of permutations of dimensions that the optimizer must consider when determining the best execution plan is reduced. Also, the view results are cached after the first execution, which prevents the execution of multiple small table joins (i.e., between the zip code, city, state, and country dimension tables) during a query.

To make the view results available to a large number of queries that access the view, the NO_MERGE hint is specified during the view definition. The NO_MERGE hint designates that the optimizer should not merge the view's SQL syntax with the syntax of a query when the view is used in a query. This hint defines the view as an independent entity so that the view results are cached and reused for multiple queries that access the physical geography dimension. If the NO_MERGE hint were not used, the view results would only be reused in the unlikely case where exactly the same query is issued multiple times, since the view SQL normally replaces (i.e., is merged into) the view reference in a query's SQL at query execution time.

Star Transformations

The star transformation is a query transformation that causes star joins to execute more efficiently than the standard star query execution path explained in the previous section. Rather than computing a Cartesian product of the dimension tables, the star transformation is based on combining bitmap indexes on the foreign key columns in the fact table. The foreign key columns in the fact table must have bitmap indexes defined on them for the approach to be used by the optimizer. Let's work through a transformation example based on the query from the star query section, the number of clickthroughs delivered by DoubleClick (External Promotion dimension) for users in the European Region (Physical Geography dimension) in January 2001 (User Time dimension). We assume that bitmap indexes have been defined on user_time_key, physical_geography_key, and external_promotion_key in the page_activity_fact table.

```
SELECT ut.month, ut.year, pg.region, ep.ad_engine,
       SUM(paf.number_clickthroughs) clickthroughs
FROM user_time_dimension ut,
     physical_geography_dimension pg,
     external_promotion_dimension ep,
     page_activity_fact paf
WHERE ut.month = 'January' AND
      ut.year = '2001' AND
      pg.region = 'European' AND
      ep.ad_engine = 'DoubleClick' AND
      ut.user_time_key = paf.user_time_key AND
```

```
            pg.physical_geography_key = paf.physical_geography_key AND
            ep.external_promotion_key = paf.external_promotion_key
      GROUP BY ut.month, ut.year, pg.region, ep.ad_engine;
```

The star transformation augments the query with new constraints that allow a bitmap index access path to the fact table. The following constraints are added to the above query by the optimizer when the star transformation is performed.

```
AND paf.user_time_key IN
      (SELECT ut1.time_key FROM user_time_dimension ut1
       WHERE ut1.month = 'January')
AND paf.user_time_key IN
      (SELECT ut2.time_key FROM user_time_dimension ut2
       WHERE ut2.year = '2001')
AND paf.physical_geography_key IN
      (SELECT pg1.geography_key FROM physical_geography_dimension pg1
       WHERE pg1.region = 'European')
AND paf.external_promotion_key IN
      (SELECT ep1.external_promotion_key
       FROM external_promotion_dimension ep1
          WHERE ep1.ad_engine = 'DoubleClick');
```

For each row returned from a subquery in the additional constraint, the corresponding bitmap for that value is retrieved from the bitmap index on the foreign key in the fact table. For example, the User Time dimension's user time keys for "January" are returned by the subquery in the first constraint. The IN operator in the additional constraint is equivalent to the join between the fact and dimension table. By AND-ing the bitmaps from the index that match the results of the subquery, the result is a bitmap that identifies the fact rows that satisfy the constraint. Continuing with the example, the merged bitmap from the first constraint represents the rows in the fact table that occurred in "January." By performing an AND operation with the merged bitmap from the second constraint, the fact table rows are further restricted to those that occurred in the month of "January" and the year, "2001." After combining the bitmaps from the four constraints, the rows in the fact table are identified that contain information on advertising delivered by "DoubleClick" in the "European" Region for "January 2001." Now that the necessary fact rows are identified, the joins are executed against the dimension tables to retrieve the header information: month name, region name, and ad engine name, since these values are not in the fact table, only surrogate keys to the dimensions where the values reside.

The star transformation is an alternative for more efficient star query execution in cases where the Cartesian product of the dimension tables becomes too large. Factors that may negatively influence the performance of the Cartesian product include a large number of dimensions in the star schema, queries where not all dimensions are constrained, and sparse fact tables. When there are a large number of dimensions in the star schema, there are many different possible combinations of key column values between tables that are created in the Cartesian product. Similarly, if all dimensions aren't constrained to a small set of values, the number of combinations of key column values in the Cartesian product grows quite large. A sparse fact table refers to the existence of keys in the dimension tables that don't have corresponding transaction rows in the fact table. If the Cartesian product of dimension key values contains large numbers of key value combinations that have no corresponding match in the fact table, then their creation was a waste of processing time since those key values will necessarily not be in the query results.

As of this writing, there are no optimizer hints to suggest a star transformation to the optimizer. Assuming the appropriate bitmap indexes exist, the optimizer determines whether to apply the star transformation over a full table scan of the fact table based on the cost estimates of the two approaches. A query accessing a large percentage of the fact table rows performs better with a full table scan. More selective query constraints that require only a small portion of the fact table perform much better with star transformations.

Partition-Wise Joins

A partition-wise join utilizes the partitioning methods of one or both tables involved in the join to divide a massive join into smaller pieces. The join executes by processing pairs of partitions from the tables. If the query is executed serially, the joins of partition pairs are executed serially. If the query is executed in parallel, a separate query slave joins each pair in parallel. The number of partitions in the table(s) limits the degree of parallelism for the join, so the degree of parallelism for the query should be set to a maximum of the number of table partitions. In general, the degree of parallelism should always be evenly divisible into the number of partitions to ensure that all the parallel query processes will finish processing at about the same time.

Partition-wise joins reduce interprocess communications overhead between parallel query slave processes during parallel join execution since the partitioning scheme is used to divide the tables among the slaves for parallel processing. This approach can give better join performance than other types of parallel join operations.

Full Partition-Wise Join

A full partition-wise join on two partitioned tables can be performed if both tables are equi-partitioned on the join key, which is illustrated in Figure 7.9. To be equi-partitioned, the tables must have the same partitioning method, number of partitions, and partition boundaries. Consider an example where the

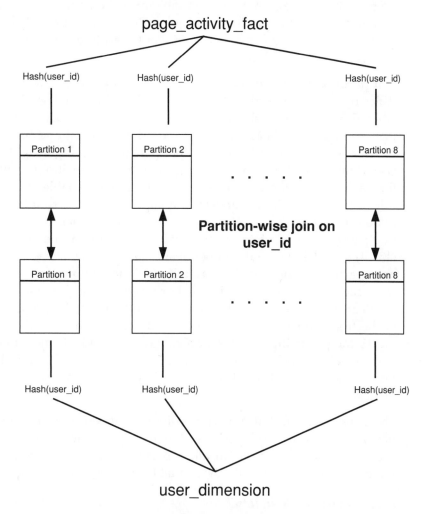

Figure 7.9 A full partition-wise join of the Page Activity fact table with the User dimension table.

Page Activity fact table and the User dimension table are both hash partitioned on the user_id. With serial execution of a partition-wise join between these two tables, one pair of table partitions will be joined at a time until all eight partitions have been completed. Parallel execution of the join can be performed with a maximum degree of eight to match the number of partitions.

If the fact and dimension table are both range-partitioned on the same key, full partition-wise joins are possible. But this is difficult to configure properly, since the range partitions of both tables need to produce uniform distribution of data across the partitions of each table. Consider, for example, a User dimension of 10 million users, range partitioned into 10 partitions of 1 million users each. The Page Activity fact table must be equi-partitioned using the user_id to enable full partition-wise joins. But it is very unlikely that partitioning the Page Activity facts by user_id would result in evenly sized partitions, as it did for the User dimension.

Full partition-wise joins can also be enabled on composite partitioned fact tables by hash partitioning the dimension based on the hash level of the fact table. From the composite partitioned example of the Page Activity fact table that is range partitioned by month (i.e., 13 partitions) and hash partitioned by user_id (i.e., four subpartitions per partition), configuring the associated User dimension to be equi-partitioned using hash partitioning by user_id (at the hash level of the composite partitioned table) enables the execution of full partition-wise joins between the Page Activity fact table and the User dimension table. That is, the User dimension only needs to be hashed into four partitions to match the number of hash partitions rather than 52 partitions (13 * 4) to match the total number of subpartitions. Oracle will build the four hash partitions from the Page Activity fact table by taking one subpartition from each of the range partitions. For example, the first hash partition for the Page Activity fact table that is involved in the partition-wise join consists of the first subpartition (hash of user_id) from each month's partition (i.e., the 13 range partitions). This implementation is ideal since it enables both partition elimination through the range partitioning of the fact table and partition-wise joins with the User dimension through the hash partitioning of the fact table.

The User table could also be composite partitioned if desired and full partition-wise joins are still possible. For example, composite partitioning by user_type and user_id would allow partition elimination by user_type and full partition-wise joins with the fact table on user_id.

Partial Partition-Wise Join

Partial partition-wise joins are possible for each type of partitioned table including hash, range, and composite partitioning. In a partial partition-wise join, only one of the tables involved in the join is partitioned on the join keys; the other table is dynamically partitioned at query execution time to match the pre-existing partitioning method of the partitioned table so that a partition-wise join can occur. Partial partition-wise joins can only be performed in parallel. The example in Figure 7.10 illustrates a partial partition-wise join of the Page Activity fact table that is partitioned with a hash on user_id, with an unpartitioned User dimension table.

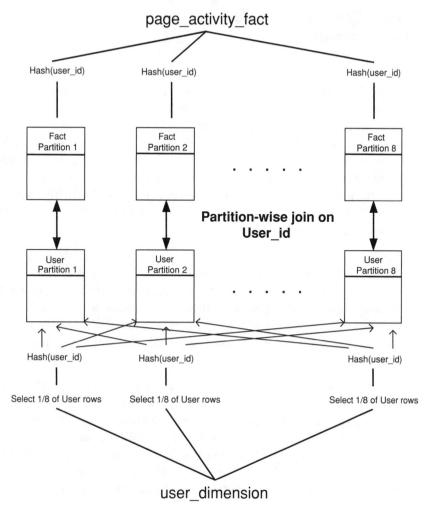

Figure 7.10 Partial partition-wise join of the Page Activity fact table with the User dimension table.

Given a parallel degree of eight, the User table is scanned at query run time by eight scanners who each hash one-eighth of the rows in the User table into eight hash partitions based on the user_id. After this is done, the User dimension rows in User partition one, for example, include the Users that also have Page Activity in fact table partition one. This result is guaranteed because both tables are partitioned using the same hashing algorithm—the fact table *a priori*, and the User table at run time. Now the partition-wise join can be computed against the partition pairs in parallel. We will explore the use of parallel operations more fully in the Parallelism section below.

Aggregate Creation, Awareness, and Management

Mimicking the pathways of their thought processes, clickstream analysts usually follow certain well-worn trails through the data in a clickstream data warehouse. These trails often follow a data path starting with the more general and going to the more specific. But base-level clickstream data warehouse fact tables are geared toward the specific, typically storing data at the lowest level of granularity—the site hit. This makes answering general questions like, "How many users clicked-through from advertising promotions to the Web site in the first quarter?", difficult to process, potentially involving millions of table accesses as the individual clickthroughs in the fact table are rolled up to produce the answer.

Furthermore, various levels of management may only deal with summarized data, never looking at the underlying detail. Many executives are only concerned with summarized key performance indicators and never look at the underlying detail that produces them. This means that most executive queries against the data warehouse will be computationally intensive summaries with lengthy response times—a bad usage model for busy, impatient managerial users.

A way out of this query performance dilemma, for both the analytical and managerial users, is to precompute summaries as part of the extract, transformation, and load process, so they are available for analytical drill-down and rolled up key performance indicator reports. But these are not just a collection of random precomputed summaries. Instead, they are a specific kind of summary, called dimensional aggregates, which follow the data hierarchies and join paths of the clickstream data warehouse star schema.

Because there are fewer rows to process using aggregates, fewer system resources are needed to produce query results, leaving additional resources to service other query requests. Alternatively, if the same amount of system resources are used to produce query results from the smaller aggregate data set, query response time will be much quicker, often orders of magnitude quicker.

The trade-off is that aggregates require additional space to store the aggregated data as well as the additional extract, transformation, and load processing resources to maintain the aggregate tables. The cost of the creation and maintenance of aggregate tables includes:

- The cost of recreating or updating aggregate tables
- The cost of rebuilding indexes

- The overhead associated with data validation and data quality analysis
- Storage costs for the physical aggregate tables
- Maintenance costs such as backup of the physical tables

For these reasons, careful consideration must be given to the decision to build a dimensional aggregate. There are a great number of aggregates that can be created based on different combinations of the dimensions and the levels of detail within each dimension. The following sections address the determination of the appropriate aggregation strategy and the database technology that is available for maintaining the strategy.

Aggregate Creation

How do we create an aggregate? A dimensional aggregate is created by rolling up fact table detail to some higher level of granularity according to the data hierarchy contained in one or more of the dimension tables in a star schema. If the aggregate is against only one dimension table hierarchy, usually called a one-way aggregate, then the result of aggregation is an additional summarized fact table and an additional dimension table with the rolled up levels of the dimensional data hierarchy omitted from it. If the aggregation is against two or more tables, the result is an additional summarized fact table, and as many new aggregated dimension tables as there are dimensions in the aggregate.

Depending on the dimension that is aggregated, the cardinality of the aggregate table may be much lower than the cardinality of the original fact table. In fact, the best aggregation strategy is one that produces the smallest aggregate tables that can satisfy user query requirements.

Consider the following instantiation of the clickstream data warehouse meta-schema shown in Figure 7.11. As before, let's assume that the grain of the Page Activity fact table is a single page view with the supporting dimensional information in the following dimension tables:

- The time of the page view (the User and Fiscal Time dimensions)
- The user's physical location when he viewed the page (the Physical Geography dimension)
- The referring URL (the Web Geography dimension)
- The site page that was viewed (the Site Geography dimension)
- What promotion, if any, got the user to the page view (the Internal and External Promotion dimensions)
- The identity of the user viewing the page (the User dimension)

- The activity performed on the page when it was viewed (the Activity dimension)

- The type of content on the page (the Content dimension)

A dimensional hierarchy defines tiers of granularity for a set of attributes, based on business rules. Examples of dimensions that might have a hierarchy defined within their table structure for the clickstream data warehouse meta-schema are illustrated in Figure 7.12. For example, within the External Promotion dimension, a particular promotion can be categorized by the promoted brand, category or product. Using this hierarchy, a clickstream analyst can obtain a summary view of user activity generated by promotions of a particular type. Similarly, the Physical Geography dimension associates a user's physical location with different levels in a hierarchy based on postal, city, county, state, and country boundaries. Finally, the Fiscal Time dimension has a hierarchy from the day level up to year level based on the enterprise's fiscal calendar.

Suppose that a significant portion of the analysis that is executed against the Page Activity fact table requires that the activity information be summarized by fiscal week to examine how activity has trended over time. To simplify our example, we will eliminate User Time Dimension from the meta-schema since

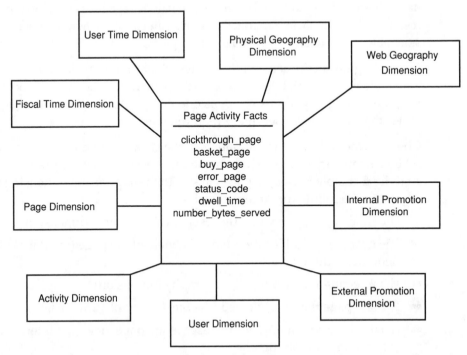

Figure 7.11 Page Activity fact table and associated dimensions used in the dimensional aggregate example.

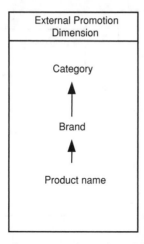
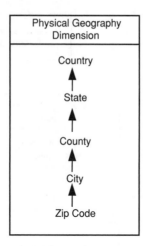

Figure 7.12 Examples of dimensional hierarchies.

Fiscal Time and User Time really represent alternate calendars at the same level of granularity, i.e., timestamp. Every query that is executed where the Fiscal Time dimension is constrained on week causes the Page Activity facts for each week to be summarized to weekly totals. An aggregate table that summarizes user page views by fiscal week rather than the original fact table granularity of GMT timestamp (i.e., seconds) would significantly reduce the number of rows processed during analysis and improve response times for the weekly queries. The resulting star schema associated with the Fiscal Week aggregate is shown in Figure 7.13.

In the new aggregate fact table, all measures are summed to the fiscal week level. For example, the original number_clickthroughs attribute is now aggregated, meaning it now contains the total number of clickthroughs on a page for a given week. The new Fiscal Week dimension contains only the levels in the hierarchy for the week level and above since there is no longer any lower level data like the day and GMT seconds in the new aggregated fact table. A code sample that generates the aggregated fact table is shown below. The key value in the aggregate for the Fiscal Time dimension now specifies a particular week rather than a seconds-level timestamp, and all page views within each week are summarized to the week level:

```
SELECT fiscal_time_week_key, physical_geography_key,
    web_geography_key, page_key, internal_promotion_key,
    external_promotion_key, user_id, activity_key, content_key,
        SUM(number_clickthroughs) number_clickthroughs,
        SUM(number_baskets) number_baskets,
        SUM(number_buys) number_buys,
        SUM(number_errors) number_errors,
        SUM(dwell_time) dwell_time,
```

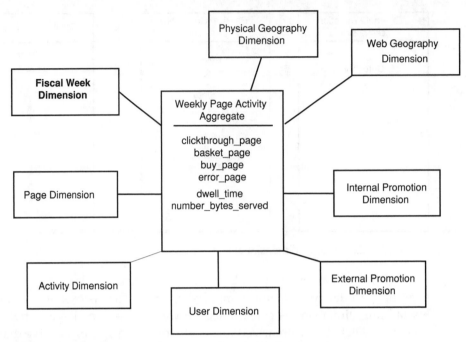

Figure 7.13 Resulting star schema associated with fiscal week aggregate.

```
      SUM(number_bytes_served) number_bytes_served
FROM page_activity_fact
GROUP BY fiscal_time_week_key, physical_geography_key,
   web_geography_key, page_key, internal_promotion_key,
   external_promotion_key, user_id, activity_key, content_key;
```

A special case of dimensional aggregation is when an entire dimension is removed to produce the aggregate. Carrying the schema of the previous example forward, consider the case where certain analytical pathways through the schema may not be concerned with the Physical Geography of where a page view happened. These pathways may only examine traffic statistics from a site perspective, with no Physical Geography component. By completely aggregating out the Physical Geography dimension, a new aggregate fact table that rolls up results over all Physical Geographies is created, producing a view of user activity regardless of physical geography. This aggregate is shown in Figure 7.14. In this aggregate, page views for the same user that were issued from multiple physical geographies (e.g., home and work locations) would be SUMmed into a single aggregated record of the user's activity regardless of location.

Below is a code sample used to create the aggregate that knocks out the Physical Geography dimension. By excluding the Physical Geography key from the SELECT, each metric in the resultant aggregate is automatically computed as

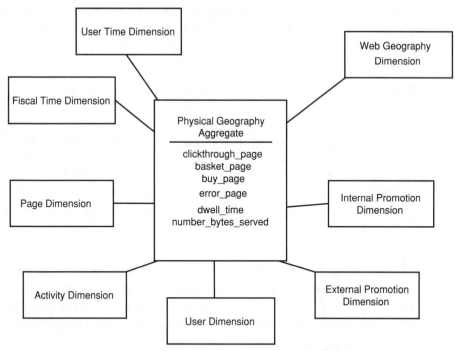

Figure 7.14 Resulting star schema associated with removing the physical geography dimension.

the SUM of the underlying detailed measures without regard to the physical location (i.e., the Physical Geography).

```
SELECT fiscal_time_key, user_time_key, web_geography_key,
    site_geography_key, internal_promotion_key,
    external_promotion_key,
    user_id, activity_key, content_key,
      SUM(number_clickthroughs) number_clickthroughs,
      SUM(number_baskets) number_baskets,
      SUM(number_buys) number_buys,
      SUM(number_errors) number_errors,
            SUM(dwell_time) dwell_time,
      SUM(number_bytes_served) number_bytes_served
FROM page_activity_fact
GROUP BY fiscal_time_key, user_time_key, web_geography_key,
    site_geography_key, internal_promotion_key,
    external_promotion_key, user_id, activity_key, content_key;
```

Under what circumstances should one create aggregates? The base fact table must be large enough to justify building aggregates. If it is a small table that can fit in memory, aggregates are unnecessary. But if it is a large table, with millions of rows that cannot fit in memory, aggregates may be able to significantly reduce database page cache and I/O overhead.

Which aggregates are the best to create? The best aggregates have a cardinality that is much lower than the cardinality of the original fact table. In fact, the best aggregation strategy is one that produces the smallest aggregate tables that still satisfy user analytical requirements.

The rollup ratio is a good way to measure the compression of a base fact table under aggregation. The rollup ratio is computed by dividing the number of rows in the base fact table by the expected number of rows in the aggregate. So, an aggregate of 800,000 rows from a fact table of 10,000,000 rows has a rollup ratio of $100/8 = 12.5$ for a rollup ratio of 12.5:1. A rule of thumb is that the size reduction of resulting aggregate (the rollup ratio) be at least 10:1 and preferably up to 20:1 to justify the cost of maintaining and storing the aggregate table. With smaller rollup ratios, the performance of queries that use these aggregates may still improve, but that benefit may not outweigh the high costs of aggregate creation.

To calculate the rollup ratio, we need to find the expected number of rows in the aggregate table. The following query template calculates the number of rows for any fact table aggregate. The *foreign_key_* * list in the query template is the concatenated (primary) key of whatever aggregate is under consideration.

```
SELECT COUNT(*)
FROM (SELECT DISTINCT foreign_key_1,... foreign_key_n
     FROM page_activity_fact);
```

Using this result as the dividend, and the number of rows in the fact table as the divisor, we can calculate the rollup ratio for any given aggregate.

The dimensional attributes of an aggregate table determine not only its size, but also generally correspond to the range of queries that the aggregate can satisfy. As a general rule, the more summarized the aggregate table, the smaller the range of queries that the aggregate will satisfy.

In certain cases, one aggregate can be used to solve more than one type of query request. For example, a query for *quarterly* page activity can be satisfied by the aggregate of Page Activity by *week* described in Figure 7.13 because the aggregate table is built at a lower level, i.e., week, in the dimensional hierarchy. The quarterly data can be summarized from the weekly data when the query is executed. This solution is not as fast as querying against the ideal aggregate of Page Activity by *quarter*, but it certainly performs better than executing the query against the millions of rows in the base User Activity fact table.

Another factor influencing which aggregates to create is query frequency. The more frequent a particular query, the more the benefit from an aggregate that would satisfy it. Query frequency can be estimated by interviewing analytical users for their query usage patterns. Certain query tools and data warehouse management tools can also yield query frequency statistics.

By populating a table similar to Table 7.1, one can determine which aggregates are most urgently needed.

The first column is a description of the candidate aggregate table, summarized to the *month* level in this case, followed by the cardinality and usage data for that table including the expected number of rows in the aggregate, rollup ratio (from above calculations), and the percentage of queries that will be satisfied by the aggregate. One should consider building the aggregates that have a good rollup ratio (greater than 10:1) and which have a high frequency of execution. Of course, these are guidelines for building aggregates, not absolute rules. For instance, high execution frequency for a particular query or group of queries may dictate the creation of an aggregate, even if the rollup ratio is less than ideal.

Aggregate Navigation

Assuming that aggregates have been created, what ensures that a user query is utilizing the best aggregate during execution? The answer to this question is especially difficult when there are multiple aggregates at differing hierarchical levels in the dimensions accessed by the query. *Aggregate navigation* refers to the process of choosing the optimal aggregate from those available based on the query constraints. Aggregate navigation is one of the primary functionalities of query tools like Business Objects, Cognos, and MicroStrategy. Aggregate navigation insulates analytical users from the complexity of the aggregation strategy because user queries are written against the simple star schema base tables, as if there were no aggregates. With aggregate navigation, query tools choose the optimal aggregate table, if any, and the query's SQL is automatically translated to target the appropriate aggregate tables.

To illustrate aggregate navigation, let's continue with the page-granularity schema used in the examples in the previous section. The base Page Activity fact table has a Fiscal Time dimension down to the GMT timestamp level (i.e., seconds) as well as an aggregate table representing a weekly summary of the base table, as shown in Figure 7.15.

Table 7.1 Aggregate Rollup Ratio and Frequency of Execution Table

AGGREGATE	# ROWS	ROLLUP RATIO	FREQUENCY OF EXECUTION (% OF TOTAL)
Page Activity by Geography by Promotion by User by Content by Activity by User Time by Fiscal Time **(Month)**	4 million	15:1	12
...			

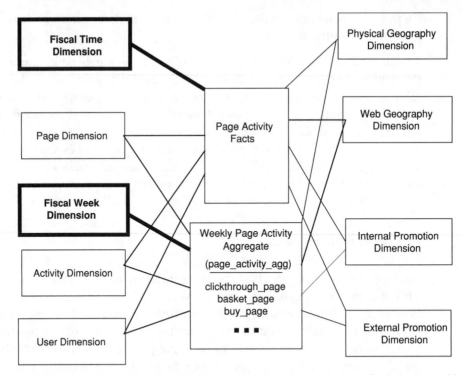

Figure 7.15 Star schema depicting the aggregate navigation path from the base fact table to the aggregate fact table.

Suppose an analytical user executes the following query against the Page Activity fact table to return the basket-to-clickthrough ratio (i.e., the number of clickthroughs that then went to putting an item in the shopping basket, divided by the total number of clickthroughs, basket or otherwise) for advertisements placed with the DoubleClick advertising engine (External Promotion dimension) by week for April 2000 (Fiscal Time dimension):

```
SELECT fiscal_time_dimension.week,
     SUM(page_activity_fact.number_baskets)/
     SUM(page_activity_fact.number_clickthroughs)
     basket_to_clickthrough_ratio
FROM page_activity_fact, fiscal_time_dimension,
     external_promotion_dimension
WHERE
     External_promotion_dimension.ad_engine_name = 'DoubleClick' AND
     fiscal_time_dimension.month = 'April' AND
     fiscal_time_dimension.year = '2000' AND
     external_promotion_dimension.external_promotion_key =
     page_activity_fact.external_promotion_key AND
     fiscal_time_dimension.fiscal_time_key =
     page_activity_fact.fiscal_time_key
GROUP BY fiscal_time_dimension.week;
```

In this case, the query request is for weekly totals, meaning the weekly aggregate table should be used to produce the results rather than the base table. Through aggregate navigation functionality, the user's query tool would modify the SQL statement to access the weekly aggregate fact table rather than the base fact table and to constrain on the Fiscal Week dimensional aggregate rather than the timestamp-level dimension table (i.e., Fiscal Time dimension). Any other dimensions involved in the query, such as the External Promotion dimension, are shared as conformed dimensions between the base fact table and the aggregate fact table so that no further modifications are required. The query translation is transparent to the user and the resulting SQL is shown below:

```
SELECT fiscal_week_dimension.week,
     SUM(page_activity_agg.number_baskets)/
     SUM(page_activity_agg.number_clickthroughs)
     basket_to_clickthrough_ratio
FROM page_activity_agg,
     fiscal_week_dimension,
     external_promotion_dimension
WHERE
     external_promotion_dimension.ad_engine_name = 'DoubleClick' AND
     fiscal_week_dimension.month = 'April' AND
     fiscal_week_dimension.year = '2000' AND
     external_promotion_dimension.external_promotion_key =
     page_activity_agg.external_promotion_key AND
     fiscal_week_dimension.fiscal_week_key =
     page_activity_agg.fiscal_week_key
GROUP BY fiscal_week_dimension.week;
```

There is more information about query tools and their use of aggregate navigation query translation in Chapter 9.

Materialized View and Query Rewrite

As we saw in the last section, query tools use aggregate navigation techniques to rewrite query SQL so that the optimal aggregate pathway is used to execute a query. Each query tool has its own proprietary method of aggregate navigation, and all the data warehouse tables, indexes, and aggregates need to be defined inside the query tool as well as in the data warehouse itself, creating a lot of double bookkeeping issues that are further exacerbated by extract, transformation, and load. A more efficient solution would be to create aggregate awareness inside the database engine itself, and have it rewrite the queries at query optimization time.

In order to accomplish this, Oracle uses the new CREATE DIMENSION data definition statement to define dimensions and hierarchies, and then it uses *materialized views* on these dimensions to create the aggregates.

Remember, a normal *SQL view* is a logical representation of a relation, which has no direct physical instantiation. The SQL that defines the view is executed every time the view is accessed, obtaining its data from the underlying physical attributes on which the view is based. Unlike normal views, materialized view results are stored in a corresponding physical table when the materialized view is defined. The advantages of a materialized view include all the advantages of a regular table such as indexing and partitioning, as well as the fact that the view definition is only executed once to populate the table. The disadvantages of the materialized view include the cost of the storage for the resulting table and the maintenance of refreshing the view periodically.

If an aggregate table is created using a materialized view, the database optimizer is able to modify queries during parsing to use the view rather than the base table. The key point is that the aggregate table must be created as a materialized view rather than a regular table outside of a materialized view for the query rewrites to take place. Also, like any other physical table, the materialized view must be refreshed after the base table is updated during ETL processing, otherwise the view will not reflect the newly loaded data.

For query rewrites to translate queries for materialized view aggregates within a dimensional hierarchy, the dimension and its hierarchy must be explicitly defined for the database optimizer. Returning to our previous example, an aggregate at the week level for the Fiscal Time dimension (Figure 7.16) cannot be used for a query at the month level unless we specify that, in the Fiscal Time dimension, weeks are grouped into or *roll up* to months. By roll up, we mean that there is a one-to-many relationship between months and weeks in the Fiscal Time dimension. So a month in the Fiscal Time dimension has multiple weeks associated with it, and a week belongs to only one month.

Oracle uses the new DIMENSION schema object type to declare the hierarchical relationships within a dimension table or across related dimension tables, which would be the case for a snowflake schema design. In addition to enabling query rewrites within the dimensional hierarchy, the dimension hierarchy explicitly documents the hierarchical structure and allows for validation of the data within the hierarchy, using Oracle's DBMS_OLAP.validate_dimension package. Let's build a Dimension definition for the Fiscal Time dimension table:

```
CREATE DIMENSION fiscal_time_dim
    LEVEL year IS fiscal_time_dimension.year_key
    LEVEL quarter IS fiscal_time_dimension.quarter_key
```

table or index. The query optimizer determines the best degree of parallelism for a particular SQL statement, even if it is defined differently in multiple places. The order of precedence for the degree parallelism varies among the many different types of SQL operations, but, in general, hints have the highest precedence, followed by the degree of parallelism specified in table and index definitions, followed by default parallel behavior. Here are some guidelines for specifying an appropriate degree of parallelism:

- An ideal degree of parallelism for a batch mode, CPU-intensive operation on nonpartitioned tables/indexes is to set the degree of parallelism to the number of CPUs, so the operation can fully utilize the CPU resources. Be aware that if multiple users execute parallel operations concurrently using this maximum formula, available CPU, memory, and disk resources would be rapidly exhausted and overall throughput may actually decrease.

- If the operation is I/O intensive, set the degree of parallelism to the number of devices across which the table/index is spread to maximize the I/O without introducing disk contention.

- For operations that do partition-wise parallelization on partitioned objects, set the degree of parallelism to be equal to evenly divisible into the number of partitions. This approach balances the partition workload evenly across the resultant parallel processes. For example, a table with eight partitions and a parallel degree of four allows for each parallel process to handle two (8/4 = 2) partitions during a parallel operation.

In a multiuser environment, the degree of parallelism can be set relatively low to prohibit multiple users from consuming all the available resources. Another alternative is to set the degree of parallelism to the maximum realistic value, like the number of CPUs or the number of table partitions, and then limit the resource utilization using Oracle's adaptive multiuser parallel performance algorithm. Under the adaptive multiuser algorithm, the degree of parallelism is automatically reduced as the system load increases to avoid overallocation of resources. Conversely, if there is no competition for resources, then operations run with the maximum degree of parallelism.

Parallelizing Database Operations

Oracle uses three primary methods to parallelize database operations:

Block Ranges. Operations that are not key-specific, like full table scans on nonpartitioned tables, can be parallelized by database block ranges. For example, a full table scan can dynamically partition the target table into equal sized ranges of database blocks, with each block range processed by a different thread of execution. Partitioned tables can use block range partitioning, but block ranges cannot span table partitions.

Partitioning (by key range or by hash partition). A database operation issued against a partitioned table or index can be parallelized based on the partitions or subpartitions of the table or index. Each thread executes the operation against a set containing one or more partitions and there is no intrapartition parallelism. As mentioned above, the number of parallel processes should divide evenly into the number of partitions to evenly balance the workload across the parallel processes. Specified degrees of parallelism should match the number of partitions in the table or index. If the optimizer prunes or eliminates partitions from consideration, the number of partitions processed in parallel is reduced correspondingly.

Parallel Processes. The final parallelization method is to divide the work based on the degree of parallelism defined for the operation. As mentioned above, the optimizer normally determines the best degree of parallelism for a particular SQL statement, even if it is defined differently in multiple places. The order of precedence for choosing the degree of parallelism is as follows: First use whatever is specified in any hints, if any. Next, use the degree of parallelism specified in the target table and index definitions, if any. Finally, use the default degree of parallelism based on number of partitions in the targeted objects, and if there are no partitions, use the number of CPUs on a system as the degree of parallelism.

Parallel Database Operations

Table 7.2 summarizes many of the database operations that can be executed in parallel in current versions of Oracle, including the type of table or index that the operation involves, and the method of parallelization.

Operations that involve multiple partitions in a partitioned table or index are parallelized according to the number of partitions defined in the table (Operations 2, 3, 4, 5, 7, and 12 in Table 7.2). For example, the parallel UPDATE operation is applied using one parallel process for each partition of a partitioned table. For those operations that involve a single partition of a partitioned table or index, block range partitioning is utilized to achieve intrapartition parallelism (Operations 1, 9, 10, 11, 15, and 16 in Table 7.2). For instance, the command to rebuild an index partition of a partitioned index can execute in parallel within the designated partition using block range parallelization. Finally, operations on nonpartitioned tables and indexes use the block range parallelization method (Operations 1, 8, 13, and 14 in Table 7.2). For example, a full table scan of a nonpartitioned table is parallelized by dividing the table into a number of database block ranges based on the rowIDs of the tuples in the table. The INSERT . . .

Table 7.2 Types of Parallel Database Operations

OPERATION NUMBER	PARALLEL OPERATION TYPE	PARTITIONED TABLE	NONPARTITIONED TABLE	PARTITIONED INDEX	NONPARTITIONED INDEX	PARALLELIZATION METHOD
1	SQL statements using table scans	X	X			Block range
2	SQL statements using index range scans			X		Partition
3	UPDATE	X				Partition
4	DELETE	X				Partition
5	INSERT... SELECT	X				Partition
6	INSERT... SELECT		X			Parallel processes
7	CREATE TABLE ... AS SELECT	X				Partition
8	CREATE TABLE... AS SELECT		X			Block range
9	ALTER TABLE... MOVE partition	X				Block range
10	ALTER TABLE... SPLIT partition	X				Block range
11	ALTER TABLE... COALESCE partition	X				Block range
12	CREATE INDEX			X		Partition
13	CREATE INDEX				X	Block range
14	ALTER INDEX... REBUILD				X	Block range
15	ALTER INDEX... REBUILD partition			X		Block range
16	ALTER INDEX... SPLIT partition			X		Block range

SELECT on a nonpartitioned object (Operation 6 in Table 7.2) is a special case that is discussed in more detail below.

Each parallel process involved in a data modification or an object maintenance operation requires a rollback segment to record undo information for recovery in case of failure. This needs to be considered when configuring rollback segments, since a table maintenance operation of degree N requires concurrent use of N rollback segments. While multiple transactions can share a rollback segment, for best performance rollback segments should be configured to have a maximum of two parallel threads concurrently accessing a particular segment. Ideally, each parallel process should have its own rollback segment.

Parallel Queries

Parallel queries include SQL SELECT statements, the query portion of data modification statements, and the query portion of data definition statements like parallel CREATE TABLE ... AS SELECT, etc. When the Parallel Query Option (PQO) is enabled in Oracle, the optimizer attempts to parallelize as many of the steps of the query as possible. The following is a list of operators within an SQL statement that can be executed in parallel:

- Full table scan
- Index range scan on a partitioned index
- Sorts due to ORDER BY clauses
- Sorts due to GROUP BY clauses
- NOT IN specification in WHERE clauses
- SELECT DISTINCT
- UNION and UNION ALL
- Nested loop join
- Sort merge join
- Hash join
- Star transformation
- CUBE
- ROLLUP

Parallel UPDATE/DELETE

Extract, transformation, and load, or ETL, typically requires massive update and delete operations on the fact table and dimension tables of clickstream data warehouse. The tight ETL time windows force database administrators to manually parallelize these operations by breaking them into multiple SQL statements that work on specific key ranges or partitions in the effected tables. These are executed simultaneously using complex scripts that must be able to detect errors, and idempotently reexecute failed portions of the ETL.

Fortunately, both Oracle and DB2 now support parallel UPDATE and DELETE operations on partitioned tables (confer Operations 3 and 4 in Table 7.2). With these operations, the database engine guarantees the integrity of the parallel transaction stream, not the administrator's scripts. The division of work among the parallel processes by partition and there is no parallelism within a partition. Thus, the maximum degree of parallelism is the number of partitions in the target table.

INSERT. . .SELECT

Another very important part of clickstream data warehouse ETL is insertion of new data into the fact table, aggregates, and even some dimensions. As with DELETE and UPDATE statements, an INSERT statement can be manually parallelized, with all the same issues of errors and idempotency as mentioned above.

In order to operate in parallel, the source data for the INSERT must come from another SELECTed table (confer Operations 5, 6 in Table 7.2). Assuming the ETL architecture supports a posting schema staging area for clickstream log file records that are ready for loading, then the INSERT to load a table can be the result of a SELECT from the posting schema. For partitioned tables, the INSERT...SELECT statement is parallelized by partition and the maximum degree of parallelism is equal to the number of partitions. Parallel inserts on nonpartitioned tables, however, are parallelized using parallel processes specified by degree of parallelism. The data to be inserted for the INSERT portion of the operation is divided equally among the number of parallel processes allocated for the operation. This division is possible since the rows to be inserted do not yet have rowIDs associated with them. Of course, the SELECT portion of the operation would also be parallelized using the operators described in the "Parallel Queries" section above.

The performance of a parallel INSERT... SELECT operation has been improved by integrating the Direct Path SQL*Loader functionality into the INSERT operation, enabling a direct-load INSERT. The direct path execution allows the data to be formatted and written directly to Oracle datafiles without using the database buffer cache as an intermediate resting spot for the data. For each parallel process, rows are formatted and inserted into a temporary segment, which is subsequently appended to the applicable data segment above the previous high-water mark for the datafile. After the data append is completed, the high-water mark is moved and rowIDs are assigned to the new rows. Special consideration must be given to the storage parameters and space management of the tables that are involved in these operations since free space is not effectively reused. A serial INSERT...SELECT can also take advantage of direct path execution by including the "APPEND" hint with the INSERT command specification.

Another performance enhancement for direct-load inserts is to insert the data while generating no redo log entries and minimal undo entries with the NOLOGGING mode. The idea behind this mode is that there is no real advantage to incremental recovery of a direct load when it can simply be repeated if there is an error, by starting from the previous high-water mark in the effected datafile. NOLOGGING can be specified for tables, partitions, indexes, or tablespaces. This mode is discussed further in the section below.

Table Maintenance Operations

The table definition and maintenance operations that can be executed in parallel include the CREATE TABLE... AS SELECT command and the ALTER TABLE commands on partitioned tables, including MOVE, SPLIT, COALESCE (confer operations 7, 8, 9, 10, and 11 in Table 7.2).

The CREATE TABLE ... AS SELECT operation contains two statements that can be executed in parallel, the SELECT statement on the data source table(s) and the CREATE of the new table. In the ideal scenario, the SELECT and CREATE statements are both executed in parallel. CREATE TABLE ... AS SELECT is ideal for a host of ETL operations, including efficiently recreating dimensional aggregates.

The CREATE statement is parallelized by partition if the table being created is a partitioned table. At most, one parallel process is assigned for each partition of the table, so the maximum degree of parallelism is equal to the number of partitions in the table. For a nonpartitioned table, the rows returned from the SELECT statement are parallelized by block range for the CREATE statement.

The ALTER TABLE commands for partitioned tables are parallelized based on the static partition definitions for the table.

Index Maintenance Operations

Parallel CREATE INDEX uses different algorithms for parallelization depending on whether the underlying table is partitioned or non-partitioned (confer Operations 12 and 13 in Table 7.2). Partitioned table indexes are created with a maximum of one parallel process per index partition and intrapartition parallelism is not supported. Non-partitioned indexes are parallelized by block range based on the degree of parallelism specified for the operation. Non-partitioned index REBUILDs are also parallelized by block range (confer Operation 14 in Table 7.2).

If a clickstream data warehouse has a User Activity Fact table partitioned by Time, and it has a time-based, partitioned index on the rows in the table, it is probably faster to issue a REBUILD operation on partitions in the index after updating the fact table, rather than dropping and recreating the entire index (confer Operation 15 in Table 7.2). Block range parallelism is used within a partition to get parallel execution. To do a partitioned index REBUILD in parallel across multiple partitions, multiple ALTER INDEX REBUILD <partition> operations must be simultaneously issued for all the effected index partitions.

The SPLIT operation, which splits an existing index partition into two or more new partitions, also uses block range partitioning to parallelize its execution (confer Operation 16 in Table 7.2).

Parallel Load

The posting schema for a clickstream data warehouse will likely have a number of tables that are loaded from flat files like Web server log files. The fastest way to load flat file data into a table is via the parallel direct path load in the Oracle SQL*Loader utility. As discussed earlier, a direct path load eliminates much of the database overhead by formatting Oracle data blocks and writing the blocks directly to the data files, bypassing the database buffer cache. The direct path loader can load data at rates approaching the speed at which data can be written to the physical disk(s). Multiple direct path load operations can be issued simultaneously to load multiple objects (e.g., table, table partitions) concurrently or to load a single object with multiple parallel processes like the clickstream data warehouse User Activity fact table. In each of these cases, the database administrator manages parallelism by appropriately dividing the input files among the parallel processes prior to issuing the load operations.

If a partition of a partitioned table is being loaded, the administrator must ensure that input data meets the range criteria for inclusion in a partition or performance will suffer from record rejections encountered during the load. If multiple, independent direct path load processes are invoked against a single object, the indexes, constraints, and triggers must be dropped/disabled prior to the load and subsequently recreated, since they cannot be maintained during a multiprocess load. The data load processes can be marked as UNRECOVERABLE to minimize redo log overhead during the data load. Setting NOLOGGING on the target objects accomplishes the same thing. Special consideration must be given to the space requirements of the parallel direct path operations since each operation obtains its own object extents for loading and this may lead to space fragmentation if the extents are grossly oversized.

NOLOGGING Mode

If you are using parallel execution to improve the performance of table object maintenance operations in ETL, then you should consider suppressing logging with the NOLOGGING option to further enhance performance. The NOLOG-GING mode causes no redo and only minimal undo log records to be generated for the object under modification. As mentioned earlier, reducing the amount of undo and redo log traffic can significantly improve the performance of bulk, parallel operations. Because there is no recovery information, the database administrator becomes responsible for the recovery of NOLOG-GING object(s) if an error occurs. An immediate backup of objects that are created/modified with NOLOGGING is absolutely required to avoid subsequent loss of data due to media or other failures. The operations in the list below can be executed in NOLOGGING mode:

- CREATE TABLE... AS SELECT
- ALTER TABLE... MOVE PARTITION
- ALTER TABLE... SPLIT PARTITION
- CREATE INDEX
- ALTER INDEX... REBUILD
- ALTER INDEX... REBUILD PARTITION
- ALTER INDEX... SPLIT PARTITION
- Direct-Load INSERT... SELECT
- Direct-Load in SQL*Loader

Temporary Tables

Application developers or administrators frequently utilize intermediate tables to store the results of a particular step in multi-step operations. Examples of operations that may utilize intermediate tables include building dimensional aggregates and completing data transformations like calculating the page dwell time during ETL processing, which requires subtracting the GMT timestamp from one user log record to the next to calculate it. Since these intermediate tables are not needed beyond the next step in a multi-step operation, it can be a good idea to make them temporary tables, rather than permanent tables occupying space forever.

Temporary tables are created so that the table data is local to the session in which it is created and temporary space is dynamically allocated to the table as rows are inserted. Space is allocated for the table data first in the user's sort space, which is sized according to the init.ora parameter sort_area_size, and, if this is exhausted, then in the user's temporary tablespace. A temporary tablespace is created using the GLOBAL TEMPORARY option of the CREATE TABLE command with keywords that specify whether table data persists for only the duration of a transaction, by using the ON COMMIT DELETE ROWS option, or the duration of a session, by using the ON COMMIT PRESERVE ROWS option. Each session that utilizes a temporary table has exclusive access to the data it inserts. No locks are acquired as the table is accessed or manipulated since table data is not shared among sessions. Additionally, no redo logs are generated for data modifications, since the data is dropped at transaction or session termination. Indexes can be created that have the same scope as the data in the temporary table. Unfortunately, temporary tables do not currently support any parallel SQL operations.

Useful Analytical Extensions to SQL

For those of us who follow these things, one of the most active marketing debates of the past decade has surrounded the deficiencies in the analytical capabilities of SQL. Niche data warehouse database engine Red Brick would chide standard SQL engines like Oracle for its inability to directly output a ranked Top 10 list, while noting that Red Brick's SQL extensions did have this functionality. Data cube vendors like Cognos would point out that it was impossible to produce a cross-tabulated report, that is, one that had running totals and a grand total, without resorting to writing a program with embedded SQL. These deficiencies in SQL's analytical capabilities gave rise to entire new classes of software like the OLAP data cubes and the relational data warehouse query tools.

Amidst the thunder of the marketing debates, most SQL engines have quietly fixed these problems. This does not mean it is time to throw away Business Objects or Cognos and do standard SQL analysis and reporting, but what it does mean is that much of the computational overhead in the analytical tools can now be performed much more efficiently inside the database engine. It is important to note that analytical tools must be configured to utilize these new operators otherwise they will continue to perform these operations internally, with all the associated overhead.

Top-N SQL

OLAP analysis tools have functionality that limits the number of results displayed in a ranking to the top-N rows, since those are the most important to the business user. As mentioned above, until recently, SQL could not rank-limit its output. In order to solve this problem, SQL has been extended so that subqueries now allow an ORDER BY clause. Previously, this clause was only available to the outermost query block, which is not sufficient to limit output to the top-N rows. For example, the SQL to return the 10 most clicked-to Web pages on a site, in descending order, is shown below:

```
SELECT *
FROM (SELECT page_key, weekly_clickthroughs
        FROM page_activity_agg
        ORDER BY weekly_clickthroughs DESC)
WHERE rownum < 10;
```

Instead of having an analytical tool fetch all rows from the fact table to calculate a particular ranking, the database engine can now perform the ranking internally, saving tremendous amounts of network traffic and analytical tool computational overhead. And an interesting sidelight, having a result set with a maximum of 10 rows also enhances the sort performance of the ranking operation. As each additional row beyond the tenth is read, the row with the lowest page byte count is discarded. At the end of the operation, only 10 rows need to be sorted to produce the final result.

Rollup Aggregate Operator

Table 7.3 shows the result of a query against Page Activity fact table for the number of clickthroughs by region, by month, for Q1 of 2001. The results are produced from the page-level fact table by summing the number of clickthroughs over the user time and physical geography dimensions as illustrated below:

```
SELECT ut.month, pg.region, SUM(paf.number_clickthroughs)
FROM page_activity_fact paf,
     user_time_dimension ut,
     physical_geography_dimension pg
WHERE ut.month IN ('January','February','March') AND
      ut.year = '2001' AND
      ut.user_time_key = paf.user_time_key AND
      pg.physical_geography_key = paf.physical_geography_key
GROUP BY ut.month, pg.region;
```

A similar report generated by an OLAP tool would also provide cross-tabulated subtotals by month and by region, as well as the grand total of clickthroughs for the first quarter over all months/regions. For example, an OLAP

Table 7.3 A Simple SQL Rollup

MONTH	REGION		
	East	West	Central
January	14	28	10
February	25	22	12
March	33	25	15

tool would subtotal the ad clickthroughs for January, 14 + 28 + 10 = 52, and subtotal the ad impressions for the Eastern Region, 14 + 25 + 33 = 72, along with all other month and region subtotals. This kind of cross-tabulation capability is now provided by the database engine using the ROLLUP operator.

The ROLLUP operator is an extension to the GROUP BY clause that produces subtotals for each group as well as a grand total for all the groups. The subtotals and grand totals are produced for the first dimension specified in the ROLLUP clause, so the order of dimensions is important. Table 7.4 shows the result of the previous query with the addition of a ROLLUP by month:

```
SELECT ut.month, pg.region, SUM(paf.number_clickthroughs)
FROM page_activity_fact paf,
    user_time_dimension ut,
    physical_geography_dimension pg
WHERE ut.month IN ('January','February','March') AND
    ut.year = '2001' AND
    ut.user_time_key = paf.user_time_key AND
      pg.physical_geography_key = paf.physical_geography_key
GROUP BY ROLLUP(ut.month, pg.region);
```

The query now returns not only the number of clickthroughs by region by month, but also subtotals of the number of clickthroughs by month rolled up into a grand total of the number of ad impressions for all months.

Table 7.5 shows the result set if the first dimension in the ROLLUP clause is region, instead of month.

```
SELECT ut.month, pg.region, SUM(paf.number_clickthroughs)
FROM page_activity_fact paf,
    user_time_dimension ut,
    physical_geography_dimension pg
WHERE ut.month IN ('January','February','March') AND
    ut.year = '2001' AND
    ut.user_time_key = paf.user_time_key AND
    pg.physical_geography_key = paf.physical_geography_key
GROUP BY ROLLUP(pg.region, ut.month);
```

In this case, the subtotals are by region, with a grand total of the number of ad impressions for all regions.

Table 7.4 Subtotals and Grand Totals by Month Using ROLLUP

MONTH	REGION			
	East	West	Central	Total
January	14	28	10	52
February	25	22	12	59
March	33	25	15	73
				184 *

*Grand Total

Table 7.5 Subtotals and Grand Totals by Region Using ROLLUP

MONTH	REGION			
	East	West	Central	Total
January	14	28	10	
February	25	22	12	
March	33	25	15	
Total	72	75	37	184 *

*Grand Total

The ROLLUP construct is especially useful for creating materialized aggregate views against a defined dimension (CREATE DIMENSION…).

CUBE Aggregate Operator

The CUBE aggregate operator is an extension to the GROUP BY clause in an SQL statement that produces subtotals for all combinations of the columns or expressions in the GROUP BY clause. Returning to our above example, the Q1 regional clickthrough query with the CUBE operator produces a cross-tabulated report that subtotals clickthroughs by month and clickthroughs by region along with the grand total over all months and regions. The results are shown in Table 7.6.

```
SELECT ut.month, pg.region, SUM(paf.number_clickthroughs)
FROM page_activity_fact paf,
    user_time_dimension ut,
    physical_geography_dimension pg
WHERE ut.month IN ('January','February','March') AND
    ut.year = '2001' AND
    ut.user_time_key = paf.user_time_key AND
    pg.physical_geography_key = paf.physical_geography_key
GROUP BY CUBE(pg.region, ut.month);
```

Table 7.6 Subtotals and Grand Totals by Region and Month Using ROLLUP

MONTH	REGION			
	East	West	Central	Total
January	14	28	10	52
February	25	22	12	59
March	33	25	15	73
Total	72	75	37	184 *

*Grand Total

Similar to ROLLUP, the CUBE operator is very useful for producing materialized aggregate views in a single SQL statement.

Disk Drive and Volume Management

All clickstream data warehouse data resides on physical disk drives, and the layout of database objects on those disks is one of the most important design elements of data warehouse architecture. In order to implement the physical design of the data warehouse, a collection of technologies, including disk arrays, disk controllers, disk management software, operating system software, and database software are combined into a hardware and software technology complex that is key to data warehouse performance. Once this technology complex is implemented, the decisions made during that process are not easily reversed or readdressed.

At many sites, there is a great gulf between the data warehouse design team and the database and system administrators who implement the physical layout of the clickstream data warehouse. Neither side understands the other side's craft very well, and this leads to a kind of fatalism in physical design choices that is the undoing of many data warehouse projects. The authors of this book have often heard data warehouse design team members say that they have "absolutely no control" over the physical design of the data warehouse, when what they really mean is that they don't understand the physical design issues and solutions. On the flip side, we see many data warehouse layouts that could only have been done by administrative staff that had little understanding of data warehouse query and performance issues.

Using the information in this section, the data warehouse design team and the database administration team can develop a common framework for understanding the implications and trade-offs of the elements of physical data warehouse design. Enabled with this information, the two sides can intelligently discuss the alternatives, and arrive at the best solution.

Our discussion starts out with the disk drives and works its way upward to data warehouse objects like tables, indexes, dimensions, and aggregates. As in the previous section, we presume the clickstream data warehouse is an open systems implementation using an Oracle database engine, unless otherwise specified.

Logical Volume Management

While database objects like tablespaces can map directly onto disk drives, most systems choose to use an intermediate mapping called logical volumes.

Logical volumes have many advantages over a direct disk mapping, including performance-oriented capabilities like striping, and redundancy capabilities like mirroring and RAID-5, etc. Logical volume management is almost always done in software, which may come from third-parties like Veritas, or from the system vendors themselves.

Third-party disk array manufacturers often provide some level of logical volume management as a standard feature of their hardware products. At least mirroring and probably some additional level of RAID redundancy are almost always provided inside the hardware of these products. But even if your site is using something as sophisticated as EMC disk arrays, you probably still use logical volume management software to map database objects to plexes on the disk array, to do maintenance tasks like archiving, backup, and restore.

There are hardware and software solutions available for open systems. A hardware solution is by nature made for plug-and-play and is therefore less flexible. A software solution requires more design and configuration on the part of the data warehouse team.

Terminology

By discussing your physical disk architecture with your database and system administrators, you should be able to produce a diagram of the I/O subsystem similar to the example in Figure 7.18.

In this example, there are 18 physical *disk drives* connected to *I/O Controller 1*. The I/O Controller has four *Channels*. From left to right, Channels 1 and 2 each have five disk drives connected to them and Channels 3 and 4 each have four disk drives connected. The I/O Controller is directly connected to one of the I/O slots on the System Bus. The design goal for the disk layout is to place the database objects on the disks to maximize the I/O spread across disks, channels, and controllers, while minimizing conflicts between objects that are accessed concurrently.

Logical volume management (LVM) software allows you to create file systems that are composed of multiple disk partitions across multiple physical disks. It gives you options for distributing I/O across multiple disks using techniques such as concatenation, mirroring, striping, and striping with parity checking. Disk administration is enhanced by a configuration database and an administrative interface to manage the disk configurations. Administrative software simplifies tasks like backup, restore, and replacing failed disk drives.

The building blocks of a logical volume include:

Subdisk. A subdisk is the lowest level building block, consisting of a contiguous portion of all or part of a physical disk drive.

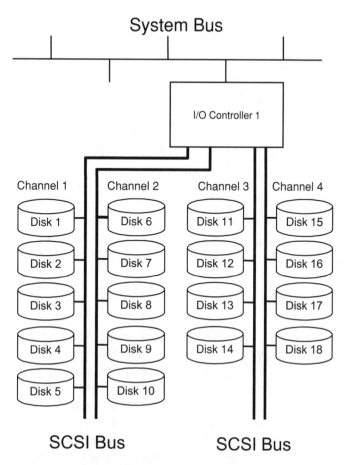

Figure 7.18 Disk I/O subsystem diagram.

Plex. A plex is an ordered collection of subdisk objects. A subdisk in a plex is said to be associated with the plex. Subdisks in a plex typically reside on multiple physical disks. The way in which new data is appended to a database object, like concatenation or striping, is defined at the plex level.

Volume. A volume is an ordered collection of plexes. If a volume is comprised of multiple plexes, then each plex contains a copy of the volume's data and the volume is mirrored. A mirrored volume could have one striped and one mirrored plex, although it is more common in a data warehousing environment for the configurations of the plexes to match.

Figure 7.19 shows one example of a volume containing two plexes.

Volume 1 has two plexes attached to it, meaning that the volume is *mirrored*, or contains two copies of the same data. Each of the plexes has four associated subdisks; the subdisks consume 500MB on each of the underlying physical disk drives such that the total volume size is 2 GB. It is not clear from this dia-

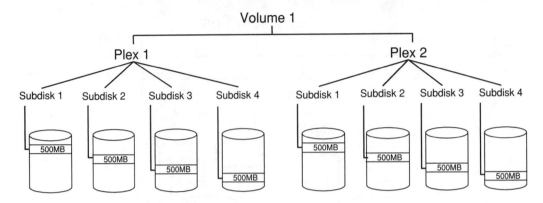

Figure 7.19 Volume containing two plexes.

gram whether the plexes are concatenated or striped. We will discuss concatenation, mirroring, and striping in the sections that follow.

Concatenation

Subdisks are concatenated in a plex to distribute I/O across multiple disks and allow the creation of a volume that has more capacity than a single disk. Joining subdisks in a plex using concatenation forms a linear address space where each subdisk is filled in its entirety before moving to the next subdisk. In Figure 7.20, a sequential read from the beginning of the plex reads all 500MB from subdisk 1, and then moves sequentially to subdisks 2, 3, and 4, in that order. The database sees the plex as a contiguous 2 GB expanse of space while the underlying implementation employs four physical disks to house the 2 GB expanse.

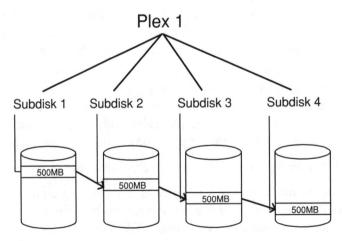

Figure 7.20 Subdisks concatenated in a plex.

Mirroring

Mirroring, or RAID Level 1, is when the LVM mirroring software automatically maintains the integrity and consistency of two or more copies (plexes) of data in a volume. In event of a disk failure, data access continues on the unaffected copy of the data. Read performance is improved over a single copy of the data since multiple reads of the same information can be serviced concurrently across mirrors of the data. The accelerated read performance is ideal for a multiuser, read-only clickstream data warehouse query environment. A mirrored configuration also enables a host of online administrative operations. For example, data can be backed up using one mirror without prohibiting application access to the other copies.

There are some drawbacks to mirroring that need to be considered. Write performance decreases slightly, since all copies of the data must be updated on a write operation, and disk writes are not typically synchronized across disk devices. But the multiple write operations can occur in parallel, and it is likely that overall write performance is increased by only a fraction of the time it takes to do a single write. The biggest drawback to mirroring is the hardware cost of purchasing twice as many disks, or more if there are multiple mirrors, to store the redundant copies of the data.

In Figure 7.21, there are two 2 GB mirrored instances, or plexes, identified that consist of four subdisks each. A disk read can be serviced by either of the two plexes whereas a disk write must update both plexes. If the shaded subdisk 4 in plex 1 fails, subdisk 4 in plex 2 continues to service read and write requests until the disk can be replaced. Upon replacement, plex 1 is resynchronized or *resilvered* to match the data on plex 2. The LVM software handles these processes with minimal intervention from the system administrator and no service outage for the data warehouse.

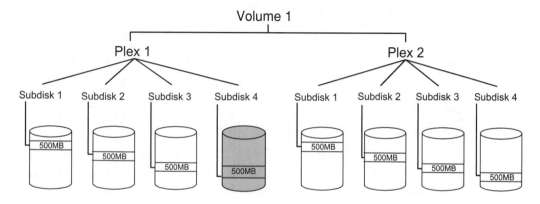

Figure 7.21 Volume containing two mirrored plexes.

The most reliable form of mirroring, called *duplexing*, recognizes the possibility that an I/O controller can fail, just as a disk can fail. Duplexing ensures that mirrors are placed on separate I/O controllers, so that a single controller failure cannot take out an entire mirrored volume. This feature removes a single point of failure that exists when mirrored disks reside on the same I/O Controller. Duplexing is utilized in one of the disk layout examples below.

Striping

Database objects are *striped* by interleaving blocks of data between subdisks in a plex. Blocks are written in round-robin fashion to a portion, or stripe, of each subdisk of a plex. The stripe width is the size of each stripe and is configurable by the administrator when the plex is defined. As shown in Figure 7.22, a 2 GB striped plex is defined across four subdisks. Assuming the stripe width is 64K, a sequential write of the plex would proceed as follows:

- A write of 64K to subdisk 1, corresponding to the portion (or stripe) of the subdisk 1 labeled with an "A."

- A write of 64K to subdisk 2, corresponding to the B stripe of subdisk 2.

- Subsequent writes of 64K to stripes C, D, E, F, G, and H on their given subdisks.

This process continues until the entire 2 GB plex has been written. Striping is also referred to as RAID Level 0, or RAID-0 for short.

By distributing I/O across multiple disks, a striped configuration increases bandwidth for sequential applications by allowing read-ahead algorithms to

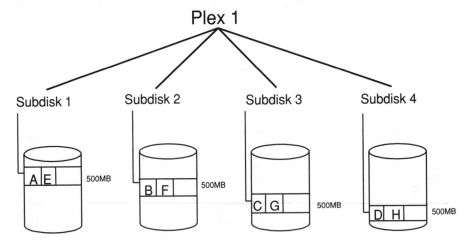

Figure 7.22 Striped plex defined across four subdisks.

read ahead on more than one physical device. Striping also enhances multi-user throughput by spreading hot spots of I/O activity over more disk drives.

For sequential operations, like full table scans, the underlying table should be striped so that one I/O request is serviced by all disks in the plex. Consider the plex defined in the example above with a stripe width of 64K. If the sequential block reads for the table scan are 256K, or a 64KB stripe on each of four subdisks, then each sequential I/O is serviced by all four physical disks in the striped configuration. Using this technique, the 256K read is serviced much faster than if the data was read from a single disk drive, and the time to service the request will approach the combined transfer rates of all four drives.

If concurrent access is the goal, it is better to configure the stripe so that an average I/O request is serviced by only one of the disks. Returning to our example, if all I/O requests from the application are less than 64K, then up to four processes may read from the striped configuration concurrently. We use the word *may* here because there is no guarantee that the data necessary to satisfy the I/O request won't spill over a block boundary and span two subdisks, in which case two physical disk I/Os will be necessary to service the request. Nevertheless, with striping, multiple simultaneous I/O requests can be serviced concurrently, whereas I/O is serialized if all the data sits on a single disk drive.

Stripe Width

Clickstream data warehouses can have both sequential and multiuser query access requirements. An example of a sequential query operation is a full table scan of the User Activity Fact Table. Conversely, indexed access to a particular row in a table accesses, at most, a few blocks of the table. In order to deliver the best concurrent query throughput, one has to create an environment where the majority of the users get their result sets through indexed access to tables or through precomputed aggregates, minimizing the number of full table scans. But for many query workloads, there is no way to completely eliminate sequential operations, so we need to find a stripe width that gives good concurrent I/O bandwidth, as well as reasonable sequential I/O performance.

One way to walk this middle path is to configure the stripe width to match the actual database I/O size, which must also match the operating system I/O size. We want one database I/O to be serviced by only one stripe, if possible. For example, if our database has a db_block_size of 8KB and a db_file_multiblock_read_count of 4, then the database I/O size is 32KB for a sequential I/O. A stripe size of 32KB and an operating system physical I/O size of 32KB would match our sequential I/O size.

One common problem with striping is misalignment of database blocks within a stripe. If the starting addresses database blocks are not aligned with the beginning of the stripe, then two I/Os will be required to read the desired group of blocks, because the last block will spill over into the next stripe. One cause of this problem is database object overhead bytes that cause the starting addresses of subsequent database blocks to be offset by the size of the over-head bytes. Guaranteeing block alignment of physical I/Os is a tricky business. If you can guarantee it, stripe width can be limited to the number of blocks in the db_file_multiblock_read_count. But if you can't guarantee alignment, a good compromise choice is to increase the stripe size to k * db_block_size * db_file_multiblock_read_count, where k=2, 3, 4, ... In practice, the authors have often used this method, with k set to 2, and obtained good indexed and sequential performance results. If we apply this method to our example, the stripe width would be 2 * db_block_size * db_file_multiblock_read_count = 2 * 8KB * 4 or 64KB.

Stripe Set Size

The *stripe set* is the number of physical disks over which data is striped in a plex. Plexes consist of a set of subdisks, and the number of subdisks in a plex should be an exact multiple of the number of physical disks over which the subdisks are spread. If the multiple is 1, there is a one-to-one relationship between the number of subdisks and the number of disk drives in the plex. If the multiple is greater than 1, the subdisks in the plex are distributed in round-robin fashion among the disk drives in the plex. In general, the more physical disks in the stripe set, the better the plex can service both indexed and sequential I/Os.

One problem with spreading the stripe over too many devices is that the probability of volume failure increases correspondingly. The more disk drives and disk controllers in a plex, the more likely the plex will have one of its disks or controllers fail. Another related issue is the cost of the storage array, and each new spindle adds cost to the disk subsystem.

Striping Plus Mirroring

Striping and mirroring can be combined in a volume definition, giving the reliability and read performance of mirroring with the sequential I/O performance benefits of striping. This is done by defining a volume consisting of two plexes to create the mirror, with each plex consisting of a striped set of subdisks. Just like regular mirroring, the approach doubles the number of the disks required to store the volume. Striping plus mirroring is also known as RAID-0+1, RAID-10, or RAID-1+0.

If the budget permits doubling the size of the disk subsystem, then this approach has the best overall performance and reliability characteristics.

Striping with Parity Checking

Striping can be combined with parity calculations to create volumes that are fault tolerant without requiring the doubling of storage needed by mirroring. RAID levels 2 through 5 all use parity calculation to reduce the total amount of storage required to guarantee reliability, but only RAID-5 stripes both the data blocks and the parity block across all the disk drives. By striping the parity blocks across all disks in a plex, RAID-5 reduces I/O contention for parity data. Figure 7.23 shows a four-disk RAID-5 plex. For each set of four stripes across the subdisks, three stripes hold data and one stripe stores the result of the parity calculations on the three data stripes. As more stripes are distributed over the subdisks in a RAID-5 plex, the stripe that contains the parity information is distributed round-robin across the subdisks in order to reduce parity-related I/O bottlenecks. This is shown in the example below:

■ Data is placed on subdisks 1, 2, and 3 in the locations marked by "A," "B," and "C." Location "P" on subdisk 4 is reserved for the parity information needed to recreate information stored on "A," "B," and "C."

■ Continuing, data is placed on subdisks 1, 2, and 4 in the locations marked by "D," "E," and "F." Location "P" on subdisk 3 is reserved for parity information needed to re-create information stored on "D," "E," and "F."

Similarly, in the last RAID-5 stripe set, data is stored at "G," "H," and "I" on subdisks 1, 3, and 4, and subdisk 2 is reserved for parity.

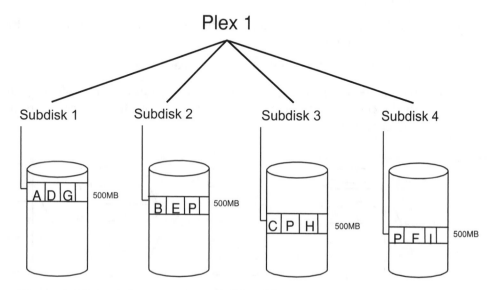

Figure 7.23 Striped plex across four subdisks with parity.

The location of the parity information rotates from subdisk 4 to subdisk 3 to subdisk 2 to subdisk 1, and then back to subdisk 4 on each pass over the four subdisks. A more detailed representation of the subdisks, shown in Figure 7.24, better illustrates where the parity stripes are located on the subdisks.

A RAID-5 plex must contain at least three disks, so the parity block can be calculated from at least two data blocks. As disks are added to the RAID-5 plex, the parity calculation becomes more I/O intensive, because more data blocks participate in the parity calculation.

A RAID-5 volume can theoretically have mirrored plexes, but that would defeat the purpose of using parity, which is to reduce the expense of purchasing disk drives. Normally, a RAID-5 volume is associated with only one plex.

When a stripe is written to disk, the parity information necessary to recreate the data in that stripe is computed with an exclusive OR (XOR) calculation and stored in the parity area. In the event of a disk failure, a new disk is inserted and the information is recreated using the parity information and the data on the other disks in the RAID-5 stripe. In the interim, the array can continue to service I/O requests by recalculating the data for the failed disk on demand, with no interruption in service. Obviously, performance will suffer because of the overhead needed to recreate the data on the fly.

RAID-5 plexes have higher write I/O overhead than any other disk configuration. For each write, the storage system performs the following steps:

1. Read the surrounding data blocks in the stripe group, as well as its parity block.

2. Recalculate the parity data using the surrounding data blocks and the new block to be written.

3. Write the new data block and the new parity data.

RAID-5 write performance can be dramatically improved by caching data and parity blocks in memory, which is a feature of storage arrays from EMC and other vendors.

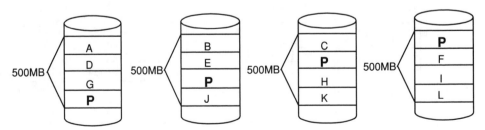

Figure 7.24 Detailed representation of parity stripes across four subdisks within a plex.

One other problem with RAID-5 is that it cannot withstand the loss of multiple disks in a plex at the same time. Regular backups are still a necessity.

In a clickstream data warehouse, RAID-5 write I/O overhead can severely degrade the performance of the load phase of extract, transformation, and load. Unless write overhead is reduced by large memory caches that use RAID-5 sensitive algorithms, like those offered by EMC and some other vendors, it is difficult to justify RAID-5 for large clickstream data warehouse environments.

Database Objects

Now that we understand logical volume management, we need to establish the mapping between data warehouse objects like tables, indexes, aggregates, and the underlying volumes. In this section, we show how space is allocated for these database objects. We also present the general guidelines for separating database objects to minimize I/O contention.

Terminology

A *database* is a set of tables and other related objects. A *tablespace* is a logical division of a database that contains one or more tables. Each Oracle database has at least one tablespace, the system tablespace. The System tablespace stores the data dictionary tables, which contain information about all database objects, and a system rollback segment. It can also hold user created tables, but in a clickstream data warehouse environment, separate table spaces should be created for different types of data warehouse objects. Each tablespace is comprised of one or more underlying *datafiles*. The datafiles map one-to-one onto LVM volumes. A volume maps to one or more physical disks based on one of the storage models presented in the previous section. These relationships are illustrated in Figure 7.25.

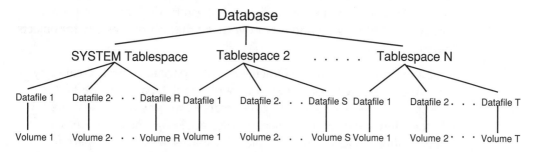

Figure 7.25 Hierarchical relationship among database objects.

Without the logical volume management software, each datafile in the database would be associated with a partition of a physical disk. In the sections that follow we explain how each warehouse object occupies its disk space.

Clickstream Data Warehouse Tablespaces

The following is a list of the types of tablespaces used in a clickstream data warehouse:

- **Table Data Tablespaces:** A clickstream data warehouse requires separate tablespaces for its table objects including the fact, dimension, aggregate, and staging area tables. We use a standard naming convention for these tablespaces:

  - Fact tablespaces are named <table-name>_FACT, and *_FACT indicates the collection of all such tablespaces.

  - Dimension tablespaces are named <table-name>_DIM, and *_DIM indicates the collection of all such tables.

  - Aggregate tablespaces are named <table-name>_AGG, and *_AGG indicates the collection of all such tables.

  - Staging Area Tablespaces are named <table-name>_STAGE, and *_STAGE indicates the collection of all such tables.

  Isolating these different types of tables into their own tablespaces will improve maintenance and monitoring efforts and allow more flexibility in separating these objects in the physical disk layout.

- **Index Tablespaces:** Every table data tablespace should have a corresponding index tablespace, named *_<table-type>_INDEX, to house the indexes on those tables.

- **Temporary Tablespaces:** Queries that produce large intermediate results, ORDER BY or GROUP BY sorts, need temporary space to store sort runs and other temporary data. The Temp tablespace is used for all temporary storage. When the tablespace is defined, it can be declared "temporary," which turns off logging and other overhead that is unnecessary for objects that are not permanent.

- **User and Tool Tablespaces:** Oracle reserves space for objects created by users and software tools that interact with the database. The default user tablespace, called Users, is the space reserved for any database users whether they are direct end users or tools accessing the database. The Users is often divided into multiple tablespaces, with a tablespace for each group of users having a particular usage profile. For example, developers may require more space for cursors and result sets than business users, and the Users tablespace can be divided accordingly. Typical click-stream data warehouse installations also tend to use software tools, like query tools, to access the database. It is a good idea to create a separate Tools tablespace for their use, which can be surprisingly data intensive.

- **Rollback Segment Tablespaces:** Database transactions use *rollback segments* to record the before image of data that is being modified. In the case of Oracle, the rollback segments serve two purposes:

    - They are used to roll back transactions in the case of a failure prior to COMMIT. For example, during a DELETE operation, entries that include the deleted data are recorded in rollback segments; in the event of a failure before the delete completes and the data is committed, the table is returned to its state before the delete operation was issued.

    - Rollback segments are used to maintain read consistency among multiple users of the data. The premise is that a long-running query should have the same view of the data throughout its execution, even if the data in the table is simultaneously being changed by other transactions. As data changes during the execution of a long-running query, the before images in the rollback segment are used to reconstruct data back to the form it was in when the query started running. It is good practice to avoid executing transactions that change data while long-running queries are running, since the data reconstruction adversely impacts query performance.

Unless NOLOGGING is turned on during ETL, it is a good idea to configure rollback segments that are sized for large transactions executed by ETL processes. Separate this rollback segment into its own tablespace (e.g., *_BIG_RBS) so that it will not interfere with the smaller rollback segments used for other types of transactions.

The remaining external objects—the control files, redo log files, trace files, the alert log, and Oracle software itself—are all stored outside the database's tablespaces.

External Objects

External objects are all stored outside the tablespaces of a database. They include:

- **Control Files:** The control file is a binary file that is necessary for database startup and operations. The file is created and maintained by the database; it is used to maintain internal consistency and to guide recovery operations.

The database needs to keep multiple copies of the control files, because losing the control file makes the database unstartable. At least two copies should be stored on different disks, and many sites maintain three copies.

■ **Redo Log Files:** The online redo log files record after-images of all data modifications to support database roll forward recovery operations.

A history of archived redo log files is stored along with backups, so that a database can be rolled forward from the point of the last backup in case of a catastrophic failure.

Space must be allocated for the online and archived redo logs. Both online and archived redo log files may be defined as mirrored and maintained by the database. Of course, logical volume management software can also be used to mirror these files.

The Oracle log writer process writes to online redo logs sequentially, as shown in Figure 7.26. The process appends new log records to redo log 1 until it fills, then proceeds to redo log 2, and so on, as illustrated Figure 7.26. The archiver process reads filled online redo logs and writes archived log files to the archive area. Each process moves through the available redo logs in the same order, with the archiver trailing the log writer. If archiving is enabled, there must be enough online redo logs so that the processes don't interfere with each other. Otherwise, during periods of extreme transaction activity, like ETL processing, the log writer process catches up to the archiver, and will try to write to the same online redo log file that the archiver process is archiving. When this happens, the entire database must wait until the archiver completes its activity.

Redo logging can be suppressed during extract, transformation and load by setting the NOLOGGING option on table and index creates and the UNRECOVERABLE option on data loads. If redo logging is suppressed, the database administrator is responsible for ensuring the integrity of the ETL transactions after a failure.

■ **Oracle Software Files, Trace Files, and the Alert Log**: Oracle software files and configuration information should be stored on a different disk device than the database datafiles. Examples of these files include the binary executable files, the parameter configuration file, trace files, dump files, and the alert log. The parameter configuration file, or the "init.ora" file, contains information such as database tuning parameters and their values, rollback segment identification, and file locations for control files, dump files, and archived redo log files. Trace files are associated with each user database background process and are useful for debugging applications and finding performance problems. The alert log contains

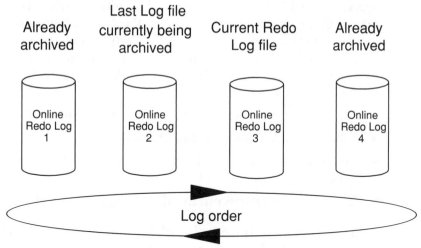

Figure 7.26 Sequential use and reuse of redo logs by the Log Writer.

records of all administrative commands, command results, and internal error entries. The alert log also contains database events such as startup or shutdown and redo log switches.

Guidelines for Database Object Disk Layout

In the last section, we established which database objects need tablespaces or file-based storage, as well as the usage model of each type of object. From this knowledge we can develop a set of guidelines for distributing these objects over the available disk space. These guidelines are designed to:

- Maximize overall query throughput and eliminate I/O bottlenecks.
- Speed database object maintenance, especially ETL and log file maintenance.
- Reduce the scope of maintenance operations and backup and restore to the affected object, rather than all objects at once.

Tablespace Guidelines

The following list gives performance-driven guidelines for placing the various types of tablespaces on disk storage:

- **Table data tablespaces:** Table data tablespaces (*_FACT, *_DIM, *_AGG, *_STAGE) should be separated from their corresponding index tablespaces (*_INDEX) to spread query I/O activity and improve ETL performance. By separating these objects into their own tablespaces, they can be placed on the disk drives so that the I/O activity on one object is isolated from the I/O activity on the other objects. For example, suppose we execute an UPDATE operation that uses an index. The operation will access the following objects:

- The index tablespace to find the rows for update,
- The data tablespace to update the rows,
- The rollback segment tablespace to record the before images of the update,
- The redo log file to record the after images of the update.

If all these objects are physically isolated from one another on the disk drives, the I/O performance of the UPDATE will be optimized.

- **Fact tablespaces:** Clickstream data warehouse fact table tablespaces (*_FACT) should be separated from dimension table tablespaces (*_DIM) in order optimize join performance. Fact tables also have special maintenance considerations because of their huge size. They are usually partitioned by time and they are subject to massive data modification during ETL. By separating the fact tablespace from the other data warehouse schema tablespaces, fact table maintenance can be optimized.

- **Aggregate tablespaces:** Aggregate tables should be separated into their own tablespace so that they can be created as quickly as possible. Very large aggregate fact tables may warrant their own tablespaces.

- **Dimension tablespaces:** Dimension tables are small and relatively static compared to fact tables, and they can be grouped together in a tablespace. But large dimensions that are subject to frequent update, like the User dimension, may require their own tablespaces.

- **Rollback Segment tablespaces:** Rollback segment tablespaces (*_RBS) should be separated from the table data and index tablespaces since all three are concurrently accessed during ETL unless logging is turned off.

- **Temp tablespace:** The Temp tablespace should have its own tablespace, due to its dynamic nature and the fact that it does not need to be logged. This tablespace should be separated from data, indexes, rollback segments, and redo logs as much as possible, since it will get quite a workout during operations like query sorts and ETL index builds.

- **Users and Tools tablespaces:** If possible, separate user created objects in the Users tablespace from the rest of the database to minimize their impact database operations. This tablespace gives developers and power users a "sandbox" to create tables and indexes that are locally inside the Users tablespace, without negatively impacting the database data or indexes. Similar arguments dictate that third-party database access and development tools use a separate Tools tablespace.

- **System tablespace:** Finally, it is best to separate user-created tablespaces from the data dictionary System tablespace. The System tablespace is accessed multiple times for each database operation, and it can be a performance bottleneck if it is not separated from other I/O activity.

Log File Guidelines

Redo log files should be physically isolated from database datafiles, especially the system and *_RBS tablespaces, as well as the active portions of the table and index tablespaces. At least a couple of records are written to the redo log for every database transaction, and it is important to make redo log writes as efficient as possible.

Similarly, archived log files should be separated from other tablespace objects to ensure that archiving proceeds as expeditiously as possible.

Guideline Implications

The general policy of separating each database object into its own disjoint set of disks means that a clickstream data warehouse is going to require a large disk farm with a lot of spindles. And because disks have become so large, it is quite likely that much of the potential storage on a drive will not be utilized, because the database objects need to spread their data over more spindles to improve I/O performance. Some objects, like backup files and old archived log files, can occupy the otherwise unoccupied space on the large disk drives. It may also be possible to store objects in tandem on the same set of drives if I/O is distributed well, using techniques like striping. But, in order to get the best performance characteristics, there is no easy alternative to a large disk subsystem with a lot of spindles.

Choosing the Appropriate Infrastructure Vendors

Now that we have discussed everything from parallel database algorithms to mapping database objects onto disk drives, it is time to make some specific comments about clickstream data warehouse infrastructure vendors. All of these comments are valid at the time of this writing. Because clickstream data warehouses tend to be so large, our comments are colored by the need to efficiently perform large-scale ETL and query analysis. If your environment is not so large, the number of possible implementation choices will increase accordingly.

Database Software

In our experience, the vast majority of clickstream data warehouses are implemented using either Oracle or DB2 RDBMS software on large-scale symmetric multiprocessors, like those from Sun Microsystems, IBM, and HP. There are some other possible choices, but they come with the caveats explained below.

Choosing an appropriate database engine is one of the critical decisions for the clickstream data warehouse infrastructure. The possible choices include:

- Oracle

- DB2

- Teradata

- Microsoft SQL Server

- Open source MySQL or PostgreSQL

- Column-major, bitmap index databases (Sybase Adaptive Server IQ-M, Sand Technologies Nucleus, and Synera Systems Intelligent Exploration Suite)

We will now discuss each of these in greater detail.

Oracle. Oracle is the most common database engine for large clickstream data warehouses. As explained earlier in this chapter, Oracle has many features that specifically address the problems associated with clickstream data warehouse environments. Because it is open system software, Oracle runs well on all the large symmetric multiprocessor systems that are commonly used to house clickstream data warehouses.

DB2. Like Oracle, DB2 also has relatively strong support for large clickstream data warehouse environments, and is a good possible alternative for competitive bidding. Recently, DB2 software has been opened up and ported to non-IBM platforms like Sun and HP. We rarely see DB2 outside an IBM environment, but this may change with time.

Teradata. Unlike all the other database software in this list, Teradata software is designed to run best in a loosely coupled, nonsymmetric multiprocessor environment. Until recently, Teradata software ran only on NCR systems, but it has recently been ported to run on loosely coupled collections of systems running Microsoft Windows 2000 (NT). Because of its loosely coupled architecture, Teradata can theoretically be scaled to run extremely large data warehouse systems that could not be serviced by a single large SMP server. Unless you have a clickstream data warehouse that is greater than approximately 25 Terabytes, Teradata may not be an appropriate choice, because it is not very open. While the Microsoft partnership may eventually yield more analytical application options and new potential hardware vendors other than NCR, right now a Teradata choice locks the site into NCR as both the hardware and RDBMS software vendor.

Microsoft SQL Server. Microsoft SQL Server continues to suffer from the scalability problems of Windows 2000 (NT). Since very few NT systems scale well beyond four to eight processors, SQL Server is only an option for smaller clickstream data warehouses. Furthermore, much of the parallel functionality present in Oracle and DB2 is still missing from SQL Server. There is no specialized join functionality, and aggregate recognition only works with Microsoft OLAP (also known as Analysis) Services. Configurable parallel INSERT, UPDATE, and DELETE are also missing for ETL.

Open Source MySQL or PostgreSQL. Many Web sites already utilize open source SQL databases like MySQL or PostgreSQL, so there may be a tendency to want to implement a clickstream data warehouse on top of these open source engines. Because of their unsophisticated implementations, lacking parallel query functionality and doing locking at the file level, they are not yet suitable for clickstream data warehouse implementations.

Column-Major, Bitmap Index Databases. This includes Sybase Adaptive Server IQ-M, Sand Technologies Nucleus, and Synera Systems Intelligent Exploration Suite. These niche products store data column-wise, not row-wise like traditional database engines. The column values are stored as bitmapped vectors, and unique values are only stored one time, rather than again and again, as in row-wise implementations. There is no concept of dimension tables, because all the data in all the columns is essentially prejoined by the bitmap vectors. Because clickstream data has a lot of redundant values, like page URLs, IP addresses, etc., these database engines may have some attraction. Unfortunately, they do not, strictly speaking, process SQL, which is a row-wise language, and they usually require a proprietary front end to process the data. Some products have partial SQL interfaces, with restricted functionality. These products will not perform well if there are a great number of unique values in many of the columns, which is often the case for user information and other types of clickstream data. Load times are also problematic, since none of these products has a good partitioning strategy because new data can potentially touch all pieces of the bitmap vector storage structure.

As you can see, it is safest to go with Oracle or DB2 for most clickstream data warehouse environments. Teradata can be considered for particularly large data warehouses that cannot be supported by a single symmetric multiprocessor system. For smaller clickstream data warehouses that will not grow beyond a few hundred gigabytes, Microsoft SQL Server may be an adequate choice.

Logical Volume Management (LVM) Software and Disk Subsystems

Veritas has a near monopoly on the open logical volume management software market, with the only competition being some similar, proprietary, disk vendor LVM software implementations. The more important issue is the choice of the disk subsystem vendor. EMC dominates the third-party disk subsystem marketplace. Because an EMC disk subsystem is really a computer with a huge page cache, not just a bunch of disks (JBOD), it implements much of the normal LVM software functionality, like plexing and a variant of RAID-5, inside itself.

It is very important to avoid implementing LVM software functionality on top of the same functionality that is already implemented inside the disk subsystem, like creating LVM plexes on top of subsystem plexes, etc. Otherwise the combined performance impacts of competing volume definitions will be, at best, unpredictable, and there can also be severe data reliability issues.

It is not clear what will prevail in the end, intelligent disk subsystems like EMC, or JBOD disk farms running Veritas software. But both choices can be used right now to run large clickstream data warehouses.

Summary

In this chapter, we discussed the seven categories of database software support for clickstream data warehouses in great detail. We also discussed logical volume management and how to map database objects onto disk drives for the best query and load performance. We concluded with some data warehouse vendor recommendations, based on the information presented earlier in the chapter. Armed with this knowledge, the explanation of extract, transformation, and load (ETL) in the next chapter will be much easier to digest.

Building the Clickstream Extract, Transformation, and Load Mechanism

In the last chapter, we discussed the technology infrastructure surrounding the clickstream data warehouse. Now we turn our attention to the last major step in creating a clickstream data warehouse—building the extract, transformation, and load (ETL) mechanism. In this chapter we review the clickstream ETL architecture and process flow and discuss the major issues surrounding the extraction, transformation, and loading of Web-based clickstream data. Much of this chapter consists of a detailed clickstream extraction and load example based on the meta-schema from Chapter 6.

A complete discussion of general data warehouse ETL processing is beyond the scope of this book. Instead we focus on the issues that make clickstream data warehouse ETL different from a data warehouse with no Web-based data sources. For a rigorous discussion of the general data warehouse ETL process we recommend reading one of the many general data warehousing ETL books that describe the process.

Extract, Transformation, and Load Architecture

We start this chapter with a brief review of the ETL architecture of nonclickstream data warehouse environments. Once we have established this architectural foundation, we can then add Web data sources to the architecture and turn our attention to clickstream-specific ETL.

At its simplest, ETL is just getting data from where it is created to the data warehouse where it will be used. Since the requirement is easily captured at a high level, many people believe that it should be straightforward. Unfortunately, the ETL tasks consume the lion's share of the project schedule and are the most frequently underestimated tasks on data warehouse projects.

One of the biggest challenges facing any data warehouse project is extracting the data from source systems and transforming it into a form suitable for use. Figure 8.1 shows an example of the environment in which many data warehouses operate. In most companies there are a number of applications performing various tasks in the enterprise. Some applications are specific to a certain business function, like sales or human resources, and some span the enterprise, such as ERP systems. Some of the applications are tightly integrated, like the various modules of an ERP package, while others have no connections to one another or may be completely outsourced, like payroll systems. In addition, there are usually undocumented links between applications that send data back and forth, often for reporting purposes, and these are shown in Figure 8.1 as "hidden" data feeds. Add to this complexity the numerous data problems

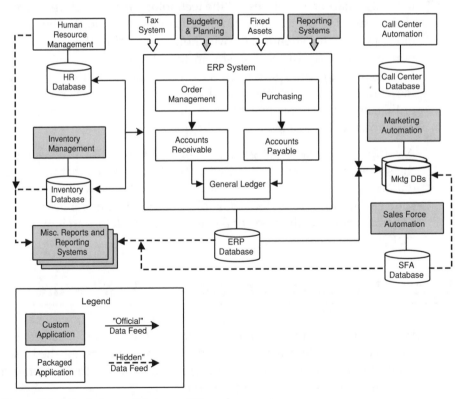

Figure 8.1 A Typical nonclickstream ETL environment.

that are unknown at the outset of the project, from bad or missing data to different representations of the same data in different applications, and you begin to see why ETL development takes up most of a project's timeline.

The multiplicity of business applications is usually mirrored by a similarly large collection of different system technologies used to implement the applications. This multisystem ETL environment is quite a challenge for many companies. The data source systems are built on different operating systems, databases, and languages. The systems frequently span generations of development technologies, from COBOL systems with hierarchical databases to the latest relational databases on open-source platforms.

The data source systems typically execute transactions aligned to one or more functional processes within the organization. There are often ancillary systems that handle some specific tasks, or provide information to end users. Because business functions often overlap, or the same data is needed to support two independent functions, data is duplicated across two or more systems. This duplication of data frequently results in inconsistent data across the application systems.

These applications and the technologies in use are the data source environment in which the data warehouse operates. Before discussing ETL in more detail it is important to understand how ETL fits into the basic architectural framework of a clickstream data warehouse. Figure 8.2 shows a high-level diagram of the data-flow architecture for a generic clickstream data warehouse.

The clickstream data warehouse architecture consists of the ETL programs that process data into the warehouse, the database and data models that store the data in a queryable form, information-based applications that make use of the information, and the underlying data and process management infrastructure that supports all of these components. The project plan, described in Chapter 5, is constructed with this architecture in mind.

The meta-schema data model and technology infrastructure for database storage were discussed in Chapters 6 and 7. In this chapter the focus is mostly on clickstream ETL, although we will mention pertinent details about other data sources and infrastructure components.

ETL, as its name implies, is separated into three high-level components:

- **Data extraction.** This component is concerned with extracting relevant data from the data sources on an ongoing basis. The data extracts can be from application databases, Web server log files, and any other sources that contain data required by the users of the data warehouse. The mechanisms for transfer of the data from the source systems to the data warehouse system are included in the data extraction component. Often

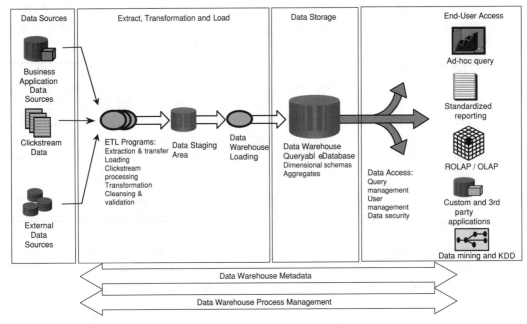

Figure 8.2 A data-flow view of clickstream data warehouse architecture.

overlooked are the data source change tracking and notification procedures and the automated mechanisms for managing changes in the production systems. If source change tracking is not implemented, then extraction can grind to a halt when a data source changes, causing the data extract to fail.

- **Data transformation.** The data transformation programs perform most of the work in the ETL process, since they handle all of the preparation of data for loading into the data warehouse. The data transformation programs do basic translations such as character set conversion or translating codes into human-readable equivalents. They also perform more involved work like the merging of data streams from multiple sources and the interrecord analysis required to process Web server logs.

- **Data loading.** The data loading process is often more complex than one would think. Before data can be loaded into the data warehouse, new or changed dimension data must be processed. This processing can be quite involved since it may mean changes to dimension rows, which can in turn require updates to existing rows in the fact tables. Once all of the data for the dimensions has been staged, the data that is destined for the fact table must be validated and all of the keys generated and checked against the dimension tables. Reindexing of fact and dimension tables and data archiving for backup and restore will also be required. Typically, the final step is updating or regenerating the aggregate tables. If nonrelational OLAP tools are used for end-user applications, you probably will have to add steps to take data from the data warehouse and process it into whatever storage format the OLAP product uses.

One thing these components have in common is that they are built on top of a common data staging area. The staging schema is designed specifically to support all the ETL processing steps prior to the final data load into the warehouse schema.

We did not mention data quality or data cleansing because these tasks should be incorporated throughout the entire ETL process. Data quality is a process-oriented issue, and so should be built into each component of the system rather than treated as a single separate step. Most systems will still do a final validation step once the data warehouse has been loaded in order to catch bad data or loading problems that may have slipped through the process undetected.

While the ETL process consists of the three high-level components, the actual design and implementation will probably not be cleanly divided along these boundaries. In practice, it is common to do some or even all of the data transformation work directly on the source systems prior to sending the data to the staging area. The decisions about how and where to perform specific processing are made when the system architecture is defined, as well as during the ETL design phase.

The ETL components of the data warehouse make the most demands of the underlying software infrastructure shown in Figure 8.2. Meta data is shown as a separate component, although in many data warehouses it is simply incorporated into various components of the system and not managed separately.

Mechanisms to support the scheduling and dependencies of ETL jobs, handling of exceptions, and the management of data are vital once the data warehouse is in production. This framework for process automation can be as simple as a few programming standards and some scripts, or as complex as a full-featured batch scheduling system like the Tivoli Workload Scheduler (formerly Maestro) product.

Clickstream ETL Architecture

There are few changes in the basic architecture of a clickstream data warehouse from a data warehouse that does not include Web-based data. The primary differences are the data sources, ETL design details, and the warehouse schema design. All of these influence the design, and they have an evolutionary impact on the overall architecture.

The More Complex Clickstream Environment

The additional data sources for a clickstream data warehouse add a level of complexity to the environment. Figure 8.3 extends the standard environment in Figure 8.1, showing additional systems under the organization's control, as well as systems that may be controlled by other entities. This Web infrastructure has already been discussed in detail in Part 1 of this book. Internally controlled infrastructure components include firewalls, proxy servers, Web application servers, and Web servers, as well as other systems that may be in use like media servers.

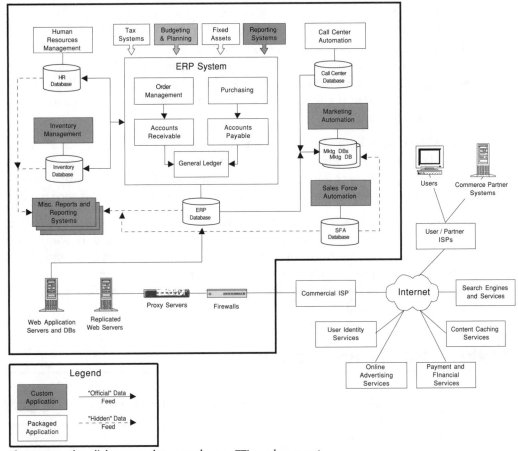

Figure 8.3 The clickstream data warehouse ETL environment.

Data sources that may be outside the organization's control include content caching servers, user tracking services, search engines, and online advertising engines. The companies that provide these services are generally willing to provide data to their clients, although negotiating a service level agreement that includes quick turnaround for data loads may be difficult. To make matters more difficult, some of these companies would prefer you to pay them for their online analysis rather than provide you the source data.

The dissimilar nature of clickstream and traditional data sources means that analysis of source systems and source data during the schema design tasks will be more difficult. The differing technologies can make extraction more challenging as well. For example, a reliance on data from external sources is almost unheard of in a data warehouse with no Web data sources, while many Web sites outsource functions like content caching. The need to extract data from multiple sources that is part of the same transaction is also a rarity in non-Web data warehouses. Replicated Web servers and Web application servers guarantee that data for a single user's session will be spread throughout the environment, making this a common ETL problem for Web data.

The project plan in Chapter 5 maintains a separate set of tasks for the analysis of Web data sources, partly to make it easier to create time estimates and partly because the work can require different skills and staff. These tasks are critical to understanding how the Web site works, what data is present, and what changes to the Web site may be coming during the data warehouse project's development.

A big part of Web data source analysis is identifying the problems and limitations of the currently available data. Many times, this analysis highlights the need to make changes to the Web applications underlying the Web site in order to capture required data. Making a Web site more clickstream-friendly often becomes a subproject that runs in parallel with ETL development. We will discuss some of these issues in the section on building the ETL components of the warehouse.

The Clickstream ETL Architecture

Before going into the steps involved in building the ETL subsystem, we need to review a generalized model of the ETL subsystem for the entire clickstream data warehouse. Figure 8.4 shows the clickstream ETL portion of the data-flow architecture shown earlier in Figure 8.2.

In the figure, the components that perform the different processing stages can be seen, as well as the general order in which the work is done. One element that is different from the traditional data warehouse data-flow is that there is a

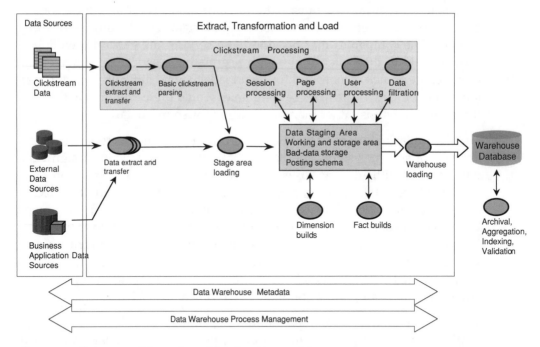

Figure 8.4 Clickstream ETL portion of the data-flow architecture.

separate clickstream data path. Clickstream data requires supplementary processing before it can be integrated with data from other sources.

The clickstream components are shown in the upper half of the diagram. In general, there will be a mechanism, which might be as simple as a file transfer or copy, to move the clickstream data to the location where it will be processed. The next step is basic parsing and loading into the data staging area. At the same time, data from other systems is also extracted and loaded into the data staging area.

Once the data is present in the staging area, the clickstream data must pass through a number of programs that map hits to user sessions, identify users, and perform the processing associated with pages, such as linking hits for page elements to pages or interpreting content codes. Depending on the requirements, there may be a step to filter unwanted data such as the hits for images or other page elements. Sometimes this filtration task is performed at the time data is loaded into the staging area. Usually, this is to reduce the volume of data, but we recommend filtering at the end of the processing because there is derived information that depends on having every hit available.

After all of the clickstream data is processed into a usable form, data for the dimension tables is assembled. The fact tables are derived last because there are data dependencies between the fact tables and the dimensions. Often, the data to be loaded into the warehouse schema is placed into a posting schema consisting of tables in the data staging area that mirror the actual clickstream warehouse tables in structure. This makes loading as fast as possible.

Postload processing is commonly included as part of the ETL subsystem, even though it is more related to query performance and DBA tasks than strict ETL. Postload activities include archiving data that is older than the data warehouse time window, creating aggregate tables and reindexing the database. A final step is validation of the newly loaded data, although this is sometimes omitted because data has been checked prior to placing it into the posting schema.

The framework that supports all this processing is also part of the ETL subsystem. Common elements of the framework are process scheduling, job control, and exception handling. The mechanisms to resolve problems such as bad data are included as part of this supporting framework.

Building the ETL Subsystem

The project plan in Appendix A shows the individual tasks that are involved in ETL development, but it does not really say much about the dependencies or about how to go about the work. Designing and building the ETL subsystem is a large undertaking, so we divide the work into eight basic steps. The remainder of this section discusses each step in the implementation process and discusses the technical or clickstream-relevant details in that step. Where applicable, we mention at what phase of the project the step normally occurs.

Step 1: Data Analysis

Data analysis work actually begins during the requirements phase with interviews. During requirements gathering the team will do both end-user and technical interviews. The technical interviews are aimed at identifying what systems are potential sources for particular types of data, and whether there is any data that might not be available.

The results from this first high-level pass at data analysis are an initial list of the traditional and Web-based source data systems for the clickstream data warehouse. This is the point where one usually discovers whether the Web site is tracking user identity and sessions, as well as what other data is available for extraction.

This is a good point in the project for the team to meet with the Web site developers to discuss various Web site design and data logging issues. Since most software defaults to the NCSA Common Log File format, one of the most common changes we see at this time is a switch from the minimal CLF format to one of the extended logging formats, mostly because changing log formats is easily done with minimal impact on the Web site. There will also be some investigation that the Web developers need to do to answer basic user and behavior tracking questions, such what technique is used to assign user IDs.

The ETL implementation really starts progressing during the design phase of the project when the in-depth data analysis is performed. Designing the data warehouse schema and mapping possible source data to that schema are usually done together, with data mapping slightly lagging the schema design. Data mapping is where the ETL process starts to get interesting.

It is at this point that the project team will meet with the technical staff who are most familiar with the source systems. Many, if not most, of the data issues faced by the project will be identified by this work. The end result of the data analysis is an updated data mapping with much more information about the data sources, as well as a document describing the known data problems.

Most data warehouse projects require minor modifications to some source systems, at the least. This holds true for the Web applications as well. Our experience with clickstream data is that most Web data problems stem from a lack of data rather than data quality issues. In some cases, the project may not be able to move forward until changes are made to the Web site to log the needed data.

Step 2: Making the Web Site Clickstream-Friendly

Since most projects identify problems with the clickstream data, the next step in ETL development is determining what options are available to deal with those problems. In many cases, the only possibility is to make changes to the Web site or Web applications.

The earlier you examine the Web site and data, the more time you have to make the case for changes to the Web site. The Web team must determine what the development impacts will be, and they must plan for that work. The last thing you want is a stalled data warehouse project while you wait for Web site changes. For that reason, the best approach is to feed problems to the Web developers as you uncover those problems, and solicit their advice early. In many cases, the Web site modifications can be completed by the time the project is ready for the ETL programming.

In Chapters 3 and 4 we reviewed many of the common data sources and some of the problems that accompany their data. Knowing some of the major pitfalls with clickstream data, there are a number of technical solutions that make it easier to gather data from the Web site.

The three items that most often drive Web site changes are user tracking, page tagging, and time synchronization. Problems with user tracking and content identification are widespread, especially with sites that have dynamically generated Web pages. These problem-prone source data items also comprise the bulk of the data needed for analysis, so any issues need to be resolved or the usefulness of the data warehouse will suffer.

User Tracking

We find that many Web sites track customers, but do not track all visitors to the Web site, leaving a large gap in the data collected. User identification and tracking was described in detail in Chapter 4. Most important is the ability to track a given user across multiple visits. The Web site must generate a unique identifier for every user and use that identifier to track the user.

To recap the alternatives for user tracking we described in Chapter 4: the Web application can generate IDs and manage user tracking; you can implement a user-ID server that is integrated with the Web application; or you can use a third-party user tracking service. Whatever the choice, modifications to the Web site are likely.

Uniquely identifying customers or external users, online or not, is a task that is difficult for many organizations. Multiple independent systems will contain customer data, and the norm is for each system to utilize its own method keying customer data. This becomes apparent whenever someone asks for aggregated information about customers, such as, What percentage of revenue is generated by the top 10 customers? Trying to assemble the data to answer this simple question is confounded by each system's own unique identifiers.

With a Web site, this problem is magnified because many Web sites do not keep user IDs under rigorous control. We've encountered numerous companies with loose user-ID management, making user tracking over time difficult, if not impossible.

The resolution to these problems for clickstream data is twofold. First, one application must be responsible for generating unique user IDs. The simplest approach is to create a user-ID server that can be called by Web applications, and turn responsibility of the process over to the user-ID server. This process does not solve everything, because it is still relatively easy to end up with multiple user IDs for a single user. For example, if a user without a user ID visits the Web site, the user automatically receives a new identifier. No effort is made to match the new user against existing information to see if this is a redundant user ID.

The second part of the resolution is to integrate the disparate user or customer data in one place, typically the data warehouse. Apart from relying on common IDs, the Web site *and all non-Web-based systems* should provide customer data to the data warehouse. Through appropriate ETL processing, duplicate users and other inaccuracies can be removed. The cleaned data can then be used for analysis purposes. More important, the data warehouse can send the cleaned data back to the originating systems so that they are updated.

By implementing a user-ID server in this way, the data warehouse has a much easier time processing user data. Even better, errors in the data will decrease over time and all systems will converge on a single unique identifier for every user or customer.

Page Tagging and Content Coding

Clickstream analysis can greatly benefit from page tagging. The goal is to ensure that every Web page can be categorized by function and content. This allows analysts to do much more detailed work than would otherwise be possible. If your Web site is static then page tagging is not quite so important, provided that the URLs have the right information embedded and they are uniquely named. The difficulty is that in most cases, the URL can't be relied on to provide all the information desired by analysts, particularly if pages are dynamically generated.

There are two parts to page tagging: content coding, and building a mechanism to tag each page. Content coding is driven by the end users' analysis needs. Therefore it is important that they define the standards for the attributes they are interested in tracking for each page, or at least sign off on the attribute list created by the project team. If your organization uses content management tools to support the Web site, then you may have some content coding already in place since some of these tools require it. Table 8.1 shows some of the possible attributes that might be useful for analysis. Someone will also need to maintain the content coding standard, usually the data administrator.

The second part, building a mechanism to tag pages, is part process and part technology. The process component is tied to how the Web site deveopers and authors create pages. If pages are manually assembled then the implementer must remember to insert the appropriate information into the page. If the pages are dynamic then the Web application must create a page tagging mechanism. No matter how the page is created, there must be a way to uniquely identify each page on the Web site, and store that ID inside the page.

Table 8.1 Sample Attributes for Content Coding

CODE TYPE	ATTRIBUTE
Content Purpose	Home page
Content Purpose	Section entry/portal
Content Purpose	Registration
Content Purpose	Navigation
Content Purpose	Search
Content Purpose	Content
Content Purpose	Product display
Content Purpose	Order form
Content Purpose	Cancellation form
Content Purpose	Product return form
Content Purpose	Status
Content Purpose	User feedback
Content Type	Site index
Content Type	Product information
Content Type	Site search results
Content Type	Product search results
Content Type	Order information
Content Type	FAQ
Content Type	Press release
Content Details	Last modified date
Content Details	Page version
Content Details	Web application version
Content Details	HTML version
Content Details	Departmental owner
Content Details	Author

Page tagging can be done internally or externally. With internal tagging, the attributes are placed inside the HTML for the page as Meta tags, formatted comments, or in some other fashion. External tagging uses the URL query string to store the attributes for a page. In general, internal tagging can be used for static HTML sites, while external tagging is more suitable to dynamically generated pages.

Time Synchronization

The third item that often drives technical changes is time synchronization. When there is more than one server providing clickstream data then the servers must have their clocks synchronized. For example, if the Web site uses load balancing across three Web servers and the Web application server runs on yet another machine, these machines must be synchronized.

If these machines are not synchronized then it is possible that event records will have incorrect timestamps. When the data from all servers is assembled, this will lead to an incorrect ordering of events, thus generating bad data for the clickstream warehouse. For example, if the clock on one machine running a Web server is slow, then it would be possible for the record of a user's first visit to be dated after they placed an order during that same session.

Synchronizing the various servers is a relatively simple task. Programs to support synchronization via the Network Time Protocol (NTP) are freely available for all major operating systems. Further, it is not vital that the time be exactly correct, only that the time be consistent across every server so event records can be reassembled in the correct order.

One area where you may run into difficulties is when the Web site uses servers in multiple time zones, as might be the case with a replicated site or with content caching services. If the Web site uses any external services that will provide clickstream data to the warehouse, then it is important to ensure that these services are synchronizing their clocks as well.

Fortunately, time synchronization is a task that does not involve any changes to the Web site. It only requires some minor system administration tasks to install and configure. The only place where this may not be so minor is with special-purpose server appliances that do not allow for easy configuration or software installation.

Log Identification

Apart from synchronizing clocks, the use of multiple Web or other servers drives the need to track the source of event records. This can be managed at the log level by naming files during extraction, assuming you are using log files.

A better method is to place the hostname or IP address of the server in the log record itself. Most Web, media, and application servers have this ability through standard logging, by adding the *s-dns* or *s-ip* element to a log in W3C Extended Log File Format, for example. While the extra data in each record might seem redundant, it makes processing and troubleshooting simpler. Putting the server name or address in the log record also facilitates real-time log processing, where the event records are immediately sent to the data warehouse.

Exit Marking and End-of-Session Events

In Chapter 3 we mentioned the problem of identifying the last page of a user's visit and calculating page dwell and session duration times. While there is no way to track a user who ends their session by typing in a URL, using a bookmark, or turning off their browser, you can track them if they use a link from your Web site to another site. This is normally the addition of a simple redirection program and a modification to the link HTML in the pages, templates, or Web application, as described in "Identifying Exit Pages" in Chapter 3. Also, there is a simple example of a PHP redirection script in Chapter 2.

Exit marking is part of a solution to the larger problem of identifying when a user's session ends. Much of the time there is no way to know that a session has ended, so the Web site usually considers a session to be terminated after a predetermined time period, like 15 minutes of inactivity. If the Web application terminates a session, explicitly logging that event is very helpful to the clickstream warehouse. This saves the warehouse from grouping records and serially processing the records looking for the gaps in time that indicate implicit end-of-session events.

Some server scripting environments and many Web application servers will terminate sessions after a time-out period. The problem with many of the products is that they do not log that information. In some cases, the session management code is so deeply buried in the application server that only the vendor's technical consultants have the ability to modify the code so the end-of-session can be logged. If this is the case, you will need to work with the vendor to try to capture this information.

Decoding of Parameters or Cookies

In Chapter 3 we mentioned the possibility that cookies or parameters in query strings might be encrypted. In a dynamic page generation environment the Web application that generates pages will probably use codes in the query string that are meaningful only within the application. For example, the following three URLs taken from real Web sites (the names are obscured) show parameters that are meaningless unless you know how to interpret them.

```
http://www.egad.com/bb/movie/new_releases/0,4277,,00.html?id=52683
http://www.yikes.com?bhfv=5&bhqs=1
http://www.zoiks.com/news.asp?nid=7CD11824-D1EB-4D8C
```

The page name and parameter from the first site might be meaningful to a Web developer familiar with the ATG Dynamo application server used at this site, but it is probably meaningless to an ETL developer. The second line shows an encrypted query string. The third line shows an encoded parameter. These are the URLs that would show up in the event logs of the Web sites.

In all of these cases, the ETL programmer must work with the Web site developers to determine how to process this data. In some cases, the encryption or encoding is not really needed and can be disabled, making the logs more legible. The more likely case is that the ETL developer must duplicate the algorithms used to generate, encode, or encrypt the parameters in the ETL subsystem. This usually requires integration with the Web site, and active participation by the Web developers. Implementing Web application code in such a way that it can be called externally is a good way to make the site more clickstream warehouse friendly.

Implementing a Logging Server

Use of a logging server to track page views makes the processing of Web log file data much easier. The general mechanism is described in the section entitled "Alternative Logging Techniques" in Chapter 4, so we won't repeat it here.

If you do choose to implement a logging server then a few processes must be put under tighter control. Every Web page that is manually created or dynamically generated must have the appropriate logging element inserted into it, like a logging Web bug or a call to the log server application. This implies that the parameters you track must all be embedded in the logging element's query string so the logging server can process them. These changes are not particularly difficult to make on most Web sites, but determining what data to track and ensuring that the procedures for linking page tagging to the log server can be a challenge. If the page tagging is not linked with the logging elements then the log files generated will be of limited use.

Step 3: Create the High-Level ETL Design and Architecture

The third step in ETL development is the high-level design of the components that make up the ETL subsystem. The project plan in Chapter 5 lists a number of tasks associated with the high-level design, most of which center on defining approaches to take for various process or technical aspects of ETL. The goal is to create an architecture that serves as a framework for the detailed design and programming to follow. A secondary goal is to define the requirements that ETL technologies must meet.

The high-level ETL design is usually held back until the schema design and at least some of the source data analysis has been completed. While the project plan shows technology selection happening during the earlier warehouse design phase, we often find that there is not enough information available to make wise choices for ETL technologies until this stage in the project. Therefore, in the project plan we show ETL design tasks in the implementation phase to reflect the normal dependencies and lag time.

It is useful to start the ETL design process by creating a system level mapping that diagrams the basic data sources and shows where data originates and where it ends up. This is the high-level counterpart to the column-level data mapping done during the schema design. Together with these, one should add all of the information learned during data analysis about the extraction and transformation processing. Collectively, all of this information forms the basis upon which to make design decisions.

Because there are so many ways to build ETL components, our objective in this part of the book is to cover the principal decisions that are made as part of the high-level ETL design and architecture. The most important design decisions are determining how one should handle aspects of the processing. We will step through these decisions in a simplified manner, looking first at those related to data extraction, then to data transformation, and finally to data loading. Keep in mind that in reality the ETL programs are rarely this discrete. For example, there will be many cases where data transformation is performed during the extract or load.

Design Decisions for Data Extraction

The basic decisions that constrain all of the data extract programs are how data should be extracted from the sources, the preferred approach for data transfer, and the preferred data-transfer mechanism.

Data can be extracted incrementally or in full during each extract cycle. Most data warehouses use incremental extracts that only retrieve data that has been added or changed since the prior extract. Incremental extracts are the most efficient because they minimize the volume of data that must be extracted and processed.

One reason incremental extracts may not work is that some systems do not keep accurate track of changes. In the transaction processing system it may not be important to keep information about events between the initial step and the final step in a transaction, such as a change in the billing address of a customer. We've encountered order entry systems that simply delete orders rather than marking them as cancelled, thus making it impossible to look at cancellation rates and reasons for cancellation. In these cases, the way to determine that there is new or altered data is to compare the prior and current extracts, and this requires a full data extract to accomplish.

An alternative method is to use some form of changed-data capture to identify altered or missing data. Changed-data capture normally makes use of specialized software to identify before and after images from application or database logs.

There is a third method of data extraction that is a variant of the incremental extract—the use of a transaction stream. With extracts built in this fashion, the events that one is interested in are sent to the data warehouse as a real-time trickle feed. In order to do this one must work directly on the transaction systems to capture the relevant data and send it to the data warehouse.

Streaming transactions as the events occur is relevant when there are real-time analytical requirements, such as hourly reporting of Web site activity. One of the problems with real-time analytical requirements is that all of the data for various dimensions or facts may not be immediately available, hampering analysis.

Because of this and the complexity of implementing streaming transaction ETL, we see transaction streaming limited to reporting and monitoring for site traffic statistics. For example, an enterprise may want to monitor the volume of visitors and number of inbound orders so that the enterprise can make changes to meet the demand. Event-driven businesses in the consumer space, like online florists, are a good example of firms that can use real-time information to adjust both online and offline activities in this fashion.

Our experience is that most clickstream data warehouses use incremental extracts, with the occasional use of a full extract where it is easier. We rarely see the use of changed-data capture, largely due to complexity and cost. It's often easier to change the source system than to implement a complex ETL process. Web log files are a special case in data extraction since they are a largely self-contained data source.

A fundamental decision related to the data extracts is how to transfer data from the source systems to the data warehouse. The choice boils down to whether data extracts should be pushed or pulled from the source system. The preferred approach has a large impact on the ETL architecture.

A "push" approach relies on the OLTP system to run and store the extract data. This means the ETL developers will write programs that run on the OLTP system, which means they must be familiar with the tools or technologies used by the source system. Data extracted in this way is often, but not always, extracted to a flat file that must be transported over the network to the data warehouse staging area for further processing.

In contrast, programs written using a "pull" approach are initiated by the data warehouse. Surprisingly, this does not always give the ETL developer more control over the technology used. When programming outside the confines of the source system there can be restrictions. For example, by accessing a source system from the outside, the only nonnative mechanism available may be something like screen scraping. This places a different set of requirements on the ETL technology architecture than using the native programming environments on the source systems.

Using nonnative applications is typically less efficient than running native code on the source system, particularly when using gateways or screen-scraping technologies. When data is pulled from the source system, it is more likely to be brought directly into the data-staging database, eliminating the need to write flat files, transfer them, and load them into the data staging area. This may counter some of the inefficiencies in using a nonnative application, so it is part of what must be weighed in the ETL design.

With either the "push" or "pull" approach, there will be other considerations such as when extract jobs may be run so they do not impact normal system activity, how the extract programs will be initiated, how to monitor them for successful completion, and how the data warehouse can be notified of error conditions.

Related to the approach for extracting data is the preferred data transfer mechanism. The mechanism could be file-based using the File Transfer Protocol (ftp), named pipes to avoid the need for file polling, or via shared storage such as NFS or a Windows share. A different mechanism is the use of database methods such as database links or replication of the extract tables to the data-staging area. Transaction-based mechanisms are another family of options, including database triggers that execute after a transaction, a network daemon called via remote procedure call, or messaging using a product such as IBM's MQ-Series or Tibco.

It should be apparent that the preferred data extract approaches—incremental versus full, and push versus pull—limit the choice of transfer mechanisms. For example, if you are using file-based extracts then there is no need to consider any of the database or transaction-based mechanisms. Likewise, a reliance on transaction-based mechanisms means that none of the file-based mechanisms will be relevant.

Clickstream data can impose restrictions on the choice of transfer methods. If your only option is to receive Web server and cache server log files then the bulk of the data will come in the form of files. If the Web site uses an e-commerce platform then you may also be forced to extract much of the event data from an underlying relational or object-relational database.

Making things more difficult is the fact that some Web servers, such as Apache, can write log records to a named pipe or program, facilitating transaction-stream approaches. If you want to provide real-time Web analytics then you must use a mechanism like this, or you must implement a logging server as described in Chapter 3, and treat the logging server as a component of the ETL subsystem.

A final complication is the use of a data extract product, which may impose a set of constraints on all of the above decisions. We will discuss this further in the section on custom development versus buying an ETL tool. In most organizations clickstream data will be available only in the form of log files, which leads us to the next set of decisions involving data transformation.

Design Decisions for Data Transformation

The two major decisions to make about data transformation are the location where most of the processing is to be done, and whether the majority of processing will be done in files or the database.

The location of processing may be constrained by the earlier decisions about data extraction and transfer. The basic choice is whether to incorporate most of the transformation processing with extract processing at the point of origin, in an intermediate location, or within the data warehouse. If the preferred approach for data extraction is to use a "pull" model and nonnative tools, then it will be very hard to do much work on the source system. If the choice is to use native push extracts then it probably makes sense to do as much processing on the local system as possible prior to transferring the data.

As always, there are trade-offs to make when deciding where best to handle processing. Doing the processing in transit or within the data warehouse makes the data extraction code simpler. However, this may be at the expense of moving more data in order to complete transformations. For example, it may be easier to perform all of the transformations of lookup codes to user-friendly descriptions on the source system and ship the resulting data, saving the need to extract all of the lookup tables so the work can be done later. However, the extract jobs can be slowed by the additional processing. In contrast, you have much more control over performance issues if you do transformation processing in a data-staging area.

Data transformation can also be done by a process that sits between the source system and the data warehouse. This is most common when using an off-the-shelf ETL product, but we have seen some ETL components built in this way. They typically operate by applying all steps of the data transformation process to each record in turn, as compared with the traditional approach of processing all of the records through each step before moving to the next.

Using a transaction approach where one row is processed through all of the steps is almost always less efficient than processing records in batches, resulting in lower performance or the need for larger computing resources. The implication is that this approach should be used when data volumes are not extremely large.

If you have chosen to implement real-time reporting, however, this may be the only approach that works because you are receiving event records one at a time. Processing the clickstream as it comes in will add complexity to the data transformation stage. For example, it is not possible to calculate facts like page dwell times or session duration until the appropriate successor records have been received. This means that the fact table can have holes in the data that may impact reporting capabilities.

The other decision that will influence the overall architecture is whether to do the bulk of processing in files or in the database. We have seen both file-based and relational ETL in use at different companies. Part of the decision is based on the tools and technologies on hand, and the familiarity of the developers with them. Our preference is to do as much of the work as possible in the database because it provides a richer and more efficient environment for data manipulation. Chapter 7 contains a wealth of information on how to use database algorithms effectively for ETL.

As we've mentioned several times, clickstream data is most often sourced from log files. Since flat files are the starting point, some of the processing may be better done using native facilities. Our experience is that certain tasks, like parsing out query strings or cookies and performing name resolution, can often be accomplished more efficiently outside the database. The enhanced data is then loaded into the data-staging area for final processing in a database before being loaded into the data warehouse.

Design Decisions for Data Loading

Loading of the production database is usually a completely separate step from the data transformation processes. Even so, certain aspects of warehouse data loading should be considered up front. The primary decisions one must make at this point are whether to recreate the dimensions at each load or simply update them, and whether to completely rebuild the fact table or perform incremental inserts.

Recreating the facts and dimensions is usually feasible only with small data volumes. However, if you are using a nonrelational OLAP product as the final data store then you may not have a choice. Some OLAP products do not allow for dynamic updates. The addition of new data requires a complete recalculation of the entire data cube.

The majority of clickstream data warehouses use incremental loads rather than full refreshes. While the programming is slightly more complex, this is the usually the only way to meet load time constraints. Incremental loading has the added benefit that it allows for more flexibility when making changes to the system.

Whether using incremental loads or full refreshes, you must also decide on the approach for loading the final data into the data warehouse. One option is to process the new data so that it is in its final form. This means that the data staging area has a set of tables that mirror the production schema in structure. Loading is then a simple move of data from the staging tables to their counterparts in the production schema.

The other option is to process the data into the staging area but not go through the added work of creating surrogate keys for the dimension rows, generating the fact table keys and making the data load-ready. Instead, the data load process creates the dimension and fact table rows from the staging area and inserts them into the production schema. The advantage of this approach is that there is no redundant storage of data to be loaded. The disadvantage is that the actual load will take longer, which means the data warehouse will be unavailable for a longer period of time.

Most data warehouses do not keep data indefinitely. Instead, they keep data for a predetermined time window and then either purge or archive the old data. Purging is relatively simple—the past-due data is deleted from the tables. Archiving can be more challenging because it implies that you might need that data at some future time. You are at the mercy of your enterprise's data retention policies at this point.

When designing the data load, one flaw that often creeps into the design is an inability to roll back the data load if there is a problem with data. There are many mechanisms to handle this, from "last modified" table columns to dropping the database and restoring it from the prior day's backups. This is an area where ETL architecture crosses over into operational aspects of the system.

The last step in data loading, data validation, should also be thought through during the high-level design phase. There are simple functional validations, like ensuring that the number of new rows generated is the same as the number of new rows in the data warehouse. The more complex validations are those aimed at determining whether the data is valid.

Checking the data quality is an ongoing process. Much of the data extraction and transformation is also cleaning the data prior to loading it into the data warehouse. When doing the postload validation, keep in mind that very often there can be conflicting results between the clickstream data warehouse and production or reporting systems. Our experience is that the data warehouse is often correct, and the comparison has uncovered a flaw in the other system.

The "Buy versus Build" Decision

Every data warehouse project examines the question of whether to buy an ETL product or custom-build the ETL components. Because each software vendor has preferred approaches and assumptions built into their product architecture, it is best to first work through your preferred approaches to handling extraction, transformation, and loading. Once you've done this, you will be much better prepared to decide which, if any, ETL products are suitable for your project. Otherwise you may purchase an ETL tool, work through the project's ETL requirements and approaches, and encounter unexpected limitations in the product that lead to undesirable compromises in design.

There are good arguments supporting both sides of the decision, so it boils down to what best fits your organization's needs. Below we list some of the major factors involved in evaluating an ETL product for clickstream data warehouse.

Prebuilt Components

One of the most compelling arguments in favor of ETL products is that they sometimes include prebuilt solutions for particular tasks. If an enterprise resource planning application such as SAP or Peoplesoft is in use, you can often find vendors who have done most of the difficult data mapping work. The major ETL players, such as Informatica, Ascential (formerly Ardent), and Sagent, provide a rich set of facilities for common data warehouse tasks like key generation, dimension update, and aggregation. These extract and data management facilities can save the development team significant time.

When it comes to clickstream data, the products are not nearly as compelling. Some vendors have rudimentary support for clickstream data. This is often limited to an understanding of one or two of the most common Web server log file formats so that the data may be extracted. Parsing the log files is the simplest element of processing clickstream data. More complex interrecord processing to calculate page dwell time, entry and exit pages, and the like, is rarely provided. At the time of this writing, the authors have not encountered an ETL product that understands the ins and outs of Web-based data well enough to save ETL developers from custom development of a large portion of the clickstream processing.

An Integrated Meta Data Repository

Almost every ETL product on the market comes with its own meta data repository, capable of storing all of the information relevant to the data sources and targets and reporting on its usage and activity. A centralized meta data repository, accessible by all components of clickstream data warehouse, promises to ensure data consistency as well as making development and maintenance easier.

Because every component of the data warehouse, from the query tools on front to the job scheduler supporting the ETL processes, needs access to some portion of the total data warehouse meta data, each individual product typically comes with its own meta data model. The developers must enter the information required by an individual product manually, once per product. To make matters worse, different products are interested in different aspects of the meta data, some of which is unique to the tool and some that overlaps into other tools. This creates a redundant sea of meta data across the data warehouse that becomes increasingly difficult to maintain over time.

To resolve this problem, many ETL products offer support for the exchange of meta data with other products. For example, many ETL products can import schema information from a database design tool like ERwin and then export that meta data to a query tool so that manual data entry is not required. In this way, the ETL vendors often promise to synchronize meta data throughout the data warehouse. But, due to the different interpretations of meta data by the products and the difficulty coordinating product releases between vendors, these features rarely work as advertised.

In the end, the repository is important to the ETL components because that is where the product goes for its source and target meta data. Unfortunately, with all of the integration problems, the only other useful aspect of the repository that meets expectations is its use as a source of documentation for the data warehouse. Further information about meta data can be found on our companion Web site at www.wiley.com/compbooks/sweiger.

Simplified Development

One promise that ETL vendors often make is that their tool will increase developer productivity by simplifying the programming model and environment, providing a more task-specific environment, and by allowing for better reusability of code. Some vendors deliver on the promise of simplifying development tasks, while others have a long way to go before their products make the work any easier.

In general, once the menial work of entering all the meta data is complete, the development tasks will be far simpler than hand-coding in a 3GL or 4GL. The problem some tools have is their lack of flexibility, which either leads to poor performance or the inability to perform certain types of processing. Developers then work around the problem by creating program exits that call custom code they develop outside of the ETL product, which also has the side effect of lost visibility in the meta data.

Apart from prebuilt and reusable components, many of the products provide the ability to reuse the same ETL code in multiple data extracts. When the original code is modified, for example by adding a new data element to an extract, the product can automatically propagate the modification to all components that use this code. In cases where the data flows through a number of modules, the ETL product can tell the developer what downstream modules will be affected by the change. This is a vast improvement over the "cut and paste" model that is often employed when hand-coding data extracts.

Integrated Scheduling and Job Control

Almost all ETL tools on the market provide facilities to schedule and execute ETL jobs based on time schedules and events like the arrival of a flat file in a directory. The more advanced products include features to manage job dependencies, handle partial execution when some jobs fail while others complete, and restart the ETL process from the point where the last job failed. These features are a terrific time-saver for the warehouse administrator once the data warehouse is in production.

In addition to running independent ETL job streams concurrently to maximize throughput, many of these schedulers can prevent unnecessary jobs from running if the preconditions for a job are not met. For example, if there is a problem with one dimension table extract, all of the other, unrelated dimension and fact table extracts can still run. When the fact table load is ready, it can be made to wait until the problem with the dimension extract is resolved. This maximizes throughput by allowing as much work to complete as possible while the administrator corrects the problem.

Some view these scheduler features as redundant since most organizations already have cross-platform job schedulers, and many operating systems provide basic scheduling and job control facilities. The applicability of these features depends on what is available in your organization and how easy it is to use and manage.

Performance and Resource Use

One problem common to most ETL tools is poor performance and scalability. It is not uncommon to see custom extract code outperform an ETL tool by an order of magnitude while using fewer computing resources. This is one of the trade-offs made to gain some of the benefits from a simpler development environment.

Many ETL products choose an engine-based architecture to do their processing. When implemented in an architecturally sound manner, this is not a problem. However, many products have artificially imposed constraints that lead to performance bottlenecks, or to problems maintaining a consistent level of performance as workloads increase.

Numerous engine-based product designs extract all of the data through the ETL server for processing, then send all of the data on to the data warehouse server for loading. Since the data must be moved across the network twice, these products can create network bottlenecks where there was formerly no problem.

In order to remain database-neutral or to maintain control over how their code executes, many ETL products do not make use of the best features databases have available for them to use. For example, a native database file loading facility will be far faster than the tool's use of ODBC or native SQL inserts, yet most ETL tools do not use these facilities. The performance problems become more apparent when the tool is performing in-memory or on-disk sorts and joins that would be much faster as database operations.

The solution often recommended by tool vendors is to add more resources, usually memory and processors, to the server running the ETL software, or to add servers and divide the processing load. This "poor man's parallelism" can be a costly solution, so many developers give up using some of the resource-intensive ETL features instead.

Sometimes the problem is not the product design, but the limited number of platforms the product can run on. Many ETL products run only on Windows platforms because the vendors believe that an inexpensive server with a cheap operating system has broader appeal. While this is largely true, the limited scalability of the platform and the many reliability issues can impose serious limitations on the system. In response, the leading ETL vendors have ported or will soon complete ports to some of the major UNIX platforms, thus removing the hardware and operating system scalability and reliability problems.

Cost

The most compelling argument against buying commercial ETL tools is the high costs of these products. Calculating the cost of an ETL product is often a challenging proposition. Because the total cost of ownership goes beyond the initial client and server software licenses, the hidden costs can double the expense associated with an ETL product.

The price shown in many advertisements and articles does not include maintenance and support costs. Like the leading database vendors, the leading ETL vendors have adopted complicated pricing models. The simpler models charge a fee per dedicated server or per processor within a dedicated ETL server. If growth of the systems requires more hardware, you will pay additional fees. Some vendors have unbundled their products, so they will also charge for different product options such as their meta data repository or an add-on module to process clickstream data.

The convoluted models impose additional license fees for each type of data source, data target, or instance of a data source or target. The most intrusive models even charge by the amount of source data processed! If your environment includes different operating systems, databases, or multiple servers then the initial price can quickly shoot through the roof.

Depending on the product, you may need dedicated hardware for the ETL server and meta data repository. This adds direct costs of hardware, as well as the cost of administering that hardware. Typically, the meta data repository is stored in a database. Some vendors bundle the database and add this cost to their license fees, while others require you to supply the database. If you supply the database then you must also add that license cost, and the annual maintenance or support costs as well.

The staffing costs are the last item to factor into the total. Before the ETL developers can start they will probably require training. The learning curve on the tools will also add time to the development schedule. Many projects get around this by hiring a consultant familiar with the tool to work with the developers on the initial tasks, getting them up to speed faster but also adding to the total cost.

One staffing cost that is often missed is related to retention. ETL implementation is a full-time job during the project. When the system is in production, ongoing ETL development and maintenance will probably become a part-time job. If the project manager does not pay attention to this problem, there is a good chance the organization will lose the ETL developers it worked so hard to train.

When comparing costs, custom development appears to be much more attractive. In-house staff can work on the project with only minimal training, since they are already familiar with the technologies in use. If required, outside developers with standard programming skills will be cheaper and easier to find than specialists in a particular ETL tool. And after the project, it will be much easier for staff to move on to other projects in the organization.

We have excluded from our "buy versus build" discussion the many technical criteria one might use to evaluate ETL products because this level of detail is outside the scope of our discussion. For additional information and technical criteria, including some product information, refer to our companion Web site at www.wiley.com/compbooks/sweiger.

Observations on Clickstream ETL Design

When designing the ETL architecture and deciding whether to purchase a product, it is important to consider your preferences for how to approach ETL, as well as all of the technical requirements, and weigh the alternatives. Avoid the expectation that a single product will meet all of your project's needs, as this is almost guaranteed not to be the case.

Industry observers still remark that most data warehouse projects build their own ETL components, although the percentage of companies using tools is increasing. At the time of this writing, the few ETL vendors that do support clickstream processing supply simple log parsing modules that will not shave huge amounts of time off the development process, so the use of clickstream-specific ETL tools is highly unlikely. Since clickstream data is still relatively new to most of these vendors, expect their products to improve over time. A case in point is Ascential's DataStage, whose Web module has some nice basic clickstream features but is still missing commonly needed but more complex processing.

Our experience with clickstream data warehouse projects is that simplicity is almost always better than a feature-rich technical solution to the ETL problems. Several industry award-winning data warehouses made use of nothing more than simple SQL scripts and programs to handle all of the ETL tasks.

This discussion wouldn't be complete without considering a third alternative: development using specialized data processing tools designed to handle large volumes of data. Products like Torrent and Ab Initio are being used in large data warehouses to meet performance expectations while also simplifying the development environment. If your project includes significant clickstream data volumes then one of these products might make a suitable alternative to either ETL tools or completely custom development.

As we've mentioned many times, it is important to fully document the work that has been completed. In this case, the end result should be a concise high-level architecture that specifies the preferred approaches to solving ETL problems, and the preferred technologies to use for different ETL components. This document should be presented to and read by every member of the ETL development team.

With all of the high-level work out of the way, and the basic tools and technologies in place, the next step is to design the clickstream processing components.

Step 4: Design the Clickstream-Specific Components

The design of the clickstream processing components is dependent on the ETL architecture of your system. For example, your preferred approach may be to process entire Web logs outside the database, or you may want to stream the data in real time rather than processing it in batches. Each of these would result in radically different designs.

Because of the many variations, Figure 8.5 shows the general stages of processing clickstream data. We separate the initial clickstream processing from the dimension and fact builds because this work is often done separately from the other ETL tasks. However, it is possible to start building some of the dimensions and storing data for some of the fact rows while processing the clickstream data. Our discussions will focus on the specific clickstream preprocessing that must be done before the data is ready for use in the dimensions and facts.

Processing the clickstream need not be done serially as shown in the diagram. Many of the tasks can be performed concurrently, although the session, page,

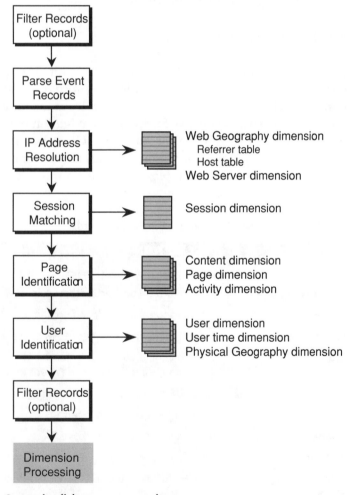

Figure 8.5 Stages in clickstream processing.

and user stages are frequently done sequentially to allow for more efficient aggregating of the data. The rest of this section reviews the design of each stage in the order shown in Figure 8.5.

Throughout the rest of this chapter we will assume that the basic request data, whatever the source, is in a format that contains the fields listed in Table 8.2. Here we are using the NCSA Combined Log Format (ECLF) with the addition of the server host, page transfer time and the user's cookies. Special cases, such as media servers, will be discussed separately.

Much of the remaining discussion in this chapter builds on information we covered in "Realities of Log File Data" in Chapter 4. It may be helpful to refer back to that section for details about some of the data problems that must be addressed during clickstream processing.

Filter Records (Optional)

The clickstream warehouse may not track every hit. The reason may be that the organization does not have the budget to process and store the large data volumes associated with fully detailed fact tables at the hit level. Filtering less interesting data, such as images for icons or navigation bars, can significantly reduce the number of rows in the fact table. Other possible reasons include lack of end-user requirements for some of the analyses or derived metrics that need all of the detail. For example, if there is no interest in Web site perfor-

Table 8.2 Data Assumed to Be Present in Event Records

FIELD	DESCRIPTION
Hostname	The user's client IP addresses
Rfc931 (username)	Expected to be unused, and contain a '-'
Authuser	Expected to be unused, and contain a '-'
Time received	The date and time the request was received
Request	The protocol, method, URL stem, and query string (if present) of the client request
Status	The HTTP status code
Bytes	The number of bytes transferred
Referrer	The URL of the last page visited
User agent	The client browser type
Server host	The IP address of the server that handled the request
Transfer time	The time the server completed the request
Cookies	The names and values of any cookies received

mance or in seeing when users stopped loading pages, then the detailed records may not be required.

Whatever the case, this would be a reasonable point at which to filter the unneeded data out of the clickstream. Filtering can also be done after parsing the records, since it requires some minimal field parsing to determine which objects are necessary and which may be discarded.

Because some of the facts can be derived only from a full set of data, it is common to keep as much detail as possible until after the dimension and fact tables are built.

Parse Event Records

With the event log available, the first stage in processing is relatively simple parsing operations. We say "relatively simple" because much of the complexity in parsing is dependent on the environment. For example, multiple network devices like proxy or cache servers, application servers and even the use of multiple Web servers all add complexity to an otherwise straightforward undertaking.

There are several different tasks that must be completed to parse the event records. The first task is separating the fields and disassembling each of the multipart fields to its basic elements. We will use the sample log record below to demonstrate the parsing that is normally required. The record has the data format shown in Figure 8.1.

```
205.188.208.40 - - [04/Jul/2001:12:37:02 -0600] "GET /article.php?Id=42
HTTP/1.0" 200 8437
"http://mysearch.com/search?q=clickstream+warehouse&geo=no"
"Mozilla/4.75 - (Win98; U)" 255.2.248.10 1 "uid=609; last=030701162402"
```

Because most event records are logged in a standard format like the above, we don't have a common field delimiter. Some of the fields are delimited by spaces, while others are enclosed in brackets or quotation marks. The result of separating each of the fields is shown in Table 8.3.

Note that *Time received, Request, Referrer, User agent,* and *Cookies* are all multipart fields. Each of these must be broken into its constituents. For example, the *Request* field contains the method, the URL, a query string, the protocol, and the protocol version. After exploding some of the fields and doing some basic reformatting, such as for dates, we end up with the data listed in Table 8.4.

Now that the data is in its simplest form, we can move on to some of the other parsing. Query strings in the request URL are from your own Web site, so it is logical to tackle these next. At this stage we just separate the query string variable names and values.

Table 8.3 Fields in the Example Log Record

FIELD	VALUE
Hostname	205.188.208.40
Rfc931 (username)	–
Authuser	–
Time received	[04/Jul/2001:12:37:02 -0600]
Request	GET /article.php?Id=42 HTTP/1.0
Status	200
Bytes	8437
Referrer	http://mysearch.com/search?q=clickstream+warehouse&geo=no
User agent	Mozilla/4.75 [en] (Win98; U)
Server host	255.2.248.10
Transfer time	1
Cookies	"uid=609; last=030701162402"

In our example, we record the transfer time rather than the time the request was completed.

We wait to interpret the variables and contents because this is often an involved process that is better delayed until we are ready to build the dimension and fact tables. In order to interpret query strings, you must know exactly what data to expect. Are your session IDs stored in the query string? Is page-tagging done with the query string? Does every page include the same page-tagging variables? Are you interested in the values on form fields? Do any of the form or page-tagging variables use the same names? If so, can you differentiate them from one another? Do you know how to extract codes used by the Web application in order to interpret the values of the variables?

Parsing the value portion of the name-value pairs requires some additional work as well. Recall that some characters have special meaning and can't be transmitted openly in the query string. These values will be specially encoded, for example by replacing blank spaces with plus signs, or placing the octal or hexadecimal representation in place of the character.

To make matters more difficult, the Web application might encode or encrypt the query string, resulting in a jumble of text. To properly decode the query string, the ETL developers will need access to the algorithm that does the encoding, or the routine and key used for encryption.

You must know the semantics of the query strings that contain required information. In our example above, the Web site serves articles dynamically and

Table 8.4 All Data Elements in the Example Log Record

DATA ELEMENT	VALUE
Hostname	205.188.208.40
Rfc931 (username)	-
Authuser	-
Date received	July 4, 2001
Time received	12:37:02
GMT offset	-0600
Request method	GET
Request URL	/article.php
Request query string	Id=42
Request protocol	HTTP
Request protocol version	1.0
Status	200
Bytes	8437
Referrer hostname	mysearch.com
Referrer URL	http://mysearch.com/search
Referrer query string	q=clickstream+warehouse&geo=no
User agent	Mozilla/4.75 [en] (Win98; U)
Server host	255.2.248.10
Transfer time	1
Cookies	"uid=609; last=030701162402"

Take note that the query strings have not yet been processed, nor has the cookie or user agent. As we will see, these elements usually require more than simply separating values.

requires an article number as input. The article number is passed to the program that serves up the content (article.php) via a variable named "Id". If we were to interpret the query string now, we would take the value of the variable and store it in a field or column labeled "Article Number" rather than the current "Request Query String" field.

The case is the same when interpreting cookies. Cookies have the same functional and semantic questions, as well as issues with encoding or encryption. Cookies are more of a challenge because of programming practices and visibility. Remember that a cookie may be valid for only a specific server, a portion of a domain or an entire domain, affecting when they show up in the log. Programming techniques like using concatenated strings in a single cookie instead of using multiple cookies, or using the cookie as a reference to variables stored at the server also affect processing.

One last thing to deal with is that there are often multiple variables in query strings or you may receive multiple cookies from the user. When parsing the records into flat files, the multiple variables must be properly delimited. Every Web site has its own idiosyncrasies. When it comes to query strings and cookies, be prepared for unexpected challenges.

The next parsing step is to synchronize the timestamps in the records, if they are not already synchronized. For example, if there are Web servers physically located in different time zones then the timestamps may be logged in local time. If this is true, the timestamps must be recast to all be in the same time zone.

There is also a possibility that different Web servers or other applications may record different values. Some Web servers record the time a request was received, while others record the time that serving the request was completed. It is partly for this reason that we specified that our event record format contain both a timestamp of when the request was received and the time it took to process the request. Most Web and application servers can log the transfer time, which we can then use to normalize the values.

The final data elements and values parsed from the example log record are shown in Table 8.5.

One complication when parsing event records is that there may be different sources for the data. Cache servers, proxy servers, and media servers may all be in use in the organization. The result is that you may need to create parsing programs for different log file formats. When this is the case, the best approach is to develop a standardized format that all of these records can be mapped to.

While this is optimal, there are always exceptions. For example, in Chapter 4 we discussed the log file from a streaming media server. This log can potentially contain much more detailed information about the user's actions than would be available in a standardized format. In this case, we would create a program to parse the additional data and handle it downstream when we build our dimension and fact tables.

IP Address Resolution

Now that all of the records have been parsed, the remaining stages can be executed. In this stage we want to look up the user-friendly host and domain names of the client IP addresses that show up in the event log. We do this because it is less helpful to know that 20 percent of user traffic comes from the 205.188 class B address space than to know that traffic is from users at AOL.com.

Table 8.5 The Fully Parsed Log Record

DATA ELEMENT	VALUE
Client IP address	205.188.208.40
Rfc931	-
Authuser	-
Date received	July 4, 2001
Time received	12:37:02
GMT offset	-0600
Request method	GET
Request URL	/article.php
Request query string	Id=42
Query string variable 1	Id
Query string value 1	42
Request protocol	HTTP
Request protocol version	1.0
Status	200
Status text	OK
Bytes	8437
Referrer hostname	mysearch.com
Referrer URL	http://mysearch.com/search
Referrer query string	q=clickstream+warehouse&geo=no
User agent	Mozilla/4.75 [en] (Win98; U)
Server host	255.2.248.10
Transfer time	1
Cookie 1	uid=609
Cookie 1 variable name	Uid
Cookie 1 value	609
Cookie 2	last=030701162402
Cookie 2 variable name	Last
Cookie 2 value	030701162402

We would normally drop any unused data elements and keep only the information we're interested in. We show all data elements in this table for completeness.

As we mentioned before, it is possible to execute some of the stages concurrently in order to speed up processing. Resolving IP addresses into names is an example of why running multiple stages concurrently can be a good idea.

Looking up the name for an IP address is the clickstream ETL stage that usually takes longer than all of the remaining stages combined. If possible, the clickstream preprocessing should be designed to execute name resolution tasks while the other processing stages run in parallel, then merging the results at the end.

Name resolution requires the use of the Domain Name Service (DNS), specifically the reverse name lookup functions. These functions resolve host and domain names and are easily accessible on most server platforms. Some of the more familiar programs for getting DNS information on the command line are nslookup, whois, and dig.

To address the performance problem, operations can be sped up by executing multiple lookups in parallel. It's a good idea to involve the network or system administrator in this task, since it is possible to overwhelm your organization's DNS servers and bring your entire network to a crawl if you aren't careful.

There is no way around the resource-intensive process of name lookups using DNS when you first start processing clickstream data. The programs that do the lookups can be made more efficient through a few simple additions:

- Save all of the address and name data into domain lookup tables in the staging area. Then it will be available during the next ETL cycle and a fast database lookup will replace the resource-intensive DNS query.

- Process the IP addresses in batches by domain. Since you may not be interested in host-level detail, resolving a single domain means not having to process the remaining rows. However, when resolving names we usually try to resolve the full address and hostname.

- When doing an extremely large number of lookups, as when first loading the clickstream warehouse, try to identify the domains and store the DNS data for those domains locally. Downloading all of the data for a domain, called a "zone transfer," is something to do sparingly since it affects that domain's DNS server. However, a zone transfer may be preferable to performing thousands of individual lookups.

The simple storing of names and addresses for local lookup has the biggest impact on performance. When doing this it is important to keep track of when the data was stored and refresh it after three to six months. Domain names expire or change hands periodically, invalidating the names you've stored.

Do not expect every IP address to resolve to a unique hostname. It is possible that some of the IP addresses may not resolve to valid hosts or domains. You will need a placeholder for these addresses, although there will usually be a domain registered at a higher level.

Apart from simple name resolution, you may want to access and store other data that is relevant to the IP address. The company or individual who registered the domain can be identified via the whois database. Information available can include the mailing address, phone number, and administrative contact.

Apart from the client IP addresses, the log may contain the IP address of the server that handled the request. In our example record format, we included the *Server Host* field so that we could determine the data source for each record. Most servers record their IP address rather than a hostname. In some cases, these servers may not have a hostname assigned through DNS. In one case, we encountered a Web server farm with six Web servers behind a cache server and load redirector. Every request to www.thewebsite.com that was not met by the cache server was directed to the least-loaded Web server. We decided to create name mappings in the ETL stage for the cache server and Web servers, so the Web administrators could monitor usage and performance more easily.

Session Matching

The primary purpose of the session matching stage is the reconstruction of a visitor's path through the Web site. Since a visit is spread throughout the log as a set of noncontiguous records, they must be properly grouped together. In order to tie a session together, the ETL program must make sure that every event record is properly associated with the visit that generated that record. The program to do this can range from simple to convoluted depending on how the Web site tracks sessions.

The simplest case is when the Web site assigns every visitor a session identifier that is captured in the query string or a cookie. The only potential additional work in this case is the creation of a unique session identifier for each Web site session ID. We may do this if the Web site doesn't provide unique session IDs reliably. A reused session ID would cause serious complications downstream.

Unfortunately, it is rare to find every event record with an associated session identifier. There are many reasons for this. The Web site could use cookies with no fallback mechanism, in which case any user who disables cookies in their browser will not have a session ID. The Web site may only assign session IDs during the transactional portion of a visit, ignoring browsing activity. The Web site may only track registered users or customers, ignoring visitors. A final possibility is that the hits could be generated by a search engine robot.

If the Web site has more than one mechanism to store session IDs , for example using cookies but reverting to query strings when cookies are not enabled, then you must look first at the primary and then the secondary locations, before moving on to more complex alternatives.

What you do depends partly on the end-user requirements. For example, at an online retailer we worked with the end-users were only interested in customers, and chose to ignore anonymous visitors. That meant we could effectively ignore the sessions for these users, even though the result was incomplete analysis since a wealth of information about potential customers was ignored.

Assuming you do want to assign sessions to all of the site's visitors, the next step is to find a way to link all of the event records that make up a session. This is where the programming can become more complex.

In most designs, the first pass through the records will group them by IP address in time series order, and look for records with a time difference that is less than some arbitrary session timeout period. While workable for a subset of the records, this can generate incorrect results. For example, if multiple users visit the Web site at the same time from behind a single proxy server, they will all have the same IP address. This first pass will group all of these visitors into a single session. The opposite is also possible: one user can have several IP addresses in a single session, as is the case with AOL and MSN users which have dynamically assigned IP addresses for each HTTP transaction. In this instance, those records would be marked as separate sessions even though they belong to a single session.

The most effective designs use a combination of elements, usually the IP address, domain, user-agent, and time series analysis, to properly assign a session ID to every record. This approach, done in a successive series of steps designed to winnow records, works for the vast majority of data. Nevertheless, you will probably have a few leftover records to deal with from time to time.

One nontrivial part of the process is identifying the end of a session. The most common approach is to use an arbitrary timeout, usually in the range of 15 to 30 minutes. If there is a gap in the records that is longer than the timeout period, the session is ended. New records with the same grouping information are then treated as a new session.

When going through the records in a session, the last possible record in the series should be marked as the last page visited. Some clickstream schemas include generated records for events like this. Instead of ending at the last hit, a new "hit" is created that reflects the end of the user's visit.

Page Identification

The page identification stage is where each hit is identified as either being a primary page or a page element. All hits that are associated with a single page view are associated with their primary page. For example, an HTML page with a logo, a picture of the company's office building, and navigation bar would generate four hits—one for the page itself and one for each of the images. Our goal is to associate all of the hits with the HTML page.

Associating hits with pages is not terribly difficult, since the page from the Web site will appear in the log as the referrer for each of the page elements loaded. So each image in our example will have the HTML page listed as the referrer.

The next step in page identification is to make sure that each page is uniquely identified. This is easy with static pages, since the URL for the page is the same for every visitor. We can use the data for the Site Geography dimension as a way to look up the unique identifier for the static pages, since that dimension already contains URLs and identifiers.

One thing that complicates page identification is trying to associate the hit for a page element with the correct page record. Since many people may be accessing the same page at the same time, knowing which of the many HTML page records is the right record can be troublesome. It is for this reason that we have the session matching stage prior to the page identification stage. With every hit matched to a session, finding the correct page becomes a trivial task. Putting session matching after page matching is a common mistake in clickstream ETL implementations.

Page identification gets even more complicated when we introduce dynamic pages. With dynamic pages, the URL may be different for different users, or even for the same user visiting a page twice. The only hope in these situations is to find a way to interpret the Web application's URLs, or to use a page-tagging technique on the Web site.

Our log parsing example highlights a different problem. We have a page called "article.php" that takes an article number as input and sends back the text of the article referenced. In this case, every hit would look exactly the same, with only the article number in the query string showing variations. What we really want to know is what article a user is reading, so that means we may need to process cookies or query strings to properly identify what was sent back by article.php. Ideally, the Web site would use page tagging to attach meaningful information to pages like this.

These kinds of problems make page tagging and content coding necessary for dynamic Web sites. Rarely do Web applications log the right kind information by default. By tagging the pages and associated elements, the clickstream ETL tasks become much simpler.

User Identification

The purpose of user identification at this stage is not complete user identification and profiling—all we want to do is assign each event record an identifier that ties it back to the user we believe generated it. The goal is to prepare the data so that building the user dimension is simpler. Even so, this is likely to be the most complex portion of the clickstream preprocessing.

There are several parts to this processing. Since we are not trying to deal with the real user identities at this point, the focus is on determining whether a record is from a user we know about, an anonymous visitor, or a robot. The assignment of profiles, determination of offline identity, and removal of duplicates are performed when we build the user dimension.

Once again, what is being tracked by the Web site is an issue. Before design can start, it is important that the user tracking mechanisms be thoroughly understood. Is the Web site assigning unique user IDs? Is the Web site tracking only registered users or customers, or is it tracking all visitors to the site? Is it using cookies, query strings, or a Web site login? Is there a backup tracking mechanism in case the primary is not working, as in the case of disabled cookies in the browser?

With questions like this answered, it is possible to start designing the user identification mechanism. As with sessions, the idea is to process the records through successively more involved steps until all are properly marked.

The easiest step is to first look for a user ID assigned by the Web site's primary mechanism. If the user ID is stored in a cookie or query string, the value can be extracted and used. It is important to know whether this is a new or returning user. If the Web site is not the authoritative source for use IDs then you may be able to perform a lookup to cross reference the Web site's user ID with the authoritative user ID. If the lookup succeeds then the user is a returning user and can be flagged as such, and the authoritative user ID assigned.

Users who do not show up in the authoritative list are probably new users, although this is not assured since they may have lost their user ID through changing clients or any of a number of other means listed in Chapter 4. These users should simply be marked as potential new users. The program that builds the user dimension can then work through the more involved process of matching new user IDs to existing user IDs.

If the primary user tracking mechanism does not provide a user value, then the next step is to look in the alternate user identification mechanism, if the Web site has one. For example, if cookies are disabled in the user's browser and the Web site instead passes the user ID via the query string, then parsing the query string would be required. These records can then be processed as outlined above.

After going through these steps, there may still be records from unidentified users. If the Web site does not employ any user tracking mechanism then all of the records will start at this point in the process.

In Chapter 3 we discussed robots and how they traverse a Web site looking for pages to process. Before going further, it is best to identify all of the records created by robot visits. This will mark records that might otherwise complicate further user identification. The question is how to identify records as being from robots rather users?

Note that we are marking robot records, not filtering them out of the clickstream. It might appear that robot users are not important to analysis, but this is not true. Analysis of robot users can tell whether and how often the Web site is being indexed by search engines, about pages being overlooked by search engines, and can tell you about abusive robots or security risks.

Abusive robots are those that do any of the following:

- Ignore the robots.txt file that specifies what robots should not access.
- Use the entries in robots.txt to access files they are supposed to ignore.
- Index the entire Web site so quickly they slow down performance for real users.
- Follow links through dynamic pages that you do not want indexed.
- Collect data from the Web site and sell it or use it in a competitive manner.

Not all robots are search engines. There are also robots for translation services, experimental search and processing services, and other purposes. Some robots can be security risks. For example, there are email harvester robots that search the Web for email addresses to add to lists that are then sold to spammers. There are robots that examine the robots.txt file and probe for files that are specifically mentioned as off-limits to robots. There are robots that scan sites for particular vulnerabilities in certain Web applications, which is not the same as scanning for server or platform vulnerabilities.

Web administrators can find out about misbehaving robots by using the clickstream data warehouse, provided the robot users are included. It is then possible to take measures to prevent these robots from accessing the Web site.

Identifying robots is a three-step process. The first is to use the User-agent field, since well-behaved robots will identify themselves by sending an identifiable user agent. The ETL developer creates a program that looks up known robot user agents and marks the records. Fortunately, there are many lists of search engine spiders and other robots freely available on the Internet, making this a simple task.

Because not all companies have well-behaved robots, it may be necessary to examine the IP address of the domain where the requests originated. As with robot user agents, there are lists of IP addresses and domains that are known origins for robots. The ETL developer need only create a program to look up the domains and unresolved IP addresses, and download these address lists periodically.

If records make it through these two steps then they are most likely not robots. One last step is to look for accesses to the robots.txt file, which should be stored in every Web server's root directory. Only robots—or people snooping—will access this file. If the user agent is unknown and there is a hit on the robots.txt file, then odds are good that all records in that session are from a robot. Bear in mind that seeing an unknown user agent does not indicate a robot—there are many niche browsers out there that are neither Netscape nor Internet Explorer.

There is a large community of people who are interested in robots and search engines. Some have created freely available programs that can process the log file and identify the robots. Before embarking on custom development, it is worth examining some of these programs to see if they may be used for this portion of the user identification process.

At this point, all of the robot records should be marked, leaving only unidentified user records. These records may be present because the user is running anonymously, or simply due to the Web site not assigning user identifiers.

The anonymous visitor problem is the hardest part of this process to handle. If we are not trying to track repeat visits by anonymous users then there are the two basic methods we can use to mark these records. One method is to assign a single anonymous user ID to all unidentified records, regardless of the session they belong to. This is easy, but it masks information about visits that might otherwise be useful. A second method is to assign separate anonymous user IDs to each set of records in an unidentified session. The latter retains more information for analysis, but it will show each session as a separate visitor.

If we do want to track repeat visits by anonymous visitors then more work is required. We can do this work here, or when we build the user dimension. Most of the time, identification based on record attributes and visit characteristics is performed when building the user dimension. The marking of records with individual anonymous user IDs is sufficient at this point.

Filter Records (Optional)

This is the same processing that we discussed as an optional first stage. Many times the filtering of extraneous records is held until the end because the records are needed for clickstream processing up to this point, but not in the queryable schema. If so, they may be safely discarded at this point. We should reiterate here that our preference is to include all of the hits in the base fact table. Analysis that does not need this information will not see it when using a properly designed interface, and aggregate tables will resolve performance issues due to the fact table's size.

At this point we've completed all of the clickstream preprocessing stages. The resulting clickstream data, regardless of source, should now be in a common format. Based on the sample log record we used at the beginning of this section (repeated below), we list all of the data elements we've processed in Table 8.6.

```
255.199.225.190 - - [04/Jul/2001:12:37:02 -0600] "GET /article.php?Id=42
HTTP/1.0" 200 8437
"http://mysearch.com/search?q=clickstream+warehouse&geo=no"
"Mozilla/4.75 [en] (Win98; U)" 255.2.248.10 1 "uid=609;
last=030701162402"
```

If this data is not processed inside the data warehouse, this would be the time to load it into the data staging area.

Step 5: Design and Build the Dimension Table ETL Components

With the clickstream data now preprocessed and loaded into the data staging area, it's time to build the dimension tables. We will mention any dependencies that might be encountered when building the dimensions. Many of the dimensions do not have dependencies between them, which means they may be built concurrently to shorten the processing window.

One thing that all of the meta-schema dimensions have in common is that they use surrogate keys. It is up to the ETL designer and the DBA to decide exactly how keys will be created and managed for all of these tables. We will omit surrogate key generation from the design discussions.

When starting the implementation, you should already have the data mapping between the data sources and the dimensions completed. This includes mapping the processed clickstream data fields to their related dimension tables. Steps 5 and 6 both assume that this work was done during the initial analysis and design phase of the project.

We will discuss the ETL design for each dimension separately as we work through this section, starting with the time dimensions. You should be familiar with the meta-schema tables described in Chapter 6 when reading through this section.

Time Dimensions

The time dimension is the only one that is normally generated by a program using no clickstream data sources. *All* the dates and times in the rolling history

Table 8.6 Final Results of All Clickstream Processing

DATA ELEMENT	VALUE
Client IP address	205.188.208.40
Client hostname	cache-dc01.proxy.aol.com
Client domain	aol.com
Domain owner	America Online, Inc.
Domain owner address	22080 Pacific Blvd, Sterling, VA 20166 US
Domain owner phone	703-265-4670
Rfc931	-
Authuser	-
Date received	July 4, 2001
Time received	12:37:02
GMT offset	-0600
Request method	GET
Request URL	/article.php
Request query string	Id=42
Query string variable 1	Id
Query string value 1	42
Request protocol	HTTP
Request protocol version	1.0
Request page ID	54
Request page name	Articles that answer fundamental questions
Status	200
Status text	OK
Bytes	8437
Referrer hostname	mysearch.com
Referrer URL	http://mysearch.com/search
Referrer query string	q=clickstream+warehouse&geo=no
User agent	Mozilla/4.75 [en] (Win98; U)
User agent type	Browser
User agent software	Netscape
User agent version	4.75
User agent language	English
User agent platform	Windows 98

(continued)

Table 8.6 (*Continued*)

DATA ELEMENT	VALUE
Server host	255.2.248.10
Server name	www1.guide.com
Transfer time	1
Cookie 1	uid=609
Cookie 1 variable name	Uid
Cookie 1 value	609
Cookie 2	last=030701162402
Cookie 2 variable name	Last
Cookie 2 value	030701162402
ETL-assigned session ID	54
Web site user ID	42

Note that in our ETL implementation we decided to break out the details in the User-agent field so that we could more effectively identify users and robots. We again show all data elements, including nonessential fields, in this table for completeness.

window of the clickstream data warehouse are precreated so they can be used as time constraints in queries.

As explained in Chapter 6, in a clickstream environment the time dimension splits in to several dimension tables: *User Date*, *User Time-of-Day*, *Fiscal Date*, and *Fiscal Time-of-Day*. Some ETL tools have built-in functions to generate the Date portions of these dimensional tables, although it is doubtful they will be able to generate the Time-of-Day component since this is not a common requirement outside the clickstream environment. When creating these dimensional tables, they need to span the entire time history of the data warehouse including dates and times all the way to the end of the current year. New segments of dates and times are added on an annual basis, at least one quarter before the end of the current span of time values.

Web Geography: Host and Referrer Tables

As explained in Chapter 6, the Web Geography dimension consists of two dimension tables: *Host Geography* and *Referrer Geography*. The former contains the information about the origins of Web site traffic, while the latter contains information about the referring and referred-to pages in a session.

Building the *Host Geography* table from our clickstream data is usually a simple matter of mapping of the data straight from the processed event records into

Table 8.7 Host Geography Dimension

HOST GEOGRAPHY ATTRIBUTES	DATA ELEMENT VALUES
Surrogate Web Geography Key	132098
Host 32-bit v4 IP address string	205.188.208.40
Byte 1 of IP address	205
Byte 2 of IP address	188
Byte 3 of IP address	208
Byte 4 of IP address	40
Host 128 bit IPv6 address	*null*
Host Name	cache-dc01.proxy.aol.com
Domain Name	aol.com
Host Country	US
Host State or Province	Virginia
Host City	Sterling

this table. The only exceptions are the surrogate key, which must be generated, and possibly some parsing of address information from the domain registration database.

Table 8.7 shows the attributes of the *Host Geography* dimension and where to source the data. We again use the example event record from step 4, containing the processed data shown in Table 8.6.

The *Host* dimension is one that you can build while doing the clickstream processing instead of waiting until the clickstream process is complete. It would be built during the IP address resolution stage of the clickstream process.

Table 8.8 Referrer Dimension

REFERRER ATTRIBUTES	DATA ELEMENT VALUES
Surrogate Referrer Key	432987
Referring URL	http://mysearch.com/search
Referring Page ID	null
Query String	q=clickstream+warehouse&geo=no
Referring Domain	mysearch.com
External/Internal Flag	External
Referred URL	/article.php?Id=42
Referred Page ID	54

The Referring Page ID is *null* because we do not have any page identifiers for external pages outside of the Web site.

The *Referrer* dimension is equally simple to build. Again, we just map the appropriate fields from the processed event record into the fields of the dimension. The only additional work, apart from key generation, is flagging whether the referrer is internal or external to the Web site, and looking up the *Referring Page ID* for the referring page if it is an internal page. In Table 8.8, we did one addition step: We reassembled the *Referred URL* so that it again includes its query string.

Site Geography

The *Site Geography* dimension contains the page structure of the entire Web site. It normally contains a row for every HTML page served by the Web site, but may also include images or streaming media documents if they are integral components.

This dimension can be extremely difficult to construct. Normally, there is no easy source from which to obtain all of the data that is required. In the section describing ways to make the Web site clickstream-friendly, we mentioned page tagging as a useful method. In order to implement page tagging properly, one must maintain a list of every page, its unique identifier, and its content coding. If this is the case, you can extract the bulk of the information directly from the application used to maintain the page tagging and content coding.

Assuming that you do not have page tagging implemented—likely since this usually trails behind the clickstream data warehouse project—an alternative is to create a program that crawls the Web site and extracts the data from the HTML pages, in much the same way that a search engine does.

If the Web site is static, the job is easier because the program must only search the Web site's directory structure looking for page and image objects to process. Since most Web sites are dynamic, you will likely have to create a primitive robot to go through the actual Web site.

While tricky, this is not as difficult as you may expect. There are a number of open source search or robot tools that you can download and customize. We once used a freely available tool called "htdig" to do the site crawling, and created some simple scripts to extract the data we needed. The hard part was not the programming; it was getting the Web site developers to embed content codes in all of the Web site's HTML pages to make our job easier.

Finally, if you have access to the tools used by the Web site developers, you may find that one of the tools maintains the site structure and pages. If you are lucky, this tool may be able to dump out the site structure in a format that you can then read with a custom program.

Table 8.9 Site Geography Dimension

SITE GEOGRAPHY ATTRIBUTES	DATA ELEMENT VALUES
Surrogate Site Geography Key	842
Page URL	/article.php?Id=42
Page Identifier	54
Parent URL	/index.html
Total Page Size	4096
Page Version	2
Date of Last Revision	04/02/2002
Primary Page Purpose	Technical information

The Total Page Size field can be tricky to calculate. If the Web page contains multiple images, each of these must be added to the size of the HTML page itself. The same applies to Java applets that might be downloaded with the page. Surprisingly, sizes for streaming media clips are usually not as difficult to compute because the media server usually has that information available.

With dynamic pages, this calculation may be impossible, or very hard to get. For example, while the page URL is "article.php", this script simply looks up an article based on a parameter. The actual page size will vary depending on which article is displayed.

In cases like this, we probably want to track every article that can be displayed, rather than just the script that looks up and displays the article. The only way to do this is to use page tagging for the articles that are supplied, mainly to tag each article with a unique page identifier. Then we can add each of these articles to the dimension individually with its own value in the Page Identifier field. What to put in the Page URL field is up the developer. In this case, we put the URL with the query string attached since that's the best way to map into the article.

Table 8.9 shows what the Site Geography dimension might look like for the page that was referenced in our example event record (the page in the *Request URL* field of the parsed record). Note that we do not build this dimension from the clickstream. However, every requested URL from the clickstream that shows up as a hit in the fact table must have a corresponding row in this table.

Content

Building the *Content* dimension is almost identical to building the *Site Geography* dimension. It is not sourced from the clickstream either. The primary difference between the two dimensions is that this dimension contains a row for every element of the Web site, whether it is an image used for navigation, an HTML page, or a Java applet.

To properly populate all of the fields in this dimension your Web developers must do content coding. Without content coding, it will not be possible to fill many of the attributes in the table. If you don't do content coding, then the Content Type, Group, and Purpose fields should all be omitted from the schema.

Using our example event record, the Content Identifier field is the same as the Page Identifier. Other objects, like images, would not have page identifiers but would have a unique content identifier. The Associated Page field is *null* in our example because this is an HTML page. The Associated Page field should only be filled in for components of displayable Web pages, such as logo or navigation images that are part of another page.

There is a complication here, and that is the many-to-one nature of some page elements. For example, it is unlikely to have a logo image for every Web page. Instead, all pages refer to the same image. When building out the dimension, you must decide how you want to handle this problem in the schema you create.

The values we might populate into the *Content* dimension related to the requested URL from our example record are shown in Table 8.10.

Table 8.10 Content Dimension

CONTENT ATTRIBUTES	DATA ELEMENT VALUES
Surrogate Content Key	842
Content Identifier	54
Content URL	/article.php?Id=42
Content Type	Dynamic content display page
Content Group	Technical information
Content Purpose	Educational
Associated Page	*null*
Content Size	2048
Content Version	HTML 4.0
Date Created	04/01/2002
Date of Last Revision	04/02/2002
Last Modified By	dadams
Date Removed From Site	*null*

There is normally a dependency between the page identification stage of the clickstream processing and either the content coding application or this dimension. When the page identification algorithm processes the clickstream, this dimension is a convenient place to look up the unique content identifiers.

There is also a dependency between this dimension and the *Site Geography* dimension. Every row in the *Site Geography* dimension should have an entry in the Content dimension, although the reverse is not true. Because of this derivative nature, many ETL developers build the *Content* dimension first, and then extract the data for *Site Geography* from *Content*.

Managing history in this dimension can also be a challenge. With both *Site Geography* and *Content* we need to see the objects in the Web site as they are now, but we may also want (or need) to see the objects are they were. For example, if a page moves from one location to another, or all of the page templates are changed, the old and new information must be recorded. Addressing the problem of slowly changing dimensions is outside the scope of this book. We suggest reading the appropriate sections of either the *Data Warehouse Toolkit* (Wiley, 1996) or the *Data Warehouse Lifecycle Toolkit* (Wiley, 1998) for more information on this topic.

Activity

The purpose of the *Activity* dimension is to track the basic types of user actions that may be performed on the Web site, such as reading product information or checking on the status of an order. Your end users normally want to analyze activity by looking at how and where visitors spend time performing different activities. This dimension provides a way to analyze user behavior at a higher level where they do not need to concern themselves with the details of hits or page views.

The *Activity* dimension is normally dependent on the Web site's content coding. If no content coding has been done, then this dimension will probably be manually assembled based on the values determined by end users. This means that the ETL developer must build a small maintenance application to maintain the activity codes, and to link those codes to the Web pages on the site. This linkage is crucial—without it, there is no easy way to tie the activity to the event records.

When building the dimension and loading fact tables, the ETL program should cross reference the activity to the Page ID in the *Site Geography* and *Content* dimensions. If a single Page or Content ID has more than one activity associated with it, then there is something wrong with the activity dimension or with the keying in the fact table.

Table 8.11 Activity Dimension

ACTIVITY ATTRIBUTES	DATA ELEMENT VALUES
Surrogate Activity Key	24
Activity/Event Identifier	12
Activity Type	Access article
Activity Group	Browsing/reading content

Table 8.11 shows the values we might populate in the Activity dimensions for our example event record where a user requested an article.

Internal Promotion and External Promotion

Internal promotions consist of internal advertisements, affiliated links to related external sites, or other internal links that promote internal or external content. Unless the promotion itself is dynamically generated, the *Internal Promotion* dimension is *not* sourced from clickstream data. Since the site designers create all internal promotions, they need to add data to this dimension as part of the process of creating new promotion content.

Even if the internal promotion is dynamically generated, an end user still has to enter the parameters to create the promotion into a promotion display application used by the Web site. Sometimes, these parameters will be passed upon clickthrough in the promotion's query string, so they can be collected for clickstream analysis. If not, the ETL developer must extract the promotion data from the Web application.

Dynamically generated promotions require that the dimension table row be constructed with data from the clickstream contained in the *Clickthrough URL* log record, which is generated when the user clicks through on the link to the promoted item. This record contains the *Clickthrough URL*, the *Internal Promotion URL* (the referring URL), and any parameters that are passed as part of the promotion's query string. These parameters should contain the *Internal Promotion Identifier*, the *Internal Promotion Type*, the Internal Promotion Version, and the *Internally Promoted Product or Service, Brand*, and *Category*, if any. This dimension is a good example of an area where a thorough understanding of the syntax and semantics of the Web site's query strings is required.

An example row in the Internal Promotion dimension is shown in Table 8.12.

External promotions include banner ads delivered by advertising engines on external sites, external affiliated links, and other external promotions in which the user can clickthrough back to the sponsoring site.

Table 8.12 Internal Promotion Dimension

INTERNAL PROMOTION ATTRIBUTES	DATA ELEMENT VALUES
Surrogate Internal Promotion Key	121
Internal Promotion URL	www.mysite.com/InternetSpecial4.html
Internal Promotion Identifier	ipromo23
Clickthrough URL	www.mysite.com/CampingStoveSale.html
Internal Promotion Type	Internal ad
Internal Promotion Version	2
Internal Promoted Product or Service	30383-95851 (SKU number)
Internal Promoted Brand	Coleman
Internal Promoted Category	Camp stoves

Unlike the *Internal Promotion* dimension, the *External Promotion* dimension is sourced completely from the clickstream. The referring URL in the log record of the external promotion clickthrough provides the necessary data to fill in the attributes of this dimension. The referring URL and the parameters in its query string contain the unique *External Promotion Identifier*, the *External Promotion Engine/Sponsor*, like DoubleClick or AOL, the *External Promotion Format*, the *External Promotion Version*, and the *Externally Promoted Product or Service, Brand*, and *Category*, if any.

All of these values will be stored in the query string. In the case of promotions that are configured and sold internally, the ETL developer should have access to the information that is embedded in the query string. In the case of promotions delivered via a third party such as an advertising engine, the ETL developer must read through the documentation provided by that vendor. In some cases, more information may be required in order to properly decode the values in the query string.

In the example row for the External Promotion dimension shown in Table 8.13, the developer would need to parse the External Promotion URL and extract the document name, *epromo99.jhtml*, in order to identify the actual promotion. This is something that could only be learned from the external advertising vendor's documentation.

User and Physical Geography

We present the *User* and *Physical Geography* dimensions together because the processing for them is frequently linked. Further, many clickstream implementations will collapse the physical geography into the user dimension. We show them separately in the meta-schema because end-user analysis may

Table 8.13 External Promotion Dimension

EXTERNAL PROMOTION ATTRIBUTES	DATA ELEMENT VALUES
Surrogate External Promotion Key	121
External Promotion URL (referring URL)	www.doubleclick.com/mysite/ epromo99.jhtml? format=banner…
External Promotion Identifier	Epromo99
External Promotion Engine/Sponsor	Doubleclick.com
External Promotion Format	Banner
External Promotion Version	3
External Promoted Product or Service	21841-33772
External Promoted Brand	John Wiley
External Promoted Category	Technical book

require that the dimensions be separate, and there is sometimes a many-to-one aspect between the physical geography and a user.

Creation of the *User* dimension is a complex task that normally requires that data go through a series of stages. Each stage addresses a particular set of data requirements and processing. The number of stages needed in a given click-stream data warehouse depends on the end-user requirements related to user behavior analysis. We will cover all of the steps involved here, since we are aiming to create a fully detailed user dimension.

The user identification stage of the clickstream preprocessor did some of the preliminary work needed to build the User dimension. Every record should already be marked with a user identifier of some sort, so the first step is to extract a list of all of the robots that were identified. The data for robots is processed along a different path since the data is different.

When the clickstream preprocessor identified records associated with a robot, it places a unique ID for the robot in place of the user ID in the event record. The robot ID is used to look up the robot identification information that needs to be inserted in the User dimension. Unless the identity information is already there from previous data loads, the User dimension is populated with the information associated with the company that sent the robot, assuming the company can be identified.

After creating the rows for robots, the next step is to extract a list of known user IDs from the clickstream records. These IDs are from the Web site's user tracking mechanism and identify both returning users and new users. If the clickstream preprocessor did not look up the IDs to see whether these were new or returning users then we must separate the two types of users now.

UserID lookup can be a problem if the Web site and clickstream data warehouse do not use the same mechanisms for assigning the IDs. If the IDs are not synchronized then the ETL developer must build a cross-reference table to link Web site and data warehouse user IDs. The problem becomes apparent when the data warehouse is expected to remove duplicate records and merge user profiles together. There will be a many-to-one relationship between the Web site's users and the users tracked by the data warehouse.

Assuming the returning users have been identified, there is no new processing required for them at this point since they should already have rows in the dimension. We save the returning user ID list at this point because there may be additional processing at a later stage.

Normally, we do not immediately add rows to the dimension for the new users. It is a good idea to first check and see if any of the new users are in fact returning users who somehow lost their user tracking information. The remapping of new user IDs to existing IDs is a valuable feature to have in the data warehouse, since it helps to avoid inflated user counts and misdirected analysis.

In order to match a new user ID with a preexisting ID, the ETL program must find a way to uniquely identify a user based on the information in the event records. This process is almost identical to the session matching mechanism used in the clickstream processor. Odds are good that some of that code can be reused here.

In addition, the user may have supplied additional information to the Web site. If the Web site requires user registration, or if the user conducted a transaction, then there should be additional information such as an email address or physical address. These can be used to compare records and match new and existing user profiles together.

There is an obvious dependency here: We must first extract user data from the Web application that stores it. The user dimension is not often sourced directly from the clickstream. Rather, we make use of the clickstream, data from HTML forms, the Web site's supporting applications and databases, and possibly external data suppliers. If any of these sources are available, their data must be extracted and put into the staging area for use at this time. Because of the number and variety of applications that might contain user-related data, we can't provide a more detailed explanation than this. The available data and its storage are entirely dependent on your infrastructure.

Assuming all robots and identified users have been processed, the next stage is dealing with any unidentified users. How you handle unidentified users depends on the end-user requirements. The two common approaches are to assign all visits with no identified user to a single anonymous user ID, or to assign one unique user ID for each anonymous session that was identified.

Our preference is to always mark anonymous visits with their own unique identifier. Then we can track related information, like the user agent, for all of the visits. A single anonymous user record means we lose some of this data. In either case, one should set the *User Type* field to "Anonymous User." This will help differentiate the anonymous users from identified users or robots.

It is a good idea to try to remove duplicate unidentified users if possible. The process is almost the same as removing duplicates for identified users, except that we are likely to be relying on clickstream data only, since an unidentified user probably never supplied us with any registration or other information. This is not always the case though. It is possible to use a Web site with cookies disabled, thus leaving the event records unmarked, even though there was an initial registration event to enter the Web site. Depending on how clever the ETL developer is, it may be possible to pull registration data from parameters in the log for the registration page and link them to the anonymous user.

One opportunity that is overlooked by many consumer-oriented Web sites is that the user may be one of two parties involved in the transaction. For example, if one purchases an item online as a gift to be sent to someone else, there will be personal information available on two individuals. The user who purchased the item will be represented in the clickstream data, but the recipient will only be in the data implicitly. Often, these recipients become users in the future, so it is useful to extract this recipient data and create "dummy" rows for them in the user dimension. Then, if they ever do use the Web site, it will be possible to tie the records together and note that they were both a direct and an indirect customer.

For basic user data, this is all the processing that is required. If we assume that the log record we've been using through this chapter as an example were tied to a real user, we might be able to store the data shown in Table 8.14.

More advanced user profiling is only effective when the Web site has made provisions to capture the required information. Chapter 5 discussed many of these user-tracking and identity mechanisms. When the Web site captures this additional information, the clickstream data warehouse must extract it. The extraction will probably be from an application server database supporting the Web site, but may also be from the clickstream in HTML form fields passed as parameters in the query strings of specific Web pages.

If the mechanisms to identify and profile users are more involved, such as with our successive revelation example in Chapter 4, then the Web site developers must work with the clickstream data warehouse developers on the design for both data capture and data extraction. Proper profiling is best done with all parties involved.

Table 8.14 User Dimension

USER ATTRIBUTES	EXAMPLE VALUES
Surrogate User Key	243978
User Identifier	609
User Agent Type	Web browser
User Agent Name	Netscape
User Type	Identified user
Gender	Male
Registered Username	Fordp
Email Address	fordp@guide.com
Email Domain	guide.com
Market Segment	None available
Demographic Information	None available
Timestamp of last Purchase	August 2, 2001
Credit Profile	None available
Daytime Telephone Number	None available
Evening Telephone Number	None available
Home Telephone Number	None available
Work Telephone Number	None available
Billing Address	None available
Shipping Address	None available

When building more advanced profiling capabilities, the designer of the profiling programs should take the Web site's privacy policy into consideration. We have seen several cases where the management of some high-profile Web sites were not aware that their internal clickstream data warehouses were in direct violation of their own privacy policies.

User profiling requires quite a few decisions regarding what data is being stored, what techniques will be used, whether external data will be involved, and how the schema will be designed. In our previous profiling discussion in Chapter 4 we talked about many of these issues, such as whether one goes to the effort of building profiles for unidentified users or all users. Many times, user profiles are built or enhanced using third-party data.

The ETL design is not a lot easier when using an external user-tracking service or purchasing syndicated demographic data. Some user services provide direct access to the information, but attempting to perform a bulk transfer of this data over the Internet can be a slow process, as well as a possible privacy

Table 8.15 Physical Geography Dimension

PHYSICAL GEOGRAPHY ATTRIBUTES	EXAMPLE VALUES
Surrogate Physical Geography Key	23883
Country	USA
State or Province	California
County or Township	Santa Clara
City	San Jose
Street Number	1587
Address 1	Shasta Ave.
Address 2	Suite 100
Zip or Postal Code	95126
Zip or Postal Code Extension	2534
Region	North America
Type of Location	Main Office

policy violation. Other services send data periodically. Still others require that you send them your user data, which they then process and merge with demographic information before sending it back.

If the Web site has a personalization engine that is making recommendations, the ETL process should attempt to extract the data stored in that application. This data may be useful in enhancing individual user profiles. There is a distinct possibility that the user profile in the warehouse might be more detailed than what the application stores, in which case a reverse feed might be created.

If we gathered address data as part of building the user dimension, we can use that data to populate the Physical Geography dimension shown in Table 8.15. When the only user information we have is an email or IP address, it is still possible to get physical location data, although it will often be at a city level or higher. There are a number of products and services that provide this information linked to either email or IP addresses. At the worst, we can simply use the information about the ISP we gathered from the IP address and fill this in as an approximation of the user's physical location.

If we obtained information about the user's time zone, either by obtaining a timestamp from within a Web page and sending it back to the Web site, or via the user's physical geography, we may need to insert rows into the User Time dimension tables. The reason for this is that it is not always possible to cover every possibility in those tables. For example, your Web site may not anticipate any traffic from outside the country, so only the in-country time zones were considered when building the User Time dimension. If an out-of-country user visits the Web site and you detect it during this dimension build, new rows may be inserted into the User Time dimension.

Aggregated Dimensions

The meta-schema chapter introduced several aggregated dimensions to go with the aggregated page view and session fact tables. Each of these dimensions is discussed below.

Page Dimension

Strictly speaking, the Page dimension is intended to be a page-level aggregate of the site-hit granularity Content dimension. When the fact table is rolled up to the page level from the hit level, all of the Content dimension rows containing page element information are suppressed to produce the Page dimension. In addition, *Total Page Size* is added as a new attribute. The Total Page Size is calculated by adding together the sizes of all elements associated with a page to the size of the HTML page. Keep in mind that with dynamic pages this calculation is not always possible. When the content varies from one page view to another, perhaps from changing the images that are displayed, then the size can only be stored as a range. If this is the case, the size is usually omitted or stored as the size of the actual HTML page source without the dynamic components.

You may have noted the similarity between the Page dimension and the Site Geography dimension. Because the Site Geography dimension is a page level view of site structure and content, they are very similar, with the Site Geography dimension carrying more site structure information in the form of the Parent URL and a little less content-related information. If you choose to have a Page dimension at both the site hit and page levels of granularity, then it is best to combine the attributes of the Site Geography dimension with those in the Page dimension, leaving just a single Page dimension. The Content dimension would then aggregate-out above the site-hit level of granularity. If you choose to have the Page dimension at only the page level of granularity, you may want to add the Site Geography Parent URL attribute to the Page dimension, which would aggregate out the Site Geography dimension from this level of schema granularity.

Example values for the Page dimension are shown in Table 8.16.

Web Geography Page-Referrer Dimension

The Page-Referrer dimension is another dimension that is aggregated when the fact table is rolled up from the hit level to the page level. As with the Page dimension, Page-Referrer is an aggregate of the lower level Referrer Geography

Table 8.16 Page Dimension

PAGE ATTRIBUTES	EXAMPLE VALUES
Surrogate Page Key	842
Page URL	/article.php
Page Identifier	54
Page Type	Dynamically generated
Page Content	Technical information
Page Purpose	Content display
Page Size	2048
Total Page Size	2048 - 8192
Page Version	1.0
Date Created	04/01/2002
Date of Last Revision	04/14/2002
Last Modified By	dadams
Date Removed From Site	*null*

dimension table. We show it here for completeness, although some clickstream data warehouses will treat it as a level in a page-element/page hierarchy within the Referrer Geography dimension. Table 8.17 shows the values that would be present for the example event record.

One problem that sometimes causes trouble with this dimension is the ISPs that use multiple IP addresses for a user during a single session. Inserting every IP address into this dimension is not a problem at the hit-level fact table. However, when aggregating to the page or session levels, multiple IP addresses cause problems. For this reason, developers sometimes insert only

Table 8.17 Page-Referrer Geography Dimension Attributes and Values

PAGE-REFERRER GEOGRAPHY ATTRIBUTES	EXAMPLE VALUES
Surrogate Page-Referrer Key	432987
Referring URL	http://mysearch.com/search
Referring Page ID	*null*
Query String	q=clickstream+warehouse&geo=no
Referring Domain	mysearch.com
External/Internal Flag	External
Referred URL	/article.php?Id=42
Referred Page ID	54

the first IP address into this table and then carry that same address forward for all subsequent records that belong to a given session. This choice provides for some consistency in the fact table keys, although some of actual IP address information is then lost.

Session Dimension

The Session dimension (Table 8.18) is the last aggregated dimension we will discuss. The meta-schema did not introduce this dimension until the discussion of aggregate level fact tables in order to better explain the schema, but this dimension will likely be built for use at both the hit and page granularities of the schema.

Sourcing the Session dimension is done straight from the processed clickstream records. The session matching stage of the clickstream preprocessor marked every hit with a session identifier. Building the dimension takes each *Session Identifier* in turn and looks up the user ID associated with this record. This implies that the User dimension has been built so that we can join the user ID we have from the processed event record to a potentially deduped user record.

The *Session Type* is populated based on rules that come from the analytical users of the data warehouse. The ETL developer must program these rules to determine the specific value for the field. For example, a visit to an e-commerce site might be labeled "browsing" until the user placed an item in their basket, at which point it would be labeled "shopping." This means that potentially all of the clickstream records in a session must be examined prior to populating the field.

The *Session Status* is similarly based on analytical requirements, although it is usually simpler. When session status is used, hopefully the most common value will be "success." Other possible session statuses include "error," if there was a problem on the Web site, or "abandoned" if we detected that the user hit the stop button and left the site, or the user abandoned his shopping cart before making a purchase.

Table 8.18 Session Dimension

LEVEL	SESSION DIMENSION ATTRIBUTES	EXAMPLE VALUES
1	Surrogate Session Key	Unique integer identifier
1	Session Identifier	36789896
1	User Identifier	609
1	Session Type	Information search
1	Session Status	Success

While the Session dimension is valid at the hit and page levels, it does not apply when the schema is aggregated to the session level. At the session level, there will be a one to one correspondence between rows in the fact table and rows in the dimension table. In dimensional modeling terms this is called a degenerate dimension, and a degenerate dimension is dropped at the level where it no longer applies.

Step 6: Design and Build the Fact Table ETL Components

Once the ETL programs to build the dimension tables have been implemented, it's time to start working on the fact tables. Creating the clickstream fact tables is normally less difficult than building the dimensions. Most of the data is present in nearly final form in the preprocessed clickstream. The most difficult part is creating the multipart key for the fact table.

Base Level User Activity Fact Table

Mapping the facts is straightforward. The *Site Hit Load Time* is the Transfer Time from the event record. If your event records do not contain a transfer time, hopefully you can record the time the request was received and the time the request was completed. Then the field is simply populated by subtracting the time received from the time completed.

The *Time Received* field is populated from the timestamp in the event record, assuming that the event records have been normalized as described in the section on clickstream record parsing. The *Time Completed* field is either populated from the event record if that field is present, or calculated by adding the *Site Hit Load Time* to the *Time Received*. For both fields we use an SQL date type rather than any parsed representation of the date and time.

The *Bytes Transferred* field is populated straight from the Bytes field in the event record, and the *HTTP Status* field straight from the Status filed in the event record. To make the schema more user-friendly, many implementations will either include the text description of the HTTP status in the fact table, or add a lookup table that acts as a pseudo-dimension table.

Table 8.19 shows the values we would put into the fact table for our sample clickstream record. We omitted keys for dimensions because they would not be meaningful in our example.

Creating the surrogate keys for each row of the fact table involves a lot of cross-referencing and lookups in dimension tables. Many novice ETL developers run into trouble with this at first because they do not save the required data in the staging area while building the dimensions. When it is time to link the fact rows to the dimension tables there is not enough information to locate the correct keys.

Since a fact row is built directly from an event record, linking to dimensions like the Host Geography or Referrer Geography is trivial because the host and referring URL information is already in the event record. The complexity of lookups increases with rows for the Promotion dimensions or the Activity dimension, since there is usually no direct link from the event record to these dimensions. When there is a link it normally requires some parsing of the URL, query string, or cookies.

The User dimension is the one that causes the most trouble. The problems are due to Web site and data warehouse user IDs being out of sync with one another, and the merging of duplicate user IDs. When duplicates are removed, the ETL developer must make sure to keep a cross-reference table linking the user ID in the event record with the new or merged user ID in the User dimension. Without this cross reference, there is no way to tie the fact table to the User dimension.

There are countless ways to handle the final assembly and loading of the base level fact rows, many of which are discussed in general data warehousing books. Performing this task for clickstream data is not much different than for a nonclickstream data warehouse, so we will not go into it further here.

Page Level Fact Table

Once the User Activity fact table has been built at the base granularity of hits, the next step is to aggregate it to the page level. The aggregation of hits to page views is not a true dimensional aggregate of our base granularity because we are substituting different facts when we consolidate the hits for a page.

When populating the fields, the *Page Start Time* is the time the first hit was received for the HTML page or tracked object in the case of streaming media or image-only pages. The *Page End Time* is the *Time Hit Completed* from the hit level fact table for the last element that was loaded on the page. Fortunately, the clickstream preprocessor already did the work of traversing the referral paths to label every hit with the page that generated it. This data did not make it into the base level fact table, but it should still be present in the processed clickstream records. All that we need to do is look for the latest *Time Hit Completed* in the hits linked to this page, or *Time Hit Received* plus *Transfer Time* in the case where we do not have the time completed in the event records. This value will become our *Page End Time*.

Table 8.19 Base Level User Activity Fact Table

USER ACTIVITY/SITE HIT FACT ATTRIBUTES	DATA MAPPING
Surrogate User Key	Unique integer identifier
Surrogate Fiscal Date Key	Unique integer identifier
Surrogate Fiscal Time-of-Day Key	Unique integer identifier
Surrogate User Date Key	Unique integer identifier
Surrogate User Time-of-Day Key	Unique integer identifier
Surrogate Physical Geography Key	Unique integer identifier
Surrogate Host Geography Key	Unique integer identifier
Surrogate Referrer Geography Key	Unique integer identifier
Surrogate Site Geography Key	Unique integer identifier
Surrogate Content Key	Unique integer identifier
Surrogate Activity Key	Unique integer identifier
Surrogate Internal Promotion Key	Unique integer identifier
Surrogate External Promotion Key	Unique integer identifier
Site Hit Load Time	1
Time Hit Received	04/Jul/2001:12:37:02
Time Hit Completed	04/Jul/2001:12:37:03
Bytes Transferred in Hit	8437
Site Hit HTTP Status Code	200

The *Page Dwell Time* calculation is similar in nature to the Page End Time, but with an added twist. The basic formula for the dwell time is:

```
Page Dwell Time = Page Start Time of the next page - Page End Time of
the current page
```

What we are really saying is that the dwell time is the period the user looked at a page after all elements of the page loaded, and before the user made another request.

One problem with Dwell Time occurs with exit pages. The calculation assumes we know when the user left the Web site. If the user did not log out or click on a link out of our site then we have no way of knowing exactly when they left. In these cases, we have to use the information generated by the session matching stage of the clickstream preprocessor. Since it determines when a session ends, it can tell us when the current session ended or timed out. Most of the time, the preprocessor inserts a "fake" event record containing the end-of-session event so that we can perform these kinds of calculations.

In Chapter 3 we reviewed inaccuracies that can creep in to this calculation from loss of visibility due to Internet caching, browser caching, and end-of-session timeouts, among other things. The best one can do is keep these problems in mind and try to design around them. Sometimes it is possible to estimate the impact of these issues by conducting tests, and then incorporate a statistical variation into your calculations so the numbers are more accurate.

When dealing with streaming media, the *Page Bytes Transferred, Start, End,* and *Dwell Time* calculations are often done for you by the media server. In Chapter 4 we discussed the log file for a common media server, and showed a sample log format. If you need to populate these values for a media clip, chances are good that the task will be a simple exercise in data mapping from such a log format.

Page Bytes Transferred is calculated by totaling the number of bytes transferred for all hits that comprise a particular page. Again, we benefit from the work done by the clickstream preprocessor, since it already marked all of the hits that belong to the page we are working with.

The last field to populate is the *HTTP Status Code*. At the page level, this is not as simple as looking at the Status field for the hit on the page. It is possible that the HTML page completed loading, but the user did not wait for the entire page to load before leaving the page. In this case, you would need to scan through all of the hits associated with the page and see if the page loaded completely.

You can't rely on a comparison of the Page Bytes Transferred to the *Total Page Size* in the Page or Site Geography dimension to determine success, since caching or dynamic pages can alter how much data was transferred to the client. Nor can you assume that a status other than 200 for a hit is what should be populated in the field. This is because many other status codes for page elements are actually indicators of success. For example, conditional GETs result in a status of 304, and redirects can have a number of different statuses.

The ETL developer must determine which HTTP status codes are indicators of success and which are not, and then decide what to put into this field. Sometimes these rules require discussion with end users. For example, suppose an impatient user hits the Stop button after the HTML page has loaded but before all the other elements have loaded. The page is perfectly readable, although the full set of navigation images are not present. The rule for HTTP status must determine whether complete loading of HTML but not other elements is a success, failure, or some area in between.

Table 8.20 shows what the data for our sample event record might look like when aggregated to the page level.

Table 8.20 Page Activity Fact Table

PAGE ACTIVITY FACT ATTRIBUTES	EXAMPLE VALUES
Surrogate User Key	Unique integer identifier
Surrogate Fiscal Date Key	Unique integer identifier
Surrogate Fiscal Time-of-Day Key	Unique integer identifier
Surrogate User Date Key	Unique integer identifier
Surrogate User Time-of-Day Key	Unique integer identifier
Surrogate Physical Geography Key	Unique integer identifier
Surrogate Host Geography Key	Unique integer identifier
Surrogate Page Referrer Geography Key	Unique integer identifier
Surrogate Site Geography Key	Unique integer identifier
Surrogate Activity Key	Unique integer identifier
Surrogate Internal Promotion Key	Unique integer identifier
Surrogate External Promotion Key	Unique integer identifier
Surrogate Page Key	Unique integer identifier
Page Start Time	04/Jul/2001:12:37:02
Page End Time	04/Jul/2001:12:37:06
Page Dwell Time	86
Page Bytes Transferred	18677
Page HTTP Status Code	200

Session Level Fact Table

The last fact table that we need to build is the Session fact table. As with the page-level fact table, we are not dealing with a true dimensional aggregate table. Because analysis at the session level is important, we add a number of new facts. We also lose several dimensions at this level, because they are only applicable when dealing with hits or page views.

The clickstream preprocessor has already done some of the work to make populating the fact rows easier. However, an even simpler method is to make use of the Session dimension, which should be built by the time we get to this stage of the ETL process. Because the Session dimension is a degenerate dimension at this level, it is not a dimension of the aggregated Session fact table. But we can use all of the newly inserted rows in the Session dimension as the starting point for the fact rows in the session-level fact table.

The rows from the Session dimension provide the *Session Identifier, Session Type,* and *Session Status.* The remaining fields must be derived for each session.

Most of this derivation is based on serial processing of the fully parsed log records associated with a session. For this reason, it can be useful to design the session matching stage of the clickstream processor so that it either numbers every hit in a session sequentially, or accumulates the desired information as it processes the sessions.

The *Session Start Time* is the *Time Received* of the first hit in the session. The *Session End Time* is harder to determine because there is not usually an event for the end of the session unless the session matching stage inserts a "fake" end-of-session event as we described earlier. The Session Length is simply the *Session End Time* minus the *Session Start Time*.

The *Entry Page URL* and *Identifier* are the *Request URL* and *Content ID* of the first hit in the session. Likewise, the *Exit Page URL* and *Identifier* are the *Request URL* and *Content ID* of the last page in the session.

When counting the *Number of Pages Visited in Session*, it is important to define what is meant by "page." For example, does a media clip count as a page? What about a link to a full-screen product image? In general, the rules for what defines a page should be the equivalent of what shows up in the Site Geography dimension, since this is where all of the primary objects for the Web site are listed.

Finally, *Total Bytes Transferred* is a simple summation of the bytes transferred for every hit that is part of the session.

Table 8.21 shows what the data might look like in this fact table for the session containing the sample event record we've been using.

One problem that will come up when building the page-level or session-level aggregate tables is the users who have more than one IP address during their session. At the hit level, there is no problem assigning each hit to the appropriate IP address in the Web Geography dimension. At the page level, you must decided whether to use the address attached to the page or carry a single IP address through all the fact rows for a given visit. At the session level, there can be only one IP address, so the choice comes down to which one will be used. Whatever the decision, it should be documented and remain consistent through the evolution of the warehouse.

Another problem is the issue of filtering in the clickstream preprocessor. If data, such as images, is filtered in the clickstream preprocessor then there will be hits that are missing from the fact table. Therefore, when we aggregate to page views we will have inaccurate facts that are assembled from incomplete data. If you filter records in the clickstream preprocessor, be sure to perform the required calculations at that time so that the page-level and session-level fact tables can be properly built.

Table 8.21 Session Activity Fact Table

SESSION ACTIVITY FACT ATTRIBUTES	EXAMPLE VALUES
Surrogate User Key	Unique integer identifier
Surrogate Fiscal Date Key	Unique integer identifier
Surrogate Fiscal Time-of-Day Key	Unique integer identifier
Surrogate User Date Key	Unique integer identifier
Surrogate User Time-of-Day Key	Unique integer identifier
Surrogate Physical Geography Key	Unique integer identifier
Surrogate Host Geography Key	Unique integer identifier
Surrogate External Geography Key	Unique integer identifier
Surrogate Internal Promotion Key	Unique integer identifier
Surrogate External Promotion Key	Unique integer identifier
Session Identifier	36789896
Session Start Time	04/Jul/2001:12:26:02
Session End Time	04/Jul/2001:12:37:06
Session Length	664
Entry Page URL	/index.html
Entry Page Identifier	1
Exit Page URL	/article.php?Id=42
Exit Page Identifier	54
Number of Pages Visited in Session	12
Total Bytes Transferred	218326
Session Type	Information search
Session Status	Success

In our discussion we've stayed close to the meta-schema discussed in Chapter 6. When working with an extended schema, as in the examples at the end of that chapter, the ETL process simply extends to encompass those new dimension and fact tables. The most challenging part is getting through the processing for the meta-schema, which we have already described in detail in steps 4, 5, and 6 in this chapter.

Step 7: Build the Data Loading Mechanism and Integrate the ETL Programs

In step 3 we discussed some of the design decisions related to the final data load in the target schema. Most clickstream data warehouses do not use a build-and-insert mechanism to load the final data. Instead they place the new data into a set of tables in the data staging area that mirror the tables in the data warehouse, often called a posting schema.

By using a posting schema, it is possible to ensure that there are no orphan fact rows (fact rows missing one or more dimension keys) prior to inserting the data into the queryable database. The more pressing need for a posting schema is for performance, particularly for very large data volumes. When using a posting schema, it is possible to perform most of the data validation on the new data so that the load process becomes a simple insertion into the final tables. This shortens the window of time that the database will be unavailable to users.

If your data warehouse does make use of any hybrid or multidimensional OLAP products, you are still not done with the data loading. Now that the data is loaded into the data warehouse schema, the next step is to feed the appropriate data into the mechanism that builds the data cubes, or whatever representation your OLAP product uses to store data.

Loading the dimension and fact tables is not the end of the ETL processing. There are data archival, aggregation, table indexing, and backup tasks that must be performed prior to opening up the database for use. These tasks are mostly related to data warehouse management and database administration. Chapter 7 described some of the basic tools and techniques, as well as some of the DBA tasks that go along with them. For more information on these post-load tasks, including more detailed information about building dimensional aggregates, refer to the companion Web site at www.wiley.com/compbooks/sweiger.

It is at this point in a project that the ETL development tasks and development tasks on the project plan, like building a process automation framework, begin to converge. After completing the ETL and data-loading programs, the final step is to integrate all of these programs within the process automation framework.

As you have seen from the prior steps, the ETL programs that build the dimension and fact tables are not created in isolation. Some of the programs depend on others, and most depend on the clickstream preprocessor. Inserting new data into the fact table requires that the new data for each of the associated dimensions be ready. This means that the process of integration should be relatively straightforward because the ETL developers had to work in concert to create these programs.

The other element of integration is linking all of the ETL programs to the process automation framework. This may involve creating wrappers for the ETL programs so they pass appropriate values for success or failure, writing scripts to launch the programs, or simply entering the ETL program information into a job control application such as Tivoli Workload Scheduler.

Step 8: Build Support for Data Administration

The final step in building the ETL subsystem is to build the required support for data administration. Most of the time, this involves creating programs to manage data quality. These can be simple data validation programs for data that has been loaded into the warehouse, or complex applications that sift through the data looking for problems.

The reality of clickstream data warehouses is that data quality will be an ongoing issue, because problems with data quality have little to do with the data warehouse and everything to do with the data sources. Because of the nature of clickstream data, there will be some data problems that are simply not resolvable, like the issue of perfectly tracking Web site users. These data problems will result in errors during processing and loading.

In order for the data warehouse manager or data administrator to identify and correct these data problems, they require programs and interfaces that allow them to look at data in the staging area and determine the cause of problems. In some cases, data must be manually corrected in order for ETL processing to continue. Data administration is a difficult task, and doing it well requires support and the ability to automate solutions once the causes are understood. For more information on the topic of data quality, we suggest *Improving Data Warehouse and Business Information Quality* (Wiley, 1999) by Larry English as a starting point.

The Basics of Data Quality

At a macro level there are two different types of data quality: content quality and definitional quality. Data content quality is a measure of the quality of the data stored in your system, while definitional quality is a measure of the quality of both the meta data and the content.

When talking about data quality it is also important to differentiate between metrics and measurements. Metrics define what aspect of data quality you are trying to measure, while measurements define how you will track and measure those metrics.

There are many data-quality metrics that may be used in the clickstream data warehouse. Table 8.22 shows some of the data-quality metrics that might be included. Each metric has many possible attributes associated with the data being managed.

(continued)

The Basics of Data Quality *(Continued)*

Table 8.22 Example Data Quality Metrics

DATA QUALITY METRICS	METRIC DESCRIPTION	POSSIBLE MEASUREMENTS
Accuracy	The degree of agreement between the data element values and the specified tolerance. Accuracy must be measured relative to a defined quality standard.	Percentage of data element within tolerable limits
Completeness	The degree to which elements contain values and have complete associations to other elements. Completeness pertains to both single data elements and collections of data elements, such as "customer."	Percentage complete or the percentage that passed referential integrity checks
Consistency	A measure of the logical coherence between elements in multiple locations and systems, including coherence between definition and use.	Percentage of data elements between two systems that match
Timeliness	A measure of availability within specified periods. Timeliness should always be measured from the perspective of the end users of the data warehouse.	Percentage of data available within specified time or the amount of time a data element was available within a specific time frame
Uniqueness	A constraint on the number of occurrences of data within or across systems. Where possible, there should be one occurrence of an element; where not possible the element should be standardized and related across systems.	Percentage of data with multiple sources or the total number of occurrences of individual data elements

Beyond the data quality issues, the data warehouse manager must also deal with changes to data sources that affect the warehouse. This requires good communication procedures as well as technology support. The data warehouse manager must be involved in design meetings for the Web site so that there is no unforeseen disruption to the data warehouse.

Summary

The clickstream ETL subsystem is the most challenging portion of the clickstream data warehouse to build. By approaching the design and implementation in a top-down manner, starting with a generic data warehouse architecture and adding clickstream components, we provided a roadmap to building the necessary ETL components.

The roadmap, when combined with eight steps to build a clickstream ETL subsystem, should provide a guide to completing this difficult work. Our goal with the eight steps is to offer in-depth information about clickstream processing that is not normally provided in other data warehousing texts, while retaining enough context to tie it to generic data warehouse ETL issues.

The next chapter, which is the last one in this book, describes the analytical technologies that one can use to build the front-end interface to the clickstream data warehouse.

Analyzing the Data in the Clickstream Data Warehouse

The sheer size of a clickstream data warehouse presents several significant challenges to the data warehouse design and implementation team. Once you have overcome the challenges of extracting, transforming, and loading hundreds of millions of rows into the database within a narrow batch window while preserving the referential integrity and quality of the data, you must also ensure that widely differing user audiences can access the data quickly and easily. As users navigate through the mountains of clickstream data, they expect rich analytical toolsets to enable ad hoc analysis that also provide speedy and consistent response times.

Online Analytical Processing (OLAP) tools are the primary mechanism used to satisfy these stringent analytical requirements. In this chapter we explore the benefits and limitations of different OLAP architectures. We also describe several novel analytical techniques that can dramatically improve the scalability, functionality, and query performance of your clickstream data warehouse.

OLAP Tools

Taking the spreadsheet metaphor to the next level, OLAP tools provide multidimensional, dynamic slice-and-dice as well as drill-down/drill-up and pivot capabilities necessary for clickstream analysis. As users slice, drill, and pivot through the clickstream data, they expect little or no latency between mouse clicks to interrupt their stream-of-thought. At the same time, the chosen OLAP architecture must also be sufficiently scalable to allow thousands of users to navigate through potentially terabytes of clickstream data. Finding the right balance of analytic functionality, consistent response time, and sufficient scalability becomes one of the greatest critical success factors in deploying a successful clickstream data warehouse.

There are three basic OLAP architectures: pure Multidimensional OLAP (MOLAP) at one extreme, pure Relational OLAP (ROLAP) at the other extreme, and Hybrid OLAP (HOLAP), which combines features from both MOLAP and ROLAP. Table 9.1 compares each of the OLAP architectures against some of the significant features necessary for a successful clickstream data warehouse implementation. Each architecture has its own set of benefits and drawbacks, with HOLAP being the compromise that offers the best overall benefits.

MOLAP Overview

MAJOR MOLAP VENDORS

Cognos, Hyperion/Essbase, Oracle Express, and Microsoft OLAP Services

When relational database engines are used to house operational data within a normalized OLTP schema, analytical queries against massive amounts of data

Table 9.1 Feature versus Type of OLAP Comparison Chart

FEATURE	TYPE OF OLAP SOFTWARE		
	MOLAP	**HOLAP**	**ROLAP**
Potential Size of Clickstream Data Warehouse	Very Small (data cube only)	Very Large (data cubes and relational databases)	Very Large (relational databases only)
Initial Query Performance	Fastest	Moderate	Unpredictable
Drill/Pivot Response Time	Consistent	Relatively Consistent	Inconsistent (depends on query)
Advanced Analytical Capabilities (time series analysis, ranking, statistical exceptions, etc.)	High	High	Low (limited by SQL)
Load Time Efficiency	Very Low (single-threaded load of data cubes)	Medium (impacted by data cubes)	Very High (parallel SQL)

yield poor performance and consume tremendous amounts of server resources. An OLTP schema is optimized for efficiently storing rather than retrieving data. Template-driven and ad hoc queries place a tremendous burden on the operational systems, resulting in strict limitations imposed by IT to prevent rogue queries from impacting OLTP response times.

Prior to the advent of modern-day data warehousing, this problem was solved using specialized databases called Multidimensional Databases, or MDDBs. MDDBs were optimized to support analytical queries, known as Multidimensional OLAP, or MOLAP. More recently, MDDBs have been populated using extracts from the underlying data warehouse, rather than directly from the operational systems, in order to support drill-through from the MDDB into the data warehouse. Figure 9.1 shows a three-dimensional MOLAP data cube that supports analysis of internal promotions by user and time.

You can think of a MOLAP cube as a data structure that contains all the base and aggregated measures from a fact table, pre-joined with each hierarchical attribute of all related dimensions. This structure is called a data hypercube, or data cube for short. By multiplying the number of rows and columns in the fact table by the number of rows and columns in each of the associated dimensions, you can determine the total number of elements, or cells, in the resulting MOLAP cube. Because loading data into MOLAP data cubes is equivalent to precomputing all the possible joins in a star schema, most MOLAP tools have limitations on how large the resulting number of cells can be, how many dimension tables may be included, the number of dimensional attributes and levels in each hierarchy, and set maximum row limits on input data from both the fact table and the largest dimension table.

MOLAP and the accompanying MDDBs require a dedicated server, source data from the clickstream data warehouse, and a sufficiently large batch window in

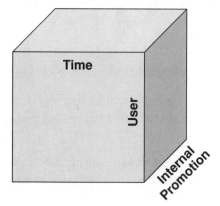

Figure 9.1 Sample MOLAP data cube.

which to compute and populate the proprietary cube structures. In addition, each MDDB uses proprietary client software that processes user queries against the data cube.

MOLAP Benefits

MDDB response times are relatively quick when compared to an equivalent query against a relational database. Each slice of the cube, stored on the server, is delivered across the network to the requesting client. Advanced analytics, such as ranking and time series, are typically built in to the client data access software, providing the user with a powerful framework for performing speedy stream-of-thought analysis.

MOLAP Limitations

MDDB limitations include strictures on the amount of data can be loaded into a cube (100 GB would be extremely large) as well as the number of dimension attributes can be included in a single cube (10 would be a lot). This size dimension limitation often leads to splitting cubes into subcubes, requiring more server hardware, memory, and disk storage, lengthening the batch window to load and build the cubes, and ultimately imposing complexity on the user who may need to stitch slices from different cubes back together to perform analysis.

In addition to burdening the batch window by populating MDDB cubes with every anticipated combination of precomputed values across relevant dimensions and hierarchies, additional server and storage capacity is required to house the resultant MDDB cubes on top of the disk space already consumed by the underlying data warehouse. Also, as the volume of clickstream data grows, data availability can become compromised when the batch data load window spills over into the promised user data warehouse availability window.

ROLAP Overview

MAJOR ROLAP VENDORS

There are only a few pure ROLAP vendors, with Microstrategy dominating the market. IBM/Informix Metacube and CA/Information Advantage play much smaller roles.

Because of the capacity limitations, redundant storage requirements, and long data cube creation times associated with MDDBs, an alternative to supporting analytical processing was developed called Relational OLAP, or ROLAP. With ROLAP, no cubes are built and as a result there are no requirements for a specialized database engine with the accompanying proprietary client software. Instead, the same relational database engine used to store the data warehouse is used to support SQL-based queries in a star-schema ROLAP environment. ROLAP products assume that the underlying data warehouse has a dimensional data model. Many of these tools can utilize relational database features like partitioning, materialized views, star joins, and specialized indexing capabilities like bitmaps and hashing to improve query performance. Figure 9.2 shows a dimensional data schema, based on the clickstream data warehouse meta-schema.

ROLAP Benefits

The most significant benefit of ROLAP is its ability to handle large quantities of data. Since the data warehouse itself is used as the data store, as opposed to MOLAP's redundant and proprietary cube structure, scalability of a ROLAP environment is constrained only by the robustness of the underlying infrastructure, namely the server hardware, disk space, network bandwidth, and the relational database engine.

ROLAP Limitations

Since ROLAP relies upon the underlying relational database engine, it also relies on SQL to perform query select, constrain, sort, and group functions. This can limit the types of analyses that can be performed, such as ranking and time series, due to limitations in capabilities of some versions of SQL. MOLAP products overcome this through the use of analytical extensions embedded both within the MDDB itself and within the proprietary client software. Some ROLAP products mitigate SQL's limitations through an intermediate analysis engine that intercepts the results returned from the database and reformats the results by applying statistical functions, including ranking and time series analysis.

In addition to the analytical limitations of ROLAP, there can be significant and unpredictable query overhead when slicing and drilling into data. Each request to reformat the data, drill up/down, sort, group, or pivot the data results in a new SQL statement, which must be sent to the server, parsed, and executed. The volume of activity on the network, contention on the ROLAP server, the efficiency of the SQL statement's execution plan, the ROLAP tool's

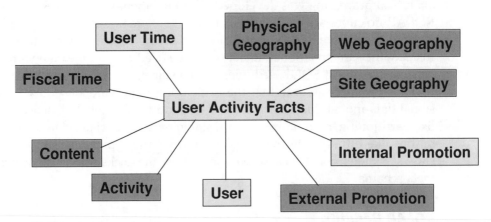

Figure 9.2 Sample ROLAP data warehouse schema.

ability to navigate relational aggregates, and the volume of data to be retrieved can cause variations in response times often frustrate users who need consistent response times to support their thought processes.

HOLAP Overview

MAJOR HOLAP VENDORS

The rapidly growing HOLAP market segment includes Brio, Business Objects, and Sagent.

To leverage the advantages of MOLAP and ROLAP while minimizing the disadvantages, a hybrid approach has been taken by several vendors, which is called Hybrid OLAP or HOLAP. Most HOLAP products rely on the relational database of the data warehouse to store the data while relying on a proprietary MOLAP-like client-based or middle-tier-based analytical engine to perform advanced calculations and present the data in the form of a proprietary microcube. Figure 9.3 shows a HOLAP query environment with data stored in both a data cube and a dimensional schema relational database.

HOLAP Benefits

HOLAP products rely on an inherently dimensional data model and can automatically take advantage of the data warehousing-specific features of the relational database engine (e.g., partitioning, materialized views, star joins, etc.). They also provide the MOLAP-like analytical extensions required to support complex OLAP analysis. Rather than return a single slice of data to the client, as is the case in both the MOLAP and ROLAP environments, several slices of

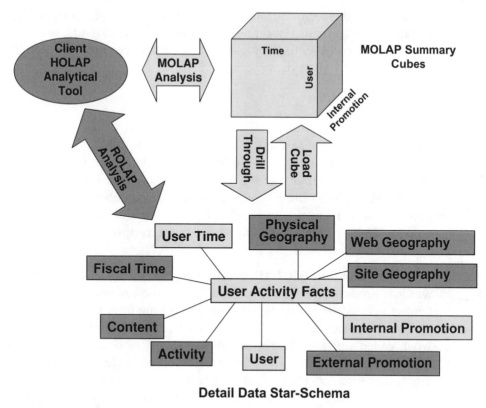

Figure 9.3 A sample HOLAP query environment.

data can be requested at run time and stored within a microcube. These microcubes reside within local memory on the desktop, and are manipulated using zero-admin, Web browser-based applets, resulting in very low latency slice, drill, sort, group, and pivot capabilities, providing a very good analytical environment. Microcubes are typically built on demand, but may be staged during the batch window and cached on an intermediate server that also routes SQL requests. This intermediate server will look at each SQL statement, and, prior to passing it on to be executed against the relational database of the data warehouse, it will check to see if the requested result set has been previously retrieved and stored on the intermediate server. If so, the cached results are immediately sent to the requesting client, eliminating the need to send the SQL statement to the relational database.

HOLAP Limitations

HOLAP's technique of requesting multiple slices of data at run time in anticipation of drilling up or down minimizes latency during subsequent user analysis. But this technique also causes longer query run times on bigger sets of data. It also can cause larger network and server workloads, since more data is processed, and because any supporting data cubes need to be built before the data can be analyzed.

OLAP Today

The once distinctively pure MOLAP versus pure ROLAP architectures have given way to blended HOLAP architectures that attempt to maximize performance and functionality of MOLAP with the openness and scalability of ROLAP. Whether building replicated server-based cubes in advance, or using powerful server engines to build cubes on demand, which are then pulled onto the desktop using a Web-based client, each approach has an Achilles heel that must be addressed.

In the case of a pure MOLAP architecture, limited scalability and batch load window time constraints often make this an inappropriate choice for a multi-terabyte clickstream data warehouse environment. A pure ROLAP architecture, on the other hand, has robust data storage scalability, but can crumble when called upon to deliver massive amounts of data to large numbers of concurrent users who then become impacted by wide variations in response times. The blended HOLAP architectures, which combine the scalability of relational databases with powerful analytics and consistent response times of data cubes, are best for the typical clickstream data warehouse analytical environment.

Analytical Features and Techniques

The following sections discuss some of the critical query tool, data model, and database engine features that you can use to optimize your clickstream data warehouse query performance.

Query Tool Related Features and Techniques

Many query tools can efficiently analyze clickstream data, if you only know how to configure and use them. In this section we explain two useful techniques, query tool bubble-and-drill using sort-on-measure functionality inside the relational database engine, and multipass SQL OLAP analysis.

Bubble-and-Drill Using Sort-on-Measure

So how do you analyze the massive amounts of data that reside in your click-stream data warehouse? One good way is to start with the extremes and the exceptions. For example, what are the top and bottom performing Web pages, products, clients, ads? Some query tools support ranking and bucketing (i.e., quartiles, quintiles, etc.) which, due to the limitations of SQL, often require two passes through the data—one pass to select the data based on the constraints supplied and a second pass to perform the ranking or bucketing operation. Ranking is useful if you are interested in the top or bottom N rows and not the entire data set, and you have decided in advance which measures to sort, like sales amount, abandonments, dwell time, etc. But if your query tool isn't very sophisticated, you may unwittingly process hundreds of millions of rows in order to bubble-up the top 10 performers, for example, unless an index for the particular measure column already exists.

An especially useful query tool feature is called "sort-on-measure," and it enables you to sort the results based on any of the measures that have been returned in your query result set. A descending sort will reveal the top performers (or offenders) while an ascending sort will show you the bottom performers (or offenders). A bad implementation of sort-on-measure functionality would be to return the millions of rows in the result set to your PC and perform the sort locally. A more sophisticated mechanism is to perform the sort on the data warehouse server and return only the results to the client.

All OLAP tools nominally support the capability to drill up or down and to sort rows or columns. But without the sort-on-measure capability, it is much more difficult to perform bubble-and-drill analysis. This capability is at the heart of stream-of-thought analysis, and when you are descending five or six levels of several dimensional hierarchies, this technique is invaluable.

As we can see in Figure 9.4, bubble-and-drill involves selecting an initial result set at the highest level of each dimensional hierarchy that would yield a mean-ingful comparison, and sorting the results (using sort-on-measure) either ascending or descending. This is the "bubbling to the top" portion of the analysis. Then, by highlighting the top N rows in the sorted result set, the user drills down one level on one of the dimensional hierarchies—this is the "drill" part. Once the next level of results is returned from the server (or in the case of HOLAP, calculated locally, assuming the lower level resides within your local cube), you then sort again on one of the measures and perform this bubble-and-drill iteratively until you have reached the bottom of each dimension's hierarchy.

Analysis of Average Seconds Spent After Site Upgrade			
	SITE VERSION 1.1	SITE VERSION 1.2	
CONTENT	SECONDS_SPENT	SECONDS_SPENT	% CHANGE
ABOUT US TOTAL	33.4	1.8	55.09
HOME PAGE TOTAL	8.7	14.6	67.82
INVESTOR TOTAL	120.9	118.7	-1.82
PRODUCT TOTAL	159.6	194	21.55
REFERENCES TOTAL	103.1	161.3	56.45
SERVICES TOTAL	316.2	291.5	-7.81
TECH SUPPORT TOTAL	465.3	506.6	8.88

> **Go from CONTENT sorted Alphabetically Ascending to %CHANGE sorted Numerically Ascending (*Bubble*)**

Analysis of Average Seconds Spent After Site Upgrade			
	SITE VERSION 1.1	SITE VERSION 1.2	
CONTENT	SECONDS_SPENT	SECONDS_SPENT	% CHANGE
SERVICES TOTAL	316.2	291.5	-7.81
INVESTOR TOTAL	120.9	118.7	-1.82
TECH SUPPORT TOTAL	465.3	506.6	8.88
PRODUCT TOTAL	159.6	194	21.55
ABOUT US TOTAL	33.4	1.8	55.09
REFERENCES TOTAL	103.1	161.3	56.45
HOME PAGE TOTAL	8.7	14.6	67.82

Analysis of Average Seconds Spent After Site Upgrade			
	SITE VERSION 1.1	SITE VERSION 1.2	
CONTENT	SECONDS_SPENT	SECONDS_SPENT	% CHANGE
SERVICES TOTAL	316.2	291.5	-7.81
INVESTOR TOTAL	120.9	118.7	-1.82
TECH SUPPORT TOTAL	465.3	506.6	8.88
PRODUCT TOTAL	159.6	194	21.55
ABOUT US TOTAL	33.4	1.8	55.09
REFERENCES TOTAL	103.1	161.3	56.45
HOME PAGE TOTAL	8.7	14.6	67.82

> ***Drill*** **on the SERVICES TOTAL to reveal the next level of detailed results for each Page in the category, and continue to iteratively Bubble-and-Drill**

Analysis of Average Seconds Spent After Site Upgrade			
	SITE VERSION 1.1	SITE VERSION 1.2	
CONTENT	SECONDS_SPENT	SECONDS_SPENT	% CHANGE
SERVICES TOTAL	316.2	291.5	-7.81
SERVICES MAIN	77.1	32.1	-58.37
SERVICES SUB X	11.2	27.5	145.54
SERVICES SUB Y	155.3	188.3	21.25
SERVICES SUB Z	72.6	43.6	-39.94

Figure 9.4 Bubble-and-drill example.

Assuming your query tool supports the sort-on-measure feature, sort-on-measure can be combined with the bubble-and-drill analytical technique, enabling you to attack even the largest clickstream data warehouse efficiently. Since you start at the higher levels of the dimensional hierarchies and work your way down, there is no reason to return a massive result set to the client, and most of the work can be done on the clickstream data warehouse server.

Multipass SQL Enables Mixed-Grain Queries

Multipass SQL enables users to perform several passes through the data warehouse from the OLAP tool, with each result set becoming a source from which subsequent relationships are derived and additional calculations are performed. Instead of the more typical scenario of using an OLAP tool to generate a single SQL statement to return a result set for further analysis, several result sets are retrieved. Calculations are performed that combine result sets, or use the first set of results as the numerator, and the second set of results as the denominator, to compare actuals against averages, or individual results against aggregates.

Not all OLAP tools support multipass SQL, and those that do sometimes impose limitations. For example, unless the semantic layer of the OLAP tool has been configured to include all fact tables and their associated dimension tables within a single subject area, multipass SQL capabilities, even if provided within the tool, will be limited to those measures and dimensional attributes that reside within the same subject area. In other cases, like ROLAP products, multipass SQL is the core of the query tool engine and may require special consideration in the data model design since there is little post-processing capability on the client side of the ROLAP tool.

Comparing daily page hit totals to monthly averages, banner ad clickthrough actuals versus forecasts, or shopping cart abandonments for a particular product against that product's category performance are typical examples of analyses that rely on multipass SQL, which are often called mixed grain queries. In some cases results can be selected from the same fact table over different date ranges, comparing daily activity to a monthly average, for example. More complex scenarios will compare result sets from different fact tables sharing conformed dimensions, especially when investigating clickstream activity as it relates to the brick-and-mortar areas of the business, such as product sales. OLAP tools with the capability to support multipass SQL can help avoid dreaded fact table to fact table joins, and instead provide individual result sets from each fact table, with the individual results then joined locally within the OLAP tool.

Data Model–Related Features and Techniques

The analytical mechanisms discussed in this section rely on special data model-dependent features and techniques that are implemented by the clickstream data warehouse design team.

Table Partitioning Enables Data Elimination

Partitioning is a very important technique for improving query performance. With proper partitioning, the database engine can eliminate 90 percent or more of the data from query consideration even before the first index is accessed. As we discussed in Chapter 7, partitioning is a feature of some relational database engines, like Oracle and DB2. If your database has this feature and, more importantly, your data model has been designed and your database has been loaded to implement this feature, you can get the database server to weed out most of the data before it is even considered or returned to you for analysis. The fact tables in clickstream data warehouses are often partitioned by a time key, such as visit date, order date, or event date. There may be further partitioning by an additional dimension within the time partition, such as Content, User, or Referring URL, with the larger dimensions also being partitioned.

Partition elimination depends on the user query to supply a range of partition key values in order to activate the feature. For example, if you were to supply a begin date and end date in your query, all data in partitions outside of the range would be eliminated from consideration by the database engine before any indexes were searched or tables scanned. Furthermore, if your database engine supports subpartitioning and your schema was further subpartitioned by User, and you supply a value or range of values for User, you will get an even quicker response by eliminating unnecessary User dimension partitions from query consideration.

Additional "Measure Statistics" Dimensions Speed Fact Table Analysis

Your clickstream data warehouse can contain hundreds of millions, even billions of fact table rows. Partitioning will help you eliminate most of the data from consideration by your query assuming you constrain on several dimensions and you are interested in a narrow date range or you are performing year over year, same period comparisons.

But what if you are interested in a range of values for a particular measure within a fact table across a broad date range with few or no constraints on any of the other dimensions? Such a query could produce tens or hundreds of millions of rows joined to the Date dimension, with a subsequent sequential scan of each record in the result set to determine whether the measure was within the range of values constraint. If your date range is too broad, a full table scan of the entire fact table might be performed, resulting in significant resource usage, long response times, and unhappy users.

Often, users are forced by data warehouse management to select constraints for several dimensions in order to ensure a relatively small result set from which the measures are tested against a range constraint. Users battle back by selecting all values for some of the dimensions to ensure they don't artificially restrict the scope of their analysis, resulting in a long query "IN" list that usually forces a sub-optimal query execution plan. Fortunately, there is a way to augment the data model to broaden the scope of analysis without artificially reducing the result set.

When your fact table contains mostly keys and just a few measures, and you are dealing with hundreds of millions or billions of fact table rows, additional Measure Statistics dimensions can be built, possibly as many as one dimension for each measure in the fact table. This adds an additional key to the fact table for each measure that has an associated dimension, along with the lookup overhead of determining the dimension table natural key value at ETL time. However, applying measure-related constraints through a Measure Statistics dimension rather than sequentially performing range checks on the measures in the fact table will result in significant query performance improvements. The larger the fact table and the more often users constrain measures based on a range of values with few other dimensional constraints, the more appropriate it is to implement this non-traditional feature.

As shown in the example in Figure 9.5, if the range of values for the dwell_time measure in an individual fact table record was 0 to 1000.0 with a decimal precision of 1, this new dimension would contain 10,000 rows, one for each distinct value. At query run time, rather than constraining on a fact table dwell_time value range, which could result in a full table scan or a sequential scan of a very large result set, a new Dwell Time Measure Statistics dimension would be constrained instead, resulting in an additional join to the fact table. The result set from this operation would not have to be subsequently scanned since the range check constraint is applied to the new Dwell Time dimension, not the fact table itself. Measure Statistics dimensions typically summarize measure values into discrete attributes, like Low, Medium, and High, or Normal and Abnormal. Department-specific and even user-specific attribute values can be added to this dimension, making this technique even more useful.

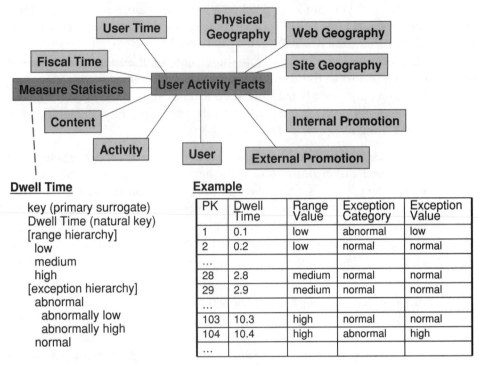

Dwell Time

    key (primary surrogate)
    Dwell Time (natural key)
    [range hierarchy]
      low
      medium
      high
    [exception hierarchy]
      abnormal
        abnormally low
        abnormally high
      normal

Example

PK	Dwell Time	Range Value	Exception Category	Exception Value
1	0.1	low	abnormal	low
2	0.2	low	normal	normal
...				
28	2.8	medium	normal	normal
29	2.9	medium	normal	normal
...				
103	10.3	high	normal	normal
104	10.4	high	abnormal	high
...				

Figure 9.5 Measure Statistics dimension example.

Split Date/Time Dimensions Enable Time-of-Day Analysis

The Time dimension is one of the most critical components of any clickstream data warehouse dimensional data model. Clickstream data warehouses are unusual when compared to many other types of data warehouses in that the granularity of the Time dimension goes down to at least the seconds in a day level. In older brick-and-mortar data warehouses the lowest level of time granularity is usually at the day level. The analysis of transaction activity and trends over days, weeks, months, or years provides the insight needed to determine the business impact of past decisions while providing a baseline for current and future decisions. However, the capability to efficiently analyze intraday visitor traffic and Web page usage patterns irrespective of date is critical for those e-businesses looking to understand capacity planning, performance impact, response times, Web site denial of service rates, and service level agreement compliance for peak-hour demand for bandwidth.

The Telco industry was probably the first industry to use a highly granular Time dimension, down to at least the minute level of detail, for call-detail record analysis. The Telco call-detail data warehouses used the granular time dimension to analyze the trade-off between the costs of increasing network bandwidth to handle peak-hour call demand versus the lost revenue and customer dissatisfaction resulting from intermittent denial of service. The same kind of granular clickstream analysis provides the foundation to quantify the value of increased Web site capacity versus lost revenue and dissatisfied users.

For brick-and-mortar businesses that capture transactions down to the date and hour of the day, it seems natural to capture the entire date/timestamp within a single Time dimension, relying on the query tool or SQL to parse out the date for interday analysis, and to parse out the time-of-day for intraday analysis. However, when it is necessary to perform time-of-day analysis down to the minute or second, irrespective of date, in order to develop a Web usage profile for a typical weekday, this parsing requirement results in very inefficient queries.

As we originally introduced in Chapter 6, streamlining time-of-day analysis involves splitting the usual User Time or Fiscal Time dimension into a Date dimension for the date component, and a Time-of-Day dimension for the time-stamp component. A single Time dimension covering just a one-year period down to the second (YYYY:MM:DD:HH:MM:SS) requires 31,536,000 records. This single Time dimension increases linearly for each additional year covered by the dimension, so that a five-year Time dimension would be 157 million records—hardly leveraging the benefits of a dimensional data model. Instead, splitting the Time dimension into a Date dimension and Time-of-Day dimension to cover a one-year period would result in a Date dimension of 365 records (YYYY:MM:DD) and a Time-of-Day dimension of 86,400 records (HH:MM:SS). And to cover a five-year period, the Date dimension would increase to only 1825 records. The Time-of-Day dimension would not grow at all, since it covers every one-second interval of a 24-hour day, and is orthogonal to the Date. Figure 9.6 shows how the User Time dimension can be split into separate Date and Time-of-Day tables.

By building the data model with separate Date and Time-of-Day dimensions, analysis of data at the daily, weekly, monthly, quarterly, or annual level involves constraining on the Date dimension, involving only hundreds or a few thousand records, rather than tens or hundreds of millions of records. Peak-hour analysis involves constraining on a subset of the 86,400 records in the Time-of-Day dimension. As you can see, each type of analysis alone is far more efficient by using separate Date and Time-of-Day dimensions than by constraining on a single Time dimension containing both date and timestamp. And when the Date and Time-of-Day dimensions are used together, interesting business analyses are possible, such as peak hour analysis for the same period year-over-year, weekday versus weekend, holiday versus non-holiday, or Monday versus Friday.

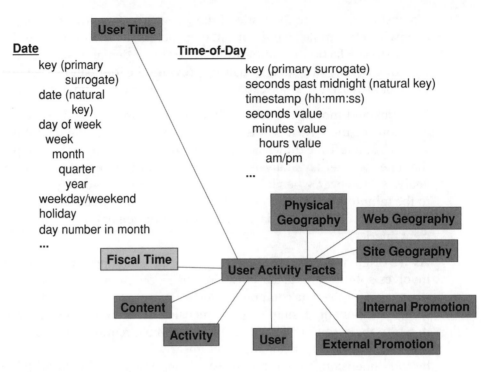

Figure 9.6 Splitting the time dimension into Date and Time-of-Day.

Database Engine Related Features and Techniques

The following technique uses a new database engine capability—materialized views.

Materialized Views Enable Server-Side Aggregate Awareness

Materialized views move aggregate awareness functionality from the client side to the server side, greatly increasing query efficiency. As we discussed in Chapter 7, you can think of a materialized view (which is called a materialized view in Oracle, and summary table in DB2) as a relational aggregate, which can be dynamically evaluated by the database optimizer and used at query run time to improve performance. Unlike traditional relational aggregates that are built through DBA-coded scripts using SQL commands, materialized views are built and refreshed by the database in response to special SQL commands. The database stores materialized view meta data that records the aggregate hierarchies and is used to determine when it would be more efficient for the optimizer to rewrite the query to use a smaller materialized view rather than to dynamically perform the aggregation against the underlying base table.

Aggregate navigation was once the exclusive domain of the OLAP tools. Relational aggregates were built by the DBA and mapped by the OLAP tool from data in the base fact table, often with limited success. To take advantage of the performance benefits of using relational aggregates, permutations of suggested query templates would be built, with each new relational aggregate paired with one or more corresponding query templates. This proliferation of unending aggregates and query templates often led users to choose to wait for the base level query to run rather than spend time to find the right template that would return the result set at the desired level of aggregation.

The problem of choosing the right aggregate can now be solved entirely within the RDMBS by using materialized views. The example below shows how a materialized view can improve the efficiency of a query to count the number of page abandonments, by content type, activity type, by date, and by hour, within a three-month data history range.

```
SELECT time_of_day.hour, date.date,
   activity.activity_type, content.content_type,
SUM(page_activity_fact.abandonments)
FROM time_of_day, activity, content, page_activity_fact
WHERE date.date >= '2000:11:01'
  AND date.date <= '2001:01:31'
  AND activity.activity_type = 'ABANDONMENT'
  [… more joins …]
  GROUP BY time_of_day.hour, date.date,
           activity.activity_type, content.content_type
```

In the absence of a materialized view, all qualifying rows from the Page Activity fact table, potentially millions per day, would be selected with the SUM function performed on the abandonments column as specified in the GROUP BY clause, ultimately resulting in one row being returned per hour, per day, in the date range. This means there will be 24 hours * 92 days = 2208 rows in the final result set.

If we had created a relational aggregate by date and by hour for the abandonment column as a materialized view using the same GROUP BY clause, the RDBMS optimizer would recognize that this materialized view already contains the rows to satisfy the query without performing the expensive SUM/GROUP BY against the base Page Activity fact table. The query would be rewritten to use this materialized view instead of the base fact table, and would essentially select and bring back one row for each hour of the day per day in the date range.

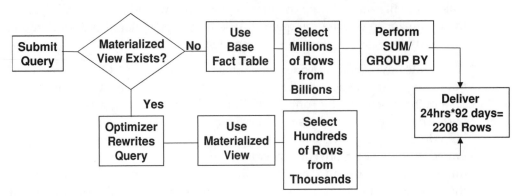

Figure 9.7 Materialized views greatly improve query performance.

Figure 9.7 summarizes how much more efficient the materialized view query processing is versus the brute force, non-materialized view processing.

Using materialized views for aggregate awareness is one of the most significant recent advances by the database vendors for improving query performance. Rather than having to maintain a myriad of aggregation tables and their corresponding query templates, with materialized views only one set of query templates at base level of granularity is maintained. In order to navigate up or down any dimensional aggregates defined by a materialized view, the query must specify that GROUP BYs are performed on the server side at query run time. Often this is can be done by creating a predefined, server-calculated aggregate measure in the semantic layer of the query tool. Accessing this predefined measure causes the optimizer to consider appropriate materialized views, rewrite the query to use the materialized view, retrieve the precalculated aggregate rows from the materialized view, and return the result set back to the client as if the original query performed the grouping against the base table.

Summary

The huge size and complexity of clickstream data warehouses rival those of the retail industry's Point-of-Sale (POS) and even the Telco industry's Call Detail Record (CDR) data warehouses. Multibillion row fact tables are quite common and analytical users need to identify, navigate through, and drill down to individual sessions, visits, and even page hits. The hardware, operating system, and database technology vendors already have the capability to store billions of rows across terabytes of disk. Unfortunately, the analytical tools have not kept pace with this data explosion. But by using the data modeling, database engine, and analytical techniques described in this chapter in conjunction with the OLAP tool with the right set of features, clickstream data warehouse analysts can greatly improve their query performance.

This is the last chapter in our book, and we hope you have found it instructive. We also hope that this book encourages you to create a clickstream data warehouse for your enterprise. To access all the supplemental material referenced in this book, as well as new information on clickstream data warehousing and other data warehouse topics, please go to our companion Web site, www.wiley .com/compbooks/sweiger.

Clickstream Data Warehouse Project Plan

Phase 1: Project Definition

PROJECT PREPARATION

Define Initial Project Scope

Determine Project Feasibility and Justification

Create project steering committee

PROJECT PLANNING

Assign Project Staff

Prepare Initial Project Plan

PROJECT INITIATION

Conduct Project Kickoff Meeting

    Review Project Scope and Goals

    Perform Team Introductions

    Review Roles and Responsibilities

    Review Project Plan

Develop Training Plan for Project Team

    Prepare and distribute skills assessment questionnaire

    Consolidate skills assessment results

    Perform gap analysis

    Develop training plan

Develop Project Communication Plan

Develop Change Management Process

Develop Issue Tracking Process

Define Development Process

Define Source Code Control Procedures

Define Documentation Standards (business, requirements, design, test plans, etc.)

Define Coding Standards (programs, scripts, SQL)

Define Data Modeling Standards

Define Quality Control Process

ONGOING PROJECT MANAGEMENT

Project Communication

Change Management

Issue Tracking

Project Plan Maintenance

Phase 2: Requirements Definition

GATHER BUSINESS REQUIREMENTS

Create Interview Team

Select End-user Interviewees

Schedule Interviews

Interview Preparation

Conduct Interview Kickoff Meeting

Conduct End-user Interviews

Analyze Interview Findings

GATHER TECHNICAL REQUIREMENTS

Conduct IT Interviews - Web Site

Conduct IT Interviews - Other Systems

Analyze Interview Findings

DOCUMENT REQUIREMENTS

Document Interview Findings

Publish Requirements Documents

Provide Feedback to Web Site Group

Revise Full Project Scope

> Define Initial Pilot Scope
>
> Update Project Plan
>
> Conduct User Signoff Meeting

Phase 3: System Design

DATA AND DATABASE TRACK
DATA WAREHOUSE SCHEMA DESIGN

> Determine dimensions
>
> Determine fact tables
>
> Determine base level fact granularity
>
> Define detailed facts and derived metrics
>
> Define dimension hierarchies and details
>
> Create initial schema design documentation
>
> Initial database sizing

WEB SOURCE DATA ANALYSIS

> Identify potential web data sources
>
> Source data mapping
>
> Analyze logged data
>
> Meet with web development team to discuss web site design / logging issues
>
> Document data issues

STANDARD SOURCE DATA ANALYSIS

> Identify data source systems
>
> Source data mapping
>
> Analyze and Document Source Data Issues
>
> Determine data retention needs
>
> Determine data security needs
>
> Determine approach for slowly changing dimensions
>
> Update schema design documentation
>
> User schema review and feedback

APPLICATION TRACK
DOCUMENT HIGH LEVEL APPLICATION REQUIREMENTS

> Define user interface needs
>
> Determine data access tool categories required

Determine data / application security requirements

Identify Initial Reports / Analysis Applications

Define User Interface and Application Requirements

Document Initial Application Specifications

Create application test plan

ARCHITECTURE AND INFRASTRUCTURE TRACK
DEVELOP TECHNOLOGY ARCHITECTURE

Review and Document Current Technology Environment

Define Data Warehouse Components and
Integration Requirements

> Determine External System Integration Requirements

> Define Project Computing Platform Requirements

> Determine Technology / Product Needs

Determine Build / Buy Approach for Major System Components

Create Project Architecture and Infrastructure Plan

Architecture Review

PRODUCT ANALYSIS AND SELECTION

Perform following tasks for each purchased component, e.g., an ETL tool, query tool or data mining application

Prepare Product Evaluation Criteria - INCLUDE FUNCTIONALITY TEST CRITERIA

Research Available Technology and Identify Suitable Vendors

Create Short List of Vendors

Conduct Detailed Product Evaluation

> Product Evaluation

> Vendor Evaluation

> Estimate hardware and software requirements

> Perform Functionality Test / Prototype

>> Prepare test environment for tool evaluation

>> Select and build portion of data model for testing

>> Obtain test data

>> Build functionality test / prototype

>> Conduct tests

>> Document results

Analyze Results and Make Recommendation

Purchase Product

Train developers

Phase 4: System Implementation

ARCHITECTURE AND INFRASTRUCTURE TRACK
CREATE PROJECT DEVELOPMENT ENVIRONMENT

Install and configure development hardware

Install and configure development software

Create development databases

Configure environment for developers

DESIGN AND IMPLEMENT PROCESS AUTOMATION FRAMEWORK

Design and implement job scheduling and dependency mechanism

Design and implement problem notification and reporting mechanism

Integrate with ETL and client components where applicable

DESIGN AND IMPLEMENT BACKUP AND RESTORE PROCESS

Determine backup / restore volume, frequency, retention, and growth requirements

Determine backup / restore approach

Select and acquire backup software and hardware

Install and configure backup software and hardware

DATA AND DATABASE TRACK
PHYSICAL SCHEMA DESIGN

Document database development standards

Determine partitioning strategy

Determine indexing strategy

Determine aggregation strategy

Determine database-level data security requirements

Review data access tool schema requirements

Update schema design document

DEVELOPMENT DATABASE IMPLEMENTATION

Configure development and test databases

Create warehouse schema

Assign physical names

Assign data types and sizes

Assign null options

Determine keys

Determine indexes

Determine partitioning

Identify and extract / create sample data for development use

Load sample data

Implement database-level security requirements

HIGH-LEVEL ETL DESIGN

Design and document architecture for extract, transformation, cleansing, staging, and loading data

Define historical data needs and data retention requirements

Define one-time history extract approach

Define incremental extract and load approach

Design program error and exceptional handling processes

Prioritize dimension and fact table ETL development

Create ETL test plan

ETL design review

DIMENSION TABLE ETL DESIGN AND DEVELOPMENT

Perform following tasks for each dimension table, history extract may need to be separate set of tasks

Document detailed source data mapping and transformations

Develop data extraction routines

Define source system interfaces

Design extract process scheduling

Design and develop extract programs

Develop data transformation and cleansing routines

Develop staging and loading routines

Develop maintenance process for dimension

Integrate into process automation framework

FACT TABLE ETL DESIGN AND DEVELOPMENT

Perform following tasks for each fact table, history extract may need to be separate set of tasks

Document detailed source data mapping and transformations

Develop data extraction routines

    Define source system interfaces

    Design extract process scheduling

    Design and develop extract programs

Develop data transformation and cleansing routines

Develop staging and loading routines

Develop maintenance process for dimension

Integrate into process automation framework

DATA ADMINISTRATION

Define warehouse data quality rules

Design and build warehouse data QA routines

Integrate with data load and process automation framework

Design and build data archival process

Create data reconciliation plan

AGGREGATE DESIGN AND DEVELOPMENT

Design and develop aggregate creation process

Design and develop aggregate management process

Determine initial aggregate tables

APPLICATION TRACK

APPLICATION DESIGN AND DEVELOPMENT

Prioritize initial reports / applications

Create detailed specifications for each report / application

    Identify business measures, metrics, formulas

    Determine standard formulas

    Determine default summarization rules

    Prototype report / application

Review specifications and prototypes with pilot users

Complete development of reports / applications

Validate report / application results

Performance testing and tuning

APPLICATION MANAGEMENT

Create user training materials

Create user training plan

Document application administration procedures

SYSTEM INTEGRATION
INTEGRATION TESTING

Assemble all back-end product and custom ETL programs

Execute ETL test plan

Assemble all end-user / analytical applications

Execute application test plan

Run history data load

Execute data reconciliation plan for historical data

Run incremental data load

Execute data reconciliation plan for incremental data

Run entire data warehouse process from load to query

Validate results

Phase 5: System Deployment

DEPLOYMENT PLANNING

Create warehouse operation and administration manual

Define problem user support procedures

Define performance management procedures

Document system administration procedures

Document database administration procedures

Document application administration procedures

Document user and application setup procedures

Identify pilot users

Identify all remaining production users

Create pilot and full scale deployment plan

Review Plan

CREATE PRODUCTION ENVIRONMENT

Validate proposed hardware and software configuration

Complete site plan and site preparation

Install and configure production hardware

Install and configure production software

Install and configure custom software

Determine database storage requirements

Storage layout and configuration

Create production database

Document production system configuration

Establish administrator and user access

Configure production backups

Create production process schedule

    Enter ETL batch schedule

    Enter aggregate management schedule

    Enter DBA task schedule

    Enter backup schedule

DATA WAREHOUSE CREATION AND VALIDATION

Load all data

Create indexes

Create aggregates

Validate data

Run systems tests

Conduct volume and stress tests

Test production backups

PILOT DEPLOYMENT

Install client software for pilot users

Install client applications for pilot users

Train pilot users

Provide users with login / access

Coaching / one-on-one training

Obtain user feedback

Make appropriate system modifications

    Data

    Applications

    Performance

FULL SCALE DEPLOYMENT

Schedule access to client workstations for remaining users

Install client software for remaining users

Install client applications for pilot users

Train users

Provide users with login / access

Coaching / one-on-one training

Conduct system acceptance test

POST-DEPLOYMENT ACTIVITIES

Provide ongoing maintenance and support

Adjust project steering committee

Define post-deployment application development and release process

Continue application development efforts

Index